Readings in

PRODUCTIVITY IMPROVEMENTS

Complete transcripts of papers
on the topic of
Productivity Improvements
presented at the
APICS 27th Annual International Conference

October 9–12, 1984
Las Vegas, Nevada

Copyright 1984 The American Production and Inventory Control Society, Inc.
International Standard Book Number: 0-935406-57-3
Library of Congress Catalog Card Number: 84-72235

INTERNATIONAL OFFICERS, 1984
AMERICAN PRODUCTION AND INVENTORY COUNCIL SOCIETY, INC.

President
Edward M. Blackman
Elpac Power Systems
Santa Ana, CA

Past President 1983
Alphedor J. Perreault, CPIM
Fafnir Bearing Company
New Britain, CT

Past President 1982
James P. Kelleher, CPIM*
Westinghouse Electric Corp.
Baltimore, MD

President-Elect
Eugene A. Crepeau, CPIM*
American Pad & Paper
Holyoke, MA

Executive Vice President
James T. Chisholm
Westinghouse I.E.D.
Pittsburgh, PA

Vice President of Education Materials
Howard J. Bromberg, CPIM*
WABCO ABD of American Standard
Wilmerding, PA

Vice President Membership and Chapter Development
Mike Ashapa, CPIM
Nyman Manufacturing Co.
E. Providence, RI

Vice President of Education Programs
Frank Swanson, CPIM
TSR, Inc.
Lake Geneva, WI

Secretary/Treasurer
Gordon Ellis
WABCO Equipment of Canada
Paris, Ontario, Canada

Vice President of Education Research
William E. Robinson, CPIM*
IBM Corporation
Atlanta, GA

Executive Director
Henry F. Sander, CAE
American Production and
Inventory Control Society
Falls Church, VA

REGIONAL VICE PRESIDENTS

REGION I
Paul E. Sheehan, CPIM
Codman & Shurtleff, Inc.
Avon, MA

REGION VIII
Kenneth J. Hunt
Arrowhead Metals Ltd.
Toronto, Ontario, Canada

REGION II
Jeffrey K. Beightol, CPIM
Cummins Engine Co., Inc.
Lakewood, NY

REGION IX
W. Russell Blackburn, CPIM
Westinghouse Electric Corp.
Baltimore, MD

REGION III
Helen A. Berger, CPIM
Hobart Corporation
Troy, OH

REGION X
Jerry R. Murphy
Portland State University
Portland, OR

REGION IV
William J. Turiak, CPIM
Martin Marietta Data Systems
Orlando, FL

REGION XI
Ray L. Weaver
Deloitte Haskins & Sells
Greensboro, NC

REGION V
Roger F. Ahrens, CPIM*
OTC
Owatonna, MN

REGION XII
Randell Eldridge, CPIM
ICI Americas, Inc.
Charlestown, IN

REGION VI
Jim R. Schwendinger, CPIM
Touche Ross
Houston, TX

REGION XIII
Jack Seastrom
United Conveyor Corp.
Deerfield, IL

REGION VII
Robert P. Williams, CPIM
NCR Corp.
Los Angeles, CA

REGION XIV
Jack Van Acker
NCR Corp.
Milwaukee, WI

TABLE OF CONTENTS

THE FACTORY OF THE FUTURE

Ron Hubbard, CPIM*
IBM Corporation

Tremendous advances in technology have provided American industry with opportunities to dramatically increase productivity. This presentation deals with these new advances and the capabilities they offer to all aspects of manufacturing.

Let's begin by looking into the not too distant future when a prospective customer calls our company to place an order. The customer is seated at his graphics display and selects our company from a list provided by a computerized service which shows all companies that manufacture the specific products in which he is interested. He calls our company and when the connection is established he receives our welcome logo on his graphics display. He selects the product he is interested in buying from a list of products we manufacture. At his option he may view a videotaped presentation of our product or textual detailed specifications. He may enter his own order into our system or may request to speak to a company representative. The representative can appear on his display via closed circuit video camera and may also present graphics or video displays of the products on the customer's terminal. If custom engineering of the product is required, it can be done online with the customer as they both view the product on their respective graphics display terminals. Once the product is selected, pricing can be performed online and, if required, contracts including custom engineering drawings can be printed at the customer location for signature. Once signed, image copies of the contracts can be transmitted back to the manufacturer and stored for reference. The newly engineered product is scheduled for production and a shipment date committed to the customer. The scheduling of production considers all elements of manufacturing including tooling and required labor skills as well as material and capacity. The manufacturing process, required tooling, etc. are generated by the design system as well as programs for NC machines and industrial robots. Special machines or tooling may also be designed based on the volume of the order. Most dramatic and amazing, our factory of the future ships our customer the custom designed and manufactured product on time with excellent quality and price performance.

The technology to make this dream a reality is available today though not yet in common usage. Many companies have implemented portions of the technology described herein, but few are taking full advantage of the opportunities offered. Most companies have implemented "islands of automation" within specific departments, but few have developed a complete "computer integrated manufacturing" system. This concept of computer integrated manufacturing (CIM) is the blueprint for the factory of the future.

COMPUTER AIDED DESIGN & ENGINEERING - CAD & CAE

The first CAD systems were little more than computer controlled plotting pens. Engineering problems were solved by the aid of mainframe computers made available through timesharing terminals. As the plotters were replaced with large graphics display terminals and greater computer power became available to the engineer the functions of CAD and CAE were combined in an integrated system. Engineering analysis problems can be solved as the geometry of the product is being created on the graphics terminal.

Interactive graphics systems today allow the engineer and draftsman to work in two or three dimensions and utilize full color to simplify complex designs. Structural analysis can be performed utilizing wire mesh which can be automatically generated to perform finite element analysis. The results of these computer tests to analyse how the product will react under stress can be displayed in statistical form or, better yet, as a graphical display showing distorted wire mesh or color patterns of stress. These color pictures of the product provide clearer information on product performance to the engineer. Also, kinematics capability allows the engineer to see the moving parts of the product in motion. These "movies" allow the engineer to identify

proper clearances and analyse possible vibration problems in the performance of the product. Many specialized CAD systems are available for specific applications from integrated circuits to aircraft. Vary basic interactive graphics systems even run on personal computers which puts this capability within the reach of any potential user.

Data bases now increase the productivity of engineers and draftsmen by allowing the storage and retrieval of previously designed products and the incorporation of these designs into new products. Interfaces to production and business systems allow the automatic creation of bill of material and process information to more efficiently schedule the product for production. Integration with word processing systems provides the capability to include prewritten textual information on drawings and to incorporate product drawings into promotional and instructional printed material. Commercial printers now have the ability to produce good quality drawings combined with text.

COMPUTER AIDED STORAGE AND HANDLING - CASH

Efficient storage and handling of material has been the focus of attention for many years. It has become apparent with the advent of "just-in-time" techniques that the most efficient way to control inventory is to eliminate it. This makes even more sense when we consider that the inventory we have in stores in most cases is not what is needed anyway. Storage was also required for inventory in quarantine awaiting inspection. As more and more companies tie product quality control procedures as well as production scheduling to their vendors the need for the modern high bay stacker cranes is diminishing. While there has been dramatic improvement in the price performance of these systems in recent years, we are seeing an example of a technology being leapfrogged by the improvements in planning and scheduling systems and the move toward focused factories.

Where CASH systems are proving invaluable is in the transporting of material throughout the factory and in loading and unloading automated machines. Computerized conveyor systems keep track of material from receiving to shipping. Laser scanners read bar codes on the pallets to identify the products and locations within the system and automatic scales verify piece counts. Material handling robots tied to automated machines load and unload work pieces and even perform setup changes.

COMPUTER AIDED MANUFACTURING - CAM

The oldest CAM function is numerical control. The Jaquard loom developed during the early industrial revolution in Europe was probably the first NC machine. The functions of the loom were controlled by holes in cards much as modern NC machines are controlled by holes in paper or mylar tape. Early NC programming languages were unique to the specific machine or manufacturer and were difficult to learn much as early computer programming languages were. New systems integrated with CAD functions make NC programming much simpler. This allows engineers designing parts to do their own NC programming and facilitates the manufacture of complex products. Cutter path programming and tool selection can be performed as part of the design process rather than as a separate step. In addition, the routing or process can be generated to guide the manufacture of the product across several machines. Currently, work is progressing on the development of an electronic processor that creates NC instructions for generalized part shapes automatically. This will further speed the process of taking a product from design to manufacturing.

Advances in robotics technology are rapidly increasing the number of tasks that can be performed by these machines. While most industrial robots are employed in materials handling and welding operations, robots have the capability for complex assembly and sorting tasks. Vision systems provide the capability to recognize objects in any orientation and sort loose parts in bins. Robots can measure parts to the minute fraction of an inch by vision alone or by precision tactual sensors. The flexibility of arms and joints can be designed to match the requirements of the job. Design tools are available on CAD systems to assist in this design function which include the use of kinematics to see the robot arm in action on the CAD screen. While the average production worker today costs $16 per hour to keep on the job, the average robot costs only $6 per hour. Robot costs have come down dramatically as their performance has improved. Sophisticated robots can be purchased for less than the cost of an American built luxury car. The only bottleneck is the lack of experienced personnel to program and implement the applications. Fortunately, new robots do not require programming to perform tasks but can be "taught" by merely guiding the arm through the series of motions required to perform the task. In the last few years the concept of CAM has gone far beyond the mere creation of NC programs and instructions for robots. Today, "computer aided" manufacturing involves integrating many machines together into a flexible manufacturing system or FMS. FMS integrates NC machines, robots, and labor into production systems that have the ability to produce high quality, low cost parts. But also they have the ability to rapidly change over and produce a variety of products efficiently. These systems offer the best of both worlds...production efficiency and flexibility at the same time. The key to success of these systems is advance planning by all the major functions of the company to determine what products will be produced by the system, the design of those products and the manufacturing process.

COMPUTER AIDED INSPECTION - CAI

In the July 8, 1984 issue of Parade Magazine there was an interesting article about W. Edwards Deming, "the man who taught Japan about quality". Mr. Deming who is the father of statistical quality control feels that product quality is not only obtainable but essential if American industry is to be competitive in the world markets. He states that management must focus on manufacturing and the product rather than financial management. Fortunately that process has begun in Detroit with the nation's automakers. Statistical quality control is being emphasized to improve supplier quality by identifying potential quality problems before they happen.

Product quality begins with the engineering design of the product. With the kinematics and structural analysis capabilities of the CAD systems already mentioned, potential quality problems can be identified and designed out of the product before it is released to production. Control of the manufacturing process by sensors and feedback instrumentation can avoid creating scrap by correcting problems before they occur or by stopping the production process when key measurements are out of acceptable tolerances. Coordinant Measuring Machines (CMM) with scanning heads can follow complex surfaces or can measure specific checkpoints with single point probes. Also, robots offer tremendous repeatability of motion which can assure consistent quality. The new technology will probably eliminate the job of inspector by making inspection a part of every step of the manufacturing process.

OTHER IMPORTANT ADVANCES

The following five technological developments are not limited to manufacturing in scope but are extremely important to making the factory of the future a reality.

The development of data base technology has provided new capability in user access to information contained in corporate data bases. Hierarchical data base structure has long provided excellent performance. Now relational data base structure is offering better opportunities for users to perform "adhoc" queries against these data using user friendly interfaces.

Business graphics terminals are providing graphical displays of data that are much more understandable than massive columns of numbers. Many new application software systems are providing this capability for users. Also, generalized tools are available to produce graphs from current user data. The ability to present engineering drawings produced on CAD systems on these business graphics terminals greatly enhances communication between engineering and other business functions.

Image processing provides the capability to display images of actual documents such as legal documents, correspondence or photographs on computer terminals. These documents are scanned, digitized and stored as non-coded information (NCI) on computer storage devices. The savings in storage, duplication and retrieval costs is significant. The documents can be displayed whenever it is necessary to view the original. Also, copies can be produced on any graphics printer.

Personal or microcomputers provide computing power wherever it is needed at very low cost. My personal computer at home has more potential capacity than the systems installed in many large companies just fifteen or twenty years ago. The computers can be used as standalone systems or as terminals attached to mainframe computers. They can be used for limited CAD applications, to program industrial robots or NC machines, and to collect data on the shop floor. They are limited only by their internal capacity in the applications they can perform in a standalone environment.

Local area networks (LAN) are the glue that holds all these capabilities together in one integrated system. Currently a mindless babble of protocols and interfaces both software and hardware, logical and physical are being used in such devices as programmable controllers, microcomputers, host computers, word processors, terminals, etc. What is needed, but is currently unavailable, is a common wall plug (with the necessary hardware and software behind it) that any terminal or communications device can plug into and communicate with any other terminal or device. This network must handle not only data communications, but also voice and image. This would eliminate the spaghetti bowl of wires currently installed in most facilities and would allow the integration of functions that we have just discussed herein.

SUMMARY

In the March, 1984 issue of MANUFACTURING ENGINEERING, Bill Knabb of Hughes Aircraft noted, "We've developed a system in one of our plants called ADAM. The engineers design a part on the terminal, and the computer spits out the process planning and the NC tapes. The people in the shop then put the tape in the machine and run it. When they're done, they throw away the process planning and the tapes, and they don't even bother inspecting the part." Many companies are well on their way to developing computer integrated manufacturing (CIM) in their plants. But most of American industry still has a long way to go. As our success in the implementation of MRP II was determined by our ability to work together, so will our success be determined in the implementation of CIM. It is important to use the lessons we have learned to insure good working relations not only between production, marketing, engineering and finance, but also between labor and management. People make these system work, not computers. While the first industrial revolution led workers away from skilled trades into monotonous jobs, CIM offers job enrichment by increasing the scope of each workers contribution in conjunction with the use of automated machinery.

In closing let me make an observation regarding the impact that Japanese competition has had on American industry that I have not heard mentioned. I am reminded of the story about the sparrow who waited too long to fly south one winter and wound up laying in a barnyard nearly frozen. A cow happened along and dropped a load of hot manure on him and thawed him out. Was the cow the sparrow's friend or his enemy? The Japanese have historically had a way of getting our attention when we ignore what is going on around us. We have allowed ourselves to develop some bad habits in the prosperous years since World War II while the Japanese have had to work very hard during that period. The world has now changed and we must change with it. I am very excited about the changes that have taken place in our industry and in this Society in the past few years. There is no doubt that we have the technology to lead the world on into the future and now it is obvious that we also have the desire. The future looks great!

BIOGRAPHICAL SKETCH

Ron Hubbard is an Advisory Industry Specialist with the IBM National Marketing Division in Fort Wayne, Indiana. In his 18-year career with IBM, Ron has worked primarily with manufacturing companies and has assisted several in the successful implementation of manufacturing systems utilizing the MAPICS and COPICS software packages. He authored the "Make to Schedule Facility" which enhances the function of MAPICS for the repetitive manufacturer. A past president of the Fort Wayne Chapter of APICS, he is certified at the "Fellow" level and is a senior member of Robotics International of the Society of Manufacturing Engineers (RI/SME).

CAD/CAM AND SHOP FLOOR CONTROL
Victor Lippa, CPIM*
Creative Output, Inc.

As practioners, many of us remember with a dubious nostalgia those days when one of our major objectives was to justify the creation of a monolithic bill of materials data base. In fact, many still struggle to convince Finance, Manufacturing, Engineering, Production Control and other organizations that a single bill of materials data base with separate extracts for the different users is best from a maintenance and accuracy point of view. Still others are entangled in the crusade to achieve the Closed Loop Manufacturing System and to become an "A" MRP user. These "crusades", however, pale in significance in comparison to our next challenge: merging CAD/CAM with the Manufacturing Data Base. The opportunities relative to such a merger are immense and will be cited in this paper - particularly with regard to CAD/CAM's impact upon Shop Floor Control.

An almost universal concept among human endeavors which is also present in the systems field is that of synergism. While a "stand alone" system may yield a benefit, linking that single system to another and extending the link still further to additional systems will yield an overall synergistic benefit far greater than the sum of the individual benefits.

In the case of CAD/CAM and Shop Floor Control, there are two mechanisms which must be present in order to fully exploit the potential of these two systems' interaction. First, there must be a fully integrated data base so that information may be mechanically transferred between CAD/CAM and the Manufacturing Data Base. This matter has been the subject of a number of articles and will not be discussed here. Second, the key to achieving a synergistic benefit from the data base merger is finite capacity scheduling.

While the full integration of the data bases is a problem currently receiving much attention but yet unsolved, the once seemingly insolvable problem of finite capacity scheduling has been solved with the development of OPT (Optimized Production Technology). The OPT philosophy of management, together with the OPT software, have solved the problem of finite scheduling. The solution has unleashed a myriad of opportunities to the OPT user, including the ability to fully exploit CAD/CAM's benefit potential with regards to Shop Floor Control.

What is CAD?

In its simplest form CAD (Computer Aided Design) is an automated drafting system which enables the design engineer to draw straight lines. Typically, today's CAD System includes a CRT terminal and a multitude of comprehensive software which goes beyond the mere drawing of straight lines. Consider the design engineer's task of designing a printed circuit board. While the engineer knows that the circuits to be layed out must include, for example, 13 various integrated circuits, 18 various resistors, a number of diodes - all of which must be in particular sequence, - etc.; he has the task of designing the board with the components in the correct circuit positions without the respective circuits interfering with each other. Simply stated, the circuit lines may not cross the path of another circuit. Where very complex circuits are involved, such as in military electronics, the designer may have to resort to the use of MLB's (multi layer boards) in order to carry the circuitry on a non interference basis. Some boards may have 20 or more levels, each of which must be designed to function in consonance with the overall design objective of the board. The design complexity is accentuated in the case of densely packed "memory boards" such as those used by computers, with up to several hundred ICs jammed into a compact space.

In addition to PCB layout, CAD has a multitude of other uses including:
● evaluating drawing changes. Intricate drawings for complex products present the engineer with a special problem - how to assure that a minor change in one area doesn't cascade into others presenting problems impacting the original design objective. CAD allows the engineer to model the drawing via CRT, simulate the desired changes and assess the possible impact upon the overall drawing. This simulation process can be a real time saver, and reduces the amount of physical change evaluation (i.e. debugging on the shop floor) required as well.

● product design review. CAD's simulation capabilities allow the conceptual "creation" of a product via CRT using the systems memory, after which a myriad of simulated "tests" may be conducted to help eliminate a number of problems which otherwise might not have been uncovered without expensive physical modeling and testing.

● geometric modeling. The parts of an assembly must fit together, and CAD can be instrumental in simulating parts under design (again, via CRT) to assure that the completed parts will assemble correctly.

● product requirements. The computerized simulation capabilities of CAD may be used to develop product requirements - such as in the case of PCB design where a Circuit Card Assembly must have certain capabilities. CAD can help the engineer to determine what those capabilities must be within a system, and then to simulate CCA performance in order to assure that the capabilities have been achieved.

● drawing and redrawing. The iterative process of drawing development, where a series of drawings must be created to develop a design with only incremental changes with each new drawing, can be simplified with CAD. Overall drawing development time reductions of 90% have been achieved using the system.

● library of designs. Existing designs can be catalogued into a library so that new design tasks can be satisfied "from the archives": why "reinvent the wheel?"

● part evaluations. CAD can facilitate a review whereby similar parts may be grouped into one. An example would be a case where brass, iron and stainless steel fittings are used in the plant - three parts differing only in material composition but not configuration. This might be a case where the cheaper iron fitting is used in oil lines, the brass for hydraulic oil and the corrosion resistant stainless steel in water lines. Suppose the stainless steel fitting could satisfy all three applications. Such a change could eliminate two SKUs in inventory while the higher cost of the stainless steel fitting might be offset by discounted greater purchase quantities. Further, reducing the number of like parts reduces the probability of "wrong part use" instances on the shop floor.

● generation of drawings/documentation. Once a design has been finalized via CRT, a "hard copy" of the drawing may be produced for use by the model shop in prototype generation. The actual labor of creating the drawing is reduced by an approximately 4 to 1 ratio, while the generated drawing may be later used in creating manufacturing visual aides as well as inspection documentation. The variety of technical data available to the design engineers at the time of drawing creation can prove especially helpful in assuring that the correct information is annotated to the inspection drawings.

At the current time the drawing/documentation /specification output of CAD is manually converted into Bill of Materials input data for the manufacturing data base. The previously discussed development of an integrated data base will allow the more efficient mechanical transfer of this information.

● library of past failures. By creating and maintaining a library of rejected designs for future reference the design engineer can avoid expending time and effort on unacceptable design approaches. In addition, a design that was historically rejected due to a reason not pertinent to the design under evaluation can be put to use, saving even more time from the design process.

While our discussion of CAD reveals a wealth of labor saving ideas in the design engineering section - many of which "telescope" to labor and time savings on the shop floor - a more significant savings may be expected when the CAD activity is extended into CAM. In fact, studies have shown that while a 4 to 1 productivity gain can be expected through CAD, tieing CAD to CAM results in a 40 to 1 or greater productivity gain. The concept of "interlocking" systems to achieve a synergistic effect is one which will recur often in this paper. In addition, a conceptual summary of the means necessary to drive the interlocking network toward significant benefits on the shop floor will be related.

3

What Is CAM?

CAM (Computer Aided Manufacturing) applies the computer to manufacturing using a number of different approaches including the following:

● numeric control. In one of its simplest forms, CAM can be used to create a paper tape which in turn can "direct" a lathe, drill press, milling machine etc. through a series of part repetitive operations. A "higher form" of machine control involves the use of microprocessors to program the machine operations. The higher microprocessor format has other benefits in that networking is made possible, whereby two or more machine controlling microprocessors can be linked together so that the machine program in one microprocessor can be used to "drive" a second machine. This capability provides flexibility on the shop floor in coping with temporary machine overloads (easy work transfer) as well as microprocessor preventive maintenance and/or breakdowns, where a remote microprocessor tied into the network can be employed to direct the machine whose microprocessor is out of action.

● robotics. Much has been written concerning robotics that will not be recounted here, but as in the numeric control discussion CAM refers to the computer directing the robots' movements.

● CAD/CAT. The same specifications, data, etc. in the CAD data base used for CAM can be used in the automatic generation of programs to inspect (CAI-Computer Aided Inspection) and test (CAT-Computer Aided Test). On the shop floor the benefit of the CAD/CAT link is magnified through networking so that test personnel may have CRT access to the designer's specifications for a particular CCA. Test computerization also allows the retention of test history to be used in process analysis and control.

In the PCB example, it is evident that linking the CAD data base to the CAM, CAI and CAT data base through conversion programs greatly magnifies the benefit of CAD upon the manufacturing operation. In practice, while the concepts outlined herein are sound, the practical application has been limited by the state of the art level of software available to develop the links.

Linking CAD/CAM to the Manufacturing Data Base

While the technical discussion of CAD, CAM, CAI, and CAT has cited a number of potential benefit areas of each of the subsystems and magnified benefits through linking these subsystems together, the major potential benefit of these systems would be attained through the employment of what is being called CIM (Computer Integrated Manufacturing) operating from the "Corporate Data Base."

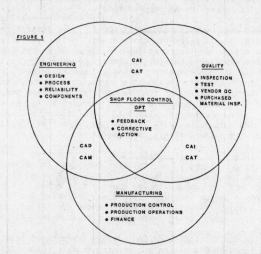

FIGURE 1

Figure 1 depicts the interaction of the different subsystems in the Corporate Data Base along the guidelines of our discussion thus far. The current state of the art has CAD/CAM developed as a separate data base and separate system from the manufacturing data base or "closed loop manufacturing system" utilizing MRP. Figure 1 breaks out the major elements of the corporate base relative to this discussion (Engineering, Quality and Manufacturing) while Figure 2 depicts the more familiar "closed loop manufacturing system" structure.

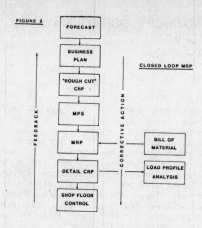

FIGURE 2

CLOSED LOOP MRP

Engineering, relegated to the position of spectator during the MRP crusade responsible only for inputting accurate data into the bill of materials, now plays a major role. The fact is that the engineering activity represents at least half of the total effort expended by many high as well as low technology companies, and many company goals have been missed due to an inability to convert engineering's concepts into product reality on the shop floor in a timely fashion. Historically, materials management people have viewed engineering as supplying the following:

- data to be used in the generation of automatic and /or manual inspection, test and manufacturing instructions.
- data to be converted into a manufacturing bill of materials.
- information for use in group technology.
- information for use in generating routings.

In actuality, this only begins to list the uses of a corporate data base. Engineering can also be viewed from these two fundamental perspectives.

1.) As an activity to be scheduled by a formal system much as manufacturing is scheduled. Product design is an activity which must be scheduled much as any manufacturing operation. In viewing the company as a whole, the design activity has priority jobs, changing schedules, capacity bottlenecks and many of the other problems encountered on the shop floor. Since it has been proven that manufacturing can achieve efficiencies through the employment of formal scheduling systems, why can't engineering? Maybe it is about time that we address the fact that the engineering function is also a part of the manufacturing process in need of effective schedules.

2.) As an active participant in the company's effort to achieve efficiencies in the scheduling of manufacturing operations. One of the objectives of "rough cut" capacity requirements planning is to identify bottleneck work centers for handling via the master production schedule, while the "bottoms up replanning" routine is an iterative (and time consuming) process for dealing with the detail capacity problems identified by the material planners in reviewing their MRP output reports. Even where this approach has met with some success, few will argue that such success comes without considerable and continuous manual effort or that the manual approach can identify and deal with a significant portion of a given schedule's problems. As accentuated by the incredible opportunities evident through the achievement of a corporate data base, the need for finite capacity requirements planning is clearly at hand.

The traditional MRP approach has been to ignore the scheduling of engineering. In addition MRP falls short of effective shop floor control for these two major reasons:

A.) MRP assumes infinite capacity. By definition, no factory has infinite capacity. While manual efforts to cope with this system deficiency are time consuming and, at best, largely ineffective, the use of OPT on a "stand alone" basis or in conjunction with MRP allows the user to achieve schedule disruption immunity through finite capacity planning.

At the current time, for all intents and purposes where OPT has not been implemented, the foreman is saddled with the manual task of dealing with MRP's assumption that his capacity is infinite. He is also expected to manually track the availability of fixtures, tools, setup people, workers, support personnel, machines and other resources in conjunction with Production Control personnel. Considering product complexity, the typical foreman's __management__ responsibilities, and the massive manual scheduling task to be completed, it is small wonder that the typical MRP generated schedule is so short lived! OPT, on the other hand, considers all of the factors necessary to support a schedule and assures that the schedule is generated in full consideration of their availability.

FIGURE 3

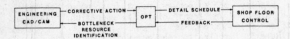

As depicted by __Figure 3__, OPT summarizes the following data from the shop schedule which can be communicated back to engineering personnel for corrective action:

• __machine loading.__ Machine utilization information can be provided to engineering identifying the bottleneck areas effecting overall system throughput. Once the bottlenecks have been identified to engineering, alternate routings can be developed which avoid the bottleneck areas. When the alternate routings have been specified using OPT, the bottlenecks will disappear and an overall throughput increase can be achieved on an ongoing automatic basis without extensive manual effort. The foreman may be freed for managing rather than "putting out fires".

• __setup man loading.__ OPT generated utilization projections can be used to identify excessive setup times and/or setup bottlenecks. Engineering can then take action to develop new setup procedures and/or implement new equipment requiring less setup effort on the shop floor. Since there is no idle time in a fully loaded, bottleneck work center, reductions in setup time increase the time available for processing material effecting an overall increase in throughput.

• __tooling and fixtures.__ Availability problems for support equipment can be identified and addressed in the same fashion as machinery bottlenecks. Engineering can take action to make process changes, alter design, process ECO's etc. as required to alleviate bottlenecks.

Since government research indicates that over 90% of the time that a product and its components spends in the American factory is spent waiting to be worked upon, increasing factory throughput (the rate at which raw materials is converted into shipments) by alleviating bottlenecks through OPT implementation results in dramatic WIP inventory reductions. Excessive WIP inventory needlessly takes up space, ties up capital, increases production cost and cuts profitability. As so appropriately summarized by Tony Friscia in the July 1983 issue of __P & IM Review__ in his article entitled "What is implied by the automatic factory?"

> The real problem...is to make the discrete manufacturing process as continuous as possible. This means bringing a part in just as it needs to be worked on, and then having it continuously flow through each of the production steps. Achieving this end is the goal of automation and integration, for the burden of industry really is an inventory and work in process problem.

An insightful article by Robert A. Richter and Harry L. Colman in the July 1984 issue of the __P & IM Review and APICS News__ underscores the problems associated with MRP's infinite capacity assumption, stresses that a maximum benefit may be accrued through evolution toward the corporate data base if net change finite capacity scheduling is employed and concludes that "net change finite capacity scheduling is an essential function" of a real time integrated manufacturing system.

B.) MRP assumes fixed lead times. In actuality, lead times - as recognized by OPT - must be __derived__. OPT rule 9 summarizes this fact by stating that "lead times are the result of a schedule and cannot be predetermined."

FIGURE 4   RULES OF OPT

1. Balance flow, not capacity.

2. The level of utilization of a non-bottleneck is not determined by its own potential, but, by some other constraint in the system.

3. Activation and utilization of a resource are not synonomous.

4. An hour lost at a bottleneck is an hour lost for the total system.

5. An hour saved at a non-bottleneck is just a mirage.

6. Bottlenecks govern both throughput and inventories.

7. The transfer batch may not, and many times should not, be equal to the process batch.

8. The process batch should be variable, not fixed.

9. Schedules should be established by looking at all of the constraints simultaneously. Lead times are the result of a schedule and cannot be predetermined.

MOTTO
The sum of the local optimums
is not equal to
the global optimum.

The relevancy of OPT rule 9 is corroborated by the casting capacity anecdote which arose from the 1974 economic boom and the 1975 recession which followed. As the boom progressed, casting suppliers found their capacity being increasingly squeezed. In order to cope with the situation, they warned their customers to increase their lead times for castings. When the customers complied, the projected load on the casting suppliers increased, inducing the casting suppliers to again warn their customers to increase their lead times still further. When the 1975 recession hit, orders were cancelled en masse. Correspondingly, lead times were halved, quartered and finally, the suppliers were hunting for orders. It was then that the people purchasing castings realized that the time required to produce castings did not really increase at all, but that as the __load__ increased the backlog increased and speed with which the order could be __started__ decreased. This story, which has been historically preferred as the "lead time spiral", is now offered as illustration of the fact that lead time is a function of __capacity load__.

The Incredible Opportunity

Resolution of the data base communication problems arising from the fact that the documented current state of the art involves only "stand alone" CAD/CAM and manufacturing system capability, together with OPT finite capacity scheduling implementation will allow the following scenario to develop within the manufacturing company:

• OPT generated tooling, fixtures, machines, setup personnel, operator personnel, etc. utilization projections highlighting bottleneck resources are provided to engineering personnel. Analysis of this information results in the identification of alternate routings, improved processes, setup time reductions, additional resources, ECOs, process changes, improved material handling techniques, etc. as required to alleviate the bottleneck situations.

• A listing of projected long term available capacity at non-bottleneck work centers is provided to engineering personnel, allowing them to design new products with the objective of making full use of this available capacity. Increased shipments associated with new products are supported by the company with virtually no increase in plant and equipment, improving return on investment by increasing plant throughput with no additional operating expense!

• A required step in ECO review becomes the generation of a simulation through OPT in order to assess the impact of the change upon shop floor capacity. Changes which may __not__ be supported are adjusted and the simulation rerun to assess the new impact, or the ECO is delayed until the necessary resources to support the change are made available.

Once the decision has been made to implement the ECO, OPT can coordinate material and resource availability on the basis of:

- changing to a new part when the old part has stocked out or its stock has fallen to a certain level.
- using a specific amount of the old part, then switching to the new part.
- changing to the new part at a given date, hour, minute.

- changing to the new part when it becomes available.

In implementing an ECO, it may be desirable to process a single prototype for evaluation before beginning mass production. OPT can model this condition. A further discussion of the OPT modeling language's extreme flexibility can be reviewed by a perusal of the excellent article on this subject by Michael Maturo (listed in the references).

● The monolithic bill of materials and routing data base would be depicted by OPT and readily available for access by all company functions including engineering. In short, OPT allows a focusing of engineerings CAD/CAM use to directly improve shop floor control and corrective action.

Bottleneck Identification is the Key

As is depicted by Figure 3, the identification of bottlenecks on the shop floor for Engineering's corrective action is this discussion's key to improving shop floor control. Many of the Figure 4 rules of OPT relate directly to the effect that bottlenecks have upon the throughput and inventory of a manufacturing concern. The bottleneck's effect may be illustrated by dividing manufacturing's resources into two categories (bottlenecks and non-bottlenecks) as in the following example:

	Bottleneck Resource	Non-Bottleneck Resource
	X	Y
Demand on resource	200 hrs./month	150 hrs./month
Potential of resource	200 hrs./month	200 hrs./month
Time Components	Process Setup	Process Setup Idle
Definition	A resource whose capacity is less than or equal to the market demand.	A resource whose capacity is greater than market demand.

Note that a resource can be anything required to convert the inventory into throughput, including machines, workers, tools, fixtures, etc.

Several rules of OPT may now be illustrated by analyzing the interaction of the X (bottleneck) and Y (non-bottleneck) resources as in the following Case 1 example:

CASE 1 - X feeding Y

	Bottleneck Resource	Non-Bottleneck Resource
	X⟶Y	
Utilization	100%	75%
Total Demand	200 hrs./mon.	150 hrs./mon.
Capacity	200 hrs./mon.	200 hrs./mon.

While Y has capacity greater than X in the example, its utilization may not exceed 75% because it would be "starved" by X. This leads to the second rule of OPT:

OPT Rule 2: The level of utilization of a non-bottleneck resource is not determined by its own potential but by some other constraint in the system.

The second case illustrating the X and Y interaction depicts the non-bottleneck operation feeding the bottleneck as follows:

CASE 2: Y feeding X

	Bottleneck Resource	Non-Bottleneck Resource
	X⟵Y	
Utilization	100%	75%
Total Demand	200 hrs./mon.	150 hrs./mon.
Capacity	200 hrs./mon.	200 hrs./mon.

While Y has a greater capacity than X, activating Y above the 75% utilization level that is equivalent to the maximum capacity of X serves no other purpose than to build an inventory in "front" of the X operation. This leads to the third rule of OPT:

OPT Rule 3: Utilization and activation of a resource are not synonymous.

Since the bottleneck resource's potential equals the demand on the resource, there is no idle time. In the non-bottleneck, however, saving setup time will only increase idle time - here larger lot sizes will not save anything. Particularly if the bottleneck's demand exceeds its potential, an hour saved at a bottleneck increases throughput while an hour saved at a non-bottleneck resource is a mirage. Since overall throughput is limited by bottleneck potentials, engineering action to save a setup hour at the bottleneck provides an extra hour of throughput for the entire system.

This discussion leads to OPT Rules 4, 5 and 6:

OPT Rule 4: An hour lost at the bottleneck is an hour lost for the total system.
OPT Rule 5: An hour saved at a non-bottleneck is a mirage.
OPT Rule 6: Bottlenecks govern both throughput and inventory.

Summary

CAD/CAM is a powerful tool which can be used by Engineering to analyze and alleviate a variety of problems impacting activity on the Shop Floor. When finite scheduling is introduced to focus Engineering's attention toward the alleviation of bottleneck producing problems on the shop floor, overall throughput is increased and inventory is decreased - allowing the attainment of our primary shop floor control objectives.

The key element in this discussion has been the employment of finite scheduling techniques to facilitate bottleneck identification. OPT has figured as the cornerstone of the discussed methodology, allowing CAD/CAM to have an impact upon Shop Floor control. While this discussion has centered upon the use of OPT primarily as a bottleneck identification and scheduling tool, the OPT concepts and software can also be utilized:

● as a scheduling philosophy which centers on the identification of critical resources within the plant and maximizing the potential of these resources.

● where conventional production language has failed, OPT provides a powerful new language to be used in the modeling of manufacturing operations.

● as a software package for master production scheduling, material and capacity requirements planning and detailed scheduling. While the OPT concepts may be implemented without software or computer support, the development of computer software to support the thoughtware of the concepts has greatly facilitated OPT utilization.

● as a finite scheduling module within the software package which develops optimized production schedules.

● as a tool to focus effort toward the maximum return from data base accuracy before 100% data base accuracy is achieved.

As this paper indicates, the use of CAD/CAM, OPT and related systems will have a profound impact upon Production and Inventory Control in the future. As practicioners, we can look forward to a wealth of opportunities arising from the employment of this new technology.

References

Brummett, Forrest D.,"Manufacturing Simplicity Guides the Successful" CAD/CAM Technology, Spring 1984,pp. 29-30.

Colman, Harry L. and Richter, Robert A., "Computer Integrated Manufacturing", P & IM Review, July 1984, pp.30-69.

Fox, Robert E.,"MRP, Kanban or OPT - What's Best?" Inventories and Production Magazine, July-August 1982.

Friscia,Tony, "What is Implied by the Automated Factory?" P & IM Review, July 1983, pp.23-26.

Klein, Leo Roth, "CAD/CAM's Impact on Production and Inventory Control: The Manufacturing Engineering Data Base.", APICS 26th Annual International Conference Proceedings, Nov. 1983, pp.157-164.

Maturo, Michael P., "The Language of OPT", APICS 26th Annual International Conference Proceedings, Nov. 1983, pp.567-571.

Biography

Victor G. Lippa is currently Manager of Consulting with Creative Output Inc. of Milford, Connecticut. Most recently serving as Manager of Materials and Production Control for Raytheon Company's Equipment Division. Vic has held positions of increasing responsibility over the past sixteen (16) years in the Manufacturing, Materials Management, Quality Control and Marketing fields. He has participated in or directed a wide variety of systems projects including four successful MRP implementations, and is currently assisting companies in applying the OPT Concepts for planning and scheduling manufacturing operations.

Vic has an MBA degree from Rochester Institute of Technology, where he graduated with highest honors. He is a member of the Honorary Society of Phi Kappa Phi, and is APICS certified in Production and Inventory Control at the Fellow Level.

Mr. Lippa has lectured throughout the United States over the past ten years, and has been a very active APICS speaker. He has served in a variety of APICS positions including Chapter President.

USING COMPUTER-AIDED MANUFACTURING IN BATCH MANUFACTURING OPERATIONS

Peter A. Boyer
Key Systems, Inc.

WHAT IS COMPUTER-AIDED MANUFACTURING?

The use of computers to operate and control machinery in the manufacturing process can reduce labor requirements, maximize raw material use, and lower production costs substantially.

This presentation addresses companies that are considering CAM implementation, and provides a brief overview of CAM applications as a basis for decisions about CAM benefits and costs.

Evolution and Objectives of CAM

Computer-aided manufacturing (CAM) began in the mid-1950s, when punched paper tape was used to control machinery cycles. The early numerical control (NC) machines have evolved into today's CAM systems, which include process planning, robotics, and factory management.

CAM differs from conventional automated manufacturing in several ways. Conventional automation, usually referred to as fixed automation, involves the replacement of labor by a special machine designed for a specific function that is usually continuous and repetitive, for example, a transfer machine in the auto industry. CAM, on the other hand, provides the versatility of computer control to perform various manufacturing functions randomly. Thus, CAM can be effectively applied in batch process manufacturing, where the lot sizes are small (from a few units to as many as a hundred). Advances in NC, robotics, automated handling systems, and common data bases make programmable batch process manufacturing possible.

CAM's primary objective is to increase productivity through adaptable, programmable systems; other more specific objects include:

- Providing random and flexible manufacturing for a set or family of work pieces (i.e., the capability to introduce any work piece or a family of parts into the system at any time without downtime)
- Applying the system's flexibility and productivity to small batch operations as well as to large batch and continuous process production
- Using the concept of machining-center manufacturing (the ability to maximize the combination of operations at a single workstation) to enhance small batch operations

When to Use CAM

Batch size and demand are critical variables in determining the most appropriate applications for CAM. Although CAM is thought to be applicable only in large batch operations, research reveals that small batch manufacturing is equally productive for CAM. CAM is ideally used for several different parts having intermittent or cyclic demand.

Other considerations for determining the advisability of using a CAM operation include:

- The level of machining complexity (the more complex the part the more applicable the use of CAM)
- Situations calling for multiple machining operations or machining more than one surface
- Conditions that call for frequent design changes or new models
- Close control of machining tolerances
- Operations that require long setup times
- Operations that demand loading and positioning of work pieces, tools, fixtures, inserts, dies, and jigs
- New parts for which no tooling exists
- Operations that require detailed operator skills and close control

A prime advantage of CAM is its flexibility; applications should therefore be sought that benefit from this flexibility. Because CAM's programs can move rapidly between complex operations, CAM enables a business to assume a wider range of jobs while increasing the productivity of each. The element of adaptiveness further allows CAM to aid in situations where lead times are shorter than usual, inventory constraints exist, setup and changeover times need to be curtailed, floor space is at a premium, and the number of work shifts can be increased.

SELECTING PARTS AND MACHINES

The first step in a CAM implementation sequence is determining which parts can be matched to available machines to maximize the cost savings compared with alternative production methods. Although many qualitative factors affect this selection, the driving concern for selecting a suitable combination of parts and machines is usually economic.

Part and machine selection can be performed either manually or with a computer. Manual methods work well when the number of candidate parts is fewer than approximately 40 and only a few CAM-type machines are being considered. A computer-based part and machine selection tool has been developed for use when a larger number of candidates is involved. In any case, both methods employ the same concept-relative production cost savings. The current cost of each candidate part--either for producing it in-house or purchasing it from a vendor--is calculated first. The costs to produce each part using CAM are then estimated. The parts with the largest savings are then chosen to fill the capacity of the machines chosen. The procedures for the manual part selection method are described in the following sections. (Computerized procedures for part selection are similar to manual methods.)

Establishment of Initial Guidelines

Certain basic issues require consideration. First, the company must determine the maximum size of the system (i.e., the number of machines). This figure can be determined by floor space availability, budgetary constraints, or simply by the number of parts currently being handled.

Another issue is total annual operating time. CAM is capital intensive: therefore, the longer it operates, the better the return on investment (ROI). This logic suggests a three-shift, seven-day-per-week operation. However, many factory environments cannot support such an operation.

The company must determine the class of parts to be produced: prismatic (boxlike, basically rectangular, solid parts), rotational (shafts and disks), or a combination. Machines for each part class will have their own design peculiarities and problems. The choice should be based on the available work content in each class as well as how familiar the organization is with the available technology for each class. Once the class is selected, it is necessary to select from among current parts, new parts, spare parts, or some combination of these.

The range of part sizes to include depends on several factors, including the average size of the parts. Small parts (six-inch machining cube or less) usually require less work content and may need to be at any given machine only for a few minutes. However, shorter cycle times mean that more parts will be in production at any one time; this may overload the production and production control systems and degrade overall production efficiency. Large parts (36-inch machining cube or more) require larger, more expensive machines. The size and weight of large parts usually necessitate special material handling considerations.

For these reasons, machining cube sizes are usually limited to less than 36 inches and more than 6 inches. This allows the parts to be transported by conventional material handling systems, permits multiple loading of small parts on one large fixture, lengthens the total time at each machine, and reduces the possibility of material handling system bottlenecks.

Preselection Process

Buyers must select from the total set of parts of potential interest, a subset suitable for computer-aided manufacture. Similarly, out of the total of CAM machines available, buyers must identify a subset suitable for the set of candidate parts. This preliminary selection step results in feasible sets of parts and machines, which can then be analyzed in more detail.

Preselection of Parts. If the candidate parts have been coded according to a group technology classification system, then the fastest and simplest approach to preselection is to have the computer sort parts according to CAM-compatible part attributes[1]. Typical attributes include:

- Desired machining cube
- Material used (e.g., aluminum or steel)

American Production & Inventory Control Society

- Form (prismatic solid, box, disk, flat)
- Types of operations (milling, drilling, boring)
- Tolerances
- Production quantity
- Machining time
- Current number of fixturings

Without a group technology classification system, manual sorting by reviewing part prints and process plans is required.

Another method of preselecting parts is to group the parts into families according to their similarities. One or two of the families can then be chosen for manufacture. Three common methods of grouping parts into families are:
- By assembly: grouping all the parts needed to produce some end item or subassembly
- By size and common manufacturing operations: grouping parts that require approximately the same machining cube and those that require the same types of machining operations (e.g., milling, drilling, tapping)
- By type: grouping all parts of the same type (e.g., transmission housings)

The drawback to this approach is that the most cost-effective combination may include parts from several families. However, if each family consists of many parts, it may be possible to choose the family with the greatest savings potential and continue the preselection and selection processes on that family alone.

In addition, the number of fixturings per part can be a criterion for preselection. One guideline is that if the part must be fixtured more than three or four times, it should be rejected because of the time and expense involved in multiple refixturings. Also, a part made of a hard material that requires extensive work will rapidly wear out tools and impose excessive requirements for tool replacements. Such intervention interrupts production and interferes with productivity.

Preselection of Machines. The class(es) of parts and the range of machining cubes chosen will limit the classes of machines that can be selected. Average accuracy requirements must also be considered, as well as part materials. Finally, experience with certain types of machines (e.g., horizontal rather than vertical machining centers), can also be a factor in limiting the number of candidate machines.

Data Collection

More detailed data must be collected for the preselected parts and machines to enable selection from among those candidates. The collected data should include:
- The machine classes that the selected parts must visit and the proper manufacturing (routing) sequence for each part.
- Total process time estimates for each machine class.
- Fixturing concepts and fixturing times.
- Current manufacturing cost estimates based on the current cost of buying the part or on the components of inhouse cost (e.g., direct labor, overhead) for each candidate part. Alternatively, the hourly machine rate cost used to quote jobs can be used. In any case, the cost concepts should not include any reference to capital recovery costs or depreciation; they should strictly reflect daily operation cost.
- Projected machine costs, based on vendor quotes for actual machines in the preselected classes. (Prices should be obtained from several vendors in each machine class, and for several machine sizes in each class.) The use of the computerized part and machine selection software may necessitate calculation of the amortized cost of the machine and the remainder of the system (based on system size). Calculating this figure requires amortizing the machine costs over the expected life of the FMS (usually 10 years), amortizing the cost of other components over the same period, and adding the two costs. The concept of salvage is important because the equipment may be sold at the end of its useful life.

Estimation of Manufacturing Costs

To estimate the savings that will result from use of CAM, the prospective buyer must calculate the approximate annual manufacturing, cost and apply it to the amount of time the part will be in production. This time is the ma-

chining time plus the load and unload time required for each part fixturing, multiplied by the part's yearly production requirement. This estimated cost is always approximate because it is based on assumptions regarding staffing requirements, machining time, and fixturing.

A company can roughly estimate the staffing requirements. Typically, the requirements for every four CAM machines in a system are one system manager, one-quarter of an electrical technician, and one-quarter of a mechanical technician. Depending on the number of tools that may be required in the system (60 tools per machine is a good guideline), one-half to one tool setter will be needed for every five machines. Finally, if part cycle times are short or each part requires many fixturings, at least two loaders will be required.

As part of staffing estimates, labor rates and overhead should be calculated. In the simplest case, the conventional direct labor cost plus overhead or the machine rate can be used. However, this figuring usually does not provide sufficient overhead allocation because overhead rates for conventional operations are generally based on the assumption of one employee per machine, which is not the case with CAM. The purchasing department must often work with the accounting department to develop new direct labor and applied overhead rates.

Assumptions about machining time are easier to make. In the simplest case, the cycle times in CAM equal those in the conventional method. This is a reasonable assumption if parts are currently being produced on NC machining centers using palletized fixtures and pallet shuttles. If standard NC machining centers and job-shop-type temporary fixtures are currently being used, the switch to CAM can cut up to 25 percent of the cycle time. If CAM is replacing conventional manual machines (especially if the equipment is old), an approximately 50-percent cut in cycle time can be anticipated.

Fixturing time is the easiest variable to estimate. Although the number of fixturings varies with each part, the average part requires two fixturings, and each fixturing requires five minutes to load and three minutes to unload.

Finally, the buyer must estimate the amortized cost of fixtures for each part. The amortized cost represents the company's annual cost of buying the fixture, based on an estimated rate of return at which the company could have invested in some other project.

Part and Machine Selection

From the candidates chosen in the preselection phase, the prospective buyer must select parts and machines. To begin the selection process, the buyer must first choose a set of machines from the available machine classes. This selection can be either arbitrary or based on the current production equipment used to produce some of the parts. The estimated number of machines from each machine class is somewhat arbitrary; however, the total number of machines from all classes should equal the maximum set by management at the beginning of this process.

To choose parts for loading into these machines, the company must calculate the saving in cost for each part; this can be done by subtracting the projected manufacturing cost from the conventional manufacturing cost. The machines should then be "loaded" with the parts having the highest values. Available machine time should be based on annual production hours available multiplied by an availability or efficiency factor (usually 65 to 80 percent) to account for such factors as downtime and preventive maintenance. If two parts have equal saving potential, the part that requires less machining time is usually preferable; therefore, machining times as well as estimated cost reductions should be compared when choosing parts. Parts should be chosen until either all machines are loaded or no parts are left, after which the cost reduction for all chosen parts should be totaled.

CAM SYSTEM OPERATING CONSIDERATIONS

Various considerations affect the design process. Among these are:
- Desired flexibility
- Machinability and process planning
- Required precision
- Required system availability
- Desired material handling system configuration
- Other desired processes (e.g., inspection, heat treatment, finishing)

Flexibility

Although flexibility is desirable, it may increase cost. By the same token, too many special-purpose machines can hamper a system's ability to handle new part types. The desired level of flexibility affects the system design. The most important aspect of flexibility is the random-processing capability that allows more than one part number in the system at one time. Usually, ratios of part types to one another can be arranged to meet current production needs, allowing rapid adaptability to changing market requirements. In addition, CAM is relatively insensitive to engineering design and tooling changes.

Some CAM systems exhibit flexibility of a second type: fault tolerance. They continue to operate almost normally in the presence of machine failures, with other machines "covering" for the one out of service.

A third type of flexibility is the ability to operate virtually unattended. Maintenance and part fixturing can be performed during the first shift, with much of the actual production occurring during the second and third shifts. Unattended second- and third-shift operation implies some automatic, online inspection. Very high system availability implies not only reliable system components but also possible redundancies, such as backup computers, duplicate machine types, and alternative routings in the material handling system.

Buyers must also consider the desired system's ability to accommodate future increases in demand or to allow a phased installation that will keep the available capital from being overtaxed. The degree expandability desired will affect the choice of the material handling system and the arrangement of equipment in the configuration.

Machinability and Process Plans

Basic data about how the part can be processed is crucial in the system design process. Overestimation of feeds and speeds, for example, can result in poor part surface finish, rapid turnover of tools, and a reduction in system throughout.

A logical approach to defining machinability data is to first obtain the optimum feeds and speeds for the part materials for each tool category from a machining data handbook. Then, the machine operators should be asked which feeds and speeds they routinely use when machining those same materials. CAM feeds and speeds should fall between these two values, adjusted for factors such as part rigidity, the increased ability of dedicated fixtures to hold the parts, and the use of new machine tools.

If a tool's feeds or speeds change during the system design process, machining time must be recalculated for all the parts using that tool; if there are many parts, this revision process can be extremely time-consuming, especially if many alternatives are being evaluated. The recalculations can be simplified by using a computer program to calculate cycle times. When the metal's characteristics are well known, it is better to assess the accuracy of machinability data before beginning configuration design, temper it with usual shop practice, and attempt to hold that data constant throughout the configuration design exercise.

Computer-Integrated Manufacturing. Process planning for an integrated CAM system differs from process planning for standalone machines in two critical areas: the fixturing approach used for each part and the selection of cutting tools. In a CAM system it is important to minimize both manual and automatic handling of the part. Careful attention to fixture designs can help. The use of window-frame and pedestal-type fixtures allows the greatest part access when either four- or five-axis machining centers are used.

The goal in system design is to have one fixture type per part type in order to have only one load-unload sequence. Although this goal is seldom attainable, each part can be analyzed to determine the best fixturing orientation with respect to the machines and required operations. Then the fixture should be designed to maintain that orientation. Also, by matching machine axes, the number of fixtures and orientations can be minimized. For example, if vertical turret lathes are being used for the rotational work content, vertical machining centers may be appropriate for the prismatic work content.

Desired Material Handling System Configuration

The simplest material handling system consists of a person using a cart to move palleted parts from machines that are under computer direction, to reduce machine wait-ing times, a shuttle loader could be added to each machine tool. This manual system works for small CAM systems in which the distance between machines is short and parts are relatively small and light. However, for larger systems or heavier parts, automatic material handling systems are more applicable. These systems consist primarily of carts, conveyors, or robots that carry pallets automatically to and from each shuttle loader. If the loader is full, the pallet will circulate in the material handling system, wait in front of the machine, or go to an offline storage area. Although a person is usually required to fixture and defixture parts at load/unload stations, the rest of the system is under direct computer control. The choice of the material handling system type is somewhat restricted in practice. Most CAM system vendors have designed their systems around one, or at most two, types of material handling systems.

Other Desirable Processes

The system design phase must address any processes, in addition to machining, that are desirable and whether these processes should be performed online. Such processes may include very high accuracy machining, washing, inspection, stress relieving, heat treating, deburring, finishing, marking, and assembly. Except for washing and inspection, these processes generally should be kept offline. A good guideline is that if the part must be removed from the pallet or fixture before an operation is started, that operation should be done offline.

However, considering the control problems created by sending parts offline and returning them, the cost of providing online equipment for some of these processes may be justifiable in some cases, though the processes need not be automated. For example, a manual inspection station could be online.

Developing Operational Strategies

At this point in the evaluation process, realistic machine loading data is estimated. Two strategies are important to the optimal work center loading:
- Batching and balancing
- Scheduling and dispatching

Production Batching and Machine Balancing. Production batching, the division of production into subgroups or lots, is necessary when tool storage capacity limitations do not allow all parts to be machined at one time. Occasionally, balancing the work load on the machines may be so difficult that batching is required.

Balancing the work load on each machine tool attempts to maximize machine-tool utilization as well as relieve or avoid potential bottlenecks in the system, with the intent of maximizing system throughput. Often, however, it will not be possible to balance everything, especially in systems with different types of machines (e.g., general-purpose machines and special machines). Balancing can also be difficult when many tools are needed for a part. The work content division and tool-changer storage limitations are crucial. Additionally, if parts are required to visit several machines, the effects of transport time and material handling system congestion may reduce system throughput.

When the batching and balancing exercises have been completed, specific parts and tools will have been allocated to specific machines in an attempt to maximize system throughput. This allocation process is iterative; optimization software greatly reduces the need for trial-and-error batching and balancing. The allocation provides realistic information for the simulation step that follows. Results of the simulation in turn may suggest modifications of the allocation, and resimulation may be required.

Scheduling and Dispatching. The strategies for batching and balancing must be implemented systematically through scheduling algorithms and dispatching rules that sequence part movement through the system. Dispatching rules must be determined so that the simulations can be realistic.

INDUSTRIAL RELATIONS IN A CAM ENVIRONMENT

Management perceptions and employee reactions to CAM can be as important in analyzing costs and benefits as are interest and depreciation expenses and operational savings. Selection of personnel to operate, program, and maintain CAM equipment is paramount. The work force must be educated to accept a CAM process rather than regard the introduction to computer-aided devices as jeopardizing job security. Similarly, union officials should be introduced to CAM and its potential benefits.

CAM can be viewed as an opportunity for employees to upgrade their jobs by being trained as programmers and maintenance mechanics, for example. Such technologically based jobs offer a change for secure employment as well as promotion. Training costs for such personnel can be high, but the company benefits in improved morale and productivity could outweigh such expenditures.

Managers might also have some misconceptions about CAM that hinder its use. Executives who pay lip service to using CAM but do not grasp its philosophy might envision a plant without operators and a better bottom line. They tend to overlook the fact that CAM plant managers will have to change their philosophy of manufacturing management.

References

Johnson, I. "Designing and Evaluating Flexible Manufacturing Systems," Computers In Manufacturing: Execution and Control Systems (Pennsauken NJ: Auerbach Publishers, April 1982)

Levulis, R.J. "Group Technology and Machine Center Identification," Computers In Manufacturing: Execution and Control Systems (Pennsauken NJ: Auerbach Publishers, April 1982)

Tombari, H. "Analyzing the Benefits and Costs of Computer-Aided Manufacturing Methods," Computers In Manufacturing: Execution and Control Systems (Pennsauken NJ: Auerbach Publishers, April 1982)

Flexible Manufacturing System Handbook - Volume III: Buyers'/User's Guide (Cambridge MA: Charles Stark Draper Laboratory Inc., 1983)

PETER A. BOYER

As an applications engineer with Key Systems Inc., a microcomputer software vendor, Peter A. Boyer is responsibile for guiding the development and implementation of customer's microcomputer-based business and manufacturing systems. Before joining Key Systems, he was an editor with Auerbach Publishers Inc., where he developed Auerbach's five-volume Computers In Manufacturing series and the Automated Material Handling and Storage volume. He has in-depth manufacturing systems experience as a representative of a major software vendor, a policies and procedures analyst, and a manufacturing systems development project manager.

Boyer is an active member of the American Production and Inventory Control Society (APICS); he is certified by APICS in material requirements planning and inventory control, has been a program reviewer for the APICS National Conference, serves on the Central Montgomery Chapter's board of directors, and publishes that organization's newsletter.

TECHNOLOGY MANAGEMENT AND FACTORY AUTOMATION

William T. Muir, CPIM
Price Waterhouse

INTRODUCTION

The introduction of state-of-the-art processing technologies into the manufacturing base of the United States will not, in and of itself, necessarily improve productivity or help contain costs. Similarly, while intangible and noneconomic factors are important to the capital investment justification process, the ultimate success of the implementation of advanced manufacturing technologies must be measured by its impact on manufacturing cost, at preplanned levels of capacity, capacity utilization and production mix. Cost-reduction (containment) success will only be accomplished by making sure that attendant financial management concepts and practices support the identification, analysis, introduction and management of new technologies and their revised cost-behavior patterns.

It can be suggested that the implementation of advanced manufacturing technologies has been hindered by antiquated cost-benefit tools which emphasize only direct labor savings. The reality of advanced manufacturing technologies is that the cost-behavior patterns are shifting to a lower percentage of direct labor and a higher percentage of other "value added" costs. This trend is even more pronounced when one considers current forecasts of the factory of the future. Therefore, if technologies are introduced which reduce direct labor, and overhead costs are allocated based on direct labor, overhead costs may seem to be reduced for individual products while, in fact, total costs have not been as favorably impacted.

The objective of emphasizing the importance of manufacturing process technology cost-benefit analysis and benefits tracking is not to replace present cost-accounting/performance measurement management systems. Rather, it is to encourage support for expanded financial management concepts. Definitions of these key financial concepts include:

Cost-Benefit Analysis: This is the financial process which assists in (1) identifying those operational areas where the introduction of enhanced technology will have the greatest financial impact, (2) evaluating the project economics of potential high-cost reduction projects, (3) preparing an analysis and plan to identify and manage project risk and (4) identifying benefits-tracking requirements so that the planning/control loop can be closed in order to monitor whether benefits are realized and, more importantly, to help manage the realization of benefits.

Benefits Tracking is the continual process of determining the actual level of project investment and associated recurring costs and savings. This information is compared to what was planned during the cost-benefit analysis phase and, subsequently, to current estimates based on any changed circumstances.

COST-BENEFIT ANALYSIS

Cost-benefit analysis uses estimates, engineered standards and/or actual cost information which has been collected on a manufacturing function basis. Based on this information, proposed capital investment projects are then analyzed according to their productivity improvement potential, economics and implementation risks.

The following guidelines have been prepared to aid the executive of the cost-benefit process. Each guideline contains (1) a statement of the guideline, (2) the current environment relative to the guideline and (3) a brief suggested approach for applying the guideline. The guidelines cover the topics of:

1. Defining manufacturing functions (activities),
2. AS IS cost baseline preparation,
3. Evaluating the efficiency and effectiveness of manufacturing functions,
4. Improvement project prioritization ("needs matrix"),
5. Selecting improvement technologies,
6. Developing cost-behavior patterns for each technology alternative,
7. Assessing exogenous factors and risk,
8. Assessing integration ("islands of technology"), and
9. Time-phased economics analysis.

Guideline No. 1

Structure the cost-benefit analysis on a manufacturing function basis.

o   Current environment

Most cost-management systems are accounting (cost-of-goods-sold and inventory valuation) oriented and do not adequately measure operations performance or the value-added cost of manufacturing functions. Likewise, the current focus of many cost/performance measurement systems is at the organizational (e.g., department/cost center) level. While this is consistent with organizational objectives as expressed in the financial budgets, there is no assurance that the cost centers are organized consistently with manufacturing functions as defined in the IDEF-type methodologies.

o   Suggested approach

Most manufacturing management improvement programs support the use of a "top-down" factory analysis that uses a Node Tree type of documentation. These approaches are structured to identify the manufacturing functions currently performed ("AS IS" or proposed ("TO BE"). Consistency between the capital expenditure, production planning and control, performance monitoring and financial monitoring processes can only be achieved by structuring the cost-benefit analysis on an equivalent basis.

Guideline No. 2

Analyze all significant costs incurred by each manufacturing function.

o   Current environment

Manufacturing cost can be thought of as the quantification of the factors of production employed to produce a product. In other words, the cost of direct labor, direct material, machinery and equipment, information systems, etc., as recorded in financial statements represents a unique mix of the factors of production as used by a particular company. It is the goal of most companies to analyze this current mix and identify areas where changes could reduce operating cost while recovering the expense of implementing the change.

For example, direct labor might be significantly reduced by replacing selected manual processes with automated robots. However, robotic technology will impact manufacturing operations in areas other than just direct labor and the cost of the robot. Manufacturing lead time, quality and the ability to respond to changes in product mix will be equally affected. In fact, it has often been observed that total manufacturing costs have risen despite demonstrated reductions in direct labor.

The source of this conflict can be attributed to traditional cost-accounting systems, which typically collect direct labor and direct material only and then allocate all remaining costs as a percentage of direct labor, making the assumption that indirect costs will change in the same proportion as direct labor costs. This relationship is not generally valid with the application of advanced manufacturing technologies. Generally, new technology involves the application of computerization and automation to processes which were previously controlled manually. This trend has resulted in a decreasing percentage of direct labor, an increasing percentage of indirect expenses, and a significant decline in manufacturing processes where the operator controls the pace of the process.

o   Suggested approach

Develop a cost model for both the facility and each manufacturing function which identifies all significant manufacturing costs. The cost model should be structured using a hierarchy of cost groupings that can be successively decomposed into a detailed analysis of significant (key success factor) cost elements. At a minimum, manufacturing technology improvement projects should analyze the following high-level cost groupings:

Manufacturing cost = Direct labor
                   + Material/Utilization
                   + Machinery and equipment
                     (including tooling)
                   + Operations support
                   + Engineering
                   + Plant and facilities
                   + Information systems
                   + Inventory
                   + G&A support
                   + Finance

The cost-behavior patterns of technology improvement projects describe the predicted impact of the technology on the factors of production as identified in the cost model. It is important that the assumptions and definitions underlying the cost-behavior pattern (both "AS IS" and "TO BE") be explicitly stated and documented.
The cost groupings of the model will vary from company to company.

Guideline No. 3

Measure the efficiency and effectiveness of the manufacturing function, as well as its cost.

o   Current environment

The goal of this guideline is to use a "top-down" approach to identify areas which represent the greatest potential for cost reduction (net of improvement implementation cost). One dimension of identifying high potential savings is to determine how efficiently and effectively a manufacturing function is currently being performed. (Efficiency is the measure of how well current resources are being used - effectiveness is the measure of productivity improvement possible from employing superior technologies). The opportunity for improvement is greatest for functions which currently have inefficient/ineffective performance and are high in value-added cost.

o   Suggested approach

Each function identified in the "top-down" model should be analyzed to determine how efficiently/effectively (relative to current company and/or accepted industry standards) the function is being executed. The analysis should emphasize the quantification of problem areas, diagnose their causes and provide benchmarks against which to measure improvements. Some of the measures used, other than cost, might include:

- throughput time   - schedule adherence
- machine utilization   - scrap and/or rework
- labor utilization   - capacity utilization

Guideline No. 4

Develop a "Needs Matrix" for use in prioritizing the improvement projects.

o   Current environment

Most improvement projects are directed at those manufacturing functions which have the highest gross cost, irrespective of how efficient or effective that function currently is. Improvement funds should be channeled to the functions and activities having the greatest cost-reduction potential. These may, or may not, be those functions having the greatest gross cost.

o   Suggested approach

The identification of high cost and low productivity can be facilitated by developing a matrix of the manufacturing functions, their associated key success factors, the current efficiency/effectiveness of the function relative to its key success factors and its gross cost.

Guideline No. 5

Evaluate the technology alternatives for improving the productivity of the functions with the highest potential payback. Select those technologies which offer the highest probability of attaining the potential.

o   Current environment

It is common, in many companies starting out on a program to upgrade the effectiveness of their manufacturing functions, to have in mind the solutions they want to implement before they have completely defined and analyzed their problems (Guidelines 1 to 4) or considered the alternatives available for reducing costs. This "solutions looking for problems" scenario often results in technologies being implemented which only relocate costs, but do not result in an overall reduction.

o   Suggested approach

Once the functions and activities having the greatest cost-reduction potential have been identified, all the available alternatives (within reason) for reducing costs within that function should be identified. Those technologies which, on the basis of their implementation history or technological promise, seem to offer the greatest potential for cost-effective implementation would be those selected for further investigation.

Guideline No. 6

Determine a cost-behavior pattern for each of the technology alternatives selected.

o   Current environment

As has been previously mentioned, many organizations expect a manufacturing improvement program to reduce only direct labor, where direct labor is defined as only that used during the actual production process. The impact of a new technology on support costs (such as indirect labor, energy, maintenance and others) is often neglected.

o   Suggested approach

Using a cost-model approach, such as that suggested by Guideline No. 2, determine the cost-behavior patterns for each of the technology alternatives being investigated within each manufacturing function. By using an analytical tool, such as the model described, there is greater assurance that all costs will be analyzed and cost reduction will be actually attained, not just cost relocation.

Guideline No. 7

Analyze the effect of exogenous factors (such as implementation risk, inflation, human factors and legislative trends) to the extent that they can be quantified.

o   Current environment

Economic conditions make any capital investment difficult to quantify. In particular, the United States economy has recently been subject to a number of problems, such as:

- Varying rates of inflation
- High rates of interest
- Increased off-shore competition and their better productivity growth

- A long-term trend toward greater leveraging of capital investments

In addition to these varying conditions, each of the technology improvement alternatives is subject to a number of risk factors related to its successful implementation. These factors include:

- Technological threshold
- External competition
- Education and training of current staff
- Other support requirements

o   Suggested approach

Each project must be assessed to determine the risk of not achieving the anticipated results, whether due to exogenous factors, economic factors or fate. The important point is to recognize most of the environmental factors which will come to bear on the project(s) and:

- Identify the most significant risk factors for each improvement opportunity which would result in the project not achieving the anticipated savings. By performing a sensitivity analysis on each cost-behavior pattern, the underlying assumptions will be analyzed to determine significant risk exposures.

- Calculate a "worst case" project cost savings for each significant risk exposure.

- Assess the technological risk for each project.

- Identify a risk-management plan that would increase the probability of project success by focusing project management attention on the previously identified risk factors.

Guideline No. 8

Determine the impact of the integration of the improvement technology.

o   Current environment

Traditionally, manufacturing advances have been incorporated on an individual basis which can be characterized as "islands of technology." Realizing the full benefits of advanced technologies will require a technology management strategy which integrates each of the new improvement technologies with each other.

o   Suggested approach

The cost-benefit analysis should quantify (to the extent possible) the synergistic effect of all projects to determine their impact on total manufacturing cost. This can best be accomplished through the use of simulation-type models.

Guideline No. 9

Determine the time-phased economics of each of the selected improvement projects.

o   Current environment

While intangible and noneconomic factors are important in a capital investment justification process, the ultimate success of the implementation of advance manufacturing technology must be measured by its impact on total manufacturing cost.

o   Suggested approach

Cost-benefit analysis should provide management with several levels of economic analysis including:

- Annualized savings
- ROI
- Payback
- Cost impact on:
  o   fixed cost
  o   variable cost (per unit)
  o   nonrecurring cost

- Risk-adjusted savings

BENEFITS TRACKING

The goal of benefits tracking is to measure the actual impact of advanced technologies on total manufacturing cost and performance measurements and compare this data to the base cost as forecasted by the cost-benefit analysis. This analysis should be derived from the same data base used to report financial requirements, but must go beyond these minimums and address significant indirect costs.

Current benefits-tracking and cost-accounting techniques are steeped in traditional accounting theory. This tradition states that manufacturing cost data should be collected by work order for direct labor and direct materials, and that all other costs should be collected in aggregate and allocated to production on a quantifiable basis (typically direct labor). This approach was developed for a manufacturing environment where direct labor and materials were the dominant portion of manufacturing cost and the direct laborer controlled the pace of the manufacturing process.

Today, however, this model is no longer universally appropriate, as evidenced by ever-increasing overhead rates. The proposed factory of the future will contain even less direct costs (other than material) than those being experienced in the factory of today. This environment dictates a revised approach to measuring the benefits attained from implementing advanced manufacturing technologies.

Guideline No. 1

Monitor those costs and performance measures which have been identified to be critical by the cost-benefit analysis.

o   Current environment

Most current cost-accounting systems collect direct labor and materials by work order, or department, for identified manufacturing activities. While factory data collection hardware has evolved to higher levels of sophistication, the type of information collected has remained the same. One of the primary reasons for this information stagnation is that the cost of collecting data in a labor-intensive environment can be significant since data collection activities are performed in lieu of production work activities. In this environment, it is often difficult to cost justify the necessary detailed data collection.

The factory of the future, however, will be highly automated and increasingly dependent on computerization. Thus, it will be possible to access a significant amount of detailed information which was not previously economically available.

o   Suggested approach

Develop a benefits-tracking plan at the conclusion of the initial cost-benefit analysis. The plan should identify the:

o   required information to be monitored by success factors
o   source of the "AS IS" data
o   source of the "TO BE" data

As advanced technology is incorporated into a manufacturing process, the type of information available from the process will change. The information required for the cost-benefit justification of the advanced technology should be evaluated relative to the information that is potentially available from the new process and from the present reporting system.

Guideline No. 2

Ensure cost and performance measures are compatible with all internal and external reporting requirements, including generally accepted accounting principles and cost-accounting standards.

o   Current environment

Financial reporting has resulted in a significant superstructure of data requirements. The purpose of these requirements is to provide reporting standardization and information necessary to determine a fair price and adequate profit. Unfortunately, there is also a significant cost associated with this compliance reporting.

o   Suggested approach

The benefits-tracking system should be structured to provide data from a common base that can be used to satisfy other compliance reporting requirements. One method of ensuring this congruence is to develop a matrix of benefits-tracking operational management and financial-reporting requirements. Any data not currently being reported should be evaluated to determine whether it is in variance with good management concepts.

Guideline No. 3

The data provided by the benefits-tracking system must be verifiable and auditable.

o   Current environment

The development of an auditable, reliable and accurate cost-management methodology is extremely important to the success of a manufacturing cost-reduction program. The system must provide feedback to management to judge the progress of the program. Problems can be highlighted and solutions implemented only if the assumptions underlying the cost projections can be scrutinized. A well-structured audit trail will facilitate a detailed analysis of variances from forecast.

o   Suggested approach

Document all sources of information which were previously identified in the cost-benefit tracking plan, including report number (by date), person or document number. Each assumption should be explained in detail with supporting documentation where appropriate.

Guideline No. 4

Cost-benefit projections should be tracked for a sufficient time to determine whether the actual savings have been achieved.

o   Current environment

Traditionally, advanced manufacturing projects are justified using corporate capital investment procedures where ROI and payback are the basis for selecting projects. An ongoing determination of whether the actual savings have been achieved is normally not an integral part of the cost-justification process. Instead, the projects become part of the normal manufacturing process and are reported through the traditional cost-management systems.

o   Suggested approach

Since most cost-management systems are not structured on the same basis as the capital-investment systems, an ongoing tracking of savings could best be achieved either by modifying the existing cost-management system, developing a dual system or performing a periodic review of the project results. The determination of whether to restructure the cost-management system should be made relative to the perceived use of the information within the management decision-making process and the cost of modifying the system. Even if the decision is made to restructure the cost-management system, the change should be evolutionary and integrated into the corporate strategic factory modernization plan.

If the decision is made to not modify the current cost-management system, periodic industrial engineering studies could be used to validate the savings. In this case, the benefits-tracking plan should include the timing and scope of the audits and the procedures used for verification of the results.

INTERFACING NEW PRODUCT INTRODUCTION WITH MRP

Ronald T. Pannesi, CPIM
Michigan State University and Eastern Michigan State University

This paper describes a method for integrating new products into a company's MRP system. The procedure was developed and used very successfully by a medium sized computer equipment manufacturing company.

INTRODUCTION

New product development can be a long and arduous process in the computer industry. Even in the case of an add-on option, extensive development and testing for compatibility and reliability often occurs. In one mid-sized manufacturer of computer equipment, new product introduction is a way of life and the company is known for its state-of-the-art products. The company also has implemented a successful MRP system. With the constant new product development activity and the basic engineering bias of company management, it had been accepted practice to fully develop a new product and then turn completed drawings, specifications and parts lists over to manufacturing for production (and integration into manufacturing systems). Recognizing the critical role of Purchasing in new product development, a full time Senior Buyer was "assigned" to Engineering to coordinate purchases of castings, plastic enclosures and other long lead tools and parts which were part of the new product. Standard components and parts which were used in the new product were "assumed" to be available.

With the advent of MRP, the task of integrating new products into the system took on a new importance. This was because of the Bill of Material structuring required and the need to identify requirements for standard parts in the new product early in the development effort. This was particularly important for long lead standard components such as Integrated Circuits.

Before system integration with MRP could be addressed, a new product development procedure had to be identified and defined.

NEW PRODUCT PROCEDURES

After analysis and discussion, a new product development cycle was defined, consisting of five phases:
*Goal and Concept Definition
*Engineering Breadboard and Mechanical Model
*Engineering Prototype
*Manufacturing Prototype and
*Pilot Production

Goals, inputs, outputs and responsibilities were carefully defined for each phase.

GOAL AND CONCEPT DEFINITION

The first phase, Goal and Concept Definition, begins with the accumulation of ideas for new products generated by a variety of company personnel. Most generally, Marketing/Sales and Design Engineering are the principal originators of new product ideas. But occasionally, other groups like Quality Assurance have generated ideas based on problems they have observed. A special department called Product Management is responsible for accumulation and evaluation of new ideas. A top management committee reviews recommendations made by the Product Management department and OK's certain ones for continued development based on market analysis and strategic goals. A Product Specification (including both functional parameters and hardware specifications) is generated for those which are approved. An overall rough schedule is also produced at this time. Basically, the question "What do we want to make?" is answered in this phase.

ENGINEERING BREADBOARD AND MECHANICAL MODEL

During the second phase, Design Engineering develops an approach to the design and tests the approach with a breadboard model. The breadboard model is an attempt to determine the feasibility of the concept. It is often put together with available components but also uses state-of-the-art components made available by vendors to "try out". More importantly, at this stage initial cost estimates are made and the first cut is made at identifying long lead items. Armed with cost and design characteristics information, Marketing begins its forecasting refinements to determine potential sales and revenues over time. The question "Can we make it?" is answered in this phase.

ENGINEERING PROTOTYPE

During the next phase, one or more Engineering Prototypes are built. There are several objectives of this phase. These include: packaging design, initial "soft" (perishable) tool design and procurement, refinement of cost information, reliability testing, selection of many standard components and finalization of options and features. The questions "What will it look like and how will it perform?" are answered during this phase.

MANUFACTURING PROTOTYPE

The following phase, Manufacturing Prototype, had been the point where the product was "turned over" to manufacturing in the past. It was at this phase that integration with existing systems began before MRP. With prints and specifications in hand, a number of objectives are designated for this phase. These include: finalization of "hard" (permanent) tooling, procurement and testing of first production pieces from suppliers, creation of processes and routings, design and purchase of assembly tooling, design of inspections and tests, setting of labor and material standards, finalization of make/buy decisions, choice of vendors and refinement of schedules for subsequent pilot and full production. Sufficient models are produced at this point for initial field testing. The question "How will we make it?" is answered in this phase.

PILOT PRODUCTION

The last phase, the Pilot run, is used to test production and assembly tools, routings, test and assembly procedures, vendor deliveries, new part performance and to train workers in production. This last phase answers the questions "Can we make it in volume and can we make it at the right price?".

The efficient integration of new product development with MRP also requires the extensive use of the company's Engineering Change Control system.

ENGINEERING CHANGE CONTROL

The company had in place, during the implementation of MRP, a comprehensive, well developed Engineering Change Control system. The objectives of the System are to provide for the orderly and timely implementation of engineering changes and new parts or assemblies and to phase out replaced or obsoleted parts.

The system is based around an Engineering Change Control Board which must unanimously approve all changes. Members of the Board include representatives from Design Engineering, Manufacturing Engineering, Industrial Engineering, Materials, The Master Scheduler, Marketing/Sales, Quality Assurance, Field Service and Cost Accounting. The Board is chaired by the manager of the Documentation Control department which was vested with responsibility for all prints, specifications and procedures for Operations.

The steps in the change process are like those in most companies. Anyone can originate a request for change by completing an ECR (Engineering Change Request) stating the requested change and the reasons for it. The change is submitted to Documentation Control which prepares an ECN (Engineering Change Notice) with marked up drawings and specifications as required (in some cases samples or models are used). The urgency of the change is indicated by a Code from 1-6 with Code 1 being the most urgent and usually indicating the potential of catastrophic failure or a safety hazard and Code 6 being the least urgent with the change instituted at the convenience of production.

Copies of the ECN "package" are then distributed to the above mentioned departments for their analysis and consideration in preparation for the weekly Board meeting where all changes are reviewed. Cost information is provided, objections are presented and modifications are decided upon where necessary.

After approval, each group has certain assigned responsibilities for implementation. Among these is file maintenance of the MRP system. Since MRP system mainte-

16

nance was a prime concern, it was not long before new product interfaces with MRP were addressed.

INTERFACING THE SYSTEMS

Basically, the interfacing of new products with MRP is done in two phases marked by the status of the Bill of Materials. In the first phase, the new product is controlled through an Experimental or "X-Bill". The product in this phase is primarily controlled by Design Engineering but is "in" the MRP system since the X-Bill is loaded into MRP files as will be described below. The second phase, uses a standard Bill of Materials and reflects the "released" version of the component, assembly or module. Parts and assemblies in this phase are controlled through the Engineering Change system.

At each of the phases of New Product development described above, there are associated interface activities with MRP. By gradually integrating the new product with the MRP system at each phase of development, early control of the new product is achieved. Additionally, long lead special purchases and additional quantities of standard components to cover new product needs are provided for.

The Goal and Concept Definition phase concludes with a rough schedule for the development being produced. The purpose of this schedule is to provide Design Engineering a control mechanism, to give Sales a proposed introduction date and to enable MRP to gain initial control over the project. As such, an overall part number is assigned to the product along with a product name. The schedule contains several key dates. These include the start-up date, breadboard design completion date, initial tooling release dates and Engineering Prototype start and completion dates. A standard lead time of 20 weeks is entered for completion of the Manufacturing Prototypes from Engineering Prototype completion. This then gives Marketing a tentative availability date for production prototypes which can be used in product literature, industry shows, etc. At the completion of this first phase, the product is entered into the Production Plan and the Master Production Schedule. Even though there is no Bill of Materials, the presence of the product in these plans provides a constant reminder to upper management of the proposed schedule and enables regular surveillance of the project. Further, Materials management begins the process of taking control of the product with the X-Bill (with no entries below the top part number) which is created at this time.

In the second phase (Engineering Breadboard and Mechanical Model), some standard and state-of-the-art components are added to the X-Bill. But most importantly, the first of the tooling required is identified. Each of the new parts or tools expected to be used is assigned a part number and added to the X-Bill with lead times added to the Item Master at the same time. Standard Parts are also added to the X-Bill as needed. As a result, the X-Bill begins to become "fleshed out" and is integrated into the system accordingly. The parts on the X-Bill are coded

so that output information from MRP and the MPS is sent automatically to the Senior Buyer who is assigned to buy experimental parts for new products as mentioned above. The information is also received by the Engineer in charge of the project since Design Engineering still retains control of bill content and part design. Marketing forecasts are refined and requirements are entered into the Production Plan and Master Production Schedule. Thus, the MRP system begins to take over control of the new product very early in the development cycle.

As the Engineering Prototypes are developed in the third phase, part selection and tool design are firmed up substantially. Since options and features are finalized at this stage, Documentation Control restructures the bills in a modular fashion compatible with MRP planning. Option bills and parts lists which are firm at this stage become "released" and any subsequent changes for released parts, assemblies and bills must be made through the normal engineering change control system. Not all bills are released at this stage since some parts and assemblies will require change or finalization after manufacturing analysis by Manufacturing and Industrial Engineers. New parts which are released are recoded to be made or purchased and planners (both materials and production) are assigned to these parts as a matter of routine. Since the release process normally takes 10-20 weeks as the design is firmed up, the structuring and coding can be done as part of the ordinary work load and do not require special major effort to accomplish.

The Manufacturing Prototype stage continues the release process until, at its completion, the entire new product is under "standard" MRP control. The designation "X" is removed from the highest level bills and with the continued refinement of marketing forecasts, early returns from field testing, and results from the pilot run, the product is incorporated fully into production. The intermediate Pilot stage is ALWAYS conducted to accomplish training and line set-up as indicated above. The new product itself, however is fully integrated with all manufacturing systems. Any changes which must be done as a result of the Pilot run are handled through the Engineering Change system.

Although the above procedures took nearly a year to formulate and implement, once in place, they worked remarkably well and new product introduction time was reduced by nearly one third.

FINAL COMMENTS

The procedure described above was not developed due to extreme foresight on the part of management but, like so many other systems and procedures, was developed in response to an unworkable situation for the company which depended so greatly on new products to remain competitive in the marketplace. It was developed mostly through a trial and error perseverance which often makes most systems and procedures really pay off.

Ron Pannesi has over 20 years of industrial experience, mostly in Manufacturing and Materials Management. A former Corporate Director of MRP for Northern Telecom Systems Corp., he was responsible for implementing MRP in a number of U.S. divisions of the company. In addition he has served as consultant for numerous other MRP implementations in the U.S. and Canada. He has lectured extensively to industry and professional organizations on MRP, Manufacturing, Materials, Purchasing, and Internal Auditing. His recent presentation, "Auditing the Materials Function", delivered to the North American Conference of Internal Auditors, was voted the best presentation at the conference. Ron is currently Assistant Professor of Management at Eastern Michigan University and is completing his doctoral work in Production and Operations Management at Michigan State University.

TOTAL QUALITY: A COMMITMENT TO EXCELLENCE

Vittal A. Rao, CPIM
Hughes Aircraft Company/Electron Dynamics Division

FOREWORD

Over the past decade with the U.S. industry moving into the age of rapidly advancing technology, managers have fallen prey to the belief that solutions to curb declining productivity problems exist only in the much heralded factory-of-the-future automation technologies supplemented with sophisticated practices like MRP and JIT inventory systems. Implementations of MRP and JIT systems almost never address Total Quality, a necessity that fosters the habit of continual quality improvement to streamline production processes and reduce the uncertainty of the coupling between parts and end-product schedules. This prerequisite becomes vital also with high-production automated facilities, since machine downtime, caused by any process failure, can be exponentially more costly.

In the light of increased customer quality expectations, foreign quality competition, and prohibitive quality failure costs, many companies would like to hop on the quality bandwagon today. In the past, a variety of stimulating programs applied by firms to improve product quality - for instance, Zero Defects, introduced by Martin Marietta in the early 1960's - produced very disappointing long-term results because they were superimposed upon existing management systems, and failed to recognize the need to be internalized and function within the established corporate culture. The recommendation is to elevate Quality into a top management responsibility, and to develop value strategies that avail of existing management planning and financial controls to accentuate and make continually visible top management's commitment to product quality.

This presentation will explore the significant interrelationships between the technical side and corporate cultures when effecting, in concert with MRP/JIT inventory systems, the concept of Total Quality to evolve the emerging new set of values into a consistent practice of manufacturing excellence.

EFFECTS OF LACK OF QUALITY

Before proceeding to develop the integrated management strategy that utilizes Quality as its pilot, it may be useful to gloss over some effects of the traditional 'after-the-fact' Quality Control/Inspection (QC/I) system and its resultant lack of quality that handicaps the U.S. company in meeting its customers' quality and reliability expectations, and in maintaining its competitive position.

Customer Dissatisfaction   Premature design releases and products that do not meet specifications repeatedly, and late product deliveries erode customer satisfaction since the expectations for service, quality, reliability, and durability are not met. Subsequent corrective action to regain market share may dramatically multiply the total costs of doing business.

Engineering Changes   Process and product design modifications are generally not synchronized for incorporation causing many a company to experience high obsolescence or nonconformances to 'Fitness-for-Use.'

Excessive Inventory   Pressure to meet delivery schedules causes management to maintain "just-in-case" levels of product inventory in the system, to allow for rejections and extra operations due to rework or reprocessing.

Informal Expediting   The vicious circle of launching recovery orders and expediting orders continues as an ineffective cure for declining process throughput quality yield and delayed orders resulting from vendor quality mismatches.

Loss in Capacity   Creation of the "hidden plant" - the proportion of plant capacity wasted to rework or repair unsatisfactory parts that did not meet 'Fitness-for-Use' the first time.

Field Failure Expenses   Costs incurred in remedying product defects - for example, warranty adjustments - come directly out of company profits, and also tie up sizable chunks of productive capacity.

In addition, the traditional QC/I system tends to be informal and harbors a number of insidious side effects. Some issues are:

Lack of Teamwork   Prevailing state of equilibrium for U.S. company individuals is to pull apart into smaller parochial groups that compete against each other. For example, an attitude commonly observed among production workers is that of having quality being inspected into the product with an excuse such as "That's not my responsibility" rather than to build it in and prevent defects the first time through. Responsibility for product quality is inherently fragmented resulting in chronic fingerpointing among the various company functions when quality problems surface.

Lack of Accountability for Cost of Quality   Customarily, quality costs are charged to the Quality function, and provide no visibility as to which upstream function caused the cost impact. Also, since most costing systems fail to categorize Cost of Quality as prevention, appraisal, or failure costs, they remain ineffective in guiding a manager to find the "holes" which are costing him lack of quality in his system.

WHY THE NEED FOR TOTAL QUALITY?

In search for productivity improvements many firms have responded to MRP/JIT inventory systems without, however, raising their quality criteria to the defect-free point. These solutions assume that a manufacturing enterprise operates the way it should, when in reality it does not. MRP's weakness, historically, has been its inability to promptly identify the impact of quality-related work hindrances, comprehend the impact on end-product schedules, and reformulate a plan of action effectively relayed to the production work force to reprioritize the work effort. Such failures have been hidden or compensated for by large move and queue times, lot sizing, buffer stock, and yield factors (7), theoretically in place to absorb the inaccuracies in materials planning and scheduling. However, both JIT and cost-efficient MRP systems are inexorably linked to a "prevention-oriented" quality management approach. For instance, the luxury of reworking or scrapping unacceptable products vanishes if the plant has to deliver parts, materials, or components at the time of need at the next process or at the customer. Suppliers to a JIT system must also be capable of supplying defect-free items requiring very minimal incoming-material inspection.

Furthermore, questions arise at boardroom reviews:

o How do we make the customer - not the goods - return?
o How can we release new product designs, on time, and "fit-for-manufacture"?
o How can we reduce WIP inventory and scrap?
o How can we increase total productivity?
o Why did it cost 25% of sales to value product quality?

Today, such questions can be answered only perfunctorily because the MRP/JIT tools are not complemented with company-wide Total Quality attitudes. To paraphrase Wickham Skinner of Harvard Business School, - "Quality is generally perceived in the wrong way at the plant level, and managed in the wrong way at the corporate level," even today.

TOTAL QUALITY MANAGEMENT

The Total Quality Management Model establishes the strategic posture a company must adopt to achieve its commitment to quality and productivity excellence, improve its profitability, and gain market share. A key foundation of the management model lies in recognizing Total Quality in its essence, -
"The capability to make certain 'Fitness-for-Use' as expected at the next process, or at the customer."
Total Quality, a systems management attitude to quality and productivity, is the fundamental pilot of the management model, and subscribes as "a supportive strategy for the achievement of manufacturing's other goals: cost, asset, utilization, dependability, and flexibility." (10)

American Production & Inventory Control Society

The Total Quality Management system develops the traditional inspection- and test-oriented Quality Control system, associated almost entirely with manufacturing, into a business-oriented system through a prevention-oriented and systemic quality program, which invokes the cooperative involvement of each company employee from conceptual design of the product, through all phases of planning, manufacture, supplier surveillance, final acceptance and shipping, on through to the continued satisfactory performance of the product at the customer. The basic principle of Total Quality is to achieve the company objectives of improved product quality, reliability, and customer satisfaction at reduced quality costs.

Total Quality Management synergistically integrates the five strategies that command the Patterns of Excellence within ten logical systems that together constitute the Total Quality Management Model. (Figure 1)

BUSINESS STRATEGY - _The Company Mission_

A key factor in improving productivity is the restoration of a "culture for quality" by management in American industry. The Japanese have achieved their current level of manufacturing excellence primarily by doing all of the basics necessary for Quality success, doing them very well, and gradually improving on them all the time. If there is any phrase that epitomizes the Japanese Total Quality philosophy, it would be, - "to concentrate on the basics, all the basics." A Japanese proverb says: "The nail that sticks out gets hammered down." Such dedication indeed permeates every aspect of Japanese manufacturing industries. American industry must recognize the fact that quality must unequivocally be given the primary attention, with cost and schedule secondary, in order to eliminate most of the waste that seems inherent in today's industrial culture.

Cultural feelings are very deep-rooted, and currently, those feelings in U.S. firms are expressed as, "Make it good enough to pass." This attitude must be reassessed today. An all-pervasive Total Quality mission needs to be introduced throughout the company, nay, the industry, to cultivate the management commitment, and leadership it takes to achieve the required cultural changes. Such a Total Quality mission may be:

"Quality is the basic business creed for the company. Quality means providing both external and internal customers with innovative products and services that totally satisfy their requirements, on time, and at affordable cost. Total Quality mindedness, a commitment to excellence, begins with each individual in the company."

Cost of Quality

Quality cost is the principal cornerstone of an integrated Total Quality effort, as managers are more concerned with cost data than with statistical data alone on the occurrence of defects. Quality costs generally represent business expenses incurred in quality-contributing activities needed to achieve 'Fitness-for-Use', and specify all costs inhibited when no lack of quality, either in design, or of conformance to requirements exists. Costs associated with quality of conformance may be classified into prevention, appraisal, and failure cost categories. Redistributing quality costs within these categories in creative fashion so as to help identify nonconformance to requirements at the earliest checkpoint

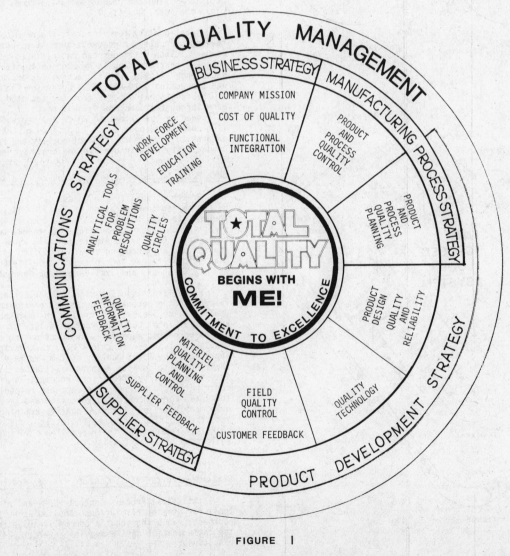

FIGURE I

in the production cycle can effect substantial savings in total quality costs. (11, Figure 2)

Recent studies indicate the typical COQ for U.S. firms is from 10 to 25% of total sales, attributable to poor quality - warranty, scrappage, repair and rework costs. As Phil Crosby notes, the costs of quality are ". . . . all a result of not doing things right the first time," and suggests that COQ should be about 2.5% of total sales. (1) Japanese automobile industry lends credibility to this estimate by showing COQ in the 2.5 to 4.0% range.

THE QUALITY COST DOLLAR

AFTER-THE-FACT TRADITIONAL INSPECTION SYSTEM	PREVENTION-ORIENTED TOTAL QUALITY SYSTEM
PREVENTION = $ 10 APPRAISAL = 110 FAILURES = 80 TOTAL QUALITY COST = $200 (per $ 1000 of Sales)	PREVENTION = $ 24 APPRAISAL = 36 FAILURES = 20 TOTAL QUALITY COST = $ 80 (per $ 1000 of Sales)
LITTLE OR NO PREVENTION COST	INCREASED PREVENTION COST

PREVENTION

FAILURES 40%

5%

APPRAISAL 55%

PREVENTION 30%

FAILURES 25%

APPRAISAL 45%

| CONTINUED HIGH FAILURES
INCREASING APPRAISAL COST
HIGHER TOTAL COST | REDUCED FAILURES
REDUCED APPRAISAL COST
REDUCED TOTAL COST |

FIGURE 2

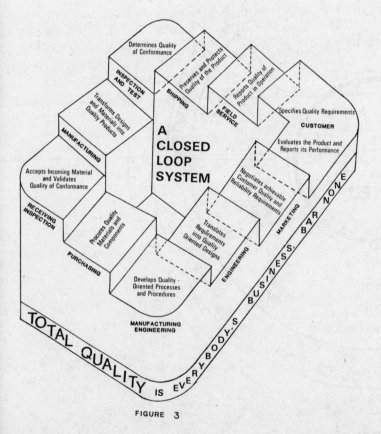

FIGURE 3

Functional Integration

Quality is the responsibility of every company function involved in performing a logical series of actions to achieve 'Fitness-for-Use'. It is essential that each function strive for excellence in its area responsibilities. It is also essential for the various functions to break down functional barriers, and to work together as a team. Total Quality Management does not look for new surefire concepts, but concentrates on the basics to improve upon the performance excellence of every company function, and integrates these efforts, synergistically, toward the achievement of Quality objectives into a Closed Loop System. Commitment to excellence is the key note in orchestrating the various functions into the habit of continual quality and productivity improvements. (Figure 3)

COMMUNICATIONS STRATEGY

To attain company-wide Total Quality the coordination of all quality-contributing functions is mandatory. The main obstacle that seems to block this coordination is the language barrier, caused by the high degrees of functional specialization that inhibit cross-functional communication. For instance, operators and inspectors may not be aware of what product characteristics are customer requirements nor how critical these characteristics are for product effectiveness. Common bridges of vocabulary and decision-making have to be erected between the product engineer, the manufacturing engineer, the shop supervisor, the buyer, the service organization, shop inspection, and the executives of each area. Inclusion of each and every quality-contributing function in the system of consensus decision-making and communications becomes essential to close the Total Quality loop.

Total Quality commitment is the development of a real feeling of quality-mindedness among the individuals in the company. Such attitudes can be initiated by encouraging employee participation in developing "patterns of excellence" within specific activities and/or functions, and conducting self-audits to determine the variability of the functional process from the targeted index of excellence. (2) Success of this phase of Total Quality is judged by the extent to which all employees in the firm come to recognize the importance of their individual efforts to improve the product quality and heighten productivity with innovative and creative ideas.

Work Force Development - Education and Training

Growth of quality-mindedness is continually fostered by customized communication of Total Quality how-to concepts to all individuals in the company. Communication is achieved through conducting educational courses which cover Total Quality tenets in general, as well as training courses and workshops on specific topics, such as SPC - Statistical Process Control, QCC - Quality Control Circles, Quality Feedback, and Small Group Improvement Activities.

Proper training is a highly important aspect with respect to the potential success of effecting Total Quality. The Japanese claim that the main barrier to a successful Total Quality program is lack of understanding of its concepts, especially in functions outside of Quality; yet, these functions need to understand and appreciate the Total Quality system, as they will execute their specific quality responsibilities as part of an integrated quality effort that encompasses all quality-contributing functions. The Japanese recognized long ago this need for concentrated education and training, and have many years of effective quality training behind them; yet, the training continues endlessly - one of the principal reasons for their excellence in applying the philosophy of Total Quality.

Statistics in the Lead, Quality Circles Follow

Statistical Process Control (SPC) and other analytical tools for problem resolutions, applied using the teamwork approach, can bring about a common language that bridges the communication gaps among inspectors, operators, and executives.

The message that "Quality is Everybody's Business" implies that everyone receive performance feedback relevant to one's handiwork, and use it to brainstorm and try out alternative approaches. Product and Process quality improvement efforts are admirably aided through statistical analysis and feedback using Control Charts. Amazing things do happen when product or process performance data are plotted and both workers and management can interpret the charts in a common language. Communication improves, mutual trust increases, and consequently, worker involvement, quality and productivity, all improve. Often, however, the objectives are misconstrued as "having charts" rather than "using charts." Statistical charts alone can accomplish nothing if nothing is done with the information displayed. The important word in 'Control Charts' is "control," not "charts." Action must be taken to remove the cause of the out-of-control condition. Indeed, statistical effort must be directed into productive channels, and "chart for chart's sake" must be avoided. In essence, statistical techniques are the tools to be used as part of a Total Quality pattern, and are not the pattern itself.

Two methods of improving quality and productivity have been: SPC and QCC. Although both methods are beneficial, it is difficult to locate many American firms that have tried both methods concurrently. Many current advocates of QCC have recognized the value of SPC. Specifically, training personnel in SPC techniques gives them more valid, reliable methods of problem solving and decision-making. By first placing training emphasis on SPC, the effectiveness of QCC later applied is meaningfully increased.

Quality Information Feedback

The quality information system provides the work force with procedures and quality data assessment reports to enable identification of potential problems and corrective action evaluation, communication of problems status, all with the intent to prevent quality problems in the future. Communication requirements enforce planned Quality data collection, for example, incoming material/supplier quality evaluation, in-process product yield and scrap analysis, process rework study, and so forth. The data collected can be analyzed either statistically or without any embellishment depending upon need. Corrective actions can be defined and implemented, and final problem closure or additional corrective action taken as needed.

SUPPLIER STRATEGY - FROM CONFRONTATION TO COOPERATION

Relationships between suppliers and purchasing departments in the U.S. tend to be confrontational, and consequently, unproductive. Nonetheless, since the net quality result in the company's products is the combined effect of the company's own quality system plus the effectiveness of the quality systems of its suppliers, it is important that the suppliers be educated to appreciate the profitable benefits of Total Quality.

Total Quality-driven supplier strategy places strong emphasis upon control of incoming-materiel at its source, in effect, upon close product-quality relationship and the building of mutual trust and cooperation between the buyer and supplier. Some of the tenets followed would be:

o Total communication of purchased materiel quality requirements to the supplier.

o The burden of quality proof placed upon the supplier, with emphasis on total validation of the supplier's own quality assurance program through process control and process capability studies.

o The communication of key supplier data, and the feedback to the supplier of incoming-materiel inspection data to assist the supplier in the development and improvement of his quality system to that index of excellence that the company will no longer need to conduct receiving inspection of incoming lots.

o Evaluation and rating of suppliers based on Cost, Quality, and Delivery, where Cost implies the total quality costs incurred, inclusive of defective, rework, or field failure costs associated with that supplier's component or subassembly materiel.

o Cultivation of a small number of Total Quality system certified suppliers seeking a symbiotic growth of mutual expectations between the supplier and company.

MANUFACTURING PROCESS STRATEGY

The strategy addresses two systems of the management model, namely, Planning for Control, and Control of Product and Process Quality. Proper Total Quality Planning provides a cross-functional perspective on quality responsibilities. By adhering to the concept of 'Fitness-for-Use' at the next process, the responsibility for in-process quality appraisal is placed where it truly belongs - namely on production operators who build the product. Production operators thus have a sense of more direct involvement in product quality, and appraisal activity is optimized. As a consequence, a new role emerges for Quality inspectors, who then serve as Quality instructors in the areas of Quality standards, SPC skills, and perform product quality and process system audits.

Process Control, a founding principle of Manufacturing Process Strategy, employs the tools of statistics to track and control process variability that affects product quality characteristics by checking the product quality or the process during production - and stopping the process if it is drifting out-of-control. This practice of constantly working to make the production process as error-free and as failsafe as possible increases substantially the likelihood that the product will be made right the first time, and enables material movements to happen "just-in-time." This technique contrasts sharply with the prevalent 'design-make-inspect-squawk-correct' methodology used so often in today's manufacturing operations, and zeroes in on the root causes of quality problems when it addresses, in a preventive mode, either product design or the efficacy of the manufacturing processes. Process Control thus fosters quality while the product is being produced, not after the fact. Properly employed, it will break the 'design-make-inspect-squawk-correct' cycle that impairs quality, increases costs, and lowers productivity.

The explanation of Process Control is basic. Nonetheless, it is often neglected in manufacturing practice, and the attention is given to only doing the minimum to pass inspection to specification, rather than to improving the process to an index of error-free excellence. This habit must be re-appraised in light of the fact that conformance to specification limits alone is no longer good enough. Indeed, a superior product can be obtained by improving the capability of the process to make certain 'Fitness-for-Use' by focusing on the transitional target value of customer requirements, and doing what it takes to be on target the first time, and every time. "Total Quality aims to continually improve the process to the point where the distribution of the chief quality characteristics of parts and materials is so narrow that the specifications are lost beyond the horizon." (3)

PRODUCT DEVELOPMENT STRATEGY

The emphasis is on integrating realistic and attainable product quality considerations through every phase from product investigation and prototype design to final production release and field service, to bring about a compatible relationship among the requirements of: the customer, product design and quality technology, materiel, and manufacturing processes. The traditional scenario, however, is often as follows:

Products receive design specifications based on the measurement ability of the engineer rather than on the functional relationship of mating parts. Manufacturing Engineering determines the process on the basis of running one or two good parts, and is also frequently excluded in the initial planning when Engineering communicates its requirements to Purchasing. Purchasing makes buys on the basis of price only, without much attention to quality considerations. Shop supervision makes undocumented changes to either increase production of products that are "unrealistically dimensioned," or to improve an "unproven" process. Results: material scrap, and costly process changes.

Product Design - Quality and Reliability

Traditional QC/I systems have limited themselves to only manufacturing type of control, 'Quality of Conformance,' while completely ignoring the element of 'Quality in Design,' - the importance of which is realized when one discovers that many of the quality difficulties met with in industry are related to inadequate or faulty design, and that such faults are immune to the controls exercised for 'Quality of Conformance.' Hence, such quality or reliability problems remain in each and every product unit shipped to customers irrespective of the excellence of conformance controls since the latter basically ensure conformance to design specification, which is already plagued with lack of quality.

Total Quality provides specific disciplines and controls to make engineering design an integrative activity, and to incorporate production knowledge in the total process to reduce total leadtime from design concept to smooth production, and insure that 'Quality in Design' as well as 'Quality of Conformance' are both accounted for.

Quality Technology

Traditional QC/I systems utilize quality measurement equipment that have the principal job of accepting or rejecting parts and products. Automation essentially speeds up the sorting the bad parts from the good. In contrast, today it is clear that the basic task of Quality Technology is not merely to inspect or test; it is also to provide rapid usable information feedback for process control and for true control of product quality.

Field Quality Analysis

Traditional QC/I systems often stop at the shipping door, with concerns beyond that point left to field service or other functions. Total Quality, however, takes an active interest in what happens after the product is delivered, - namely, on 'Quality of Performance' factors that affect product liability and quality costs, company reputation and potential future business. Specifically, Field Quality analysis seeks answers to how customers use the company product, learns its true quality characteristics through various product research, and discovers the relationship between the functional and the substitute product quality characteristics, and confirms 'Fitness-for-Use' requirements in cooperation with the customer. Through the Field Service function, Total Quality forms the critical link which closes the Quality loop. In another sense, it starts the quality cycle all over again, and the information gathered is used to constantly improve the product, the service, and the customers' continued confidence with the products and services. This is largely accomplished by effective feedback to all quality-contributing functions so that they can take rapid corrective action when and where required, or, based on this data, further improve the product.

"TOTAL QUALITY BEGINS WITH ME" - AN INDIVIDUAL EMPHASIS

In the context of a well-developed framework of business policies, practices, plans, and patterns of excellence, Total Quality Management Model emphasizes as its hub the company individual around whom the company strategies are designed. (Figure 1) Often, however, individuals do not see the need to subscribe to Total Quality because management makes perfunctory efforts to clarify why it is necessary. Indeed, quality-mindedness to management seems to be no more than a matter of lip service. Consequently, many an individual worker harbors feelings such as, "My quality contribution is so small a portion of the whole, that I really am not part of the company-wide Total Quality emphasis, nor important to it."

Traditional management systems tackle this dilemma of how to reach deeply into the organization and effectively influence behavior there with a web of information and control routines that direct from the outside what people do, but, at some point, these routines lose their charge in spurring people on to above-average performance. The inability to effect continued high-output performance with formalized strategies is one of the driving forces today behind the U.S. company's continued concern in cultivating a corporate culture aimed at internalizing in its popula-

tion the enterprise's values that interest themselves with each individual's growth and self-development, and with adopting Total Quality as a way of life. With such shared values, employees begin to see the company's interests and their own as more congruent, start understanding that Total Quality, in essence, begins with each employee producing an output that they themselves would like to receive, and slowly, but steadily, tend to commit themselves more fully to the company's mission of excellence.

TOTAL QUALITY, THE PRODUCTIVITY PRESCRIPTION

Total Quality, in concert with MRP/JIT inventory systems, provides a partnership to achieve breakthroughs in productivity, and total cost improvement. When the breakthrough occurs:

o Customer service improves effecting increased market penetration.

o Quality in Design leads to effective time-phased incorporation of engineering releases and changes into production resulting in substantially reduced obsolescence costs.

With both Quality in Design and Field Quality Control at the front end of Product Planning, valuable savings are realized in engineering time traditionally spent on warranty claims, product liability problems, and field service questions.

o Cooperative understanding between suppliers and buyers results in less expediting on the part of the buyers, and purchasing can work on more productive tasks like standardization with engineering designs, annual contracts with vendors, value analysis, etc.

o Inventories and lead times are optimized by getting the "right" material at the time of need.

o Quality begets quality. Since material shortages and substitutions disappear, and since excessive overtime needs are obviated with product quality improvements, the end of the month "push" is made unnecessary, resulting in improved employee morale and continued quality and productivity gains.

o Overtime is reduced because the "hidden plant" capacity used for rework and repair is now available as increased productive capacity.

o Direct labor productivity increases because parts shortages and resulting interrupted fabrication and assembly runs are minimized.

Indirect labor productivity is improved by "doing the job right the first time," minimizing redundant efforts.

o In the organizational context, the productivity of not only the labor force, but also that of management is increased. Perhaps the best perspective on the potential of Total Quality for improvements in productivity of leadership and management is to aptly construe what the Vice President of Tennant Corporation, speaking at an Executive Conference on May 18, 1981, said: "When management has the time to work on the real problems rather than keep on fighting fires, every area of the business can be improved."

THE CONCLUSION - THINK TOTAL QUALITY

The intent of the Total Quality Management Model has been to assess the relationship of the firm with its external and internal environments, and identify the key strategies of the managerial dimensions, both technical and cultural, that are germane to an effective organizational response to today's quality challenge. Blueprint strategies for Quality/Productivity excellence in the U.S. have many patterns that have academic appeal, but little implementation. It will not be easy, therefore, to translate theory into practice, unless Total Quality is woven into the cultural fabric of the enterprise. We must begin to think Total Quality.

Total Quality, based on defect prevention, provides the tools of SPC, QCC, and others, which, when pragmatically applied, can help achieve significant improvements in quality and productivity, and more importantly, maintain these improvements that are required in overall product design, development, and manufacturing processes to achieve the end result of a total production system, namely, MRP/JIT, the management philosophy that also involves all organizational disciplines. It needs to be recognized that although inventory and cost reductions do occur with MRP/JIT systems, it is truly the end result of a total management strategy aimed at eliminating defects, reducing quality costs, and improving both product and process quality.

Total Quality, a commitment to leadership excellence, is a comprehensive approach to steer improvements in quality and productivity throughout the company. Total Quality is the bottom line. The bottom line is a mix of systems, possessing that combination of high automation technology, and sophisticated information systems, MRP/JIT, and QUALITY that provides a clear decisive edge for competitive position. In the international economic war that our industries are engaged in, Quality is proving to be the winning strategy.

REFERENCES

1. Crosby, P. B., 'Quality is Free,' New York, McGraw-Hill, 1979

2. Day, T. C., "Strategies For Setting Up A 'Commitment To Excellence' Policy - And Making It Work," Management Review, May 1984

3. Deming, W. E., 'Quality, Productivity and Competitive Position,' MIT Center For Advanced Engineering Study, 1982

4. Feigenbaum, A. V., 'Total Quality Control,' New York, McGraw-Hill, 1983

5. Hall, R. W., 'Zero Inventories,' Homewood, IL, Dow-Jones Irwin with APICS, 1983

6. Juran, J. M., Ed., 'Quality Control Handbook' (3rd Ed.) McGraw-Hill, New York, 1974

7. Rao, V. A., "Closing the Loop with Quality Data Feedback," International Conference Proceedings, APICS, (New Orleans, LA), November 1-4, 1983

8. Schonberger, R. J., 'Japanese Manufacturing Techniques: Nine Hidden Lessons in Simplicity,' New York, The Free Press, Macmillan, 1982

9. Scott, D. C., Schleicher, W. F., Pub., "The Quality World of Allis Chalmers," Quality Assurance, December 1970

10. Wheelwright, S. C., "Japan - Where Operations Really Are Strategic," Harvard Business Review, 59 No. 1 (July - August, 1981)

11. Quality Costs - What and How (2nd Ed.), ASQC, Milwaukee, 1971

12. Athos, A. G., Pascale, R. T., 'The Art of Japanese Management,' New York, Simon & Shuster, 1981

THE AUTHOR - A SKETCH

VITTAL A. RAO, CPIM, a recognized professional practitioner and educator in the field of Manufacturing Resources Planning and Control Systems, is Management Systems Specialist at the Electron Dynamics Division of Hughes Aircraft Company in Torrance, California. His earlier experiences as Senior Industrial Engineer and Manufacturing Systems Consultant were with Ford Motor Company and Burroughs Corporation in Detroit, Michigan. In these capacities, he has developed and implemented management systems for Productivity and Quality Tracking, Configuration Control, Material Requirements Planning, Product Costing, and was responsible for the education and training of Industrial Engineering and Production Control staff in the use of MRP systems.

Vittal is professionally affiliated with AIIE, APICS, ASM, ASQC, and recently served as Director of Education for the Los Angeles APICS Chapter, and as Associate Professor of California State University Extension Program at Dominguez Hills where he conducted Production and Inventory Management courses co-sponsored by LAPICS. In addition, he has performed various counseling, consulting, training and public speaking activities for National Junior Achievement and for Toastmasters International.

Mr. Rao's academic credentials include post-graduate honors in Materials Engineering and in Industrial Administration from Purdue University in Lafayette, Indiana, and B.Tech honors from Indian Institute of Technology in Bombay, India. His previous publications are articles in APICS International Conference Proceedings, Transactions of the AIIE, Management Science, as well as in internal company documents.

ENGINEERING/MANUFACTURING INFORMATION NETWORK: A FRESH START

Joe Dietrich
Baxter Travenol Laboratories, Inc.
Mark Kuchel, CPIM
Arthur Andersen & Company

INTRODUCTION

The establishment of a single, all inclusive information network is a critical and mandatory step toward the development of a Computer Integrated Manufacturing system. This undertaking can be large and complex due to the number of groups impacted and existing "systems" involved. The level of information and scope of information are questions that must be carefully dealt with to avoid the pitfalls that surround a large information network.

SYMPTOMS OF A POOR NETWORK

Most companies are well aware of an information problem when it exists. It is also true that most companies find out about their problem when it is too late. However, indications of those problems probably were present long before the serious problem surfaced.

The first and most common problem occurs when multiple sources of nearly the same information exist. (No group will ever admit that their information is the same as any one else's). This information obviously will contain inconsistent data when multiple groups are updating the information at different time intervals for different purposes. Corporate level and plant level systems are typical examples of systems that are seldom the same.

The existence of multiple design groups usually point to additional problems. If multiple sets of standards for product drawings and documentation exist there is a definite problem. Unfortunately, a more typical problem is when no standards exist or when the standards are set by pulling an old copy of the documentation and using that as a guideline. The mechanism for enforcing drawing and documentation standards should be reviewed to insure that loopholes do not exist.

Another flag can be raised when no formal handoff exists between the product engineer and the process engineer. There very seldom is an engineer who is truly skilled in both areas of development. Companies are sometimes forced into using the same engineer for both areas due to the "handoff" problem that exists. This situation normally occurs because information is not present to allow for an efficient transfer from one group to another.

A single bill of material should exist for all users requiring information related to the structuring of component parts into assemblies. The same can be said for the routing or process step information that is required by the users of the data. Although the common rationale for having multiple bills or routings is that different information is required by the various groups using the system, this is a basic problem that will cause down-the-road problems.

An automated link to a CAD system is fast becoming a mandatory feature in an information network. Few companies who can justify a CAD system can afford to have the information in CAD be different than the information in the rest of the system. Mechanisms should be in place to insure that identical data exists in both data bases and ideally that the information is entered a single time.

The ability to retrieve identical or similar designs from the data base should be available to someone who is unfamiliar with every previous design effort. This is especially important for companies that continually change or improve the design process. A parts classification system should also provide for expansion and changes in the existing product line.

The most obvious symptom of a problem can be gauged by the amount of paper that exists related to the design and manufacturing of the product. A paper based system is laden with problems related to updating, distributing, controlling and auditing of the data in the system.

TYPICAL INFORMATION SOURCES

A review of the existing information sources should include the following types of information if available:

- o Plant Based B.O.M. system
- o Corporate Based B.O.M. systems
- o Cost B.O.M.'s
- o MRP/Quick Deck B.O.M.'s
- o Process Controlled "Recipe" Cards
- o Product Descriptions/Definitions
- o Process Drawings/Flowcharts
- o CAD Drawings
- o Manual Drawings
- o Corporate Procedures/Specifications
- o Plant Level Procedures/Specifications
- o Equipment Validation Manuals
- o Engineering Standards
- o Costing Standards
- o Parts Classification
- o Job Training Materials

The review of engineering and manufacturing related information should yield an inventory of the types of information contained in each source. Documentation on the creators, users and frequency of use of each source should also be included. This information will allow for a decision to be made on whether the consolidation of information is practical. Political considerations may not allow for documenting and discussing the systems to be combined and therefore eliminated. However, identification at an early point is necessary to determine if the effort can be cost justified based on overhead reduction rather than just on the basis of greater data accessibility.

CONSIDERATIONS

The approach toward combining and eliminating existing systems must be well planned. Thorough knowledge of the information content of these systems is mandatory. The source of updating, the group responsible for updating and the entire user community must be established for each of the sources of information.

Other considerations that may impact how each information source is ultimately handled revolve around the system's originator. The original intent of a system as well as the originating person/group may have a substantial impact on how the system is dealt with in the new information network.

The toughest issue to deal with is determining what information is necessary.

Many opinions will exist on this topic. Every information source had a purpose behind it's creation and therefore someone who thinks the information source is worthwhile and should be made available to everyone.

ACID TEST

With the wealth of information available to the new network, a determination must be made to allow for evaluating the data to be included in the system.

A high level statement from management must be solicited to assist in the evaluation. The following statement is typical of what most organizations are striving for in an engineering/manufacturing information network:

"We must include all data required to design and produce an end item."

Lower level guidelines must then be established by project management to avoid the thrashing that occurs when too much information exists to be dealt with effectively.

PARTICIPATION

It is essential to carefully select the appropriate participants responsible for organizing and executing the program. Representatives from every area of the company impacted by this program must be involved. The executives ultimately responsible for engineering, manufacturing and quality assurance within our organization employed a task force approach to resolve the issues discussed earlier. They defined the scope of activities to be addressed as those relating

American Production & Inventory Control Society

directly to the product development process, from conceptual design thru and including manufacturing operations. Each organization within the company directly responsible for those associated activities was represented on the task force at the director or V.P. level. Refer to Figure 1.

TASK FORCE MEMBERSHIP

RESEARCH AND DEVELOPMENT

PRODUCT ENGINEERING

MACHINE DESIGN ENGINEERING

PROCESS DESIGN ENGINEERING

INFORMATION SYSTEMS

MANUFACTURING AND PRODUCTION CONTROL

MANUFACTURING DATA CONTROL

RELIABILITY AND QUALITY ENGINEERING

QUALITY ASSURANCE

FINANCIAL MANUFACTURING OPERATIONS

TECHNICAL OPERATIONS/PROGRAM MANAGEMENT

FIGURE 1.

The executive group also developed a list of specific objectives and goals to be achieved by the new system as shown in Figure 2.

TASK FORCE OBJECTIVES

MAXIMUM INTEGRATION ACROSS ALL FUNCTIONS (WORLDWIDE)

MAXIMUM COMPATIBILITY WITH AUTOMATED TECHNOLOGY

OPTIMUM ASSURANCE OF PRODUCT QUALITY

SATISFACTION OF COST, MRP AND OTHER BUSINESS PLANNING SYSTEMS

AVOIDANCE OF INFORMATION REDUNDANCY

FOCUS ON DRAWING, BOM AND PROCESS INTEGRATION

MINIMIZE NECESSARY SPECIFICATIONS

ESTABLISH AUTOMATED TECHNICAL MEMORY

OPTIMUM ELECTRONIC TRANSFER OF DATA

FIGURE 2

PROGRAM SCOPE

The scope of the resulting program encompassed many practices and systems within the technical, scientific, engineering, manufacturing and quality organizations of Travenol. The entire product development cycle was subdivided into three major areas: product design and definition, process design and definition and manufacturing operations. All systems, data, practices and support activities relating to these areas were targeted for examination and inclusion.

We found several kinds of systems and structures in place in each of these three areas within our organization. However each area was dominated by one particular kind of information system. CAD was the most powerful tool we found in use in the area of product design. It's use in all aspects of product design is expanding dramatically. Process design tools

for use on our CAD equipment are also being explored, however, our primary system for managing manufacturing process and equipment data was a document based word processing system. Manufacturing operations were well managed in several key plants by a variety of in-house closed loop manufacturing control systems.

Isolated projects were bringing CAM, MRP, bar coding, and other applications into our portfolio of systems. Our major concern was that the core of fundamental systems and data structures required to support, integrate and leverage all of the systems into a comprehensive information network was extremely old or non-existent. We realized that our ability to build higher level systems such as MRP, CIM, CAM, etc. was dependent upon the quality of existing B.O.M., process router, part and equipment data bases. We knew that CAD/CAM alone was not going to be our savior, nor would CIM efforts result in an automated factory of the future for us, nor would MRP alone achieve our broad-scope objectives. They all have to work together and they all have to rely on a well structured core of engineering and manufacturing data. In short, we needed a fresh start on our information network.

PROGRAM GOAL AND ORGANIZATION

In accordance with the objectives given them, the task force defined a program to develop standards, procedures and information systems aimed at improving engineering and manufacturing efficiency and productivity. We made it clear from the start that there were a few prerequisites that were needed to even consider attempting a program of this size. First and foremost comes management commitment to the effort. Specifically that means money, resources and time, not a memo endorsing and supporting the program. The most important commitment needed was to insure our ability to change the way thousands of people had been used to doing their jobs. Informal ways and means to get information had been in use for so long the cultural change required to force people to do things by the book was staggering. Another important prerequisite to accomplishing our goals was to have in place the hardware and software necessary to deliver the network to all plants and all users, worldwide.

The sheer size and the number of people and systems involved in this effort required two important approaches to be used. The first was a matrixed program management methodology whereby project leaders, team members and even executive steering committee members transitioned into and out of the program at the appropriate time. Our organization is fortunate in that we have several executives experienced with this technique.

To provide continuity and momentum to the program an administrative team of seven people (including the program director) was formed. It was their job to continually identify tasks, deliverables and project team composition, to provide coordination and assistance, and report progress to the steering committee.

Secondly, since we could not manage all the engineering, manufacturing and quality data in our corporation at one time, a pilot approach was implemented. A few key products were selected to be used to develop the system and network structures, while keeping the amount of data processed to a manageable level. Once the system and network structures have been piloted, a cost benefit analysis will be performed to determine if and how to convert our corporate data bases.

NETWORK STRUCTURE: HARDWARE/SOFTWARE

As previously mentioned, our network had to reach everywhere in the corporation. The evolution of systems in our company followed the same patterns as most; multiple brands of hardware, multiple versions of similar software and isolated instances of both system retardation and sophistication. None the less, a pattern of hardware and software heirarchy existed between corporate headquarters and manufacturing plants. Our mainframe communication networks extend to almost all our remote sites. We therefore pursued a strategy to make use of the variety of equipment in place rather than attempt to force any group or plant to convert uneffected systems to our designated type of hardware. We had been encouraged by several hardware and software vendor announcements and commitments to move toward greater commonality and improved communications. Some key products supporting our strategy were the development and use of IGES (Initial Graphics Exchange Standard) by CAD/CAM vendors, IBM's DISOSS (Document Interchange System) product and improved communications between all IBM boxes from PC's to 3080's. Wang's announcements to interface their wordprocessed documents to DISOSS and file compatibility between their PC and IBM's further supported our strategy.

In short, although it is not a straightforward proposition, we have found every reason to believe our existing hardware and software investments will provide the necessary interfaces to create a network capable of distributing documents, graphics, data, voice, image, etc. from and to any remote location tied into our mainframe communications.

SUMMARY

To remain competitive in our industry, our company must realize significant engineering and manufacturing efficiency and productivity improvements in a relatively short time period. After analyzing our product development process, we have identified an improved information network as the single most important opportunity to realize our goals. It is not a simple task, but it is a task we cannot afford to leave undone. We believe we have taken the right steps to lead us to an environment in which computer aided engineering and manufacturing will be the norm, not a dream.

BIOGRAPHIES

Mark Kuchel is a manager in the Management Information Consulting Division of Arthur Andersen and Company. He has designed and installed manufacturing systems in the electronics, pharmaceutical, and consumer products industries in both single and decentralized manufacturing environments. He has been responsible for client education and support pertaining to all aspects of closed loop manufacturing systems. Mr. Kuchel is a CPIM and is a member of the Chicago APICS chapter.

Joe Dietrich is Group Manager of Manufacturing Data Systems Advanced Planning for Baxter Travenol Laboratories, Inc., a major health care supply company located in Deerfield, IL. He is responsible for the design and implementation of an integrated, distributed engineering, manufacturing, and quality data information network. Prior experiences include design and implementation of distributed closed loop manufacturing systems, and international financial and manufacturing system development and support.

Mr. Dietrich holds a Bachelor of Science in Engineering degree from Purdue University and is pursuing an MBA at DePaul University in Chicago. Mr. Dietrich is also a CPIM.

COMPUTER INTEGRATED MANUFACTURING—INDUSTRY'S GREATEST CHALLENGE

Paul F. Bacigalupo
International Business Machines Corporation

INTRODUCTION

What do America's best-managed factories have in common? According to the May 28, 1984 Fortune Magazine cover story so-titled the following characteristics are evident in all of the ten factories selected.

o Each factory selected was tops in its industry in either productivity or quality or both.

o They have found ways to merge product design with manufacturing, building in quality, wisely making choices about automation, developing a closer relationship with their customers, and more effectively managing their work forces. When design and manufacturing are merged, production people are concerned about product quality at the "beginning" of the manufacturing process not only at the "End" of the process. Therefore, by addressing "Manufacturability" in design, every production worker can focus on the quality of products manufactured.

o Flexible automation has been utilized to allow the same equipment to process different parts with little or no retooling or set up required.

o Quality products produced in highly efficient automated plans can actually create new jobs due in great part to increased market shares which generates greater product demand.

o A key ingredient in the success of these ten factories has been the realization on the part of the production workers that management is a partner and that competion is "the enemy".

o Experience is demonstrating that at the best plants, american workers and management can produce high quality and low cost products for the world market.

How does Computer Integrated Manufacturing (CIM) relate to the characteristics of well managed plants? CIM is the strategy applied to accomplish the results stated.

COMPUTER INTEGRATED MANUFACTURING (CIM) AS A STRATEGY

Computer Integrated Manufacturing (CIM) is a top management strategic plan addressing the competitive effectiveness of its products in its world-wide marketplace. The competitive issues that top management has to cope with are:

o Increasing market share

o Bringing "new" quality products to the marketplace at low product costs

o Striving for greater product quality while at the same time reducing product costs

o Increasing customer service through shorter product lead times and availability of product to satisfy customer demand

o Providing flexibility in the manufacturing process to satisfy new product designs and varying production volume

o Coping with increasing shortages of engineering talent and skilled machinists

o Providing increased communications within and amongst their own plants and functional organizations, as well as with vendors and customers

o Reducing indirect labor and overhead expenses

o Reviewing investment decisions in consideration of intangible benefits.

There must also be an understanding that,as with any strategic plan, planning is accomplished from the top of the organization "down" and that implementation is performed from the low levels of the organization "up". That is, CIM is not a low level plant technical issue, it is a top level strategic direction affecting all facets of the business.

SCOPE OF CIM

In determining the Scope of Computer Integrated Manufacturing (CIM) it becomes important to understand and review the flow withing the typical manufacturing company and/or plant. Please note that there is no consensus about terminology in the CIM field.

If we at the "Functional Cells" within a manufacturing facility, we can identify the flow of manufacturing operations, as well as the related organizations required to support the manufacturing of products.Figure 1. illustrates the overview of a manufacturing facility identifying twelve (12) major departments or "Functional Cells". Additionally, a company/division would also have a marketing/sales organization to complete the facility as a self-contained entity. Financial and data processing organizations are identified a "Plant-Wide Services". This pictorial view of a plant provides a visual understanding of where plant automation and communication systems may apply. However, before the role of automation is discussed, the CIM functions must be defined. CIM is an evolutionary strategy that builds upon the concepts of the past 10-15 years, that of Computer Aided Design (CAD) and Computer Aided Manufacturing (CAM). The technologies that exist today can address CAD and CAM. That is not to say that the majority of companies withing the industrial sector are necessarily utilizing these techniques, but that the "tools" are available. The thrust, however, is to integrate CAD and CAM, and then progress to the next stage of this evolution. That stage is intergrating CAD/CAM with other business related functions. This last step in this evolutionary process is CIM.

Therefore, the scope of a Computer Integrated Manufacturing (CIM) strategy would include the following major elements.

o Computer Aided Design (CAD) - in its broadest sense this area might be more properly stated as Computer Aided Engineering (CAE) in that not only is CAD (product and tool design/drafting) addressed, but also the functions of group technology, software engineering and other related engineering areas.

o Computer Aided Manufacturing (CAM) - This generic area would include utilizing robots, numerical control machines, and automated assembly/storage/inspection/material handling facilities. Concepts such as Flexible Manufacturing Systems (FMS), Automated Guided Vehicles (AGV), CNC/DNC, and sensor systems-either robotic and/or vision are all potential alternatives to address industrial automation (automation within the manufacturing process). CAM also includes the concept of being able to automatically generate manufacturing processes utilizing group technology coding schemes, sometimes identified as "computer aided process planning" (CAPP). Many of these concepts/techniques require a merging or integration with engineering.

o Business/Production Planning and Information Control Systems (B/PPICS) - provide the functional interface to the production and business master and operational plans developed, as well to the purchasing system. The inventory management systems, including the tool room, are an integral part of CIM from customer order servicing (finished goods/ service-spares inventory) to work-in-process inventory to purchased materials inventory. The ability to provide feed back to the operational plans, such as capacity planning and production scheduling, is addressed by plant floor communications systems which is an integral part of plants/industrial automation. Therefore, we see interfaces and requirements to be integrated with CAD and CAM to effectively develop, execute, and monitor production plans.

o Computing Technology - underlying the ability to perform whatever degree of automation is required for a particular company is the requirement to utilize computer technology. Whether in the CAD, CAM or B/PPICS element of the CIM strategy, computer technology will be utilized and, therefore such

CIM COMPUTER INTEGRATED MANUFACTURING

FUNCTIONAL CELLS

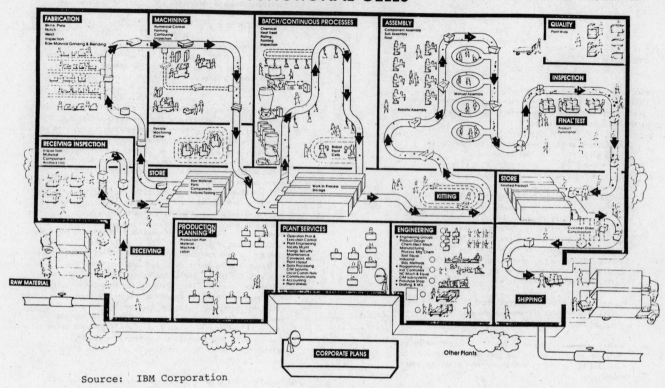

Source: IBM Corporation

Figure 1.

resources must be properly identified and planned to ensure an effective "integrated" implementation can be accomplished.

ROLE OF AUTOMATION

The projection for robots in 1990 ranges from 60,000 to 100,000 working units on plant floors. Many companies are using and will increase their use of such automated techniques. Everyone knows the auto industry story by now. However, the story bares repeating due to its applicability to other industries, such as the machine tool industry. Many have laid the auto industry problem squarely on labor wage, but this is only part of the problem that is now well understood. Although the Japan auto industry labor rate averages $12 per hour to the U.S. auto industry's $22 per hour, the bigger problem was the number of labor hours required to assemble an automobile. The U.S. labor hours required to assemble any automobile was two to three time the hours required in Japan for a like size auto. That fact plus the wage rate differential creates a severe competitive problem. The U.S. auto industry is addressing assembly time through the greater use of robots in their automated assembly lines. Other companies that face quality and cost of product problems are assessing their automation alternatives and taking appropriate actions.

Companies such as General Motors, IBM, Westinghouse, and General Electric amongst others have corporate plans to develop their own "Factory of the Future" utilizing CIM strategies. Considerations for quality, product costs, and worker impact are among the issues being assessed. A case in point, GE at their Lynn, MA plant of 8,400 union workers offered their workers an option to provide union concessions so that GE could invest $52 million for plant modernization, including a "Factory of the Future". This meant operating in a mode different from today. GE management spent much time with the union representatives to ensure their understanding of the implications of modernization, and won union support. A "No" vote meant that GE would invest the

$52 million in a neighboring plant, non-union, in New Hampshire. By a 2 to 1 vote, in June, 1984, the union workers supported the General Electric CIM strategy at the Lynn plant.

Automation means more than just providing mechanization for production processes (assembly, test, storage, material handling, etc.). Mechanization should be accomplished within a systematic plan. This plan should identify a systems approach for mechanization, as occurred within the manufacturing support systems arena (MRP, Purchasing, Production Scheduling, etc). It was important to layout a plan or blueprint of support systems to ensure that integration would be possible. This same requirement exists in the industrial automation area. That is, mechanization without systems will result in making "automation" and integration difficult and, therefore much more expensive. Each industry segment withing the industrial sector and each company within the segment must determine how far to go with automation. But it is clearly evident that companies must develop plans for automation in support of their CIM strategy. Mechanization without an automation plan would not only cost more money, but will also result in a loss of a most precious commodity-time.

ORGANIZING FOR CIM

There are many approaches to develop a strategy. Some companies will utilize a task force with a limited role, others will establish a standing committee or a committee with a broad role. The approach being reviewed is the method for developing the CIM strategy utilized by a large machine tool manufacturer.

A Computer Integrated Manufacturing (CIM) Committee has been established with twenty-five (25) members of management representing all segments of the business. There are five (5) sub-committees addressing:

o   Business Planning
o   Engineering
o   Production Planning

28

o   Manufacturing Control
o   Plant Automation.

Within each sub-committee there are task groups, which may
also include cross sub-committee members. These task forces
might focus on issues that overlap function areas, such as:

o   Office Automation
o   Resource Management
o   Management Reporting and Tracking
o   Productivity
o   Group Technology
o   Coding Systems.

Each division/plant will take its automation plan direction
form the CIM committee. This corporation is making progress
in defining its CIM strategy, and implementing a CAM
sub-strategy which includes mechanization within a plan for
automation. Within the next year we expect to see published
reports on their progress toward their CIM objectives.

INDUSTRY'S CHALLENGE

CIM offers great opportunities for the industrial sector
through productivity gains that will result in lower product
costs. higher quality products, and potential increases in
world-wide market shares. To reap these benefits companies
must be willing to prepare the strategies and plans required
to ensure that the productivity gains can be achieved.

What are the results of such CIM strategies today?
Corporations such as General Motors, IBM, General Electric,
Deere and Company, Ingersol Milling, Ford, Chrysler and
Westinghouse are all documented cases of success, amongst
many others.

o   John Deere Component Works, Waterloo, Iowa - $150
     million capital investment achieving 40-50% reduction
     in scrap; 30-40% reduction in costs of material
     storage, retrieval and handling; and reductions in
     on-site inventories, manufacturing lead time and the
     production cost per component. They utilized group
     technology, manufacturing cells, AS/RS concepts,
     automated material handling techniques, production
     information and control systems with communications
     links, etc.

o   IBM, Fishkill, NY - Huge semi conductor plant utilizing
     advanced production technologies to manufacture chip
     elements on a silicon wafer with an electron beam. The
     technology implemented is years ahead of techniques
     used by other U.S. and Japanese producers.

o   General Electric, Dishwasher Plant, Louisville, KY -
     $39 million investment in plant automation resulting in
     10% reduction in the cost of goods manufactured,
     production workers handle 78% fewer parts, and
     work-in-process inventory has been significantly
     reduced. Add to these benefits a higher quality
     dishwasher - the concepts and techniques within the CIM
     strategy are working.

Much concern has been expressed about the impact of CIM
concepts and techniques upon the production workers. There
is an impact on work patterns man-machine relationships,
etc. However, the estimates are that as the productivity
gains are achieved and market share increases, employment of
production workers will increase. There are examples of
such occurrences today. Of course, each new technology
within this continuation of the "Industrial Revolution"
creates new jobs in new industry segments.
The challenge is to develop a Computer Integrated
Manufacturing (CIM) strategy, provide sub-strategies that
allow mechanization to occur within the framework of a plan
for automation. The overall objective of CIM to achieve
productivity in manufacturing a low cost, high quality
product that is competitive in world-wide markets and to
increase market share, and therefore be more provitable. As
we have discussed, results are being achieved, the
opportunity and tools are available. Those that choose not
to take advantage of CIM may not be in business by the next
decade.

REFERENCES

Bylinsky, G. "America's Best - Managed Factories", Fortune;
May 28, 1984.

Greene, A.M., "Are Factory Systems the Path to
Productivity?" Iron Age; October 22, 1982.

Hayes, R.H. and Wheelwright, S.C. "Link Manufacturing
Process and Product Life Cycles", Harvard Business Review;
January-February, 1979.

Hegland, D.E., "The Automated Factory - A Progress Report",
Production Engineering; June, 1983.

Miller, W.H., "The Phony War Between High Tech and Low
Tech". Industry Week; October 3, 1983.

Quinlan, J.C., "Profile of CIM in Action", Tooling &
Production; January, 1983.

Schaffer, G., "Sensors: The Eyes and Ears of CIM", American
Machinist; July, 1983.

Teicholz, E., "Computer Integrated Manufacturing",
Datamation; March, 1984.

AUTHOR

Paul F. Bacigalupo is a consultant with the IBM Corporation
in a career that spans over twenty-six (26) years. He has
designed, implemented, taught, and consulted in
manufacturing and engineering management systems within the
industrial sector domestically as well as in Europe, Japan
and Mexico.

Mr. Bacigalupo has served as the 1974 International
President of the American Production and Inventory Control
Society, as well as President, in 1976, of the APICS
Educational and Research Foundation, a corporation separate
from APICS. He has served on the Editorial Board of the
Production and Inventory Management Journal since 1966. He
is a life member of APICS.

He is a member of the National Council of Physical
Distribution Management (NCPDM) and participates in the New
England Roundtable.

A graduate of Northeastern University, Mr. Bacigalupo has
also attended graduate courses at UCLA and the University of
Massachusetts.

STOREROOM PRODUCTIVITY IMPROVEMENTS WITHOUT AUTOMATION

Edward V. Ferris
Clifton Precision Special Devices

INTRODUCTION

Across America today we are seeing a large increase in the amount of money spent by the largest corporations and "mom and pop" operations to improve productivity. Computer hardware and software, CAD/CAM systems, automated storage and retrieval systems, robots, and a variety of other ideas are being employed by manufacturing as well as service industries with some good results. Estimates on future capital expenditures for these items are staggering, yet some of this money will be spent unnecessarily. By reviewing current operations carefully it may be possible to improve productivity while reducing or eliminating these planned capital expenditures. The following case study will show how significant productivity improvements are possible in a small parts stockroom without large expenditures and how these improvements resulted in an increase in inventory accuracy.

OVERVIEW OF THE FACILITY

Clifton Precision, Special Devices Division, designs, develops, and manufactures high reliability electronic and electro-mechanical instrumentation for military and commercial applications in aerospace and naval systems. As demand for aircraft and vessels is relatively low in volume, demand for our products tends to follow suit. Engineering projects and production efforts in producing shippable products are accomplished in a classic job shop environment. We have recently implemented a Material Requirements Planning system and are currently in the process of "closing the loop."

The small parts stockroom which we will examine handles 33,000 stock keeping units, all of which are considered direct cost items. These items are stored in an area which occupies approximately 4200 square feet. In order to better understand the improvements made, a review of the methods of operation and staffing requirements before the improvements were undertaken is necessary. It also must be noted that these improvements were made before the implementation of our MRP systems.

STATE OF OPERATIONS BEFORE IMPROVEMENTS MEASURES

The 33,000 items in the stockroom were stored in an alpha-numeric sequence. In many cases there were several locations for the same item. Items were not assigned location numbers. Overflow areas were essentially anywhere the material would fit and too often this material was stored without identification. In addition to a weekly computer report showing stock balances, a "cardex" type card showing the transaction history was maintained in a shelf-box for each item. This card was updated whenever a stockroom transaction took place.

Documentation of transactions for updating the computer record consisted of transferring part numbers and quantities from a scrap of paper to a data processing-designed form which was keypunched weekly. Needless to say, there was much arguement over which record was more reliable: the computer or the shelf-box card.

The stockroom was staffed by eight people who were responsible for receiving and issuing material. In addition to stockroom personnel, approximately fifteen other people were permitted totally free access to the stockroom and could issue material. Of course it was impossible to insure that each transaction went through the proper updating procedure. The walls and doors that surrounded the stockroom were useless because of the large number of people permitted access to the area. If a supervisor needed a part on the manufacturing floor he had three choices: he could go and pull the part from stock himself; he could find someone who could do it for him; or he could write the request on a scrap of paper, place it in a box at the stockroom door, and hope that it would be pulled in a day or so.

The best estimates indicated an average of five transactions per man/hour or one every twelve minutes. Inventory accuracy in the stockroom was estimated at 35%. No cycle counting program existed and the only audit of the operation was the physical inventory. Morale in the department was very low, absenteeism was extremely high and the rest of the facilitiy had little faith in anything that was done by the people in the stockroom.

IMPROVEMENT MEASURES

Realization by management of the overwhelming problems that existed in the stockroom fortunately occured when business was very good for the company. If corrective action had not been taken during the "boom" we were experiencing, results could have been devasting to the company in the long run. A critical error made by some companies is that efficiency improvements are not looked into until a firm experiences a downturn in business at which time it may be too late.

Management at this time faced two alternatives. The first was a complete revamping of the stockroom and included a state-of-the-art automated storage technique for the stockroom. The second alternative involved reviewing the current operations and streamlining these procedures to produce the most efficient non-automated system possible. Both options were considered in-depth for both cost and overall efficiency and management opted for the second alternative. The following steps detail how the stockroom was streamlined and an efficient and accurate operation was produced.

The first area targeted was the elimination of the "other personnel" from the stockroom. Management issued directives to all departments stating that Inventory Control personnel were the only employees permitted direct access to the stockroom areas. With this action the walls and doors surrounding the stockroom now served a purpose: a control point was established for the receipt and issue of material.

The second area involved the standardization of forms. One all-encompassing, four part carbonless form, no bigger than an index card, was developed to handle approximately 98% of all material issued. This form insured accurate identification of material and eliminated the likelihood of transposition errors and the mislabeling of material. In addition, two other forms were developed to handle issues of material not covered by the four part form. These actions greatly reduced the possibility of errors in reporting and helped to make the computer record more reliable, which enabled us to proceed the the third step.

Area number three slated for improvement was the elimination of the shelf-box card that was maintained with the material. This step significantly reduced transaction time by eliminating the need to record issue and receipt information manually which was both time-consuming and difficult to do. In its place a program was written by the Data Processing department which displayed a listing on a CRT screen of all issues and receipts to stock of an item. Since this display was available to all departments, it further reduced the need for outside employees to enter the stockroom to check this information while providing a valuable audit trail of all items. Further, because experienced keypunch people were entering this information, it was more reliable and much faster than the manual mode.

The fourth improvement area proved to be the most difficult and time consuming: establishing a location control system. It was decided that the current alpha-numeric system was most inefficient and that the location of material should be based on activity. Due to the lack of an MRP system and a formal master schedule at this time, we were forced to use a combination of both a shipping plan for future shipments and a past usage history on each item. Items that had the most activity or were projected to have high activity were located in an area closest to the work stations of the stockroom personnel. In addition, this material was located on shelves that were between the knees and shoulders of employees so that bending or climbing ladders to reach material was reduced to items that had low activity. Other considerations in this area included storing material in one location versus being scattered throughout the stockroom; locating material for a distinct product in one area; and setting up and maintaining floor stock for extremely high usage items. Although this was the most difficult areas to implement it far and away proved to have the most dramatic impact on decreasing the amount of time it took personnel to issue material.

At the same time we were establishing a location control system we embanked on our fifth improvement area which involved the packaging of material whenever possible in units of tens. By establishing this type of packaging system we improved our accuracy significantly. The likelihood of an error in counting ten pieces of an item is much lower than counting one-hundred or larger quantities of an item. Further, when ten pieces of an item were counted, they were placed in a sealed package or container so that any entry into this type of package would be readily visible.

The sixth improvement area was the establishment of the "Zone Concept" of stockroom operation. This idea of operation basically involves assigning each person in the stockroom a distinct area for which that person is responsible. Because of this concept it is much easier to spot trends in both the accuracy and work habits of each employee and to educate and correct problems on a one to one basis with each employee.

Following the implementation of these six major improvement areas we started our cycle count program. Accuracy at the beginning of our program was approximately 75%. However, after only three months we acheived a plus 95% accuracy and have maintained that level of accuracy ever since. Management feels that this level of accuracy could not have been achieved or maintained had the six improvements mentioned above not taken place.

MOTIVATING EMPLOYEES

As with any operation system, people are the key to a successful plan. Management recognized this and viewed employee inputs as essential to the effective implementation of each step. Before any step was implemented, it was thoroughly presented and explained to stockroom personnel. Their feedback was essential to fine-tuning the plan, and in the location-control area their suggestions were critical to its success. Thus, employees felt they were an important part of the productivity improvements and with the great deal of management attention given to the stockroom, morale moved upward while absenteeism was reduced.

Motivating employees in the stockroom was a relatively easy task as compared to changing the attitudes of employees outside of the stockroom. Because the stockroom was a free access area for so long, it seemed outside employees took personally the fact that they were unable to issue material on their own. Only through months of posting cycle count results on bulletin

boards throughout the plant and the high degree of accuracy of material issued to the manufacturing floor were attitudes changed on a plant wide basis.

PRODUCTIVITY MEASUREMENTS

Measurement of productivity can be as simple or complex as one desires. The approach that we use is a very basic one and done on a weekly basis. First we total the number of hours used by employees involved in issuing and receiving parts. Any time spent by these employees performing duties other than issuing or receiving parts is factored out. In addition, any time spent by these employees cycle counting is factored out. The remaining number of hours is the amount that is used to calculate the "average transaction time" which we use as our productivity measurement. Second, the total number of transactions are added, which includes receipts to stock and issues from stock but excludes the number of items cycle counted. The total number of hours is then divided by the total number of transactions with the result being multiplied by 60 to give an average transaction time in minutes. The same calculations are performed for cycle counted items. With these figures we are able to both measure and compare productivity rates against previous weeks as well as previously established standards. Standard times can then be adjusted as necessary or in the case of unforseen problems, we can take corrective action or education of employees as necessary.

Before we started out program to increase productivity, our average transaction time was above twelve minutes. It was hoped by management that the measures taken would reduce the time to the five minute area. Results however, have exceeded these estimates. The stockroom now has an average of 4.2 minutes per transaction and there have been numerous instances where the average transaction time has gone to 3.5 minutes. This not only exceeds managements expectations for improving the stockroom operation but also exceeds the results anticipated had management opted for an automated system.

APPLICATIONS TO LARGER WAREHOUSES

A careful review of the steps taken will reveal that these ideas can be applied to almost any size stockroom enviroment. The "zone concept" and the location of material based on activity would probably have the biggest benefits to larger warehouse operations. In all cases it is most important to restrict access to the stockroom for two reasons: to increase inventory accuracy by providing a control point for issues and receipts; and to increase stockroom productivity by eliminating disturbances to employees performing their job.

SUMMARY

By carefully reviewing your current stockroom operations it may be possible to increase productivity without incurring a large expense. It is my suggestion that a team of employees be assembled from different departments (i.e. accounting, manufacturing engineering, production planning) to review any operation under consideration for automation to insure the expense is necessary. This is not to say that I am opposed to automation. Quite the contrary I believe that automated systems are the wave of the future and in businesses where high rates of growth are projected for the future these systems are a necessity. In fact, it is my opinion that our stockroom is now in a position where we should again consider an automated system. However, we will again review our operation to see if further improvements can be made to our current non-automated operation.

ABOUT THE AUTHOR

Edward V. Ferris is an Inventory Control Supervisor at Clifton Precision Special Devices in Drexel Hill, PA. He has been employed in the Inventory Control field for the past seven years and has held positions as a Production Coordinator and Receiving Department Supervisor. He is currently a dean's list student at St. Joseph's University Evening College in Philadelphia,PA in his junior year as an Accounting major.

COMPUTER INTEGRATED MANUFACTURING: A MATTER OF SURVIVAL

Robert B. Vollum, CPIM*
Creative Output, Inc.

INTRODUCTION

Technology, nurtured by the computer, is increasing at rates never before experienced in the history of mankind. No single part of this technological explosion is having a greater impact than the revolution taking place in the processing of manufacturing information. Most of the pieces of the manufacturing puzzle have been put together in effective application programs for the processing of data. However, as an industry, we are still struggling to effectively pull the pieces together into systems that will process information to support the manner in which management makes decisions. Computer Integrated Manufacturing (CIM) addresses the framework of this problem. See figure 1.

APPLICATION INTEGRATION

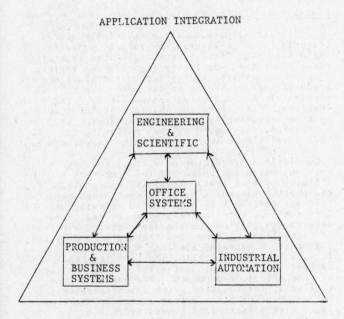

Figure 1. COMPUTER INTEGRATED MANUFACTURING

APPLICATION SYSTEMS INTEGRATION

Until recently, application systems, for the most part, have been loosely connected with self-contained logic to process data pertinent to that application only: e.g., design engineering information has, generally, been separated from process engineering; facilities management has had no interface to sales projections; purchasing, order entry, cost accounting, and general ledger accounting have often maintained an identity separate from the mainstream of manufacturing planning and control.

Most "MRP" systems have been woefully inadequate in their ability to provide ad hoc simulations of viable alternatives. Even those systems with real time "what if" capabilities have fallen short in their ability to provide management with a look at all the information available to it. Significant future advances in the management of manufacturing companies will come from the creative use of information resident in all areas of the database through unstructured, non-procedural, relational languages. In other words, we will benefit most as we learn to use the computer in the manner that we use our brains.

THE ENVIRONMENT

The manufacturing environment is one of incredible complexities. No single function operates in a vacuum. All actions are related to many other conditions which, in turn, interact with myriad other situations. Since these normally volatile conditions are further affected by the unpredictable environment of the external economy, the need for management to obtain accurate information rapidly and to form intelligent decisions is obvious. Factory operations must face and solve a continually shifting pattern of changes, and must do so under the constant tyranny of time and cost. When action is taken in one sector, other sectors will almost invariably be impacted. Consider, for example, some of the things that may happen when the Engineering department introduces a part change:

. Existing stock may be obsoleted
. Multiple products may be affected
. Part phase-in/phase-out must be coordinated on all affected products
. New tooling may be necessary
. New routings must be prepared
. Shop loading may change
. Product schedules might change
. Network schedules may be altered
. Product cost will change
. Customer orders may be impacted
. Purchasing orders may be affected
. New vendor sources may be necessary
. New part specifications and inspection procedures will be required
. And on and on

As more and more segments of the business are introduced to the computer, it becomes more urgent that those segments communicate with each other directly through the system, with relevant pieces of information being accessible from any part of the system.

PRODUCTIVITY AND TECHNOLOGY

The United States has come under severe pressure in recent years to stem the tide of flagging productivity. Where U. S. industry once dominated the world, it is now trailing in several key industries and is fighting to hold its own across the board.

Ultimately, the fight to increase productivity will be won or lost by the ability of manufacturing executives to manage effectively and creatively within the dynamics of today's business climate. That means optimizing capital investment, managing that investment to keep costs to a minimum, and taking advantage of developing technology. Of the factors involved, it has been estimated that the application of new technology will produce approximately 60 percent of all new gains in productivity. Investment in new capital will provide an additional 25 percent, while labor gains can be expected to produce only 15 percent. Clearly then, the pursuit of technology holds the key.

When speaking of technology in manufacturing operations, we are talking primarily about computer applications to control information and to control process automation. CAD/CAM, computer driven machine centers, robotics, automated warehouses, electronic scanning, and manufacturing planning and control systems are examples of recent manufacturing technology advances.

The computer is the focal point of the "factory of the future." At one end of the scale are computer driven machines performing work that was previously done by unskilled and semi-skilled labor. At the other end, the creative thought processes are augmented by computer aided design and engineering facilities. The realities of these extremes are much in evidence today. It is the middle ground between the poles that will produce the most electric movement during the decade of the eighties and into the nineties.

Advances manufacturing concepts such as group technology, cellular manufacturing, computer automated process planning, flexible manufacturing, and automated material handling systems will forge past the barriers of intellectualism and emerge as reality. Semi-intelligent, multi-dimensional robots will populate the "iron collar" work force.

The coordination of all these technologies requires advanced communications and data management systems. Planning, scheduling and control systems will need to address the issues of immediacy and profitability. Small batches, short turn-around, high inventory turns, maximum cash flow, and relief of bottleneck contentions will come center stage as true manufacturing objectives. The historical cost accounting standards of efficiency measurement, already under serious attack world-wide, will fade from use in the more enlightened companies in favor of simpler, more direct profit measurements.

ENGINEERING AND SCIENTIFIC

Engineering and scientific applications are being controlled by powerful Computer Aided Design/ Computer Aided Manufacturing (CAD/CAM) systems that interface, more and more frequently today, directly with manufacturing business systems. CAD/CAM technology is moving forward at an accelerated pace as micro computers are bringing the cost of automating the engineering process down. Today, with the increased power of the mini computers and with direct coupling to mainframes, these systems can, economically, have direct access to the massive number crunching capabilities of the mainframes to augment the flexibility and user-friendly communications of the minis. Additionally, advances in local intelligence and displays, particularly color graphics, in terminal technology have provided CAD/CAM users with a window directly into the business system. When the engineering and business systems are integrated through a common data base, the output from CAD can be used directly by CAM activities such as numerical control, robotics, process planning, and factory management.

As CAD/CAM technology closes the gap between engineering vision and factory reality, fewer people will be employed in the factory. Already, the Bureau of Labor Statistics indicates a decrease in employment in the industrial segment from 30 percent of the work force in 1960 to 25 percent in 1985, with the trend predicted to continue.

The changing workplace will produce a need for higher skill levels in factory workers. Engineers, designers, scientists, systems people and other technically educated people will be in demand. Factory management will be reduced in numbers and those that follow the manufacturing career route will need to provide a bridge between the engineering technician and the machine operator/technician.

The factory will become a much more interesting and exciting place to work. Many lower level jobs will be upgraded as workers learn to use computer assists. These workers will experience greater job satisfaction because they will be performing more interesting, more challenging work. They will understand more of how their jobs fit into the overall picture. However, there is a price to pay. One of the top priorities for the next several years will have to be the retraining of workers whose skills have become obsolete.

INDUSTRIAL AUTOMATION

Most manufacturing departments are organized along the traditional lines of either product specialization or process specialization. Those that are product oriented are normally geared for high-volume, specialized production by grouping together the processes employed in the manufacturing of a specific product. In contrast, similar processes that can be employed on a variety of products are typically grouped together in a process department. Process facilities, such as job shops, are normally highly flexible in application but relatively low-volume in capacity.

Traditional manufacturing has always been faced with the either/or organization choice of volume versus flexibility. Today, group technology has spawned the concept of group departments organized to produce families of similar items, classified by shape, material, and/or manufacturing processes. Combining machines into specific groups, or cells, to handle the requirements of broad families of similar products often produces results that resemble the high capacity of a product facility while affording the high flexibility of a process facility.

Flexible Manufacturing Systems

Historically, automation invariably addressed only the high-volume, low variety production and did so with fixed system. Computer technology now affords the opportunity to produce a variety of products simultaneously and to introduce new products and/or changes easily under the control of flexible manufacturing systems (FMS). The inherrent flexibility and multiplicity of these systems dramatically change the economics of automation. Aggregate volumes rather than individual item volumes justify the investment.

Flexible manufacturing systems consist of both automated equipment and the computers and software systems that control the equipment. The equipment employed is not only mechanized production equipment but also automated material handling systems, both interdepartmental and intradepartmental, automated storage systems, electronic recognition systems, and transfer and positioning robots. Material handling systems may include conveyors, towlines, monorails, track systems, variable-path automated guided vehicle systems (AGVS), and robots. Production is controlled by the computer which synchronizes material movement with production operations in accordance with computerized schedules.

PRODUCTION AND BUSINESS SYSTEMS

MRPII SYSTEMS

General Flow

Manufacturing planning and control systems have introduced a whole new way of doing business to the manufacturing industry, not only to factory operations but to companies as a whole. The forward looking logic of MRP has changed the philosophy of business control from an extrapolative projection of history to one of timely provisioning of the management plan for the future.

Manufacturing Resource Planning (MRPII) is focused around the dictatorial demands of a master production schedule. This schedule is a statement of planned production for the next several months. The length of the planning horizon can vary from industry to industry and company to company based on the idiosyncrasies of each company or industry. The master schedule must balance the demands of the market with the reasonable capability of the factory to produce.

Once a balance between market demand and factory capacity has been reached, the schedule is passed to the Material Requirements Planning (MRP) module which interprets it into time-phased, lot-sized manufacturing and purchasing demands (planned orders) and establishes due dates.

The planned orders generated through MRP are passed to the Capacity Requirements Planning (CRP) module. The CRP logic calculates individual order schedules and projects capacity loads at each work center for each time period across the planning horizon.

As time passes, the system recommends orders for release to the factory or to Purchasing based on system-calculated start dates. As an order progresses through the shop, all activity data affecting it will be collected and reported to the system for record updating. Labor and material assignments, scrap generation, quantity completions, and job movements are all captured and reported. The system will re-prioritize all orders in each work center every time the program is run and will sequence, or dispatch them, accordingly.

Each iteration of the system will produce an updated order status picture and will generate messages geared to keeping the factory on target to the master schedule. If circumstances prevent this meshing, actions must be taken to bring actual performance in line with the plan, or the master schedule must be changed. The master schedule must always be current and accomplishable for the system to work effectively. With the volatility, uncertainty, and continuous change attendant to the manufacturing world, maintaining schedule stability is extremely difficult, at best, and quite often virtually impossible.

Database

The heart of a system's ability to respond effectively to the continuous change of manufacturing is its database. A sound database provides a virtual mirror image of company operations. State-of-the-art systems permit direct database inquiry and real time manipulation of data.

The database contains information about the company's products, its facilities, and its plans. The central focus is on parts and the relationships of parts to each other in a variety of product structures. Those relationships establish the ability to perform bill of material explosions and where-used searches.

The facilities described in the database are the work centers and tooling used in the factory, plus the company's vendors and customers. The facilities information is cross referenced to the part records through a series of relational records. Routings, operations, and tool cross reference records link parts to work centers. Vendors and customers are linked to the parts through vendor and customer cross reference records.

The plans that are described in the database are the master production schedule, customer orders, purchase orders, and manufacturing orders. Vendors and customers are linked directly to their respective orders while manufacturing orders are tied to the applicable work centers through work-in-process records. The plans are also linked to the part records through another series of relational records. These records provide the line item details, by part, of the master schedule, each customer order, each purchase order, and each manufacturing order.

Customer Order Servicing

Customer order servicing provides the path-

way for the linkage of the marketplace to the factory. The term implies the systemic capability to:

- Enter orders
- Process orders
- Inquire into the status of orders and influence their movement

To be effective, COS software must provide for fast and accurate order entry and must facilitate the positive control of customer orders from the time they are entered into the system until they are completed. How effectively these objectives are pursued will be determined by how easily the database can be accessed and by how effectively the application software for order servicing integrates with other key programs for inventory and factory management.

Integrated Purchasing

Purchasing management has been slow to embrace the integrated technology of computerized manufacturing planning and control. This is due mainly to the failure of most of the early attempts at factory systems to provide adequate, timely provisioning to meet schedule demands.

In an integrated system, Purchasing personnel will normally have on-line access to database information and application programs to assist them. Those programs relating specifically to purchasing should operate together in a modular fashion. The purchasing module, in turn, must interface directly with MRP, Inventory Accounting, Quality Control, Receiving/Inspection, and the General Ledger, specifically Accounts Payable.

Shop Floor Control

When addressing the factory floor, the only thing that remains constant is change. Schedules change, parts are changed, material is scrapped, shortages arise, people are absent, machines break down, etc.. These circumstances present factory management with constantly changing sets of alternatives and conflicting priorities. Immediate access to current information is a must. Beyond that, it is crucial that management be able to manipulate the myriad pieces of information essential to the proper operation of a factory and to satisfy the exigencies of the moment while still maintaining the integrity of the master schedule. This is an enormously complex and difficult task.

Until recently, most of the attention of the MRP crusade of the 1970's was focused on the office functions of order planning with pitiful little value trickling down to the plant. This lack of factory control contributed to the failure of many manufacturing planning and control systems to provide the value sought. High on the list of reasons for these failures was the lack of understanding on the part of the office planning personnel of the needs of the factory and the almost total lack of knowledge about, and mistrust of, the computer and computer oriented systems by the factory workers and managers. These conditions were aggravated by the unresponsiveness and inaccessibility of those earlier systems.

Today, the tools do exist to properly plan and load work centers, analyze bottlenecks, and dispatch work and personnel to work centers based on up-to-the-minute planning and status information. Also, many systems have become friendly enough that factory personnel no longer find them threatening or cumbersome to use.

Factory operations offer the potential for enormous value to be gained from the creative and effective use of the computer. The shop is the repository, and therefore, the court of last resort for the solution of virtually all the operational problems of a company, regardless of their department of origin. The shop manager with timely and factual information at his disposal, and with the ability to manipulate that data in real time to simulate alternative solutions, has an enormous advantage over the manager who must operate by the seat of his pants. It is not enough that a system precalculate schedules and shop loads. Management must be able to change the relationships of data, at will, to pursue alternate lines of reasoning.

The most serious responsibility that shop management has is the stewardship of a company's physical assets in the pursuit of profit. In this stewardship, the most pressing concern is the control of value flowing through the facilities. The level of work-in-process and the rate at which it turns over determine the speed with which a company can generate a positive cash flow. In the short term, cash flow may be more significant to the financial well being of a concern than profit or loss. The control placed on the input and output of shop backlog heavily influences the rate at which orders turn over.

There are a variety of techniques employed to maintain consistent shop flow. The effective ones all have a basic attribute in common. They strive to maintain the value of work-in-process at a minimal level consistent with optimal flow through the factory. Beyond that, they can differ widely in their perspective. Some concentrate on plant utilization while others focus on customer service. Maximization of profit must clearly be the goal.

Regardless of the perspective, one of the keys to effective performance lies in the timely collection of operation data and the re-planning of the activities through the systemic, iterative interpretation of that data. Modern systems are introducing the use of factory data collection devices to the shop floor. Early attempts at this required the use of punched cards and met with active resistance from the labor force. The technology associated with factory data terminals has taken giant strides in recent years. The devices are less imposing, and the collection media have changed from punched cards to newer technologies such as bar code, magnetic stripe, and optical character recognition. Work is also being done on machine to machine communication and on audio input.

Cost Accounting

Cost accounting has been part of the bedrock of traditional manufacturing practices since the early days of the industrial revolution. The assignment of overhead to products through burden allocations and the measurement of departmental and individual worker efficiencies against predetermined acceptable standards are imbedded in the manufacturing culture. Recently, two new manufacturing philosophies, Just-In-Time (JIT) and Optimized Production Technology (OPT), have taken dead aim at those practices, proclaiming them to be the root cause of much of our productivity problem, as well as being profit inhibitors.

Ignoring the argument about the propriety of the practices, when associated with MRP based systems, cost accounting is a logical extension of manufacturing control. Cost accounting focuses on quantity, time, and cost. Manufacturing control focuses on quantity, time, and schedules. The matching and reconciliation is done through the common records in the database that are shared by both systems.

The major elements of cost accounting are:

. Cost build-up
. Cost center accounting
. Job order (production unit) costing

Cost build-up is the process of cascading costs on a level by level basis through the structured bills of material to arrive at total product cost or a standard value. Conventional MRP "where used" implosion logic is used in the construction of a cost build-up. The two techniques used are roll-up and fold-in. The roll-up technique maintains the integrity of each of the individual costs of material, labor, and overhead at each level of the build-up, as well as the total, cumulative cost. The fold-in technique adds the cumulative, total cost of each lower level into the material cost of each succeeding higher level, thereby losing the identity of the individual cost elements.

Cost center accounting collects and measures labor and facilities performance against budgets and standards applied to the operations performed at each work center. Overhead costs are distributed to the work centers either directly or in accordance with predetermined allocation calculations. In this manner, all the distributable costs included in the cost of goods calculation are distributed to the factory for absorption by the orders processed through the plant.

Job order costing accumulates material, labor, and overhead costs attributable to each work order. These costs are assigned at each work center as the order passes through. Material and labor are applied directly. Overhead is distributed on a prorata basis.

ALTERNATIVES TO MRP

Several thousand MRP implementations have been attempted during the past ten years. Many have achieved noteable success. Most have not. Those that have succeeded usually have done so at great expense over an expended period, and they have often settled for results that were significantly short of original expectations.

Two alternative philosophies that have achieved impressive results are the Just-In-Time (JIT) approach that originated in Japan as the Toyota KANBAN system and Optimized Production Technology (OPT) that was born in Israel. JIT has produced dramatic results where it has been employed. However, it is not suited to all types of manufacturing, and it works best when certain cultural attitudes, that are inherrent in Japan but foreign to most of the rest of the world, are in place. JIT is a manual system geared to reducing inventories and to identifying and resolving bottleneck operations.

OPT is a new technology which produces optimized schedules as part of an overall philosophy that challenges many of the fundamental precepts of traditional manufacturing practices. OPT directly attacks bottlenecks and works to reduce inventories much as JIT does. One basic difference, however, between OPT and JIT is that OPT is a computerized system that can analyze alternative approaches in advance of committing resources or creating problems on the factory floor. Although a relatively new system, OPT has already produced startling results in several of the largest corporations in the United States.

OFFICE SYSTEMS

Until recently, office automation meant word processing. Today, it also means personal computing, electronic mail, calendar control, message switching, graphics, and database access. Many of the current systems support terminal use as an independent, self-contained unit or as part of a communications network. Communication networks may be local or they may tie into global hook-ups. The world of office systems is rapidly expanding to permit desk top access to public databases as well as to corporate business systems information from a terminal that can also be a very private, one station device.

As artificial intelligence and audio capabilities expand, system use will become increasingly more adaptive to the human thought processes. Decision support systems employing unstructured, non-procedural languages, dubbed programmerless computing, have already started to take hold.

SUMMARY

Most of the elements essential for computer integrated manufacturing are in existance today. The major tasks remaining are to continually evolve these techniques into more effective tools and for management to learn how to use them properly. The keystone to the effective pursuit of full integration is the database. Most of the existing databases are hierarchically organized networks. This organization will be around for a long time. Many of the newer, more advanced systems are employing distributed and relational databases. The significant factor is that all applications become logically integrated through the database and that management have unrestricted access to that information in pursuit of the overall financial goals of the company.

ABOUT THE AUTHOR

Robert B. Vollum is Director of Consulting for Creative Output Inc. Prior to joining COI, he was the Principal Manufacturing Consultant for the Sperry Corporation. During his career, Bob has served as Chief Executive Officer and President of a capital goods manufacturing company he founded and later sold, and held previous positions as Vice President and General Manager of divisions of two major conglomerates. His experience includes several years with a major management consulting firm and extensive responsibility for Manufacturing Operations, Materials Management, Sales and Marketing.

Bob earned his BS Degree in Engineering and Science from the U. S. Naval Academy and has pursued graduate studies in Business Administration at Union College and The College Of William and Mary. He is certified at the Fellow level by the American Production and Inventory Control Society (APICS) and is a Senior Member of the Society of Manufacturing Engineers (SME) and its associated organizations CASA/SME and RI/SME. He has been published broadly on a variety of manufacturing topics and has spoken often at universities and professional society functions throughout North America and Europe.

THE FUTURE WORLD OF MANUFACTURING

Earle Steinberg, Ph.D.
Touche Ross & Company

INTRODUCTION

The explosion in computer technology that has taken place during the last ten years has changed the way American Industry does business. Today there are approximately five million stand alone computers in the world. It is estimated that by the turn of the century there will be an excess of twenty million computers. Look around you. That means that everywhere you see one computer today, you are likely to see four within the next fifteen years. Translated into production rates, this means that a new computer is born approximately every eight minutes. In addition to this phenomenal growth in the number of computers a corresponding increase is taking place in the power of computers that are being produced. If you were to measure computer power by IPS (instructions per second), you would discover that the total brain power of computers is doubling every two years. Combine these two facts together: A tremendous increase in the number of computers as well as the phenomenal growth in the power of new computers that we are producing today, and we can reach only one conclusion:

BY THE TURN OF THE CENTURY COMPUTERS WILL BE THE DOMINANT TECHNOLOGY ON THE FACE OF THE EARTH.

IMPACT ON MANUFACTURING

This explosion in computer technology and processing capability has lead to a new level of competition in manufacturing throughout the world. Ten years ago, a manufacturing firm could select as a basis for competition either cost, quality, or customer service. It was entirely impossible for a company to compete on a basis of having the highest quality goods in its marketplace regardless of cost while others found their niche in being strictly the low cost producer with the customer excepting lower quality in the product. Today, because of the abilities of advanced manufacturing technology to improve all the aspects of manufacturing the basis for competition has shifted. This translates into several key issues that all manufacturing firms must face:

... COST
... QUALITY
... CUSTOMER SERVICE
... FLEXIBILITY
... INTERNATIONAL COMPETITION

Today manufacturing firms are finding themselves in a race for survival. In order to compete effectively, companies must simultaneously strive to produce goods at an exceptionally low cost while maintaining high quality with outstanding customer service (sometimes this means short lead times), yet have tremendous flexibility to meet international competition. We are finding that many firms who used to be able to produce standard products in a make to stock environment are now faced with the prospect of demands from their customers for one of a kind products in short production runs delivered at a low cost with very high quality in a short lead time.

This requirement for flexibility is already being provided by many foreign competitors. For example, an automated forge shop in Korea can provide castings which are produced in a unique, one step process at a very low cost in a short period of time. Add to this the foundry's capability to engineer the product, develop the patterns, and produce and deliver the product in a very competitive lead time and you have an outstanding example of why American manufacturers must compete on the basis of cost, quality, customer service, and flexibility simultaneously. Several years ago, many manufacturers would have been astounded at the thought of having to go through the design engineering,

prototyping, testing, and other development in the manufacturing process for entirely new products to be produced in very small lots in a short period of time with high quality at a low cost. Yet, today more and more manufacturers are realizing that their primary hope for survival in a competitive market hinges on their ability to do precisely that. It is painful for American manufacturers to finally come to terms with the fact that manufacturing is no longer a western civilization endeavor. We are competing not only with the Europeans and Japanese, but increasingly with South Americans and even new manufacturing concerns that are springing up throughout the Middle East.

What impact has all of this had on manufacturing management? Simply put, successful firms are realizing that:

MANUFACTURING IS A STRATEGIC WEAPON.

It used to be that strategic thinking in manufacturing hinged primarily on considerations of marketing and financial arrangements. However, we are now finding that increasingly that strategic resources being developed are:

1. Outstanding product quality.
2. Substantial reduction of lead times.
3. Ability to offer customers specials in small quantities at low prices.
4. Competence to develop new products in previously undreamed of short development cycles.

These resources are providing unique strategic leverage that allows manufacturing firms to compete in an increasingly competitive international market. The fact of the matter is that no amount of marketing, advertising, or financial manipulation can make a company healthy in the long run if its physical products, facilities, technologies, and people, are not of competitive quality.

SOME CRITICAL ISSUES IN MANUFACTURING

The following are some quotes from a number of distinguished manufacturing executives who have addressed many of these issues:

"Manufacturing must take far greater initiative within U.S. companies" from Ronald Petersen, Director of Operations, Lockheed Corporation.

"Quality is the number one priority in U.S. manufacturing" from William J. Devaney, President Vidmar Corporation.

"First priority must be to use existing facilities more effectively" from Critical Issues Committee of the Society of Manufacturing Engineers.

"Manufacturing must be governed by long term strategies" from Leo Everitt, Vice President Manufacturing, FMC Corporation.

"Engineering/Manufacturing interfaces must be improved" from Robert Ochs, Director of Operations Development of Aerojet General.

If we look at these concerns expressed by some impressive manufacturing executives, we can see that some dominant themes in manufacturing are emerging in the world marketplace. The first is improved production and inventory control systems. Of course, APICS has played a critical role in undertaking a massive education effort to sell American industry on improved manufacturing control systems. This effort has been spectacularly successful by almost any measure one can devise. While there are many companies who have still not adopted MRP II or alternative systems for manufacturing control, virtually every senior manufacturing executive is at least aware of the need to consider such approaches.

Another theme that has clearly emerged is a new, rigorous emphasis on quality. We have leared from the Japanese something that we knew a long time ago: It makes much more sense to do something right the first time than to do it a lot of times, hoping that we've done it right often enough. The old American approach to quality control which emphasizes large lot sizes and tolerance of high scrap rates is simply not adequate for addressing critical issues involved in competing on the basis of cost and quality. Many American manufacturers have adopted a Total Quality Management approach where the emphasis is on discovering problems that are involved in low quality products or defective lots and addressing those problems rather than emphasizing producing in large lots in order to obtain the satisfactory yield rate.

The integration of manufacturing and other systems has become critical for American manufactureres who wish to compete in the international marketplace. Here we are not only referring to the "MRP II" concept of tying together financial and manufacturing planning at the top level. We are also concerned with a close integration of manufacturing and engineering all the way down to the shop floor. As we move toward the adoption of advanced manufacturing technology and a more automated factory, the distinction between manufacturing engineering and manufacturing begins to fade. Therefore it is important that better communication between engineering and manufacturing staffs be developed if the company is to be competitive.

The development of new physical processes is fundamental. If we look at the history of American manufacturing we recognize that the concept of a traditional job shop with like processes grouped together was originally adopted because we believed that it would provide us great flexibility when contrasted with the traditional flowshop layout. Initially, this certainly proved to be the case. However, many companies have found that, as the number of products they produce increases, and the complexity of each product also increases, an interesting phenomena occurs. The job shop layout that was originally conceived in order to provide great flexibility in production led to long, circuitous routings through the shop with a tremendous amount of backflow and criss-crossing along with excessive material handling. Recognition of this problem has forced many companies to consider a Group Technology approach, where common parts are grouped together and multiple operations are performed in a specially designed manufacturing cell which is arranged along with other manufacturing cells in a shop floor arrangement which smooths the flow of materials through the plant, thereby reducing material handling activity and reducing backflow. While group technology is not a particularly a new idea, the advent of Computer Aided Manufacturing (CAM) has allowed manufacturers to design and build manufacturing cells with dramatically increased productivity. The use of computers to control manufacturing has long been routine in continuous process industries such as chemicals, oil and oil refining. It is only during the last decade that it has been introduced in batch manufacturing industries. It now appears that the main technical barriers to automation in batch manufacturing will be overcome in this decade. Progress in development of CAM in all industrialized countries is likely to lead to construction of more fully automated factories sometime during the late 1980's. It is interesting that, in 1977 the Agency of Industrial Science and Technology (AIST) of the Ministry for International Trade and Industry (MITI) in Japan, developed a project which aimed at the completion of a fully automated factory in 1984. This factory is supposed to produce modules of its own machine tools and therefore will represent a step toward a development of a self-replicating series of machines. When fully completed, the automated plant is to produce components weighing up to 500 kilograms and measuring 1 meter in any dimension. Only ten technicians are expected to be needed to provide production, but the plant is expected to have an output similar to that of a conventional factory employing 700 workers. Eugene Merchant, Principal Scientist at Cincinnatti Milacron recently visited the Japanese project center and believes that the work appears to be on schedule although others have expressed some doubt. The impact of such an operational automated machine tool factory would be immense. These factories would be able to produce duplicates of their own equipment quite quickly, and that would lower the cost of machine tool production

within a relatively few years. Regardless of how rapidly this project advances, it is clear that it represents a significant challenge to American manufacturing in the machine tool industries.

Another interesting but often overlook trend in manufacturing throughout the world today is an increasingly strong emphasis on white collar productivity, measuring payback on indirect costs. For a long time, even manufacturers with heavy investments in NC or CNC machine tools considered the notion that they could dramatically increase productivity by motivating their labor force to greater efforts, by better relations with unions, or other incentive schemes. Now it appears possible that many of the traditional blue collar focused attempts at productivity will be dealt with by replacing many blue collar jobs with "steel collar" workers. There is however, a lack of understanding of how we can measure white collar productivity and reduce the ratio of indirect to total manufacturing costs. It is clear that performance measurement system which consider white collar productivity and which emphasize strategic, long-term view and development of better operations technology are the wave of the future. Far too many executives have viewed a tour of duty in manufacturing management as an opportunity to increase short term profits while doing very little to improve the manufacturing infrastructure of the company which determines its ability to compete in the long-run in a highly competitive marketplace. A greater emphasis on evaluating management productivity in terms of how the manufacturing infrastructure has evolved and improved during the tenure of management is critical to the success of the American manufacturing firms. It is not enough to look at this quarter's financial statements or even this year's profits. Instead, we must begin to provide incentives for manufacturing executives to take a longer term view of their responsibility to enhance and develop the companies ability to compete on a strategic basis in the world marketplace. One of the questions that many of the companies are now asking of their manufacturing executives is simply this: "How has our capability to compete in the manufacturing environment been enhanced during your tenure of management?" While it is difficult to measure progress and the development of manufacturing infrastructure, it is nonetheless critical to the long-term success of American industry to provide some incentives for management to be concerned about the long term ability to manufacture and deliver product at a low cost with high quality in a short period of time and to maintain a high degree of flexibility in order to compete in the international marketplace.

Some examples of how outstanding manufacturing companies have addressed these issues follow:

TRW
.. TRW has appointed vice-presidents of productivity, quality, technical service, manufacturing, and material to stimulate and share ideas across ninety independent divisions.

.. They have established productivity committees and projects in over seventy divisions.

.. They have initiated new corporate wide thrusts on quality.

.. They have invested in top down management development, emphasizing education in manufacturing strategy.

.. They have begun to study performance measurement systems which emphasize strategic, long term views and development of better operations technology.

GENERAL ELECTRIC
.. GE is currently developing changes in rewards systems to emphasize more long term and qualitative contributions.

.. They are investing heavily in management development for manufacturing directors and division managers, emphasizing manufacturing strategy concepts.

JOHN DEERE AND COMPANY

.. John Deere and Company has invested millions in radical new equipment and process technology to improve quality, reliability and customer service.

.. They have de-emphasized performance measures based on short term cost reduction and older notions of efficiency.

It is now clear that some dominant themes in manufacturing are emerging throughout the world. To summarize the above discussion, we can characterize those themes as:

1. Improving production inventory control systems.
2. New, rigorous emphasis on quality.
3. Integrating manufacturing and other systems.
4. Developing radical new physical processes.
5. Strong emphasis on white collar productivity, measuring payback on indirect costs.
6. Reducing intra-company competition between divisions - movement away from independent profit centers.

The last theme, that of movement away from independent profit centers in multi-plant manufacturing companies may be news to some, but has long been an accepted fact to others who are effectively competing in the manufacturing marketplace. Let's take an example of a large multi plant manufacturing company in the southwest. There are three plants that operate independently, yet sell parts to each other for production of product at a negotiated transfer price. These plants have an average gross margin of 18%. Yet when the final product leaves any of the three plants which are capable of producing it, the average gross margin is only 7%. What accounts for the difference between 18 and 7%? Simple. Each plant manager is evaluated on a basis of his own profitability in operating his individual plant. There is a tremendous amount of focus on buying and selling parts from each of the plants and striking deals which in the short run will make each plant appear to be more profitable. Yet, we all recognize that selling to each other is no way to compete in today's marketplace. It's only through delivery of low cost, high quality services to the customer that we can hope to be viable in the long run. This movement away from independent profit centers will enable companies such as this one to establish a different set of priorities. Some companies have addressed this problem by establishing transfer prices and accounting systems which force any plant to "eat" their own variances in the transfer of parts to other sister plants. A better way to approach this problem is to establish an overall corporate goal and set targets for each individual plant in such a way so that each plant contributes in its own way to the achievement of the corporate goal. Each plant is then measured not on the basis of some artificial profit measurement which can be manipulated through the process of interplant transfers, but instead on the basis of how they meet their target and contribute to the achievement of the overall corporate goal.

FACTORY OF THE FUTURE

The degree of automation that we can expect to see within the next twenty years is staggering. Unfortunately, many companies will latch on to any new technology in attempt to be ahead of the trend or to simply appear to be progressive. This clearly is one path to financial ruin. Automation is a complex and costly process. It is easy to envision some companies purchasing large numbers of robots and automated material handling equipment because it appears to be "the thing to do". If such a company has not addressed fundamental issues such as production and inventory control, it is likely that all the automated equipment will move the wrong parts around the shop floor a lot quicker so that they can get to where they can't be worked on a lot sooner. This, of course, is ridiculous. The consideration and adoption of new manufacturing technology must be done on a rational basis in light of specifically measured and identified costs and benefits and must be part of an on-going master modernization plan which is driven by the overall strategic plan of the company. It does little good for example, for a company to invest heavily in radical new processes equipment if top management has not considered what the future marketplace for that equipment is likely to be. It is entirely conceivable that expensive investment could be made in a plant which would turn out to be a "white elephant" because top management will not have considered projected technological breakthroughs. The strategic questions that we have discussed earlier, such as cost, quality, customer service and flexibility provide a basis for competition in the marketplace. Long term strategic thinking must address each one of these elements of competition in the marketplace and translate those elements into specific performance measures in functional areas such as manufacturing operations, manufacturing engineering, design engineering, finance and accounting, and data processing. Specific or expected performance measures for manufacturing operations, for example, should reflect how advanced technology will reduce cost, improve quality, shorten lead time, and increase flexibility in manufacturing. Understanding these performance measures and developing a set of targets will help guide the evaluation of particular components of advanced manufacturing technology.

General Electric is a firm which has addressed many of these issues and has expressed their basic set of philosophies and beliefs in a straightforward and simple manner. They believe that many companies, by adopting inappropriate manufacturing technology, or by developing "islands of automation" that only create bottlenecks in the shop, can move toward a "factory of the future" now. However, the real question exists whether such companies will have a "factory in the future". The key, they believe, is to take a rational approach toward automation where development of meaningful master modernization plans which will ensure that the company will not only have a "factory in the future" but will also have a factory with a future.

Very little actual data has been gathered from which we can learn some specific lessons about the process of automation. Stephen Rosenthal of Boston University, publishing in the Journal of Operations Management has indicated that what data we do have leads us to several clear conclusions:

1. Leading edge users of computer aided manufacturing processes believe in learning by doing. These companies have begun the long journey towards automation by taking small, discreet steps. In order to develop a history of success, they first considered automation and advanced manufacturing technology projects which they felt comfortable with and which could be achieved with some degree of certainty. Rigorous cost benefit analysis was performed and is generally considered imperative the success of any such effort. Performance measures are established. Specific improvements are sought and tracked and the automation project is installed on a rigorous schedule with an emphasis on developing "lessons learned along the way". After installation of an automated improvement process or project, performance is then tracked to ensure that whatever improvements have been realized are permanent.

2. Suppliers claim that most manufacturers are not sophisticated customers. Manufacturing companies that deal in providing automated equipment believe that most of their customers purchase automated equipment with neither a clear understanding of cost benefit approaches, nor a clear understanding of implementation planning or effective utilization of automated equipment. If this is true, then many decisions are being made which will result in a large number of initial failures in movement toward a "factory with a future". As far as we can tell, the only effective method of dealing with this problem is extensive education of management in both manufacturing strategy and advanced manufacturing technology. Along with this extensive education must come clearer

40

communications between engineering and
manufacturing.

SUMMARY

In this paper we have addressed some critical issues
in American manufacturing brought about by increased
international competition resulting from the explosion
in availability of computer technology and its impact on
manufacturing processees and planning. Many of the
issues are difficult and complex and will take years to
resolve. The issue however, is not whether we should
resolve them but rather how to resolve them.

To quote one of the vice presidents of manufacturing
of General Electric: "American industry has three
choices: AUTOMATE, EMIGRATE, or EVAPORATE". American
manufacturers can either choose to adopt advanced
manufacturing technology to help them compete
simultaneously on the basis of cost, quality, customer
service and flexibility, or they can lose a large share
of their marketplace to other companies and countries
that do. If that happens, they will see many of their
jobs emigrate to other parts of the world and other
regions of the country where manufacturing firms have
taken advantage of expanding computer technology to
improve their manufacturing processees significantly.
The third choice, of course, is to ignore the entire
situation, hope automation issues go away, or that
others will fail. In this case, it is most likely that
some manufacturing companies will, in the long run,
evaporate.

Those manufacturing firms who take a long term
strategic view of their own future and proceed in an
orderly manner toward adoption of advanced manufacturing
technology while using reasonable cost/benefit analysis
along the way will not only endure but probably
prosper. The key is to understand how each element of
the advanced technology helps you to compete in the long
run in your own marketplace.

GROUP TECHNOLOGY, PRODUCTION ACTIVITY
CONTROL, AND JUST-IN-TIME
John N. Petroff, CPIM
COMSERV Corporation

GROUP TECHNOLOGY LAYOUT

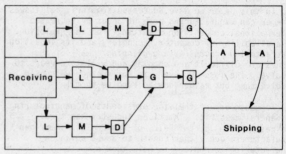

Figure 2

At one time, Group Technology and MRP were considered incompatible. But since MRP I evolved into MRP II, and especially with the new developments in the areas of Just-in-Time and Zero Inventory, Group Technology is becoming recognized as a complimentary and supporting technique.

There is some confusion on a definition of Group Technology. APICS defines Group Technology as "An engineering and manufacturing philosophy which identifies the `sameness' of parts, equipment or processes. It provides for rapid retrieval of existing designs and anticipates a cellular type production equipment layout." (1) Hyde says "GT is a technique for manufacturing small to medium lot-size batches of parts of similar process, of somewhat dissimilar materials, geometry and size, which are produced in a committed small cell of machines which have been grouped together physically, specifically tooled, and scheduled as a unit."(2) We will use Hyde's definition for the balance of this presentation.

Figure 1 depicts how shop orders travel through a factory with conventional layout. Here we see that the factory is arranged with machinery and equipment grouped according to similarity, without regard for the sequence and flow of work through the facility. Notice that even in this simple example, the pathways are very complicated, and the total travel distances great. Another thing to realize, is that each work center is preceded by its own queue. This means that if a shop order passes over five work centers, it must wait in a queue five times.

Figure 2 shows a similar factory laid out according to Group Technology. Here we see the factory laid out according to several common work sequences which accomodate the families of products being produced. In this example we see that the product lines fall into four main groups, with the machines laid out in sequence without regard for the type of machine involved.

There are many advantages that come with Group Technology, and several are important to those of us working in P&IC:
o Queue time is reduced. One of the principles of Group Technology is that once a shop order is started in a work center, it flows from operation to operation, from machine to machine, directly with no waiting in a queue. Taking one of the lines from Figure 2, we see that a shop order is processed on five machines, but experi-

PROCESS—TYPE LAYOUT

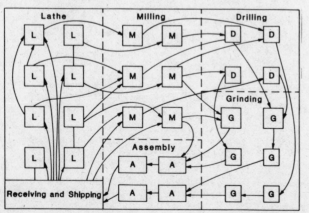

Figure 1

ences a queue only once. This reduces the queue by four-fifths, or 80%.

o Factory leadtime is reduced. In factories with conventional layout, queue time is 90% of factory leadtime, and processing time 10%. In our example, we eliminate four of the five queues, thereby reducing manufacturing leadtime by 72%.

o Work-in-process is reduced. Since shop orders in a queue are part of work-in-process, any reduction in queue will result in an equivalent reduction in wip. The cost of carrying inventory is high. Although there is no real consensus as to inventory carrying cost, it could be 12%, 24%, 36% per year or even more. Even a modest-sized manufacturing company can have $1,000.000 of work-in-process inventory. Taking this hypothetical company and our same GT example, reducing queue by four-fifths also will reduce wip by 72%, or $720,000. Using the 24% per year inventory carrying cost figure, this yields a yearly saving of $152,800. Notice that this is a contribution to profits before taxes, the popular "bottom line", and recurrs every year. This is in addition to the permanent reduction in inventory investment.

o Smaller lot sizes are possible. Because of the partial dedication of machines and equipment in a Group Technology layout, setup time automatically is reduced. This should result in a corresponding reduction of lot sizes. In an early implementation, one French company grouped two lathes, one vertical drill, and one milling machine into a GT cell. They found setup time dropped by 85%.(3) One of the supporting techniques leading to zero inventories is the reduction of setup time in order to achieve lot-for-lot lot sizing. This is one illustration of how GT supports current materials management principles.

o Enhances just-in-time performance. Shortening factory leadtime by 72% will certainly lead to much greater accuracy in getting shop orders completed on schedule. Shorter leadtime means that orders will be started much later than before, drastically increasing the likelihood that the entire pick list will be on hand at release time. Also, shorter manufacturing time reduces exposure to scheduling and production anomalies.

o Reduces the impact of engineering change orders. A few companies have a stable product line and few ECO's. They are in the minority, however. Most companies have a significant traffic in them, and many companies are plagued by them. Effectivity severity of ECO's range from next order, to in-process, to in-stock, to in-the-field. There is a very strong incentive not to recall products from stock or from customers for rework. Its easier to call for rework while an order is open on the floor. Reducing the exposure time by more than three quarters will reduce

42

rework of open orders by some noticeable amount. A few may still demand rework of stock on hand, but most will be given a "next order" severity.

o Lowers manufacturing costs. The Machinability Data Center found references claiming a 40% reduction in manufacturing cost per piece. (4) The reduction occurred mainly in operating cost. Figure 3 shows their finding. They also found evidence of a 47% reduction in manufacturing operating costs, Group Technology over conventional layout.(5) Figure 4 shows these findings. These studies are not recent, but nevertheless demonstrate that significant cost savings, beyond wip inventory reduction, come with Group Technology.

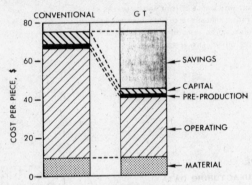

Figure 3
Comparison of manufacturing costs per piece for conventional and group technologh layouts

o Fosters standardization. The analysis techniques developed to implement and sustain GT automatically lead design engineers to current components, and encourages common usage and similar designs.

Almost every new technique exhibits some disadvantages, Group Technology included:

o Requires extensive analysis. In order to convert to a GT factory layout, the company must

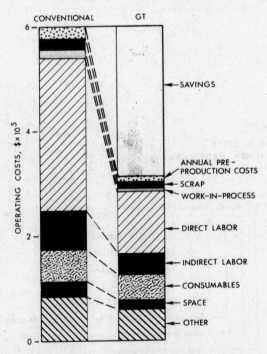

Figure 4
Comparison of annual operating costs for conventional and group technology layouts

analyze all existing items. And they must be grouped according to similarity of production steps. Since this has never been a strong requirement in traditional manufacturing, analytical tools usually are not in place. This means that some type of analysis provision must be developed and put into place, even before analysis can begin. This usually requires the addition of some kind of classification code to a new field in the item master. For companies with thousands of manufactured items, this could be a formidable job.

o Requires factory rearrangement. Carried to its logical conclusion, conversion to GT would require that the whole factory be uprooted and rearranged. The time and cost implications are obvious.

o Supervisors need retraining. Under a conventional layout, a work center supervisor usually has only one type of machine or equipment to supervise. In a GT environment, the supervisor would have to know how to supervise operators working on a wide variety of equipment.

o Inflexibility. When set, a GT cell has a degree of specialization that may inhibit or make more costly the introduction of new products, especially to the extent that they are dissimilar to current ones.

Within a closed-loop MRP II system, achieving a Group Technology layout requires a number of steps in preparation.

The first step is to adopt a classification technique that will support later analysis. No good analysis can proceed by performing a computer sort on the description field on the item master, nor on the part number field. Significant noun systems for the description field always fall short. For example, Fig 5 shows a very simple shape that can easily be given fifteen different names. And conversely, Fig 6 shows six entirely different assemblies called "Support". Even the old "Bolt, Hex" fails where a similar item is called "Screw, Machine", or "Fastener, Threaded", not to mention such variations as "Threaded Fastener", "Machine Screw",or "Hex Bolt". While the debate over significant vs nonsignificant numbering rages on perpetually, it is nonetheless evident that no significant numbering scheme seems to work sufficiently to support the kind of analysis needed, even when they grow to enormous field size.

A classification coding procedure must be able to classify the universe in order to be useful in the long term. Because of this, it is rare that a company can develop its own. There are, however, a number of successful proprietary systems available. Appendix A lists some of the major ones available in the USA and western Europe.

Time does not permit an extensive discussion of the various proprietary classification methods in this presentation. However, Figures 7, 8, 9, and 10 show how a simple washer would be classified under the Brisch-Birn, Miclass, CODE, and Opitz systems, respectively.

In an MRP II setting, each manufactured item would be given a classification, coded into a reserved field on the item master. The coding scheme adopted would need to be crafted such that it would group parts together according to the way they are manufactured.

The next step in implementing Group Technology is to analyze all manufactured items, and arrange them in groups according to how they are manufactured. This analysis must be done by experienced, talented manufacturing engineers and manufacturing managers, who will be able to reach a balance between too many highly-specialized cells, and too few of them to gain the touted benefits.

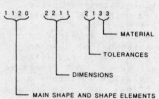

Figure 5

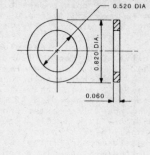

12 DIGIT DECIMAL SEMI-POLYCODE

```
1120   2211   2133
  |       |     | |____ MATERIAL
  |       |     |_____ TOLERANCES
  |       |_____ DIMENSIONS
  |_____ MAIN SHAPE AND SHAPE ELEMENTS
```

ROUND PART WITH SINGLE OUTSIDE AND DIAMETERS
WITHOUT FACES, THREADS, SLOTS, GROOVES, SPLINES,
OR ADDITIONAL HOLES. THE OUTSIDE DIAMETER AND
LENGTH ARE WITHIN CERTAIN SIZE RANGES.

Figure 8

Different Items Bearing the Name : "SUPPORTS"

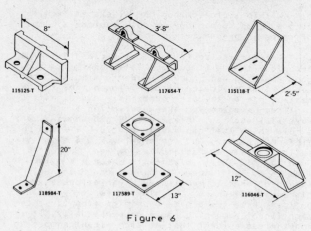

115125-T   117654-T   115118-T

118984-T   117589-T   116046-T

Figure 6

<u>CODE</u>

**MANUFACTURING DATA
SYSTEMS, INC.
(BERGEN, HARTEC)**

8 DIGIT HEXIDECIMAL SEMI POLYCODE

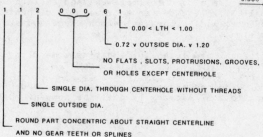

```
1  1  2   000   6  1
|  |  |    |     |  |__ 0.00 < LTH < 1.00
|  |  |    |     |_____ 0.72 v OUTSIDE DIA. v 1.20
|  |  |    |_____ NO FLATS , SLOTS, PROTRUSIONS, GROOVES,
|  |  |                 OR HOLES EXCEPT CENTERHOLE
|  |  |_____ SINGLE DIA. THROUGH CENTERHOLE WITHOUT THREADS
|  |_____ SINGLE OUTSIDE DIA.
|_____ ROUND PART CONCENTRIC ABOUT STRAIGHT CENTERLINE
                        AND NO GEAR TEETH OR SPLINES
```

Figure 9

P.N.C.

**BRISCH –BIRN TYPE
DEVELOPED FOR GENERAL MOTORS**

6 DIGIT DECIMAL MONOCODE

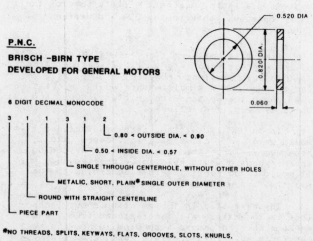

```
3  1  1  3  1  2
|  |  |  |  |  |__ 0.80 < OUTSIDE DIA. < 0.90
|  |  |  |  |_____ 0.50 < INSIDE DIA. < 0.57
|  |  |  |_____ SINGLE THROUGH CENTERHOLE, WITHOUT OTHER HOLES
|  |  |_____ METALIC, SHORT, PLAIN* SINGLE OUTER DIAMETER
|  |_____ ROUND WITH STRAIGHT CENTERLINE
|_____ PIECE PART
```

#NO THREADS, SPLITS, KEYWAYS, FLATS, GROOVES, SLOTS, KNURLS,
OR SWAGED OR ANGULAR ENDS

Figure 7

OPITZ

**DR. H. OPITZ
AACHEN, WEST GERMANY**

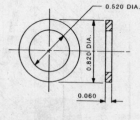

9 DIGIT DECIMAL SEMI-POLYCODE VERSION

```
0  0  1  1  0  1  6  1  0
|  |  |  |  |  |  |  |  |__ TOLERANCE CLASS
|  |  |  |  |  |  |  |_____ INITIAL MATERIAL FORM
|  |  |  |  |  |  |_____ MATERIAL TYPE AND HEAT TREAT
|  |  |  |  |  |_____ 0.80 < OUTSIDE DIA. < 2.00
|  |  |  |  |_____ NO AUXILIARY HOLES OR GEAR TEETH
|  |  |  |_____ PLANAR MACHINING OF FACES BUT NO SLOTS OR GROOVES
|  |  |_____ SINGLE INSIDE DIA. OR STEPPED TO ONE END W/O THREADS
|  |_____ SINGLE OUTSIDE DIA. W/O THREADS
|_____ ROUND PART WITH LTH/DIA. RATIO < 1/2 AND STRAIGHT CENTERLINE
```

Figure 10

After a tentative layout is achieved, a cost-benefit analysis must be done to see if the expense of an extensive factory re-arrangement is compensated by the generous cost savings possible. In a situation where a new factory is being outfitted, and no re-arrangement is needed, an attractive payback can often be expected. Another choice time for considering Group Technology is when major new equipment or new manufacturing technology is being acquired.

When commenced, implementation of GT will require extensive restructuring of bills of material and routings. Sub-assembly breaks often will fall differently, and routing and time standards will demand extensive revision.

Also, the new environment will alter sharply the old lot sizes, especially if manufacturing engineering takes the opportunity to improve tooling and equipment to reduce setup times.

Since factory lead time will drop sharply, time-fence rules and procedures, and those for master production scheduling should be reviewed and revised as needed. Reduced leadtimes could even result in sales literature and bulletins being revised to take full advantage of the new environment.

An important later step in implementing GT would be to train work center supervisors. One aspect of this would require technical training on the equipment slated for the supervisor's cell. Also important would be training in the skills needed to supervise workers in what will be a dramatically different working environment. Quality circles, for example, work well in a GT environment.

In summary, Group technology offers attractive potential improvements in terms of work-in-process inventory reduction, factory lead time reduction, and lowered costs. Implementation costs are high, however, especially in the areas of developing and recording a comprehensive classification program on the item master, possibly rearranging the factory, rewriting bills of material and routings, and in training. GT certainly supports the Society's current Just-in-time and Zero Inventory crusades.

APPENDIX A

Proprietary Classification Coding Vendors

Brisch System:
Brisch-Birn & Partners, Ltd.
1656 Southeast Tenth Terrace
Fort Lauderdale, FL 33316

Miclass System:
TNO U.S. Office
176 Second Avenue
Waltham, MA 02154

Code System:
Hartec Corp
3350 E. Atlantic Blvd.
Pompano Beach, FL 33061

Opitz System:
Dr. H. Opitz
Aachen, West Germany

Part Analog System:
Lovelace, Lawrence & Co, Inc.
4344 W. Central Ave.
Toledo, OH 43615

Footnotes

(1) "Dictionary" Fifth Edition; American Production and Inventory Control Society; Falls Church, VA; 1984, p 13.

(2) Hyde, William F.; Improving Productivity by Classification, Coding, and Data Base Standardization; Marcel Dekker, Inc.; New York and Basel; p 152.

(3) ibid; p 155.

(4) machinability Data Center, a Department of Defense Information Analysis Center; Group Technology, An Overview and Bibliography; MDC 76-601; c/o Metcut Research Associates, Inc, Cincinnati, Ohio; p 18.

(5) ibid; p19.

About the Author:

John N. Petroff, CPIM, is an Executive Consultant at Comserv Corporation, Eagan, MN. He provides consulting and education to client management in connection with implementing and operating formal manufacturing business systems.

Mr. Petroff has over 25 years of business experience including management consulting, data processing management, materials management, and manufacturing systems. He has successfully implemented and supervised MRP systems at several companies on three continents.

An accomplished speaker and seminar leader. Mr. Petroff frequently makes presentations to APICS groups, as well as to other professional societies. He has a CPIM, and a CDP (Certificate in Data Processing), a BBA and an MBA. He is currently Immediate Past President of the Twin Cities Chapter of APICS and was a founder of the Arabian Gulf Chapter. He is fluent in the German Language.

Mr. Petroff has had a number of articles published on technical as well as on general business topics, in Production and Inventory Journal, Modern Office Technology, Directions, Datamation, Handelsblatt, and VDI Nachrichten.

THE "M" IN PRODUCTION IS SILENT
Robert G. Brazenor, Jr., CPIM
Sperry Corporation

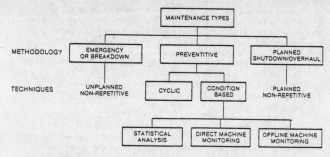

Figure 1. Maintenance Activity

The "M" is MAINTENANCE, the Poor neglected relation of manufacturing.

The objective of this presentation is to show how those principles upon which a good P&IC system is based also relate to Maintenance Management Control and secondly how maintenance management interacts with all of the manufacturing disciplines.

The major types of maintenance functions are similar in any industry even though they may be as diversified as refining, discrete manufacturing and mining. Basically, in all these operations, the same type of equipment is maintained by similarly trained maintenance workers supported by a common management commitment to profitability, thus supporting a generalized approach to maintenance management by various industries.

The problem with current maintenance systems is their failure to relate to other manufacturing disciplines.

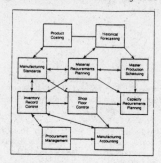

MANUFACTURING DISCIPLINE

These same disciplines, inherent to P&IC systems currently in place in most plants, which support manufacturing work order management and inventory control can also be directly applied to maintenance work order scheduling and control, spare parts inventories and maintenance costing and budgeting.

The management of maintenance and its inclusion in MRPII truly closes the manufacturing loop by including as a requirement, maintenance input to the production plan to reduce downtime. The purchasing and accounting functions can be equally impacted as costs and inventories are controlled and budget responsibilities established. BOM's can be used to pinpoint equipment assemblies and assign spare parts as well as to capture costs for future planned capital expenditures. Capacity plans for maintenance crafts/skills are as important as work center loading and utilization. ECO's/ECN's must be developed for new or obsolete equipment to insure that spare parts lists are current for good maintenance and inventory control.

Why are we so interested in Maintenance Management Control?

An article in the June 25th Industry Week states "U.S. Industry is spending hundreds of millions of dollars to create efficient, fully automated factories. That's good. However relatively little money is being spent on new maintenance practises for these facilities. And thats very bad. Production in the factory of the future will be so sensitive to downtime that even temporarily idled machinery may rout profits. Maintenance itself will become more costly in terms of labor, tools, and parts as plants begin the shift from mechanical to electrical to electronic maintenance."

"The annual maintenance bill for U.S. Business is in excess of $200 billion, and about one-third of that is wasted because of poor management"--quote from Joseph W. French, senior maintenance consultant in the applied Technology Division of DuPont Co., Wilmington, Delaware.

Maintenance costs, in industry, had been increasing at an average of 15% per year from 1972-1982. This expense is on going, whatever the economic climate, or the profitability is of a particular industry or plant.

The maintenance activity can be summarized as shown in figure 1.

The cost of maintenance at the company level represents close to 6% of the cost of goods sold based on an industry survey but:

* Dun's Review estimates that perhaps 1/3 of this amount could be saved through a well designed maintenance program.
* ZEYHER (New Guide to Cost Control - Prentice Hall) indicates that maintenance costs could be reduced 30 to 40% using cost control techniques.
* Other sources state:
  - "Normal maintenance force operates at 50% of capacity due to a lack of maintenance planning and control."
  - "Due to built-in delays and lack of management concern, productivity in the maintenance work force is usually less than 50%."
  - "Production lost time due to ineffective maintenance programs is costing firms millions of dollars per year and maintenance problems are worsening."
  - Production Engineering implies that "businesses in capital intensive industries (process) do not have effective ways to allocate maintenance resources to minimize equipment downtime."

Many Plant managers tend to treat maintenance as an uncontrollable cost or even a free service, yet actually maintenance programs are part of the production process.

Let's look at the makeup of maintenance expenses. Labor and material are the general classifications. Labor includes the plant's own maintenance staff, along with its supervision, and contract labor. Contract labor is often used to supplement the plant's staff for load leveling or for major maintenance jobs too large for the normal staff to handle. Jones & Laughlin Steel Corp. (J&L) for example, already has accomplished at several plants what other steel firms feel they must do. At its Aliquippa, Pa., plant it negotiated an agreement eliminating maintenance workers in favor of outside contractors. At its new "Worldclass" seamless tube mill in Youngstown, some 43 separate types of jobs have been cut to four. There - and at its Crucible Stainless Steel Div., in Midland, Pa., - production workers themselves do the required maintenance. Materials expense typically may include only the actual cost of the spare part. However, the costs of purchasing, stocking, and distributing those spare parts are often allocated to the maintenance functions.

I have been in plants where maintenance parts are expensed when received, no costs for parts are applied to either equipment or departments. There is no idea of the dollar value of parts inventory, the maintenance inventory is a purchasing responsibility without accounting responsibility. You can imagine the excess and obsolete parts that abound in this maintenance inventory stores.

What is the dollar value of inventory on-hand? Who knows?

Management has never looked upon maintenance as a path to glory but it is a basic part of the companys strategy and corporate plan to guarantee use of personnel, equipment, facilities, and money. Of course, management would like to minimize its maintenance expense while maintaining the operational reliability and safety of the plant and equipment. Here is where maintenance management comes into the picture.

The outcome of a successful maintenance management system should show up in both the balance sheet and the income statement and lead to improved plant safety, appearance and quality assurance of product.

To achieve these objectives we must first establish maintenance management fundamentals.
1. Organization

2. Work Orders
3. Scheduled maintenance
4. Equipment/machine/tool data input
5. Work Order planning
6. Stores inventory
7. Purchasing
8. Costing

Have we seen anything here that is that much different in principle than a good manufacturing system. The department or disciplines might be different, but the management and control are basically the same.

Remember - Maintenance Management goals are to:
* Keep down day-to-day maintenance costs
* Reduce unpredictable and costly plant breakdowns
* Support peak performance of plant

These activities also impinge on:
* Production (manufacturing) plant operations
* Spare parts/stores
* Purchasing
* Accounting and costing
* Personnel/payroll

To implement these fundamentals we must define the duties and responsibilities, selection of personnel, development of sound budgets and methods to monitor results and audit the process.

MAINTENANCE MANAGEMENT FUNDAMENTALS

1. ORGANIZATION

The establishment at the plant level that generates the work and does preventive maintenance planning.

Maintenance category overview:

Most maintenance managers adopt one or more of these philosophies for their plant:
* Run until it breaks
  - nothing done to maintain the assets
  - recondition to new condition when it fails
  - low maintenance costs
  - catastrophic risk
  - severely limits plant output

Short term benefits but high long term risk - not advisable.
* Preventive maintenance
  - maintenance tasks at definite intervals (weeks months, annually, or manufacturers recommendations)
  - a major undertaking in most plants - not the way we do it.
  - large expenditure for maintenance for several years but benefits will be realized in the long run using preventive maintenance.
* Predictive Maintenance
  - a refinement of preventive maintenance
  - equipment is closely monitored
  - as performance drops as measured by decreasing output, increased downtime, increased operating costs or other variable, maintenance tasks are performed.

Vibration analyzers, shock pulse meters, thermometers and other measuring instruments are used. According to Jesse Adams, a R.J. Reynolds Tobacco Co. maintenance specialist, the instruments have paid for themselves and the people using them ten times over and the payback came in little more than a year by predicting when machinery was going to breakdown.
* Corrective maintenance
  - non-repetitive jobs normally involving a facility that is already down or malfunctioning.
  - Emergency type tasks
  - non-planned
  - usually happens when a part has been promised to ship that day.
* Shutdown maintenance
  - not likely to be repeated in the near future
  - usually large jobs that are irregularly done

The application of these maintenance philosophies to actually getting the work done is Maintenance Management. But beings managers are involved daily with personnel matters, trade union concerns or plant emergencies, it is easy for them to lose sight of their overall maintenance goals.

Within the framework of applying adopted philosophies to the maintenance functions there are certain objectives which are essential to operating an effective maintenance department:
* Planned approach
  - ability to anticipate and plan for maintenance

- reduce emergency situations which result in overtime, a greater percentage of unproductive time, and increased costs to expedite parts delivery.
* Utilization of Resources
  - increase productivity
  - increase job skills
  - work sampling
  - multiple assignment of maintenance tasks
* Non-Productive Activities
  - reduce excessive travel time
  - reduce non-business conversation and idle time due to lack of schedules
  - reduce time spent going to stores for parts
* Analysis Capabilities
  - feedback to anticipate where and when problems might occur
  - equipment/machinery spare parts information
  - history/follow-up records
* Production Improvement
  - Downtime for maintenance planned into the production schedule to minimize the maintenance impact
  - review of history files to systematically tackle repetitive problems
  - look for instead of waiting for failure to occur
  - look for symptoms and review maintenance history to avoid major catastrophic failures.

2. WORK ORDERS

The foundation of a good maintenance system and the vehicle through which work is scheduled, required resources are identified, and the maintenance activity is monitored. Work Orders as stated in the APICS Dictionary state that the term is used to designate orders to the machine shop for tool manufacture or maintenance. Work orders support the three major classifications of maintenance:
- Preventive
- Corrective
- Shutdown

Work Order Capabilities:
* identification by part number the specific equipment and sub-assemblies to be serviced.
* equipment Bill of Materials with major assemblies and sub-assemblies identified to include a parts catalog, documentation and engineering drawings.
* data for each spare part used, description of the structures that specify relationships among the parts.

As in manufacturing, the BOM is the fundamental function for the entire maintenance system.
* the location of the equipment to be serviced.
* specifics when the work order is to be performed.
* the prioritizing of orders based on production activity.
* cost generation for each work order following job completion.

Benefits:
* leveling the work load
  - resources and materials availability and commitments are maintained to reduce overtime and increase job completions.
* Reduction of Emergency repairs
  - with maintenance procedures planned, facility downtime and excessive maintenance costs should be reduced.
* Equipment Downtime Minimized
  - coordination with production and inclusion within the production schedule should reduce equipment unavailability.
* Work Order Costing
  - detect excessive maintenance costs
  - help evaluate purchase of equipment
  - provide source data for cost accounting
  - insure departmental budgets are met.
* Spare parts tracking and control
  - reduce maintenance inventory
  - decrease the number of stockouts
  - reduce excessive expediting
  - control the purchase of spare parts.

* Increased Productivity
  - arrange work orders into a routing that reduces travel time between jobs

- specifies parts and tools needed, equipment location and special instructions to reduce time lost between stores and job.

```
┌─────────────────────────────────────────────┐
│            WORK ORDER INFORMATION            │
│                                              │
│ EQUIPMENT   : 11334E129  WORK ORDER NO.: 62392500 │
│ LOCATION    : PROD FRAC  DATE ENTERED  : 82/10/29 │
│ EXPENSE ACCT: 6345-2913  ORGINATOR     : TGB      │
│ CAPITAL ACCT:            CONTACT       : B. SERGEANT │
│ PRIORITY    : 07         UNIT          : SOLVENTS │
│                                              │
│ DATE AVAILABLE:82/11/21                      │
│ DATE REQUIRED :82/12/15                      │
│ DATE SCHEDULED:82/11/25                      │
│                                              │
│ PROBLEM: TUBES LEAKING DUE TO CARRYOVER OF ACID │
│ DESCR. : TUBE BUNDLE DUE TO BE REPLACED.     │
│         : SHELL SHOULD ALSO BE INSPECTED AND CLEANED. │
└─────────────────────────────────────────────┘
```

WORK ORDER DISPLAY

3. SCHEDULED MAINTENANCE

Repetitive tasks, including preventive maintenance and shutdown (Pre-planned) maintenance.
* Capabilities
 - When - cycle time
 - Where - location
 - Resources and parts needed
 - Estimated completion time
 - Work order status
 - Related work orders (for grouping)
 - Work order history.
Benefits:
* Optimum cycle time determination to fine tune the frequency of cyclical maintenance.
* Utilization of crafts/skills and available resources.
* Efficient maintenance scheduling
* Current status of work orders enables a super-visor to react to emergency downtime situations.
* Organization of Maintenance Planning and work-load smoothing - will enable production and maintenance to reduce downtime by scheduling maintenance as part of the Master Production schedule.

```
┌─────────────────────────────────────────────┐
│ *** PM DATA FOR   10716P004        ***       │
│                                              │
│ PM JOB      : ELECTRICAL CHECK  PRIORITY : 6 │
│ CRFT/AUX.CR: ELT07              NBR OF MEN: 2 │
│ CONTACT     : ELECT PM SUPER    MANHOURS : 16 │
│ ROUND/SEPRT: ROUND              STRT/INT/CALL: /12MO/ │
│ OP-STAT/OC : DOWN               LAST PERFMED : 82/08/19 │
│                                              │
│ OBJECT      : CHECK INSULATION               │
│ AUX.JOB     : TIGHTEN CONNECTIONS            │
│ DOCUMENT    : 2E077                          │
│                                              │
│ TOOLS       : MEGGER EQUIP, STD ELECTRICAL TOOLS │
│                                              │
│ MATERIAL    : CONNECTORS, FUSES              │
│                                              │
│ COMMENTS    : REFER TO HISTORY RECORDS BEFORE WORK TO │
│               CHECK PREVIOUS RESULTS         │
└─────────────────────────────────────────────┘
```

SCHEDULED MAINTENANCE DISPLAY

4. EQUIPMENT/MACHINE/TOOL DATA

Availability of the components, sub-assemblies and their components with part numbers and assembly drawings.
Capabilities:
* Description
* Bills of Material
* Where used data
* Equipment with same sub-assemblies and parts.
This is basically our Manufacturing BOM being used to identify equipment, sub-assemblies, spare parts, part numbers and stores location.

Is this any different than an indented, summarized or one line BOM that is used daily by production and engineering. To keep our Bills current for the mainten-

ance of equipment/machines, engineering should be responsible for updating the Bills when equipment is scrapped or parts are changed. New Bills should be created when new equipment is purchased based on the manufacturers spare parts list or the Plant engineers recommendations.

```
┌──────────────────────────────────────────────────┐
│ ***SPARE PARTS FOR  113211P117                    │
│ COMPONENT :RECYCLE PUMP   INSPECTION CLASS :3  QTY │
│ ACCESSIBLE QTY                                    │
│                                                   │
│ LINE  SP.P .DESCR   MAN./MOD  PART NO.  STORAGE POS. │
│ 001   BEARING-IB    BERCO     1935501   A17-392619 │
│                                            QTY:3  │
│ 002   BEARING-OB    BERCO     1935529   A17-392527 │
│                                            QTY:2  │
│ 003   SEAL MECH     SUPERSEAL 1762221   A18-122930 │
│                                            QTY:4  │
│ 004   SHAFT         EPCO      1110349   A03-699592 │
│                                            QTY:0  │
└──────────────────────────────────────────────────┘
```

EQUIPMENT DISPLAY

5. WORK ORDER PLANNING

All outstanding work orders for a particular piece of equipment can be reviewed and scheduled concurrently. We currently use the same information for capacity planning, rough cut planning and work center loading and scheduling. Are we really doing that much different for maintenance W-I-P.
Capabilities and Benefits:
* Parts, tools and manpower skills to complete a job are available.
* Functional information on the equipment and its components are known.
* Historical work, the spare parts used, cost, time and skills/crafts committed.
* Group jobs on the same piece of equipment.
* Ability to tie-in with Production scheduling for down-time or utilization of equipment.

```
┌──────────────────────────────────────────────────┐
│ ***AO W.O. PLAN/IN PROGRESS FOR 10716P002 ***821111 │
│                                                   │
│      PLANNED                        OPER          │
│ LINE START FINISHED CRAFT WO TYPE & JOB COND PR WO-NO │
│ 001  11/15 11/19  MECO2 REPLACE SEAL  CRIT 03 62131700 │
│                                                   │
│ 002  11/15 11/19  ELTO1 DISCONN. POWER CRIT 03 62131701 │
│                                                   │
│ 003  11/15 11/16  ELTO7 PM ROUND        06 43070900 │
└──────────────────────────────────────────────────┘
```

WORK ORDER PLANNING DISPLAY

6. STORES INVENTORY

Inventory, whatever kind, must be kept to a minimum-but you must have the right parts available when you need them. Conflicting theories, not when you have a planned maintenance program.
Capabilities:
* Control inventory
* Avoid stock-outs
* Up-to-date spare parts
* Accurate information
* Time phased delivery of parts for preventive and shut-down maintenance
* Location of parts.
Benefits:
* Management of spare parts inventories
* Start and complete jobs on time
* Increase productivity
* Value assessment
* Ability to reserve or allocate parts
* Reduce inventory levels.

Nothing different here, but these functions relate to spare parts, couldn't they be combined with production inventory to reduce stores area and personnel. Its been done and it works.

```
*** AVAILABLE STOCK FOR PART. NO. 7010739***821111

DESCRIP: EXCHNGER TUBE,FT    ORIG. DESCR.   : TUBE
MFR    : TIFAB TUBE CO.      INSPEC. CLASS  : B
MOD. NO: 0.750 X 240         COMPO/PART     : PART
CAT. NO:                     ACCT. CODE     : EXC TUBING
TECH DE:

ACCESS-QTY   : 5000          STORAGE POS  QUANTITY UNIT
RESERVED     : 10000
LOAN         : 0
UNDER REPAIR : 0
ORDERED      : 20000 REQUESTED
MIN STOCK    : 10000     ACC. PURCHASE   : 0
ORD QUANTITY : 10000     ACC. WITHDRAWAL : 0
UNIT PRICE   :           SOLD            : 0
```

STORES INVENTORY DISPLAY

7. PURCHASING

"Keep suppliers competitive with one another but treat them fairly: use the purchasing department creatively - 50% of the sales dollar is controlled by purchasing and a 10% reduction in costs can translate into a 5% increase in profits.", a recent quote by Harry Figgie in his book The Cost Reduction and Profit Improvement Handbook.

Capabilities:
* P.O.status and descriptive data
* Vendor performance
* Recommended procurement actions
* Receipt tracking
* Progress of open orders
* Receipt of parts shipments and partials.

Benefits:
* Improved leverage with suppliers
* Open purchase order contract.

Maintenance managers can be helpful with information when ordering new equipment or spare parts as to their reliability, time and expense involved to maintain or repair it and the ease of servicing.

```
*** REGISTER LINE WITHIN ORDER NO.          ***

SUPPLIER : ERIE PUMP CO.    DEL. WEEK:8305  S-CODE:L2
           17 LAKE STREET
           ERIE, PA.
LINE-NO              :003
PART-NUMBER          :6300517 IMPELLER
ORDERED QUANTITY/UNIT:2 EACH
  AND/OR AMOUNT      :
ORDER TEXT LINE 1    :7.5 INCH DIAMETER IMPELLER TO FIT
         LINE 2      :ERIE PUMP S/N 10023
         LINE 3      :
PRICE/UNIT $         :328.50
DISCOUNT, IN PERCENT :NONE      NET PRICE $328.50
AVG PRICE (RECALC             NEW DEB. PRICE:
ACCOUNT         :AFE 17633    OLD DEB. PRICE:
DELIVERY WEEK (START):8305    FIN.-WEEK:
DIST2 BUDGET YEAR            LAST LINE OF ORDER:005
```
PURCHASING DISPLAY

8. COSTING

Where are your maintenance dollars going? Budgets can be prepared by department for maintenance work. The adage that maintenance doesn't cost anything will be eliminated.

Information will be available to make decisions on whether to continue repairing equipment or to replace it. Decreases in efficiency can be determined by using costing data, and departments or plant locations can be billed for work done.

We are trying to control maintenance costs, not reduce the maintenance of equipment but control the cost of maintenance. Any different than cost criteria in manufacturing or other industries? These dollars go to the bottom-line, that is what its all about.

```
***     ACCOUNTING SUMMARY        *****821111

EQUIPMENT NO. :10716K033    WORK ORDER NO:41732600
ACCOUNT NO.   :1932-5322    DATE OPENED  :82/06/19
EQUIP YTD-COST :7360.98     DATE COMPLETE:82/07/02
  PRIORITY: 05              AFE COST:2582.80
  WO COST : 2582.80         AFE NO. :375-10

CRAFT  TIME   COST      CONTRACTOR  TIME   COST
MEC01  62.0   556.76    CERT COMPR  46.0   1380
ELT01   4.0    34.20

SPARE PARTS USED:
 PART NO    DESCRIPTION  QTY USED  COST EACH  EXT.COST
 3225619    PACKING      12 ft     2.32       27.84
 650036     PISTON ASBY  2 EACH    982.00     1964.00

COMMENTS :  INSTALLED NEW GRAPHITE PISTONS
```

ACCOUNTING (COST) DISPLAY

PRODUCTION AND MAINTENANCE MANAGEMENT

How do we get Production and Maintenance together? We do have similar systems that can operate jointly. Computers and systems do not replace management drive, judgement and commitment, but together with them in concert, can make significant improvement a genuine reality. How do we accomplish these goals:

* Hold Production responsible for the cost of not maintaining equipment. Fix budgets through cost control and use them as an incentive to hold costs down by production doing preventive maintenance.

* Hold daily meetings if possible, between the Production and Maintenance managers to review equipment status and changes in production requirements that will effect preventive and pre-planned maintenance.

* Think about putting the responsibility for ordering spare parts and equipment on the Plant Engineer or maintenance department. This is currently being done in many plants and has had some good results.

* Get Engineering, Plant Engineering and Production all involved in maintenance. Suggestions, ideas and recommendations can't hurt. Plus you are now getting involvement which can only be helpful for the manufacturing process.

* As Production managers - don't keep putting off scheduled maintenance due to your poor planning and scheduling, meeting impossible commitments and telling sales you can work miracles on the Shop Floor. Without proper preventive maintenance you will be responsible for catastrophic production problems sooner or later. Schedule the maintenance and work the schedule.

"Establish Preventive Maintenance as part of the daily routine. This is necessary to preserve the capability of the equipment for process controlled quality and to preserve the flexibility of its use." Quote form Robert W. Hall, CPIM, with the APICS, "Zero Inventory Crusade", P&IM Journal, 3rd Quarter 1983.

In the 1970's we saw the advent of MRP (Materials Requirements Planning), then MRPII (Materials Resource Planning), reduction of inventories; now in the 1980's we have KANBAN and Zero Inventory for manufacturing Search for Excellence.

Can you attain just-in-time production, flexible manufacturing systems, zero inventory and excellence in materials management?

These are all important parts of your manufacturing system, but one part is missing - MAINTENANCE CONTROL.

With the formal P&IC systems currently in place, we can interface with, and enhance the informal maintenance system most companies now have, resulting in a Maintenance Management Control System that will --

Put the "M" into ProductioM.

Biographical Sketch:

Industry Specialist with the Sperry Computer Division,
Sperry Corporation, Philadelphia District in Wayne,
Pennsylvania.
Graduate of Gettysburg College with a Degree in Business
Administration.
Retired in 1983 from the U.S. Army Reserve with the rank
of Lt. Colonel.
Active in APICS since 1969 and has been active at the
Chapter, Region and National Level. Served as Region IX
Vice President for two years and on several National
Committees.
Received the APICS Presidents Service Award as COINS
Editor.
Past Speaker at two Chapter Management Workshops.
Certified by APICS in 1982.
Bob has over 20 years in the field of Production and
Inventory Control as a P&IC and Materials Manager.

A THREE-DIMENSIONAL APPROACH TO EXCELLENCE IN PROCEDURE DOCUMENTATION

Vince K. Gulati, CPIM
Price Waterhouse

INTRODUCTION

The objective of this paper is twofold: to discuss why procedure documentation manuals have a strong tendency to be discarded soon after their publication; and to describe a Three Dimensional Approach to attaining excellence in documentation of procedures based upon case studies.

COMMON SYMPTOMS OF OBSOLETE PROCEDURES

Do any of the following statements commonly heard in distribution and manufacturing environments sound familiar to you?

"That's Jim's job, not mine."

"Cost is not important, just get it out of the back door."

"We can't help it - it's the policy."

"I am just a peon, following the rules. How about talking to my supervisor."

"We don't do it that way in our plant."

"That's been tried before."

"How does it matter? We are making a profit."

"Let's think about it some more."

"This is the 'Schafer' report."

"I put this report on Mary's desk, she does something with it."

Upon a closer look at these statements, a common underlying theme emerges. There are either no procedures in this facility or they are inadequately documented. Since, I know that these statements came from a place where written procedural manuals did exist, they were either obsolete or inadequate. Let us briefly examine why procedure documentation manuals become obsolete or get discarded by the users soon after they are published.

CAUSES OF PROCEDURE DOCUMENTATION OBSOLESCENCE

Procedure documentation in most companies is written by individual departments without a centrally defined responsibility for keeping them updated. If a department gets reorganized or some employees leave the company, updating a manual is seldom the top priority of the new employee or the supervisor.

Frequently, one may find as many formats of procedure manuals as there are departments, and even more if there has been an excessive turnover. Lack of a uniform and a structured format makes it very difficult to update the manuals, thus making the old ones obsolete.

Most procedure manuals are written by job descriptions. Whenever the tasks change or the job descriptions change the procedures manuals become obsolete, unless updated frequently.

Often, procedure manuals are so detailed and disorganized that finding a specific task requires reading through reams of pages. On the other hand, many are so broad that they provide very limited guidance to the end users who have to actually perform the tasks.

In short, the major cause of procedure documentation obsolescence are: lack of proper accountability, lack of a uniform format, frequent organizational changes and inadequate level of detail.

THREE DIMENSIONAL APPROACH TO PROCEDURE DOCUMENTATION

This approach recognizes the following basic facts which impact procedure documentation.

o Organizations do change, therefore the procedures must address the tasks rather than positions.

o Procedures are clearly broken down by functional areas and the respective supervisors are assigned the responsibility for preparing and keeping them updated.

o Uniformity of format is maintained by standardized forms.

o To overcome the difficulty of providing the adequate level of detail, the procedures are written at three levels.

1. The Overview Level - consisting of block diagrams and flowcharts depicting inputs, processing and outputs.

2. The Functional Procedure Level - consisting of tables of input processing and brief output details. These tables include originating source for each functional procedure, frequency, title of the person performing the function, the purpose of output and distribution.

3. Detailed Task Level - consisting of detailed instruction for performing the tasks and subtasks. This includes exceptions as well as sample exhibits.

CASE STUDY EXAMPLE

To describe this approach a very simple example of documenting warehousing procedures is presented below.

1. The overview level: A flow chart indicating each of the following procedures is shown in a block diagram.

    1.0 Receipt of Items from Inspection
    2.0 Receipt of Items from Receiving
    3.0 Storage of Items in the Warehouse
    4.0 Issuance of Item(s) Requested
    5.0 Entry of Material Transaction Data into the Computer System
    6.0 Delivery of input reports

    The top management may just use this part of the procedure manual and not be bothered about additional detail. (Please refer to EXHIBIT A)

2. The Functional Procedure Level: In this section brief summary of inputs and outputs is provided. This section will be most useful to the supervisory management. (Please refer to EXHIBIT B)

3. Detailed Task Level: The detailed tasks comprising each function described in the overview level is further broken down to subtasks with ultimate detail. (Please refer to EXHIBIT C)

Additionally, the exceptions to any tasks are noted separately (EXHIBIT D) and the copies of the sample forms are also included in this section.

ADVANTAGES OF THIS APPROACH

The major advantages of this approach are:
o easy to understand by all levels of concerned management
o focus on tasks rather than positions makes it outlast organizations
o easy to change and modify
o provides adequate documentation to handle potential product liability litigation
o provides a systematic means of identifying opportunities for improvement.

SUMMARY

Procedure documentation manuals become obsolete due to organizatonal changes, inadequate level of detail, lack of defined responsiblity and non-standard formats. A three dimensional approach to procedure documentation can overcome these drawbacks by focusing on tasks rather than positions, standardizing the format and detailing procedures at three different levels.

O V E R V I E W   L E V E L

B L O C K   D I A G R A M

Exhibit A

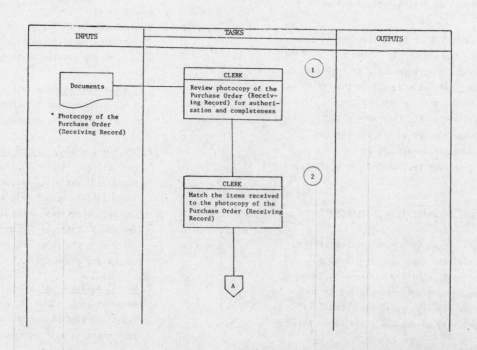

American Production & Inventory Control Society

FUNCTIONAL PROCEDURE LEVEL

FUNCTIONAL 2.0 WAREHOUSE - RECEIPT OF ITEMS FROM RECEIVING											
INPUTS				PROCESSES				OUTPUTS			
Ref.#	SOURCE	FORM, REPORT OR INFORMATION	FREQUENCY	PERFORMED BY	DESCRIPTION	REF*	FREQUENCY	REPORT OR DOCUMENT	PURPOSE	DISTRIBUTION
2.1	-Quality Control		As Needed	Clerk	Review photocopy of the Purchase Order (Receiving Record) for authorization and completeness	AP2.1 EL2.1	As Completed			
	-Receiving	-Photocopy of the Purchase Order (Receiving Record) (Exhibit 5)								
2.2				Clerk	Match the items received to the photocopy of the Purchase Order	AP2.2 EL2.2	As Completed			
2.3				Clerk	Move the items to be stocked to Warehouse staging area	AP2.3	As Completed	-Copy of Purchase Order (Receiving Record)	To place in a storage location in the warehouse	Warehouse Stocker

Exhibit C

DETAILED TASK LEVEL

Ref.#	TASKS		SUBTASKS
2.1	Review the photocopy of the Purchase Order (Receiving Record) for authorization and completeness. (Exhibit 5) (Clerk)	2.1.1	Review the following information on the photocopy of the Purchase Order (Receiving Record) for completeness: - Part Number - Description - Quantity - Input Document Stamp - Quality Contol "OK to Stock" stamp (If items are being transferred from Quality Control) If any of the above are incomplete or missing see EL 2.1.1.
2.2	Match the items received to photocopy of the Purchase Order (Receiving Record). (Exhibit 5) (Clerk)	2.2.1	Verify the following information on the photocopy of the Purchase Order (Receiving Record) to the items Received. - Part Number - Quantity If the items received and photocopy of the Purchase Order (Receiving Record) do not agree see EL 2.2.1.
		2.2.2	Sign and date the lower right hand corner of the photocopy of the Purchase Order (Receiving Record).
2.3	Move the items to the Warehouse staging area. (Exhibit 5)	2.3.1	Retain the photocopy of the Purchase Order (Receiving Record) with the items to be

LISTING OF EXCEPTIONS

Ref. #	EXCEPTIONS		REQUIRED ACTION
2.1	Information on the Move Ticket is incomplete or approval is missing. (Exhibit 5) (Clerk)	2.1.1	Refuse the items and require the Forklift Operator to return the items and the Purchase Order photocopy (Receiving Record) to the person initiating the document for correction or proper approval.
2.2	Information on the Move Ticket does not agree with the items received. (Exhibit 5) (Clerk)	2.2.1	Refuse the items and require the Forklift Operator to return both the items and the Purchase Order photocopy (Receiving Record) to the person initiating the document for correction or proper approval.

BIOGRAPHY

Vince Gulati is a manager in the Management Consulting Services Department of Price Waterhouse in Houston.

Over ten years of industrial experience includes: Advanced Planning Manager, Department Head - Engineering Specifications and Product Data Base and Production Research Engineer at International Harvester; Industrial Engineer at McLaughlin Body Co.; and Instructor in Production Management and Corporate Financial Management at a midwestern university.

He has an MBA degree from Western Illinois University; MS degree in Operations Research and Statistics from the State University of New York at Stonybrook; and a BSME degree from the Indian Institute of Technology.

He has spoken on various occasions to community clubs and is actively involved in the Greater Houston Toastmaster's Club and APICS.

Previous speaking experience includes:

o APICS 1983 Annual Conference, New Orleans, November '83

o Mini National APICS Seminar, Houston, September '83

o North Texas APICS Chapter Seminar, Dallas, October '83

o APICS Chapter, Little Rock, Ark., February '84

"TOTAL CYCLE TIME": ROAD TO PRODUCTIVITY IMPROVEMENT

Greg Henschen, CPIM
Wayne Piotrowski
Motorola, Inc.

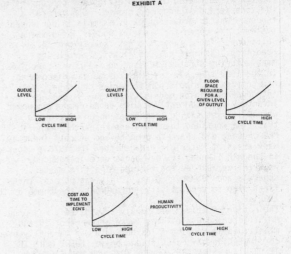

EXHIBIT A

I. INTRODUCTION

In the recent book, "Industrial Renaissance", it was reported that the manufacturing cycle time from iron ore to completed vehicle at the Ford River Rouge Facility was 48 hours in 1922. Ironically, this was not news in the 1920's; today it would be regarded as a noteworthy example of productivity. It has been fashionable to report on the many advances and techniques used to improve productivity in the 1980's; current literature is replete with examples.

As Western industry continues its thrust toward productivity improvement, many have attempted to emulate techniques thought to have been originated in the Far East (JIT, quality cycles, etc.). Few have noted potential benefits inherent to short cycle times or consciously used cycle time reduction as a strategy to stimulate productivity. The purpose of this presentation is to:

● Introduce the concept of "total cycle time" and its significance for productivity and business strategy.
● Identify determinates of total cycle time and how they can be managed.
● Present the methodology used to evaluate and improve total cycle time of an actual business.

The subject program was originated at two locations within the Industrial Electronics Unit of Motorola, where the primary businesses are: a diverse line of display systems and digital appliance controls.

WHAT IS CYCLE TIME

Historically cycle time has been defined as "wall clock time" to complete a task or series of tasks. It can be the time elapsed to complete a single manufacturing operation such as "stamping" or to complete the entire production cycle. "Total cycle time" in the present paper is defined as "wall clock time" elapsed for the entire business system to fulfill its manufacturing objective, demand management through the manufacturing process.

WHY IS "TOTAL CYCLE TIME" IMPORTANT?

"Total cycle time" is significant in that it has a direct impact on a businesses ability to meet a number of major business objectives:

● Profitability
● Customer Service
● Inventory Investment
● Efficient Plan Operations
● Long Term Growth

Typical measurements used to evaluate performance to these objectives are: RONA, ROI, asset turnover, customer service level, market share, etc, yet we seldom recognize that improvment in these measurements can be influenced by cycle time directly. Other benefits related to short cycle times are less obvious and sometimes defy precise measurement:

● Easier to implement engineering changes
● Low material queues
● Clean and more orderly work environments
● Tendency to improve quality levels
● Provides higher visibility to production problems
● Better utilization of floor space

Though strictly based on judgement, the following general cost relationships are probably valid (Exhibit A):

HISTORICAL PATTERNS--OLD TOOLS, OLD PERSPECTIVES--THE SAME RESULTS

Given that the world economy has been characterized by generally high growth and low interest rates since the 1950's, it is not surprising that productivity has lost some priority. Productivity here is used in the most general sense:

PRODUCTIVITY = OUTPUT / INPUT

The acquisition of excessive inventories and capital was acceptable business practice. Accounting conventions did little to identify declines in productivity; we regarded excessive resources as assets, not liabilities and that perception pervaded the whole organization.

The issue of time as a resource was rarely raised as an operational concern. Classic responses to common operating problems were to deploy additional inventory; as a result, cycle times were typically long and productivity tended to decline. Some of the following continue to be common practice today.

	Functional Problem	Typical Behavior
Marketing Sales	Inability to forecast accurately.	Increase finished goods levels.
Manufacturing	Maintain higher output levels when needed.	Insure availability of capital equipment and personnel.
Personnel	Absenteeism	Maintain buffer inventory.
Quality	Sub-standard quality components.	Maintain buffer stocks.
Materials Management	Scheduling problems.	Maintain work-in-process queues.
Industrial Engineering	Excessive set-up times.	Run larger lot sizes. Tendency toward "super machines".

How did these perceptions and behaviors divert U.S. industries from the productivity issue? The following is a partial list:

● Our objectives were generally stated in terms of output - - - not the relationship of output to input .
● Because this mode of operation was generally rewarding and profitable, it was perpetuated. Through periods of rapid economic growth competitive "shakeouts" were not as frequent, as world competition intensified, few Western firms were required to become "best in class" on a world scale simply to survive. Where a firm had a dominate position, few felt the need to improve on an ongoing basis.

- The age of automated data processing was concurrent to the same period of economic growth. Our general tendency was to grow complex vs. simple in our operating systems. We opted for "complex models," "software solutions," "more reports"; not "simple/practical reporting," "simple product flows", "zero-based" manufacturing strategies based on business objectives. In the 1960's we saw the MRP crusade and discovered how complex or simple our factories could be. We introduced planning models which time phased our inventory data correctly. With added computing power we applied lot sizing techniques which were up to that time confined to operations research journals. The MRP crusade did serve to promote and educate industry in many areas of Materials Management. The 1970's ushered in the MRP II era; few new tools were introduced, however, we learned the virtues of a firm master schedule and "do-able" plans. This was perhaps the first step to productivity improvement, the theme of the 1980's.
- The notion of "time" was rarely considered a resource. "Manufacturing Cycle Times" were often recorded and maintained in routing files but data was generally used for incentive pay calculations only. WHERE WERE THE THEORETICAL STANDARDS OF HOW LONG OUR MANUFACTURING CYCLES SHOULD BE? WHAT LEVELS OF PRODUCTIVITY SHOULD BE ASSOCIATED WITH THESE TIMES? SOMEHOW THESE QUESTIONS WERE NEVER ASKED!
- The notion of "continuous improvement," the drive to approximate the "theoretically best" performance given a set of resources has not been in our industrial culture. Most firms were guided by pragmatic thinking and a sense of urgency--"What's the one or two things we can do to solve most of the problems today!"

WHAT IS OUR FUTURE--OLD TOOLS, NEW PERSPECTIVES-- IMPROVED RESULTS

Economic growth, complex systems and sub-optimization of resources (including the use of time) characterized the 1960's and 70's--what will charactize the 1980's? Much has been written about "factories of the future," production systems which yield quality levels measured in parts per million (PPM) etc. The purpose of the present paper is not to review these trends. It is probable however, that cycle times will be quite different from todays standards and that improved results will be gained with minimal investments and many tools that existed in the 1950's. WHAT MUST BE CHANGED? OUR PERSPECTIVES AND EXPECTATIONS!! What would futuristic cycle times be, the benefits and implications are obvious. Ultimately the goal would be to have at the end of every work day:

- NO WORK-IN-PROCESS ON THE FACTORY FLOOR OVER WHAT IS THEORETICALLY ALLOWED
- No unplaced purchase orders
- No unentered orders
- No orders that have not had a credit check
- No unpicked stock
- No shipments waiting to be packed
- No unreceived goods
- No parts waiting for inspection
- No finished assemblies that have not moved in the last shift
- No parts on quality hold or engineering hold
- No backlog of engineering changes
- No over shipments

II. ELEMENTS AND SCOPE OF TOTAL CYCLE TIME

ADDRESSING THE TOTAL BUSINESS SYSTEM AT THE INDUSTRIAL ELECTRONICS UNIT OF MOTOROLA

Total Cycle Time reduction became a program in 1982 at the Industrial Electronics Unit. In business A all essential elements of the production system were addressed in the program; they were:
- Forecasting
- Order entry
- Material ordering
- Purchasing
- Vendor time
- Receiving
- Manufacturing

In business B, efforts to date were primarily devoted to the manufacturing cycle. The effort began with a

detailed analysis of every function which contributed to the production system, a summary is pictured below (see Exhibit B).

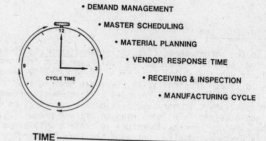

EXHIBIT B

ELEMENTS OF CYCLE TIME:

- DEMAND MANAGEMENT
- MASTER SCHEDULING
- MATERIAL PLANNING
- VENDOR RESPONSE TIME
- RECEIVING & INSPECTION
- MANUFACTURING CYCLE

TIME ————————————

The following sections describe objectives, strategies and results to date by "total cycle time" element.

FORECASTING CYCLE TIME

Major tasks or sub-element of the cycle were:

- Field preparation of forecast data, review and compile forecast data at the Unit headquarters, print forecast output and resolve discrepencies.

  Program objectives and results are summarized in Exhibit C.

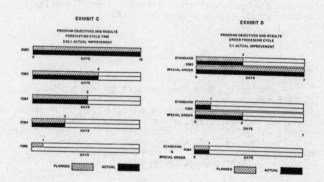

Strategies used to reduce the cycle time were:

- Week end processing, automated systems interfaces, utilization of microcomputers for communications and computation, modular planning.

ORDER PROCESSING CYCLE

Major tasks or sub-elements of the cycle were:

- Order receipt, edit (price, model number, delivery, credit), book.

  Program objectives and results are summarized in Exhibit D.
  Strategies to reduce the cycle time were:

- Revised internal procedures, improved communications network via microcomputer.

MASTER SCHEDULE CYCLE

Major tasks or sub-elements of the cycle were:

- Receive and analyze raw forecast data, detailed plant review , capacity analysis, develop final schedule and review for sign-off, input to material requirements planning systems.

  Program objectives and results are summarized in Exhibit E.

American Production & Inventory Control Society

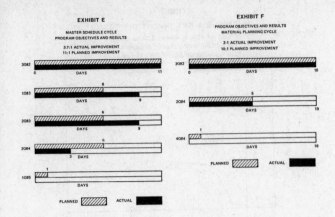

EXHIBIT E

MASTER SCHEDULE CYCLE
PROGRAM OBJECTIVES AND RESULTS

3.7:1 ACTUAL IMPROVEMENT
11:1 PLANNED IMPROVEMENT

EXHIBIT F

PROGRAM OBJECTIVES AND RESULTS
MATERIAL PLANNING CYCLE

2:1 ACTUAL IMPROVEMENT
10:1 PLANNED IMPROVEMENT

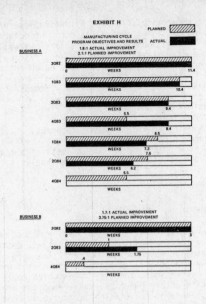

EXHIBIT H

MANUFACTURING CYCLE
PROGRAM OBJECTIVES AND RESULTS
1.8:1 ACTUAL IMPROVEMENT
2.1:1 PLANNED IMPROVEMENT

Strategies used to reduce cycle time were:

- Implemented abbreviated master schedule, weekend processing, utilized microcomputers for communications and computation, modular planning.

MATERIAL PLANNING CYCLE

Major tasks or sub-elements of the cycle were:

- Load assembly component schedules, obtain and analyze netting reports for next level, analyze data and release orders.

    Program objectives and results are summarized in Exhibit F.

    Strategies used to reduce cycle time were:

- Implement regenerative MRP, implement net change MRP.

PURCHASING CYCLE/VENDOR CYCLE

Major tasks or sub-elements of the cycle for key commodities were:

- Enter requisition, contact vendor, acknowledge order, manufacture, transportation.

    Program objectives and results for key commodities are summarized in Exhibit G.

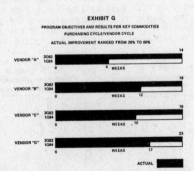

EXHIBIT G

PROGRAM OBJECTIVES AND RESULTS FOR KEY COMMODITIES
PURCHASING CYCLE/VENDOR CYCLE

ACTUAL IMPROVEMENT RANGED FROM 26% TO 60%

Strategies used to reduce cycle time were:

- Schedule sharing by module and item, capacity contracting, supplier stocking.

MANUFACTURING CYCLE

Major tasks or sub-elements of the cycle were:

- Wind, preliminary operations, assembly, impregnate/mold, auto insertion, assembly, kitting, set-up, line-wire, post-op, test, set-up, line-wire, test, pack.

    Program objectives and results are summarized in Exhibit H.

Strategies used to reduce cycle time were:

- Lot size reduction, queue control, utilizing unworked shifts, group technology, revised shop layout, parallel vs. series scheduling, eliminating quality problems, method changes.

III. ANALYSIS TOOLS

Descriptive flow charting and inventory profiling were used to detail the elements of total cycle time and identify areas of potential improvement.

DESCRIPTIVE FLOW CHARTING

All elements of total cycle time were charted in considerable detail using standard symbology. The objective was to compare "actual" and "theoretical cycles" for task content, function, timing and direction of flow. Exhibit I illustrates the basic methodology used.

EXHIBIT I

MANUFACTURING CYCLE TIME ANALYSIS

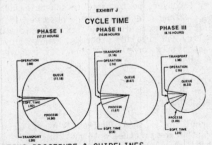

Typically results were graphed to identify areas of improvement (see Exhibit J).

EXHIBIT J

CYCLE TIME

PHASE I — PHASE II — PHASE III

FLOW CHARTING PROCEDURE & GUIDELINES

1. Define the scope of the study.
2. Create updated theoretical flows which include all tasks or operations required to complete the cycle. Existing routing sheets or systems flows are good starting points.

3. Once the theoretical flow for all operations or tasks are identified and timed, actual data can be determined by "walking through the system". Actual flows will recognize queues, delays, transport times, missing operations or tasks, inspections/tests, equipment delays, etc. Total cycle time is "wall clock time" and therefore must include unworked shifts. Because sub-elements are variable (i.e., queue) it will be necessary to make assumptions and arrive at average times based on several observations.

Flow charting requires minimum technical skills. Our study was done by personnel with no special training in operational flow development. The objective is meaningful description of activities for subsequent analysis.

INVENTORY PROFILING

Inventory profiling is a quantitative method which describes the relationship between cycle time, cost profiles, rates of inventory flow. Profiles were used to determine the theoretical investments associated with alternative cycle times, identify areas which would yield the greatest inventory benefits, rank reduction programs by relative cost/benefit relationships, arrive at reduction goals for employee involvment programs.

Several techniques of profiling are available in the current literature and texts, Exhibit K illustrates an example from one of the facilities studied. Theoretical inventory turns were modeled at various points to demonstrate the impacts of reduction activities (see Exhibit L).

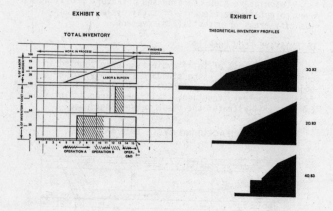

EXHIBIT K

TOTAL INVENTORY

EXHIBIT L

THEORETICAL INVENTORY PROFILES

IV. RESULTS

Overall the results of the program were significant. In addition to the cycle time reductions reported in section II, benefits directly related to the program were derived in inventory turnover, performance to schedule and required floor space. Comparable results were observed in quality, these benefits were more directly attributed to a concurrent quality and supplier programs, however, cycle time reduction was highly correlated to quality improvement.

INVENTORY PERFORMANCE

Throughout the program, Business A experienced a moderate growth rate. Actual net inventory turns improved by 46%, Exhibit M illustrates that aggressive goals were set through the program (i.e. 2:1 improvement in one year) to stimulate change. Business B underwent high rates of growth over the same and must be regarded as technologically advanced relative to business A. Actual net inventory turns improved 232% compared to planned improvement of 346% (see exhibit M).

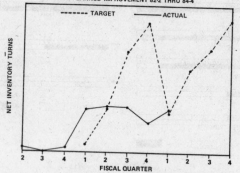

EXHIBIT M

BUSINESS A NET INVENTORY TURNS

TARGET VS ACTUAL QTR 82-2 THRU QTR 84-4
46% ACTUAL IMPROVEMENT 82-2 THRU 84-1
253% PLANNED IMPROVEMENT 82-2 THRU 84-4

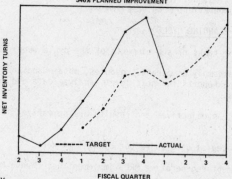

BUSINESS B NET INVENTORY TURNS

TARGET VS ACTUAL QTR 82-2 THRU QTR 84-4
232% ACTUAL IMPROVEMENT
346% PLANNED IMPROVEMENT

QUALITY

Cycle time reduction programs were concurrent to corporate quality and supplier programs, quality improvement was highly correlated to cycle time reduction as indicated by data from Business A. Exhibits N, O and P illustrate quality performance measured in PPM from areas achieving the greatest reductions, improvement ranged from 1.6:1 to 9.7:1. Areas which achieved minimal cycle time reductions showed lesser improvements or degraded. Overall outgoing quality improved dramatically, 7.2:1 see Exhibit Q. It should be noted that Business A has historically been regarded as a high quality supplier. Over the period depicted in the graphs below it has assumed the position of quality leader in its industry. Business B has always maintained the status of quality leader in its markets.

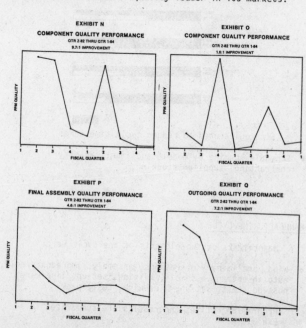

EXHIBIT N
COMPONENT QUALITY PERFORMANCE
QTR 2-82 THRU QTR 1-84
9.7:1 IMPROVEMENT

EXHIBIT O
COMPONENT QUALITY PERFORMANCE
QTR 2-82 THRU QTR 1-84
1.6:1 IMPROVEMENT

EXHIBIT P
FINAL ASSEMBLY QUALITY PERFORMANCE
QTR 2-82 THRU QTR 1-84
4.6:1 IMPROVEMENT

EXHIBIT Q
OUTGOING QUALITY PERFORMANCE
QTR 2-82 THRU QTR 1-84
7.2:1 IMPROVEMENT

PERFORMANCE TO SCHEDULE

Performance to schedule improved significantly. Assembly support areas which underwent cycle time reduction programs and overall performance to master schedule both improved from a 90% level to a 98% level for both businesses.

OTHER RESULTS

• Both businesses reported reductions in floor space required, the estimates ranged from 5-10% to date.
• PROFITS WERE IMPROVED SIGNIFICANTLY IN BOTH BUSINESSES.

V. SETTING UP A TOTAL CYCLE TIME REDUCTION PROGRAM

Initial Study

• Trace the informational flow from forecast thru shipment
• Document the material flow from supplier thru shipment
• Estimate the Cycle Time for both the informational flow and the product flow by functional area
• Determine the critical path from forecast thru shipment
• Sum the estimated critical path cycle times

Formalize the Study

• Identify and prioritize the most significant critical path cycle times
• Establish goals for the program
• Use aggressive goals (i.e. 50% reduction in total cycle time in 12 months)
• Use realistic goals (based on your assessment of the expected commitment from top management)
• Use goals that can be integrated into existing productivity improvement programs and that complement existing objectives wherever possible
• Use measureable goals (i.e. double inventory turns in 12 months)
• Remember that the program is long term and is based on the theme of continuous improvement
• Prepare a formal presentation aimed for top management

Report to Management

• Explain the program and outline the findings
• Recommend the areas to concentrate resources
• Identify and quantify both the benefits to be realized from the program and the estimated resources required
• Emphasize how the benefits address long term strategic goals
• Explain the program goals and measurement criteria
• Seek Top Management's commitment to the plan

Organizing For Improvements and Cycle Time Reduction

• Make sure that top managements commitment is communicated to all management levels
• Get agreement on the priorities for Cycle Time Reduction and select the cycle time element(s) or sub-element(s) to be improved
• Select the team members with emphasis on a broad base of skills and experience (i.e., employee involvement groups)
• Select a team leader
• Perform Total Cycle Time training at the team level
• Review the initial study results for the area(s) being addressed by the team
• Establish the teams time phased cycle time reduction goals
• Plan periodic meetings for progress reports
• Leave it up to the team to determine and execute the detailed cycle time reductions.
• The team action plans may include the following:

  • A more detailed cycle time measurement
  • Procedural changes
  • Process changes
  • People changes
  • Layout changes
  • Periodic remeasurements of cycle time
  • Capital expenditure recommendations

Special Considerations

Procurement of parts represents one of the major frontiers for cycle time reduction. We have begun to address this area thru supplier relations programs which emphasize the following:

• Partnership
• Mutual growth
• Supplier base reductions
• Quality certifications
• Cost reductions
• Schedule sharing

VI. EDUCATION

As with most major undertakings, education can play a pivotal role in the success of a Total Cycle Time Reduction Program. A well executed educational program can provide management with the insight and understanding that can greatly enhance not only management's likelihood of committing to a long term program such as Total Cycle Time Reduction, but their degree of commitment as well.

Our educational program was begun in parallel with the rest of the Total Cycle Time Reduction Program, but ideally should have preceeded the top management commitment phase. The major components of our particular approach to education is best illustrated by the following educational program matrix.

EDUCATIONAL PROGRAM MATRIX

EDUCATIONAL RESOURCE		LEVELS OF MANAGEMENT		
Seminars	Topic	Exec.	Middle	All Other
Bob Hall	Zero Inventory Crusade	X	X	
Richard Schonberger	Far East Manuf. Techniques	X	X	
Plossl & Heard	Manufacturing Cycle Time	X	X	
Rath & Strong	JIT	X	X	
Internal Experts	Total Cycle Time	X	X	X
APICS	Various	X	X	X
Facility Tours		Exec.	Middle	All Other
Far East Facilities		X	X	
Progressive U.S. Facilities		X	X	
Other Resources		Exec.	Middle	All Other
AIAG Videotapes			X	X
Pertinent Literature			X	X
Participation in Total Cycle Time Reduction Team			X	X

VII. CONCLUSIONS AND SUMMARY

A total cycle time reduction program was applied to the production systems of the Industrial Electronics Unit of Motorola. Significant benefits resulted from the program in inventory performance, customer service, performance to schedule, quality and profitability. The essentials of the method are: determine theoretical and actual cycle times, identify the reasons for variance, take action to reduce the cycle closer to the theoretical value. The approach is not fully developed, but does present alternatives to popular techniques and strategies (i.e. JIT, Kanban etc.). Cycle time as a concept has some distinctive features:

• Versatility, it can be applied to the entire production system or selected segments.
• The approach is straight forward and is easily interpreted at all levels.
• As a strategy the total cycle time approach can be deployed as a single technique or expanded to address all elements of business strategy.
• The approach provides a readily understood framework in which all contributing functions remain visable.
• The approach can be implemented quickly and lends itself to "continuous improvement."

Test the method in your own system! Identify the queues, delays, and other reasons for long cycle times. Are they acceptable? Probably not! The cost to identify and eliminate them from your system can be very low.

It will be necessary for most industries to improve productivity in 1980's, numerous programs are in progress. As firms search for the means to improve, many routes are possible; "Zero Inventories", MRP II etc. The authors have found another path . . . "Cycle Time Reduction" . . . it is a hidden road to productivity.

ABOUT THE AUTHORS

Wayne Piotrowski is presently Manager of Material Planning and Systems for the Industrial Electronics Unit of Motorola, his primary responsibilities are to manage productivity improvement and other material/business planning programs. He has over ten years of experience in Materials Management and business consulting in various industries. Prior to joining Motorola he was associated with Gould, Inc., Bally Manufacturing and Skil Corporation. He holds a Masters of Business Administration degree from Loyola University of Chicago and a Bachelors of Science from DePaul University, Chicago, Illinois. Wayne is a member of the American Production and Inventory Control Society.

Gregory P. Henschen is a Manufacturing Resource Specialist with Motorola's Industrial Electronics Unit, where his primary duties involve the formulation and implementation of productivity improvement programs.

Prior to joining Motorola, Mr. Henschen spent over eight years in materials management and manufacturing systems consulting for firms involved in the manufacturing of heavy construction equipment and telecommunications equipment. Mr. Henschen has a B.S. in Industrial Management from Purdue University and is currently pursuing an MBA at the Lake Forest School of Management. He has been a member of APICS for five years and is APICS certified.

QUALITY CIRCLES REVISITED

James F. Cox, CPIM*
The University of Georgia
Dwight R. Norris
Auburn University

Quality circle programs have received considerable attention in the last few years. Though circle programs have been very successful in Japan, not all implementations have proven successful in U.S. companies. In fact, little scientific research has taken place to substantiate successes or failures. To date, published evaluations either are anecdotal and describe or laud the technique, or probe the impact of quality circles in generalized terms of financial savings and benefits. Little is known about the causes of success or failure, or the types of employees attracted to quality circles. More rigorous empirical studies of quality circle programs are perhaps the most serious omission in this field today.

The purpose of this paper is to present results of a follow-up study of the effectiveness of a quality circle program. Some 22 months after the initial study, the authors re-visited the facility to examine longitudinal changes over the ensuring period. Results of the initial study, presented by the authors at the 1983 APICS International Conference (Cox and Norris, 1983), were somewhat unexpected. Employees who had voluntarily joined a quality circle were lower performers, reported lower job satisfaction, and had higher absenteeism rates than employees who had not joined a circle. Simultaneously, circle joiners viewed their supervisors as more considerable of their feelings, tended to have more education, and more years of service.

Due to the fact that the initial study was conducted only 26 months after the quality circle program was begun (4 circles were 26 months old and 11 circles were 18 months old), the authors wished to determine if characteristics in the initial study that distinguished circle from noncircle members continued to differentiate between these groups. Secondly, an audit designed to assess quality circle program effectiveness through study of member attitudes was repeated. An analysis of attitudinal changes toward the program of the period between the two studies is provided.

PART I – CIRCLE MEMBERS VERSUS NON-MEMBERS

Both the initial (1982) and follow-up (1984) studies were conducted among operative employees in a small electronics manufacturing plant employing approximately 280 persons. Approximately 250 employees completed a general attitude questionnaire. Eighty-five of these employees were circle members. Participants were not informed of the purpose of the study and the authors administered all questionnaires. Confidentiality was insured as management saw only summary results and the authors did not know the names of the respondents.

The company established a quality circle program, with four circles 26 months prior to the initial study and 11 circles 8 months later. Essentially, circles were formed on each shift in each department. Circles ranged in size from 5 to 13 members. Participation in the circle program was strictly voluntary. In most cases, departmental supervisors served as circle leaders. The plant employed a circle facilitator. After volunteering, circle members received training in quality control techniques before participating in circle activities.

Study Variables. A total of 14 individual variables were studied, including 3 demographic characteristics, 3 behavioral measures, and 8 attitudinal variables. Demographic variables were age (years), education level (1 = no high school degree; 7 = graduate degree), and tenure with the company (months of service). Behavioral measures were taken from company records, and included absenteeism, tardiness, and job performance. The number of absenteeism and tardiness incidences in the 12 months preceding data collection was measured. Supervisors provided an evaluation of performance based on four factors; dependability, quantity-quality of work, cooperativeness, and safety-health. Supervisors indicated whether performance was (4) exceptional, (3) exceeds normal requirements, (2) meets normal requirements, or (1) improvement is necessary.

Attitudinal measures included job satisfaction, propensity to leave, communication, and perceptions of leader behavior. Reliabilities for the attitudinal scales (Cronbach's alpha) ranged from a low of .81 for propensity to leave to .97 for superior-subordinate communication. The Minnesota Satisfaction Questionnaire (short form) was used to measure job satisfaction (Weiss, Davis, England, & Lofquist, 1967). This scale provides measures of intrinsic, extrinsic, and general job satisfaction. Propensity to leave was measured by a 3-item scale used by Lyons (1971). Higher scores indicate a greater propensity to leave.

Two measures of communication, upward and superior-subordinate, were taken from Dennis' communication climate scale (Goldhaber, Dennis, Richetto, & Wiio, 1979). Perceptions of leaders behavior (initiating structure and consideration) were assessed using the Leader Behavior Description Questionnaire developed by Stogdill (1963).

Means of the study variables for 1982 members and non-members, and 1984 members and non-members are presented in Table 1. T-test of mean differences between members and non-members for each of the two studies are remarkably similar. Members in both studies were more educated. Non-members were again higher performers. Though differences in absenteeism between members and non-members were not statistically significant in 1984, they were in the same direction as 1982 results. Tardiness for circle members was higher in both 1982 and 1984,

Table 1

Means and Standard Deviations For Members and Non-Members

Study Variables	Initial Study (1982)		Follow-up Study (1984)	
	Members (N=91)	Non-members (N=105)	Members (N=79)	Non-members (N=76)
Age	36.3	37.3**	35.2	36.5***
Education level	2.3	2.0**	2.5	2.0**
Months with company	56.8	54.2	54.8	52.7
Job satisfaction				
Intrinsic	44.6	45.4	46.7	47.6
Extrinsic	19.1	19.7	21.3	21.9
General	71.0	72.6	75.3	77.1
Propensity to leave	6.3	6.0	6.2	5.8**
Upward communication	13.8	13.1	16.0	14.0**
Superior-subordinate communication	70.9	68.0	76.1	74.8
Initiating structure	40.9	40.0	40.1	41.8
Consideration	35.2	33.5**	38.4	38.0*
Job performance	2.6	2.9*	2.7	2.9
Absenteeism	3.9	2.7*	2.0	1.4
Tardiness	4.0	3.2	2.8	1.5

*Subgroup means are significantly different, p .05
**Subgroup means are significantly different, p .01
***Subgroup means are significantly different, p .001

though differences were not statistically significant. One significant difference in 1984 was that members felt upward communication was improved. As is evident, differences that distinguish members from non-members in 1982 tended to also distinguish 1984 circle members from non-members.

Discriminant analysis was used to statistically distinguish between circle and non-circle members. A discriminating function was developed based on the characteristics of members and non-members. A prediction of membership was made for each participant and compared to actual membership to identify which of the variables did indeed discriminate.

A summary of significant variables to the discriminant function is presented in Table 2. A total of 6 of the original 14 variables were selected, with the F-to-enter values nonsignificant for all other variables. These 6 variables produced a significant degree of group separation as indicated by Wilk's lambda (R=.86) which approximates a X^2 of 19.8, significant beyond the .01 level. Group centroids were significantly different. A successful classification of members and non-members was achieved with the resultant discriminant function. Sixty percent of the subjects were correctly classified.

Considering the discriminant weights, a positive value indicates the variable was higher for non-members, while a negative value means the variable was higher for members. Non-members tended to be somewhat older, more extrinsically satisfied, reported a higher likelihood of leaving the firm, and were somewhat higher performers. Circle members had higher education levels and felt upward communication was better.

Table 2

Discriminant Analysis Summary

Study Variable	Standardized Weight	Correlation with Discriminant Function
Age	.42	.48
Education level	-.28	-.29
Extrinsic satisfaction	.71	.20
Propensity to leave	.77	.29
Upward communication	-.57	-.37
Job performance	.35	.38

NOTE: Variables are listed by order of entry. Group centroids were -.51 for members and .32 for non-members

The difference between the standardized weights and discriminant function correlation for extrinsic satisfaction and propensity to leave is substantial (approximately .5). Such a difference indicates that these two variables are not important discriminating factors until age and education level have been accounted for (statistically controlled). Once subjects are statistically matched on education and propensity to leave, then extrinsic satisfaction and propensity to leave become important.

In the 1982 study, circle members were also found to be lower performers, reported lower job satisfaction, and were more educated. Age differences, differences in propensity to leave, nor upward communication differences were significant in 1982. Across both the initial study and the follow-up study, circle members were consistently more educated, but were lower performers and felt less job satisfaction.

The results indicate that significant differences exists between members and non-members. The differences tend to persist over time. Differences between members and non-members that were evident only months after the decision to join a circle was made, were still important almost 2 years later. Whereas one longitudinal study in one organization cannot prove such differences, these studies suggest that certain long term differences are important.

PART II - ASSESSING PROGRAM EFFECTIVENESS

The large number of circle program failures, 70% or more, indicates the need for research to identify causes of program failures and problems preventing the effective operation of individual circles. Past literature suggests the most common reasons for circle and program ineffectiveness and failure are:
1. Lack of acceptance, interest and commitment by supervisors. A competent and enthusiastic supervisor as the circle leader, is critical to the effective operation of a circle.
2. Active participation by circle members in all aspects of circle activities. Each member must be actively involved in all phases of circle activities to insure circle effectiveness.
3. Education of circle members in quality circle concepts and techniques (brainstorming, Parato or ABC analysis, management presentations). The proper understanding and use of techniques are provided through adequate education and training of members prior to joining the circle and a continuing education program after circle membership.
4. Open communications are essential. Poor communications among workers and with management prevents or hinders problem identification, solving and implementation. Members and leaders must be able to effectively communicate their ideas.
5. Resistance to change is a natural reaction. Workers, supervisors, and middle and top management must overcome their resistance to changes in their work environment and relationships with others. Commitment by each group is critical to the success of a circle program.
6. Poor management and organization of circle meetings and activities can cause member frustration and dampen worker enthusiasm and participation. Effective planning and control of meetings are essential to insuring member involvement and satisfaction.

The quality circle auditing instrument presented by Cox and Norris (1983) was administered in July 1982 and May 1984 to circle members in a small electronics manufacturing plant. The original instrument consisted of 81 items covering seven areas. The first section consisted of eight items related to measuring the individual members activity level in the circle program. The remaining six sections examine member attitudes toward supervision, participation, education, communications, resistance to change, and circle management. In July 1982, one hundred and three circle members completed the instrument and in May 1984, eighty-three members completed the instrument.

The results of the general questions related to member activity level in the circle program are provided in Table 3 and Table 4. Several interesting points should be noted. Over the twenty-two month interval between questionnaire administrations average length of circle membership increased from 1.15 years to almost two years. Upon closer investigation it was found that circles did not operate in each department on each shift and that workers were moved frequently in the past therefore several past members and possible members were anxious to rejoin or join a circle, however a circle was not in operation in their area. The movement of members across departments and shifts is supported by the increasing number of workers (42%) who have been a member of two or more different circles.

Presently 82% as compared with 65% of circle members in 1982 have their immediate supervisor as their circle leader. Also, an increase from 64% to 77% of circle members thought their supervisor should be the circle leader. Across both surveys, meeting attendance remained above 96% and over 40% of members at both survey administrations indicated spending personal time on circle activities. Also at both sittings, 79% and 88% of members felt the QC presentations to management were a good idea. The responses at both administrations support managements' opinion of having a very successful circle program.

Table 3

Summary of Responses to General Questions on Quality Circle Attitude Questionnaire

1982 N = 103   1984 N = 83

Question or Statement		Responses				
		Percentages				
		1	2	3	4	5
1. Length of Quality Circle membership?						
1. years		-	-	-	-	-
2. months		-	-	-	-	-
2. How many different Quality Circles have you been a member of?						
1. one circle	1982	67	25	8	-	-
2. two circles	1984	55	30	12	-	-
3. three or more circles						
3. Who is the leader of your present Quality Circle?						
1. my supervisor	1982	65	18	1	2	14
2. another supervisor	1984	82	12	1	2	2
3. an employee in my department						
4. an employee from another department						
5. other (please specify) _____						
4. How do you feel about having a Quality Circle staff member present at Circle meetings?						
1. a facilitator is not needed	1982	14	23	17	14	32
2. need attend only 1/4 of meetings	1984	14	12	21	12	40
3. need attend only 1/2 of meetings						
4. need attend only 3/4 of meetings						
5. should attend all meetings						
5. Who should be leaders of Quality Circles?						
1. supervisors	1982	64	34	2	-	-
2. non-supervisors	1984	77	18	4	-	-
3. managers above the supervisory level						
6. How often, on the average, have you attended the Quality Circle meeting? Approximately ____ % attended.	1982 1984	- -	- -	- -	- -	- -
7. Have you spent some of your own time (lunches, breaks, etc.) on Quality Circle matters?						
1. yes	1982	46	54	-	-	-
2. no	1984	42	58	-	-	-
8. How do you feel about Quality Circle presentations to management?						
1. should be discontinued	1982	6	16	79	-	-
2. no opinion	1984	5	7	88	-	-
3. good idea--should be continued						

American Production & Inventory Control Society

Table 4

Summary of Responses to General Questions on Quality Circle Attitude Questionnaire

1982 N = 103   1984 N = 83

Question or Statement		Responses	
		Mean	Standard Deviation
1. Length of Quality Circle membership?			
1. years	1982	.82	.83
	1984	1.65	1.60
2. months	1982	3.99	3.80
	1984	2.60	2.73
2. How many different Quality Circles have you been a member of?			
1. one circle	1982	1.41	.64
2. two circles	1984	1.52	.74
3. three or more circles			
3. Who is the leader of your present Quality Circle?			
1. my supervisor	1982	1.81	1.39
2. another supervisor	1984	1.31	.82
3. an employee in my department			
4. an employee from another department			
5. other (please specify) _____			
4. How do you feel about having a Quality Circle staff member present at Circle meetings?			
1. a facilitator is not needed	1982	3.27	1.46
2. need attend only 1/4 of meetings	1984	3.48	1.52
3. need attend only 1/2 of meetings			
4. need attend only 3/4 of meetings			
5. should attend all meetings			
5. Who should be leaders of Quality Circles?			
1. supervisors	1982	1.38	.53
2. non-supervisors	1984	1.24	.53
3. managers above the supervisory level			
6. How often, on the average, have you attended the Quality Circle meeting? Approximately _____ % attended.	1982	96.09	7.77
	1984	96.26	8.60
7. Have you spent some of your own time (lunches, breaks, etc.) on Quality Circle matters?			
1. yes	1982	1.54	.50
2. no	1984	1.58	.50
8. How do you feel about Quality Circle presentations to management?			
1. should be discontinued	1982	2.73	.56
2. no opinion	1984	2.83	.49
3. good idea--should be continued			

The comparison of the responses to the 1982 and 1984 administrations for the six remaining areas is provided in Table 5. Each area consisted of several questions measured on a five-point Likert scale with 1=strongly disagree; 2=disagree; 3=neither agree or disagree; 4=agree; 5=strongly agree; unless otherwise specified. In both 1982 and 1984, scores in each area were extremely high.

An interesting point to note is that in each of the six areas scores increased while standard deviations decreased in five of the six areas over time. Again, these results support management's view of having a successful circle program. Overall improvement in the program took place over the two years between the questionnaire administrations.

Table 5

A Longitudinal Summary of Responses to the Audit of Quality Circle Program -- 1982-1984

	Number of Questions	1982 N = 103		1984 N = 83	
		Mean	Standard Deviation	Mean	Standard Deviation
Supervision	7	25.495	4.224	26.08	3.93
Participation	10	38.34	5.473	38.90	4.94
Education	11	40.314	4.836	41.19	4.96
Communications	12	44.69	5.697	45.77	5.17
Resistance to Change	11	42.86	5.567	43.40	4.53
Organization	22	81.489	9.655	82.05	9.19

REFERENCES

Cox, J.F. and Norris, D.R. Measuring Quality Circle Effectiveness. Proceedings. American Production and Inventory Control Society 26th Annual International Conference, New Orleans, Louisiana, November, 1983, pp. 178-181.

Goldhaber, G.M., Dennis, H.S. III, Richetto, G.M., & Wiio, O.A. Information Strategies. Englewood Cliffs: Prentice-Hall, Inc., 1979.

Lyons, T.F. Role clarity, need for clarity, satisfaction, tension, and withdrawal. Organizational Behavior and Human Performance, 1971, 6, 99-110.

Stogdill, R.M. Manual for the Leader Behavior Description Questionnaire-Form XII. Columbus: Ohio State University, Bureau of Business Research, 1963.

Weiss, D.J., Davis, R.V., England, G.W., & Lofquist, L.H. Manual for the Minnesota Satisfaction Questionnaire. Minneapolis: Industrial Relations Center, University of Minnesota, 1967.

ROBOTS AND FLEXIBLE MANUFACTURING SYSTEMS: A PRIMER

Alan G. Dunn, CPIM
Alan G. Dunn, Inc.

Introduction To Robots

American manufacturing companies producing everything from automobiles to blenders are welcoming a new employee to the production ranks. This employee normally works in complete silence, complete respect of management and with complete consistency. The employee's name is "Robot" and he has approximately 6,500 brothers and sisters in other manufacturing companies across the nation.

Robot technology has ushered in a new era in American re-industrialization. Technologies employed by robots are permitting manufacturers to not only improve the production process but to also improve the quality of products. This introduction of industrial robots has permitted manufacturers to perform tasks that simply could not be performed previously. An example of this is seen in the nuclear power industry where welding and patchwork must often be performed within contaminated environments. Only robots, devices that synthesize human motion, can safely perform such tasks.

The continued introduction of industrial robots into the American manufacturing economy will radically alter the economics of automation and productivity. Though the full benefits of robotics will be difficult to achieve and the barriers to successful implementation are formidable, the promise of robotics is still exceptional and exciting.

Industrial Robots Arrive In America

Surprisingly, it has been more than ten years since the first industrial robots were developed. The first real industrial robot was developed and introduced in Japan. The robot, called the "Versatran" was produced by AMF Company, a United States manufacturing company. The robot was introduced in 1967 and has since been joined by over 36,000 robots in Japan and 6,500 robots in America.

Exhibit I

Partial List Of Industrial Robot Suppliers

o General Electric	o Advanced Robotics
o General Motors	o Nordson
o Westinghouse	o Odetics
o Cincinnati Milicron	o Kearney and Trecker
	o Giddings and Lewis
o Fanua	o Sundstrand
o Hitachi	o Bendix (with Comau)
o Kawasaki	o Ingersoll Rand
o Yasukawa	o Yamazski (Mazak
o US Robots	Machine Corp.)
o Condec	o Unimation
o Textron	o Fared Robot Systems
o Nova Robotics	o Intelledex

The major suppliers of industrial robots in

the United States are listed in Exhibit II. Growth of robot manufacturers is predicted to double in the next 3 years with the major markets being captured by 3 or 4 major suppliers.

Users of industrial robots are usually large firms that have integrated together several robots with the business information management system to form a Flexible Manufacturing Systems (FMS). It is the FMS factory that provides the greatest return for manufacturers considering automation.

What Does An Industrial Robot Really Do?

In an article by Mack Corporation, a robot has been defined as a subdivision of automation science. A comprehensive definition of an industrial robot is presented in Exhibit II. The key words in the definition are "motion" and "reprogrammable". Industrial robots today are capable of being reprogrammed to perform different tasks under a variety of conditions. This reprogramming is not always electronic, it can be mechanical or fixturing type reprogramming in certain cases. In short, the defintion states that an industrial robot is a device that can be re-instructed to perform certain motions in place of human interaction. In theoretical terms, the introduction of robot technology requires a digression to a pre-industrial revolution production process, utilizing synthetic human motion instead of actual human motion.

Exhibit II

Robot Definition
Adopted By The Robot Institute of America

"A Robot is a reprogrammable multifunctional manipulator designed to move material, parts, tools or specialized devices through variable programmed motions for the performance of a variety of tasks".

Robots can perform a variety of operations including operations that simply could not be performed by human beings. An example would be an operation requiring that a human reach around an object, twist a wrist, and reach inside another operation. The human anatomy simply does not permit human limbs to bend in this manner, however, robot engineers can redesign the human anatomy in synthetic form to readily perform this task. More importantly, robot engineers can reprogram the same robot to perform a variety of other tasks, some more difficult, some less difficult but all at the same price. Certain companies utilizing robots have indicated that the robots perform a variety of tasks, 24 hours a day with little time for lunch breaks and rest periods!

Robots And Motion

To really understand the mechanics of a robots, one must understand some theory

American Production & Inventory Control Society

of motion. Motion has been defined as:

"the act or process of moving".

Additionally, robotics requires that motion be defined as:

"meaningful movement or process of moving".

It is the "meaningful" part of the definition that greatly enhances a robots chance of success in a particular manufacturing operation.

Typically, the motion of a robot can be defined across either a controlled path or a point-to-point movement.

- o Controlled path: When the robot moves along a prescribed and programmed path, one that has many directions along the X,Y and Z axes (based on the cartesian coordinate system).

- o Point-to-point: Includes motion from one point to another. This motion is normally easy to program and requires the definition of a simple sequence of events.

A company utilizing a robot to perform pick-and-place operations (picking material from one machine and placing it in the fixture of another machine) requires a robot with point-to-point motion. Certainly, a robot that can move in a programmed control path can also be programmed to move in a point-to-point path. However, the cost of the robot is much higher. Vice versa, a company requiring a robot that will follow the contours of a multi-dimentional part must have a robot that moves in a controlled path. Point-to-point motion can rarely be utilized in such an operation without extensive programming support.

Types Of Robots

There are basically three types of robots. These are:

- o Fixed sequence (sometimes called non-servo controlled)

- o Variable sequence (sometimes called servo controlled)

- o Multi-legged robot (sometimes called "functionoid")

Fixed Sequence Robots

These robots are normally inexpensive, simple to use and easy to understand. Fixed sequence robots provide point-to-point motion and are a logical choice for transferring or moving material from one process to another. These robots have good reliability and usually operate along X,Y and Z axes with one or more rotations provided. Many fixed sequence robots in use today rely less on computerized control methods and more on cam and drumtimers which sequence start and stop operations. In summary, fixed sequence robots are often used in pick and place operations where precision of point-to-point motion is demanded.

Variable Sequence Robots

These robots are truly programmable in nature. They have a wide range of capabilities providing both controlled path motion and point-to-point motion. Most variable sequence robots are utilized in manufacturing tasks that require a variety of motions, sequenced differently depending upon the item to be manufactured. Additionally, variable sequence robots can be programmed to avoid obstructions either by preprogrammed control or by sensory devices such as proximity sensors, laser sensors, fiberoptics, etc. The programming for these can be quite expensive and normally represents a high cost of the installation.

Multi-legged Robots

These robots, sometimes referred to as "functionoids", are devices that perform a variety of controlled path tasks and are capable of moving about under their own power. Because it moves about, a multi-legged robot can be used in applications where the production method must move to the production process. Applications for multi-legged robots may be in agriculture; sea, land, space exploration; security; surveillance; and defense. These robots are few in number and are not normally suited for use in stationary manufacturing facilities.

Other Physical Requirements

All robots regardless of the type, require a controller device and a manipulator device.

The controller of an industrial robot normally saves and manages the motion of the manufacturing process. In a fixed sequence robot, the controller may be simply the size and configuration of cams that create the movement. Aside from normal cam wear, the controller provides uniformity and consistency of motion. In more sophisticated variable sequence and multi-legged robots, the controller is a combination of:

- o Computer hardware

- o System software

- o Motion software (application software for the performance of a particular set of motions)

The controllers in all robot systems are responsible for managing the motion of the robot. A robot technologist at Unimation, a leading supplier of industrial robots, says that programming and control of robot motion can represent over half the total effort and expenditure of utilizing robots. In short, robot controllers are the "black box", or brains, of the system.

The manipulator is the portion of the robot that actually performs the work. Typically, robots have a series of manipulators that can be interchanged much the same that tooling is interchangeable on conventional factory equipment. All robots require a manipulator device to grasp, hold, bend, rotate, press, etc., the material being processed. One can think of a manipulator as the liason between the theory of programmed motion and the actual processing of motion. A manipulator is to a robot what a cutting bit is to a lathe.

Major classifications of manipulators include:

o End effectors for holding material while it is being processed. Usually end effectors have to be customized to match requirements of the manufacturing process. In a sense, this is exactly the way conventional machinery works. A manufacturing manager buys a conventional machine utilizing different tooling (or manipulators) to alter the capabilities of the machine.

o Rotational devices. These may be used in conjunction with end effectors. Rotational devices are needed to provide the turning and twisting ability, commonly identified as roll, pitch and yaw motions. One should think of a rotator as the device on the end of the robot that performs tasks that a human wrist would normally perform.

o Gripping devices. These can be thought of as the fingers of the robot hand. Gripping devices are fingers that open and close at preprogrammed intervals. The grippers perform end effecting duties but are not limited to a specific job or task. Grippers are a step toward standardizing a grasping process.

Industrial robots are still babies in an industrial revolution. Though we have discussed the major types of robots, we anticipate a greater variety of industrial robots as the pace of robotics acceptance picks up. We see an increased use in specialized robots targeted at vertical markets. These robots will be designed primarily for one generic type of use though a variety of motions will be necessary in the program. Also, as more robot manufacturers enter the marketplace, we see an increased use in the "low cost" variable sequence robots. As the price of these robots drop, manufacturers will begin experimenting by installing them to directly offset human laborers. Once the learning curve is underway, we expect the proliferation of robots will emulate the proliferation of computer based information systems.

Integrating Robots Into The Factory

"Industrial robots are to factory automation what MRP is to closed loop manufacturing planning". - A. Dunn

In the early days of manufacturing systems, MRP (Material Requirements Planning) was titled as a new way of planning the inventory segment of the business. Shortly, American manufacturers began to realize that a higher level tactical plan (a Master Production Schedule) was required to facilitate some orderliness on the factory floor. Shortly thereafter, manufacturers discovered that a master production schedule is driven by a forecast and requires some form of capacity planning. Many a plant had excellent material availability, yet lacked capacity and therefore missed customer deliveries.

In the middle 1970's, American manufacturing management realized that even though MRP is the hub of a formal manufacturing management system, it requires a total integration of all operating elements into a common understanding and data base.

This new understanding signalled the birth of MRP II and the integrated manufacturing business methodology. Clearly, industrial robots are the MRP of an integrated factory system (Flexible Manufacturing System, or FMS). Flexible systems radically alter not only the manufacturing process but the economics of automation. This radical alteration is due mostly to the flexible systems use of robotics and the provision for producing multiple parts of different designs sequentially. Aggregate production volumes can be high enough to justify a flexible system even though individual part volumes are low. In contrast to the conventional "Taylorized" approach which follows a preprogrammed sequence of specialized steps to make a product, a flexible manufacturing system can be programmed to alter production processes at varying times in varying sequence. An example is seen on a production line that utilizes robots to assemble electric/mechanical parts. The assembly line may produce five different types of radios in five cases with five voltage configurations, all moving down the assembly line sequencially. Robots would assembly each radio differently, altering the sequence of production steps according to the product being constructed.

Though the aggregate volume of the factory may be great, the individual item volumes may be low and can be customized through the integration of flexible manufacturing systems. Additionally, flexible manufacturing systems allow the reduction of lead times, enable additional reductions in inventory (by reducing Queue times), and increase manufacturing capacity by working more hours than humans can work. For example, Mazak Corporation, a Japanese machine tool maker, has built a plant in Florence, Kentucky based on two flexible manufacturing systems. One system produces frames and beds for Mazak Machine tools while the other system makes gear boxes and other small components. Together the two flexible manufacturing systems make 180 distinctly different parts. A plant based on the conventional "Taylorized" production methods would have required 240 workers to produce the same amount of differentiated products. In contrast, the Mazak Corporation requires only 19 workers spread between two shifts. The night shifts runs unattended except for a night watchman. The savings are obviously apparent.

A recently refurbished plant in Erie, Pennsylvania manufacturers 10 kinds of locomotive motor frames. Using industrial robots in an integrated system network, General Electric sliced its work in process inventory in half, increased capacity 38% and utilized 25% less floor space, all while reducing manufacturing cycle times from 16 days to 16 hours. In themselves, these accomplishments seem nothing less than magnificent. However, the big payoff from General Electric's FMS is faster reaction time to changing market conditions using flexibility not just to cut costs but to out distance competitors.

In summary, flexible manufacturing systems require industrial robots and more. **A complete understanding of the manufacturing process and market conditions is necessary prior to integrating robots into the manufacturing environment.** The word flexibility truly means allowing automated manufacturing of components on a random basis. FMS normally does away with long set up times, queing delays, in process inventory levels and human errors associated with a batch manufacturing process.

Exhibit III

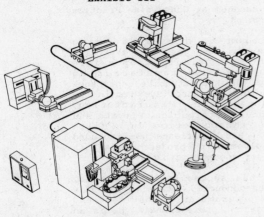

Theoreticians and current users of robots are pleading for manufacturing executives to integrate robots properly. The plea is one that says "don't make the mistakes that you made with MRP". Remember, MRP is only a scheduling tool within the integrated manufacturing methodology. Robots are also only a tool in the integrated manufacturing methodology - the only difference being that MRP is an information tool while robots are a physical tool.

How to Integrate Robot Technology Within The Manufacturing Environment

Implementing robot technology requires a systematic, methodical approach to evaluating the application of factory automation. The steps that one should follow in implementing robots are as follows:

1. Analyze the entire production process.

2. Analyze the current information system.

3. Analyze products, markets and competition.

4. Develop a flexible manu- facturing system frame- work.

5. Develop an implementation schedule.

6. Justify expenditures.

7. Begin implementation and stick to your plan.

8. Monitor progress and report results.

Identifying True Costs Of Industrial Robots

Costs of implementing industrial robots can be divided into three categories.

These are:

- o Nonrecurring costs
- o Recurring costs
- o Intuitive costs

Recurring and nonrecurring costs are often referred to as "surface costs" because they are fairly easy to determine once the MSRD is developed. Intuitive costs (sometimes known as costs of change) are more difficult to determine and nearly impossible to justify.

Cost Summary

Nonrecurring Costs

- o Hardware Costs
- o Software Costs
- o Programming Costs
- o Systems Planning Costs

Recurring Costs

- o Repair, maintenance and service costs
- o Labor costs

Intuitive Costs

- o Contingency costs
- o Employee rehabilitation costs
- o Communication costs
- o Costs of standardization
- o Productivity and quality improvements
- o Market responsiveness

The costs of implementing robots in a manufacturing facility are great, but not as great as the potential payback. Flexible manufacturing system users such as General Electric, Westinghouse, General Motors, General Dynamics, Hughes Aircraft, and Ingersoll Rand, are experiencing productivity improvements in excess of 300%. Certainly this cannot be ignored.

Conclusion

Harvard University's Dr. Robert E. Reich wrote in his recently published book, The Next American Frontier, "If American **prosperity is to be truly restored, a substantial fraction of capital and labor must shift toward flexible system production ....To make this shift, American manufacturing management must unlearn 70 years of conventional wisdom about how to run a manufacturing business. Failure to do so could possibly lead to the serious reduction and possible elimination of basic manufacturing in the United States.**

In a sense, industrial robots have been the catalyst that strengthened flexible manufacturing system technology which in turn is completely transforming the economics of production.

The transformation of the production process from batch manufacturing methods to flexible manufacturing method utilizing industrial robots should not be taken lightly, especially considering the potential productivity and profit gains. However, robotic entry costs are great and should not be undertaken without a thorough investigation of the manufacturing process. This in turn may require additional management education in the uses of flexible manufacturing systems before the investigation process and subsequent purchase of system components.

Acknowledgements

Hasegawa, Dr. Yukio "How Society Should Accept The Full-Scale Introduction of Industrial Robots". Waseda University.

Mack Corporation "Robotics...Start Simple". P & IM Review. June 1983, Vol. 2, No. 6.

Maningas, Rick "Remarks For Automation and Robotics". P & IM Review. June 1983, Vol. 2, No. 6.

Polcyn, Stanley J. "Industrial Robots Boosts Productivity 300 Percent". P & IM Review. June 1983, Vol 2. No. 6.

Longmire, Robert J. and Walker, Duane R. "Jobs In the Robot Age". P & IM Review. June 1983, Vol 2. No. 6.

Harrigan, Kathryn Rudie and Porter, Michael E. "End Game Strategies for Declining Industries". Harvard Business Revue. July 1983

Welles, Chris "Factories: Flexibility In The Future". Los Angeles Times, July 17, 1983.

"The New Economy". Time Magazine, May 30, 1983.

Kinnucan, Paul "Flexible Systems Invade The Factory". High Technology, February 1983, Vol. 3, No. 7.

Acebes, Carl "Companies Pour Into Robot Market". High Technology, February 1983, Vol. 3, No. 7.

Friscia, Tony "What Is Implied By The Automated Factory?". P & IM Review, July 1983, Vol. 3, No. 7.

James, James R. Sr. "Computerized Numerical Control (CNC) Tables". P & IM Review, Juy 1983, Vol. 3, No. 7.

Tombari, Dr. Henry "Analyzing The Benefits and Costs of CAM Methods". P & IM Review, July 1983, Vol. 3, No. 7.

Andrews, Charles G. and Kraus, Dr. William A. "The Human Face Of Automation". P & IM Review, July 1983, Vol. 3, No. 7.

Kato & Hasegawa "State Of The Art Of Robotics". pp. 21-27, Preprints, IFAC Congress VIII, 1981.

Dunn, Alan G. "Case Study - An Actual Robot Implementation". Technology Management, Vol. 4, No. 1, January 1982.

Dunn, Alan G. "Robots Require a Holistic Approach". New American Management. February 1983.

Reich, Robert B. "The Next American Frontier". Times Books.

Farrell, Kevin "Hope For Robot Makers After A Flat Year". Venture, June 1983.

Feigenbaum, Edward and McCorduck, Pamela The Fifth Generation. Addison-Wesley Publishing Company.

About The Author...

Mr. Dunn is President of Alan G. Dunn, Inc. (ADI), a firm that specializes in consulting and education to the manufacturing, distribution and related industries. Prior to founding ADI, Mr. Dunn managed the Materials Management Consulting Group of Coopers and Lybrand's Management Consulting Practice in Los Angeles.

In addition to his consulting experience, Mr. Dunn possesses over nine years of increasingly responsible distribution and manufacturing experience. He has extensive experience in Manufacturing Control Systems in the following areas: Manufacturing, Maintenance, Distribution, Private and Contract Transportation and Public Utilities. His experience has included major involvement on project teams both as a manager and participant.

Mr. Dunn has successfully developed, planned and conducted extensive in-house education programs as a Consultant and as a management professional. He is an avid speaker and author in the areas of Manufacturing Management, Distribution Management and Business Planning. He has spoken nationally for the American Production and Inventory Control Society, the National Council of Physical Distribution Management, and other professional societies. Mr. Dunn currently presents, under contract, the APICS Tutorial programs nationwide. Recent publications have appeared in Distribution Cost Digest, APICS Conference Proceedings, and the Material Handling Engineering Magazine. His most recent publications include, "Industrial Robots - What Are The True Costs?", "Managing the Training Effort", and "Improving the Material Handling Process".

Mr. Dunn is an active member of the American Production and Inventory Control Society (APICS), the National Council of Physical Distribution Management (NCPDM) and the Institute of Industrial Engineers (IIE). He is past President and Chairman of the Board for the Orange County APICS Chapter. Mr. Dunn serves on the Boards of Directors of several California companies and is currently listed in "Who's Who in California".
Education credentials include a Bachelors Degree in Business Management from California State University, Fullerton, where he has also attended graduate studies in Business Management. Mr. Dunn is recognized by APICS as a Certified Practitioner in Production and Inventory Management (CPIM).

CYCLE COUNTING USING PORTABLE COMPUTERS WITH BAR CODE READERS

Wayne E. Donnelly, CPIM
Arthur Andersen & Co.

INTRODUCTION

Zero inventory is an idea worth pursuing. But until we get rid of all of that inventory, we still have to count it. Although many companies have installed cycle counting systems, their success has been somewhat dubious. Portable data collection devices may provide some help in improving those systems.

These small, and truly portable computers have been used by the retailing industry for some time to conduct physical inventories. Recent improvements and new features in these devices now allow for interactive communications with a mainframe. Existing cycle counting programs on the mainframe can identify parts to be counted using normal selection criteria. New programs then load these parts into a portable terminal to be carried out to the warehouse. This concept offers tremendous potential for increasing the accuracy and the speed of cycle counting as well as physical inventories.

THE TERMINALS

It is important to understand the basic abilities and characteristics of portable data collection terminals. They are very lightweight, ranging from about 1 pound up to four pounds, depending upon options (bar code scanners and carrying cases). They are generally 6"-12" in length. At this size and weight they can be carried virtually anywhere by warehouse personnel. Most of the terminals offer a full alphanumeric keyboard with some precoded function keys and keyboard shift keys. The programmability of the terminals allows for a variety of combinations of data characters, special symbols and control keys to be used. Data entry on the keyboard can be reduced by the use of optional bar code scanners. This is becoming increasingly popular because of the widespread use of bar coding. There are two basic types of bar code scanners that these portable terminals use; contact and non-contact. The contact scanners are very similar to a light pen and are much lighter and less expensive than the non-contact laser scanners. A recent development now allows a single scanner to determine which type of bar code is being read and adjust accordingly. This is an important development for companies that are forced to use more than one type of code. Both types of scanners work well and which one you chose depends on your requirements and your budget.

A 16 or 32 character display is provided on terminals of this type. They can be either LED or LCD. The LCD is the most popular but, again, depending upon requirements the LED may be appropriate (low light conditions). In most situations it is advantageous to have the 32 character display. The extra characters allow for more explicit user prompting and error messages. In many cases, 32 characters is not enough. Several of the terminals offer a scrolling feature to "page" through displays requiring more than 32 characters.

Probably the most important aspect of the terminals is the memory size. The amount of space available for data storage usually ranges from 16K up to 132K. As chip technology advances so will the memory size of the terminals.

The amount of memory available for the application program is not easy to determine. There are several approaches the the manufacturers take to store programs in the terminals. One approach allows the memory for data storage to be used for program storage if the program exceeds its storage area. The result is reduced area for data storage but at least the program will work. The other approach strictly limits the size of the program. In this case the only choice you have is to reduce the functionality of the program. The latter may not be possible so it is a good idea to determine what you want the terminal to do before purchasing any equipment. Most vendors are good at estimating the size of the application program you need to accomplish the required functions.

Getting an application program into the terminal is easily accomplished. Here again, due to the numerous approaches, requirements should be understood thoroughly before hardware acquisition. One approach is to develop the program on the terminal itself, typing in the instructions on the terminal keyboard. This approach has a lot of appeal because there is little need for interfaces to other hardware devices for program development. For more sophisticated users, several manufacturers offer development systems on which the application program is created and tested.

The development systems are generally one of two types. Several manufacturers offer small minicomputers for the sole purpose of generating programs for the portable data collection terminals. Other manufacturers provide software for development that can run on a variety of personal computers. Both approaches work well it just depends on the volume of program development to be done and the complexity of the programs. After successful testing, the application program can be loaded directly into the terminal by the development system via a RS-232 cable. Most development systems can also load the application program into microchips which are then placed directly into the terminals (also called "chip burning"). An alternative to placing the programmable microchips (EPROMS) in the terminal is to put them into a program load module (PLM). The use of a PLM is very similar to plugging in game cartridge in your Atari unit. The main difference being that the program stays resident in the game unit after the cartridge is removed. It will stay there until a new PLM is inserted. The use of a program load module has several distinct advantages. First, the terminals can be used by a variety of departments or by a single department that has several uses. Whenever a new program is needed all that is required is to plug in a different PLM. Another advantage is that one PLM can be used to load an infinite number of terminals. Without a PLM, each terminal must have its EPROM microchips removed and replaced whenever a new program is required. This can be a significant effort if program requirements change frequently.

COMMUNICATIONS WITH A MAINFRAME

Transmitting data to a mainframe from the portable terminals in many cases can be easy. Communications get complicated when the requirements call for data to be loaded from the mainframe to the terminals. If an interactive conversation is required with the mainframe, things get difficult. This involves the use of the mainframes communication monitor. Some of the options that must be addressed are:

. Polling vs. non-polling
. Dial-up lines vs dedicated phone lines
. Transparent vs. non-transparent
. Baud rates

Most communications with a mainframe will require additional equipment such as modems, acoustic couplers, protocol converters and front-end communications processors. I am not going to elaborate any further on mainframe communications because it will become extremely technical. I do strongly suggest that someone knowledgeable in communications be part of the hardware selection committee.

COMMUNICATION OPTIONS

If the system does not require mainframe communications directly with the terminal (or if that is just not possible) there are several alternatives to transmit the data. Several manufacturers produce tape drives and floppy disk machines. These machines typically handle one-way communications with the terminals. Data can be stored on tape or disk in remote locations and then that storage medium can be sent to the mainframe for subsequent processing. A hard copy can also be obtained using small printers that attach directly to the terminals. The newest option for communications involves the use of personal computers. This will provide the ability to capture and analyze data on the PC and then send it to a mainframe. It is becoming much easier to communicate between mainframes and PCs and consequently this alternative offers much potential.

CASE STUDY - FORT HOOD

We designed and installed a cycle counting system used to count parts in a variety of warehouses at Fort Hood, Texas.

The typical processing cycle would proceed as follows:

1) Warehouse supervisor will dial-up mainframe, connect the hand-held computer to the acoustic coupler. He enters the warehouse number and the number of parts desired for the download.

2) After receiving a prompt on the hand-held computer indicating that the mainframe programs were finished and the download was successful, the supervisor disconnects the terminal from the telephone and acoustic coupler.

3) The supervisor then assigns each terminal to a counter and indicates the assignment in a log book. The counter then proceeds to locate and count the specified parts in the appropriate warehouse.

4) Upon completion of the counts, the counter returns the terminal to the supervisor who records the receipt in the log book. The supervisor again dials the mainframe and presses the "send" function key. After the entire set of records in their terminal is received successfully by the mainframe, the terminal is then ready for another download.

TECHNICAL DATA

This system used MSI 88s (56KB RAM memory) hand-held data collection devices with attached bar code wands. Data was uploaded and downloaded to these terminals via CICS on an IBM 4341. The terminals were connected to an MSI 2741 protocol converter so that IBM 2780/3780 protocol could be used. This allows us to verify that each data transmission was successfully received before the next data stream was sent. We also used MSI E10-5 acoustic couplers so that we could communicate to the mainframe over voice-grade telephone lines.

FUNCTIONAL HIGHLIGHTS

Listed below are the functional highlights of the portable terminal programs.

. Displayed prompts to guide the counters through the warehouse and to instruct them on the sequence of data input.

. Verified through bar code scanning that the user had found the correct bin where the cycle count part was located.

. Verified through bar code scanning that the user had found the part that was to be counted.

. Validated the format of data entry fields, i.e., numeric data, units of issue, date and time ranges, user identification number among others.

. Allowed the counters to enter exception codes indicating what problems they may have had while counting, i.e., missing labels, part not found, etc.

. Provided the capability to manually enter any data that was bar coded but not readable due to a bad label.

. Provided the ability to add records in the terminal. When records were added, a search of the data in the terminal was performed to prevent duplicate entry. In the Army's case, it was an invalid situation where a part with a certain condition code and expiration date would appear multiple times in one bin.

. Prevented data from being loaded into the terminals unless all previous count records from the terminal had been successfully sent up to the mainframe.

. Retained the entire block of count records in the terminal until the mainframe confirmed that all records had been received successfully.

. Restricted activity on the terminal to "sends" only whenever terminal battery power was low. This ensured that all counts up to that point would at least be received by the mainframe. Processing could continue without loss of records when batteries were replaced.

. Displayed error messages on the terminal so that problems could be corrected by counter rather than waiting for an analysis of the mainframe reports.

. Able to time stamp each count transaction using the real-time clock option in the terminal. This time stamp facilitates reconciliation.

. Sorted recounts to the top of the cycle count list so problem parts would be counted fist.

BENEFITS

Due to the capabilities of this system, many advantages were gained over the punched card and computer printout system that was previously used at Fort Hood.

. Error Detection - Notification of errors in the count transactions occurred at the lowest level possible, the counter. Using the programmability of the terminal we were capable of telling the counter what the error was and in some cases, how to correct it. If the counter was not able to correct it and take some alternate course of action, he could enter exception code indicating what was done. This virtually eliminated the typical turnaround time required for error detection in more cycle count systems. Even in today's on-line environment the counter cannot take the computing power with them throughout the warehouse.

. Accuracy - Bar coding technology is quite well developed. The error rate is about 1 in 3,000,000 characters.
Due to the fact bar codes where being used there were fewer keystrokes required; fewer chances to make an error.
Fewer parts were missed during counting. Many times cards were lost or destroyed. In some rare cases, counts were entered using on-hand inventory reports instead of actually counting the parts. Because the terminals were verifying that bar code labels for parts and bins had been scanned, this became very difficult to do. Any data that was manually entered when it should have been scanned was flagged as a non-fatal error.
Real time clocks were capable of time stamping each transaction. This facilitated reconciling with normal transactions during the day.

. More counts, less time - At first that statement may seem deceptive. The counters were not able to count more parts because they had to deal with more of their own data entry errors. But the statement is true when viewing the whole system. There were fewer errors for analysts to review, there were no cards to be punched, no transactions to be created from count sheets, and fewer total key strokes were required.

. Paper reduction - Count cards and count sheets were no longer required. The only reports printed were the exception reports for the analysts and a transaction audit trail report (I know, but remember I work for an accounting firm).

. Multi-use terminals - Because we had terminals that made use of PLMs, we were abe to use them in other areas on the base. They were also used to collect maintenance and fuel consumption data in the motor pool.

. Symbology standards - The military standards for the use of bar coding is quite well documented. Most manufacturers offer equipment that reads Code 39 and therefore you need not worry about the bar code itself.

. Remote sites - Fort Hood is one of the largest military bases in the free world. The warehouses involved were geographically quite far apart. We were able to dial-up the mainframe and transmit data using voice-grade telephone lines. This prevented the need for regular CRT terminals and special dedicated telephone lines.

PROBLEMS/CONSIDERATIONS

There are no free lunches and consequently there are some areas that must be given careful consideration when installing this type of system.

- Data Integrity - Controls must be included in the terminal programs to ensure integrity of the data. Some problem areas usually include: records were lost during transmissions, records were loaded into terminal before it was unloaded, records were uploaded twice, records were uploaded without being processed and communication failures.
- Label quality/durability - If labels are not changed very often you might consider highly durable, plastic laminated labels. If labels are changed frequently, inexpensive paper labels may be more appropriate. Other questions to consider: direct vs indirect sunlight, exposure to the environment and/or chemicals.
- Label design - Some questions to answer here include;
  How much human readable data is required?
  Can multiple data fields be combined into one scan?
  Are there any security problems with the data printed on the label?
  What bar coding standard is applicable to your industry and your requirements?
  Do the bins and/or the parts lend themselves to accepting a label in a place that is convenient for scanning and/or reading by humans?
- Screen size - The terminals can only display up to 32 characters at a time. If you must display long part descriptions then a scrolling feature might be necessary. The small display forces us to be creative with the messages and data displayed.
- Communications - Only in a few cases can all of this technology be used by plugging it in and turning it on. It requires design and evaluation just like any other systems project. Compatability can become a problem when hardware from several manufacturers is used. Ask for references, demonstrations, warranties and guarantees.

PRICES

The prices for this equipment will vary widely based upon the options selected. Representatives prices are listed on table 1.

Terminals	$ 800 - 4,000
Modem	$ 500 - 700
Protocol Converters	$ 1,500 - 2,500
Tape Drives	$12,000 - 15,000

Table 1

OTHER USES

If a company choses to invest in portable data collection devices, there are a myriad of other areas that could benefit from the use of these terminals:

- Receiving/shipping
- Shop floor issues
- Field quotations
- Purchasing/buyers

CONCLUSIONS

Never before have we been able to detect and correct errors when and where the actual events were occurring. Users have been tied to terminals, forced to enter data in specific locations. We now have the technology to take the computing power with the users wherever they go. As we have seen by examining the system developed for Fort Hood, these are significant improvements to be recognized by the application of this technology for cycle counting. But we must be careful not to fall in the trap of a "solution looking for a problem". As with all new technology it requires evaluation to judge its appropriateness.

WAYNE E. DONNELLY

Mr. Donnelly is a senior manager in the Management Information Consulting Division of Arthur Andersen & Co.'s Houston office. He has worked with clients in the U.S. and South America in the design and implementation of integrated manufacturing control systems, and productivity improvements. He has also had experience in reviewing, selecting and implementing third-party application software. Mr. Donnelly has both a Bachelor and Masters degree in Business Administration from the University of Texas.

AUTOMATION CONTENT VERIFICATION AND PRODUCT INSPECTION USING MACHINE VISION

David L. Hudson
Octek, Inc.

It is certain that to keep American manufacturing competitive in today's marketplace, productivity must increase, utilizing existing machinery and a great deal of automation. Alongside the demand to increase productivity, other forces are driving the rush to do more automating.

Capital expenditures are usually weighed in relation to the payback they produce. In manufacturing and consumer goods industries, measuring the goal of increased productivity can take the form of more units per hour, less cost per piece, better quality control, or a combination of these. Justifying the expense is often dependent on how quickly the investment will produce the projected productivity gain.

First, competition continues to grow as foreign companies flourish. Exchange rates are in favor of international suppliers that offer quality and value "for the price." Foreign competition places a premium on product quality and reduced costs in manufacturing. To accomplish this, industry is emphasizing improvements in the manufacturing processes and quality of goods as the key areas for near-term automation programs. Quality assurance has become a science, and it along with customer service represents the biggest area of savings to many companies.

Second, computing power at today's prices has almost become a commodity. The ability of micro-computer hardware to process data quickly and simply has spurred the growth of process control, the use of CNC tools, the adoption of bar coding and scanning, and the introduction of robots. Other new automation technologies such as machine vision for inspection and process control also rely on micro-computer technology.

YEAR	VALUE	UNITS SHIPPED	ANNUAL UNIT GROWTH RATE
1982	$50	2,600	
1983	80	3,700	30%
1984	130	5,000	35%
1985	210	7,800	56%
1986	320	12,900	65%
1987	500	21,200	64%

**Table 1: Forecasted Vision System Growth
($ Millions)**
(Source: Frost & Sullivan Inc.)

Machine vision is a key technology that is helping to automate many manufacturing operations in control and inspection. It is helping to improve product quality and reduce costs. Machine vision installations are being made with existing equipment as an integral part of many entirely new automated processes. This demand for vision systems (See Table 1) correlates closely with the dramatic growth of the robotics industry (See Table 2) which has served as a leading indicator of growth in factory automation.

	YEAR	SALES	ANNUAL GROWTH RATE	5-YEAR AVERAGE GROWTH RATE
	1980	$100		
ACTUAL	1981	150	50%	50%
	1982	215	43%	72%
	1983	$280	30%	80%
PROJECTED	1984	395	41%	112%
	1985	540	37%	136%

**Table 2: Robotics Industry Growth
($ Millions)**
(Source: Prudential-Bache Securities)

GETTING TO THE POINT

There are dozens of successful installations of machine vision in our factories. One such example is the inspecting of hypodermic needles. The manufacturer had human inspectors manually inspecting the quality of hypodermic needle points. Inspectors wore cotton gloves that would catch on the needle point if the tip was bent or had a burr. The need was for greater inspection reliability and reduced costs. So, the medical equipment company worked with a machine vision company to determine the feasibility of the automated inspection.

Briefly, the first step was to separate the vision functions from the mechanical handling requirements. This allowed the vision company to focus on building a mocked-up version of the inspection procedure. The manufacturer then approved the implementation of a prototype system including the mechanical parts handling equipment needed to properly present the needles to the cameras. Although the specific solution they arrived at is proprietary, the results of the implementation are no surprise. The payback was less than one year, and the product quality is better rated. (See Figures 1 and 2)

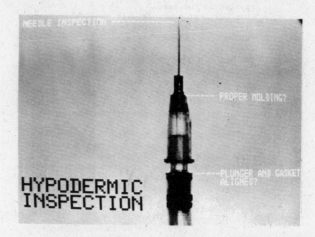

Figure 1: Digitized Hypodermic Assembly

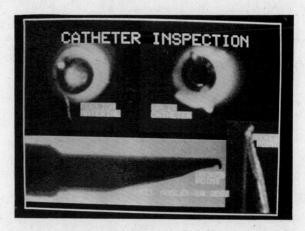

Figure 2: Defective Catheters

PEPPERONI OR SAUSAGE?

An Octek Eye-Q system is inspecting pizza crusts for a major food company. The system inspects each crust for a variety of defects and automatically rejects crusts that are defective. Defect statistics gathered by the system are used to control the production process.

Pizza crusts are produced by the company on a continuous, automated line. Pizza dough passes through a baking oven before the topping is applied. Variations in the production process can cause a variety of defects such as burned crusts, holes, cauliflowered edges, odd shapes and under or oversized crusts.

72

Manual inspection was effective in removing a number of defective crusts, but the high production volume caused many defects to pass inspection. Most defective products were removed later but only after costly toppings and condiments were added to the crusts.

The company installed an Octek vision inspection system at the output of the oven to increase inspection accuracy and reliability. The system accumulates product quality statistics and provides reports. A solid state television camera is mounted over the conveyor line with special lighting. Hoods over the line prevent plant lighting from interfering with the images that are captured at the inspection station. A video monitor displays each crust as it is inspected and shows a running total of good and defective crusts. When a defect is detected, the Eye-Q triggers an air jet that removes the crust from the conveyor. Several tests are performed on each crust to verify that it is free of defects.

Test limits are set by the process engineer using a keypad. For example, if the process engineer decides to change the crust size limits, he teaches the Eye-Q new limits by following instructions displayed on the video monitor. New limits are entered on the keypad and displayed on the monitor. The new test limits are permanently stored in a bubble memory, even when power is switched off. (See Figures 3 and 4)

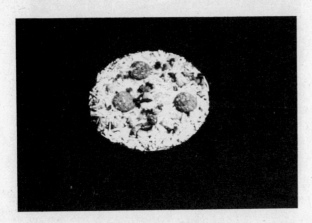

Figure 3: Frozen Pizza Pie

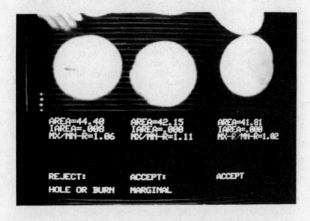

Figure 4: Crusts Inspected by Eye-Q

One major benefit of automating crust inspection was totally unanticipated. The system automatically prints defect statistics at the end of each shift. About one month after the system was installed, a worker began posting the statistics on a bulletin board. The number of rejects steadily declined after the posting. Workers were using the statistics to adjust the process in compeition with other shifts. The overall result was that the system significantly reduced waste and improved overall quality of the comapny's pizza crusts. Inspection systems are presently in development for the firm's other food lines.

SCREENTEST™ FOR VIDEO MONITORS

Video monitor performance has steadily improved during the past twenty years. The computer and graphics industries are demanding higher resolution and less geometric distortion. Yet, the adjustment and inspection procedures employed by the industry have not changed. The methods used to adjust linearity, height, width, focus and other parameters are similar to the methods employed by the television industry thirty years ago.

Manual methods are unsatisfactory today, because humans are being asked to perform measurements that are at the limits of human visual acuity and repeatability. It is difficult for a test technician to perform all of the adjustments satisfactorily and at frequent intervals. Performing the adjustments reliably during an entire eight-hour shift may be impossible.

Octek has developed an automated video monitor inspection and alignment system that is capable of performing common monitor measurements in less than 10 seconds. At this speed, the system can measure the position of a line 50 times more accurately than a human eye aided by a mask or tool. Major benefits of the system are faster monitor inspection, greater measurement accuracy and repeatability that far surpasses human inspection.

Five cameras with precise optics are mounted in a specially designed fixture. One camera scans the center of the monitor and four cameras scan the corners. During the test, the letter "H" is displayed in the center of each monitor as well as in each of the four corners. SCREENTEST scans each of these positions by selecting the appropriate camera. The "H" that appears in each field is processed and a number of features are extracted, such as character position, focus and tilt. The resulting analyses are then combined to extract the desired measurements. (See Figures 5 and 6)

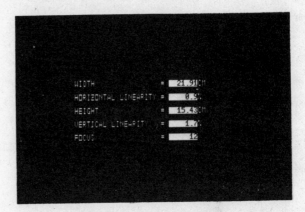

Figure 5: CRT Inspection

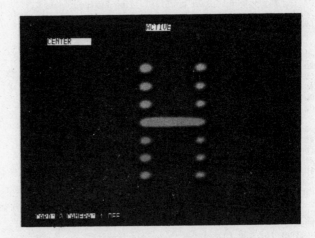

Figure 6: CRT Character Alignment

All of the desired measurements are performed in sequence automatically to conduct a complete test. Each of the measurements is compared to preset test limits. Test results are displayed at the end of the cycle together with their test limits. "Passed" or "Failed" results are highlighted for the test operator.

Adjustments are performed interactively with the SCREENTEST to eliminate human subjectivity. Each of the measurements is performed repeatedly on demand. The preset measurement limits are continuously displayed along with the actual measurement to aid in performing the adjustment. The adjustments are made easier by the magnified images that appear on the SCREENTEST display screen. Table 3 shows how rigorous the inspection criteria can be using the accuracy and reliability provided by machine vision.

MEASUREMENT	METHOD	12" MONITOR ACCURACY
Height		
Top to bottom, left & right sides		0.2%
Width		
Left to right, top & bottom		0.2%
Horizontal Line		
Left to center/right to center		0.2%
Vertical line		
Top to center - bottom to center		0.2%
Center Position		
Center of center character		0.1%
Trapezoidal Distortion		
Top width - bottom width		0.2%
Focus		
Black to white distance		0.1mm
Character Tilt		
Position of dots, top & bottom		0.1mm
Pincushion		
Requires additional cameras		0.2%

Table 3: Video monitor inspection

WHAT'S IN THE BOX?

Content verification of parts or products in packages is one of the most effective automatic vision tasks yet to be implemented. In fact, a standard system, In-Vision is now available for a wide range of content verification applications.

An early initial implementation of In-Vision was done for a major health product and food company. The system is installed on a conveyorized packaging line moving parts through a series of insertion machines, a gluing station and finally out to packing stations.

Twenty-two different food supplements (liquid vitamins) are packaged with dosage/instructional circulars and aseptically wrapped droppers. At rates up to 220 packages per minute, the machine vision system "looks" into the product boxes to verify the presence of all three components; bottle, dropper and circular. (See Figures 7 and 8)

Before the implementation of In-Vision, the manufacturer had four human inspectors positioned along the side of the conveyor to visually verify the package contents. In the manual mode, a marker was used to identify erroneously or partly filled packages. Other humans farther down the line manually removed the defective packages.

The tedium and complexity of human inspection of the packages was compounded by the use of various promotional and standard circulars with each of the 22 product types. Today, In-Vision inspects the packages hour after hour without fatigue, pay raises, coffee breaks or errors. The automated vision system communicates with the packaging line, sending signals to an on-line reject mechanism and timed signals to activate the gluing machine.

Attractive paybacks have been provided by each of the systems that has been presented. They range from less than 5 months in the best case to just under 1 year. Whether for the food industry or electronics, the costs for machine vision have been relatively low - $49,000 to $60,000.

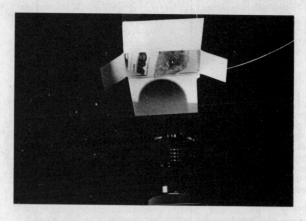

Figure 7: Camera Capturing Character Image

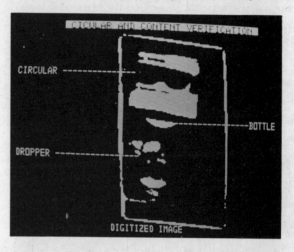

Figure 8: Verification of Circular, Bottle and Dropper

Other successful machine vision applicatins include: robot vision to assemble keyboards, the inspection of printed wiring board edge connectors, the inspection of lead solder, the sortation of nuts and fruits and verification of package seals. There is virtually no limit to the potential applications for machine vision technology in manufacturing.

That machine vision has begun to gain wider acceptance in industry is evidenced by the number of "repeat" orders for such systems as their usefulness becomes increasingly documented.

As machine vision technology continues to be improved and refined, it will surely play an even more dominant role in the upgrading of manufacturing productivity worldwide.

BIOGRAPHY OF DAVID L. HUDSON

David L. Hudson, Vice President of Octek Inc., has eighteen years experience in the high technology industry. At Octek, his responsibilities include marketing, communications, sales and business development.

Mr. Hudson's practical experience has been in machine vision, material handling, bar coding and scanning systems. His knowledge and product development expertise are key to Octek's targeted approach to the food and electronics markets.

Prior to joining Octek, Mr. Hudson has held positions in management and as a Principal with three system companies including General Electric, Distributed Systems and Dennison Intacs.

In addition to his duties in company mangement, Mr. Hudson speaks regularly on machine vision applications and development in inspection and robotics. He has recently had vision technology articles published in CIME, PHOTONIC SPECTRA and IMAGE AND VISION COMPUTING.

Active participation in APICS, IEEE and IIE helps Mr. Hudson stay abreast of industry requirements and the application of new techniques to industrial problems.

INVENTORY STORAGE TECHNIQUES—SPECIFIC, RANDOM ACCESSED OR CHAOS

Katherine A. LeBeau
CTI-Cryogenics

INTRODUCTION

"No, we don't have any inventory problems. We just need more space. You don't understand this business. We're unique."

The very first thing the managers of the three companies we will visit pointed out was their uniqueness. Yet, all three had the same inventory problem. Yes, inventory problem. Isn't "space" merely another item of inventory which needs to be controlled? Too much, too little, or the wrong mix in inventory can be a serious and costly problem.

A company may also make a costly error if more and more real estate is added to the warehousing budget before a concerted effort is made to use what is already available to its fullest potential.

DEFINITIONS

Before looking at the individual companies, I would like to briefly define the inventory storage techniques that the companies were using. Later we will see how the use of two of these techniques is improved while the third is obsoleted.

SPECIFIC OR FIXED LOCATION

This system may be described as the "place for everything and everything in its place" system. The layout drawing serves as a map for material handlers, order pickers and anyone else needing to find something. The space is allocated to a specific item whether there is inventory in it or not. This system is people friendly. Training new hires is simplified and errors are minimized when something is always to be found in the same place if there is any. If this system is so simple, why doesn't everyone use it? Space. This system results in poor space utilization. Nearly twice the amount of space must be allocated to each item than will actually be needed. This is true because your average inventory is 50% of the maximum inventory, but you must maintain space for the maximum even when the area is almost empty just before the receipt of a new lot of material. This system as it is may fit situations where you have a large number of different items going out in small quantities. Modifications to this system do exist and can be more efficient. We will see some examples of these possible modifications.

RANDOM ACCESSED

This system allows for the material being moved into the warehouse to be placed in the first available opening and its location address documented. The goal in a warehouse of this type is to minimize the handling of the material as well as to increase the efficiency of the use of warehouse space. This system is more difficult to implement because of the need for close control and supervision. Locator records must be kept accurate or the material may become lost and a physical inventory may be the only way to find the material and correct the locator records.

Keys to the effective administration of this method are:
* Proper entering of each new receipt into the locator system.
* Noting of all location changes promptly in the locator.
* Maintaining accurate locator records; (cycle counting of locations can help to accomplish this goal).
* Limiting the number of employees authorized to release material and change the locator records to minimize errors.

This system works well with large items, high-volume material movements or with items requiring unusual material handling equipment.

CHAOS

The name of this technique speaks for itself. It really is the lack of any system at all. I liken it to the way materials were stocked in the "Mom and Pop" hardware stores of the past. It is workable only as long as someone remembers where something was put. Space is not used properly as most everything is kept at or below eye level. This is the technique from which growing companies usually feel they must escape. The key is to escape before you lease or buy more space.

THE COMPANIES

The companies in this study, while sharing some of the same problems, vary in size, product line, and operating procedures. Let's visit each one briefly for the purpose of understanding their histories and their operating methods.

The first company is a surgical instrument manufacturer. Originally founded in 1838 as a sole proprietorship, it is now a division of a Fortune 100 company. Their primary space problems involved the storage of finished goods inventory for approximately 2800 different hand instruments and related operating room products.

This finished goods inventory is stored at a single location for world-wide distribution. Products arrive daily from several remote manufacturing locations and from vendors in other parts of the world. The company manufacturers 60% of its products and imports the other 40% as complementary products to their own lines.

In the past the warehouse was located in the center of the corporate headquarters building. It was given this less desirable real estate so that the space around it could be used for light manufacturing and offices. Fixed location was the technique used in this stockroom. As the business grew, this crowded location, with no room allowed for expansion, became a breeding ground for errors, inventory inaccuracies and accidents. Housekeeping and employee morale suffered. Control had been lost. In a company where first-in-first-out is not only desirable but a legal requirement new techniques needed to be introduced.

Before any new techniques were tried, a decision was made to move the finished goods operation from the corporate headquarters building to a separate central distribution facility. This move was accomplished in 1977. The new warehouse located eight miles from the headquarter's site, is a 33,000 square foot single story building. It was a perfect start. The only walls that existed were those forming the office and cafeteria areas located in the northwest corner of the building.

The objectives the company chose for the overall warehouse operations were:
* Provide minimum-cost warehousing, while maintaining service levels.
* Provide better service than the competition, regardless of costs.
* Provide competitive service at the best possible price.
* Maintain a level of housekeeping and storage that would provide a "showcase" for the company's products.

Specific objectives were also noted with regard to the warehouse layout. They were:
* Utilize space to the maximum, especially cube space.
* Provide for efficient materials handling.
* Provide the most economical storage, considering the costs of equipment, space, material damage, and handling labor.
* Provide maximum flexibility to meet changing storage and handling requirements.

A layout drawing was begun. This layout was to be used not only for the move, but as an ongoing reference tool for planning purposes. The company felt that this drawing should provide the following if it was to be of value:

* An effective means for the manager to control where materials are stored.
* A miniature view of the entire warehouse, to be used to plan future programs.

* A guide for the warehouse men telling them where to store incoming materials and where to find outgoing ones.
* A basis for determining storage rates and a means of evaluating storage and cost performance.

When it seemed as though they had planned for every eventuality, the move was made.

The flow of material was smooth. The use of cube had been addressed. This building would use both random accessed storage and a modified version of fixed location. The random accessed technique would work for the bulky, case-packaged products which produced high volume shipments. Manual locator logs were set up. Incoming material was moved into the first available slot in the pallet racks which were set up in the section reserved for these products and logged in. The release date from incoming inspection controlled the lot use sequence for these products.

For the remainder of the product lines, the modification to the fixed location system of the old stockroom was a simple one. The building would operate like a grocery store. To insure first-in-first-out all incoming materials were delivered first to a "bulk" area. This area would hold space for related products in the same general area at all times. Materials would be logged in by date and quantity. As material was needed for the pure fixed location forward picking area, requisitions were drawn from "bulk." Materials were released from the area according to their entry dates in the log book. One person was responsible for this function, backed up by his supervisor. The area was secured. This type of storage had other benefits. It minimized the amount of product open for picking at any one time, and because the product was sealed and counted upon acceptance into bulk, the physical inventory of this area was taken using the log book counts. The auditors would naturally take a sample of the bulked product and request actual counts, but the sampling proved so accurate that soon that requirement was minimized. A physical inventory which used to take three to four days was cut to one and one-half days.

Not only had the operation become more inventory efficient, but there was now time and energy available for employee training programs. These programs included both job training and safety programs. Morale went up and the facility recorded several years of accident-free operation. The operation appeared to be everything that had been planned. It was certainly the most advanced company of those in this study. What could have happened to make them go back to their layout - a growth of 100% over a three year period. Let's leave company #1 for a while and see about #2 and #3.

Company #2 began as a sole proprietorship well-drilling operation in 1915. It is now a multimillion dollar corporation which produces structural steel and concrete filled columns and distributes steel pipe and tubing. The company along with needing a large area in which to operate also needs crane, conveyor and heavy material handling support; some of its products weigh as much as 90 pounds per linear foot and are generally 40 feet long.

The company grew rather slowly until the early 1970s when the grandson of the founder was asked to join the business. He brought with him a business school degree and several years of background in manufacturing. He wanted to see progress. Until his arrival much of the handling of steel was done by brute force. The warehouse consisted of 10,000 square feet of space under roof with one bridge crane and 40,000 square feet "out in the yard." There were times when orders could not be delivered because they simply could not find the material. It was either covered with snow, mud or weeds. Inventories were inflated when duplicate material was obtained to fill these orders. Additional enclosed space was desperately needed. Suitable inventory locating methods and controls needed to be established. Housekeeping rules and safety programs were also nonexistent. Injuries were considered to be part of the job. A plan of attack was formulated. The first move was to add 17,000 square feet to the warehouse. This addition also added two heavy duty bridge cranes and several hundred feet of heavy duty conveyors. Next a warehousing foreman was hired to try to make some sense of the inventory. A layout was done. The goals were surprisingly similar to those at the surgical instrument company.

*   Allow for efficient utilization of space.
*   Permit ready accessibility to materials.
*   Allow some flexibility in the arrangement of stock.
*   Provide for ease in identifying the inventory items.
*   Allow for ease in inspection of inventory condition.

*   Allow for the efficient use of material handling equipment.
*   Provide for ease in counting the material during physical inventories.

Random accessed inventory locations were established and the inventory position was monitored by means of a physical inventory taken weekly and recorded in a log book. The situation improved from a chaotic 40% inventory accuracy record to one of 80% accuracy.

Machine operators and material handlers were made responsible for their areas and machine so that housekeeping and periodic maintenance became part of the daily procedure. As working with heavy materials can be a dangerous business, safety courses were offered. Attendance at these courses was mandatory. Some of the employees rebelled at the changes; some left the company. Those who stayed and those who were hired after the change found that they had a clean, safe and efficient environment in which to perform their tasks. This company too found a great new challenge to contend with - a 100% growth over a two year period. "Space" became a problem again, or so it appeared.

Company #3 also began as a sole proprietorship. The original product was a helicopter design which was sold to the Air Force. The company built approximately 400 of the ships over the life of the contract. During its initial growth period it outgrew its original quarters in an airport hanger and moved into two other facilities. One serves as the corporate headquarters, while the other, an old woolen mill building, has been taken over as the manufacturing plant. This company's primary inventory consists of tooling, fixtures, and master parts which are owned by the customer.

How do they amass this inventory? When they are awarded a contract, it includes the planning, tooling, detail parts and assembly required to produce the product. Each detail part must have a master part and each assembly must have an assembly fixture. Manufacturing Engineering designs the required tooling and submits fabrication orders for these tools to the tooling department and machine shop. Upon completion, all master parts and fixtures are inspected and purchased by the customer. All new tooling is kept in a specific area until it is released to production. When the contract has been completed, the tooling, now dormant, must be stored and maintained until the customer orders its disposal. The customer pays a storage fee for this service.

In addition to arriving at dormant stores because the contract has been completed, tooling may also arrive there for several other reasons. These reasons are categorized as follows:

*   Inactive - Active tools that are currently not being used by production.
*   Change of Method - Tool planner changed method of fabricating the detail part making the tool unusable.
*   Limited Part - Detail part has been placed in a limited status by engineering.
*   Redesigned Part - Engineering redesign has rendered the tool unusable.
*   Cancelled Part - Part is no longer part of the engineering design.

These dormant tools are sometimes stored for long periods of time, but must be available for customer inspection at any time. Storage of tools has been a problem at the company for many years. In-plant warehousing was achieved by using all available space, throughout the plant. Tools and fixtures are randomly stored when not in use. Outside areas and partially finished cellars are used to store larger fixtures. It is common for tooling to remain on the production floor for months after the end of the contract until space is found to house them or until the space they occupy is needed. Government contracts require that the company maintain all tools for up to ten years after the completion of the contract. The reason for the long-term storage is that future spares contracts may be issued or the line may need to be reopened to build more aircraft.

Manual locator systems were used to log in at storage and to aid in the retrieval of the tools. Sometimes the system worked but very often only part of the tool was located; then chaos set in. The hunt was on. Crib attendants and maintenance people had to look for the misplaced tool. These searches resulted in a useless loss of man hours. Lost man hours while annoying in the past, became a luxury the company could not afford in the 1980's when an upswing in business forced them into a study of how they could operate more efficiently. This upswing in business brought with it the need to build and store new and exotic tooling. This tooling could not be handled in the haphazard manner that had been used in the past. Is more "space" the answer?

Is any one of these companies truly unique? To an outsider they appear to have much in common.

* Each of the three companies is Yankee grown.
* Each began as a sole proprietorship.
* Each is now a corporation.
* Each went through a major facilities expansion in the 1970's.
* Each found itself short of space, or so it appeared, in the early 1980's.

Will additional space now, by itself, solve anyone's problems? What are the real problems? In one case, the answer was "yes, additional space is needed". In all cases space management, layout inadequacies, and employee training needed to be addressed.

It was amazing to walk through these companies and look up at 18 to 40 foot high ceilings and find material stacked on the floor. The use of the cube needed to be improved in all facilities. Where pallet racks were being used, more could be added; where shelving was being used, pallet racks would serve better, and where neither was being used some or both were needed. The purchase of material handling equipment and storage racks and shelving is usually cheaper than the cost of acquiring and maintaining additional real estate.

It virtually is impossible to control the rotation of stock when first-in-first-out is desired but last-in-first-out is practiced simply because there is no where to put new material except on top of the old.

GAME PLAN

* Objectives needed to be reaffirmed and restated.

* New layouts needed to be prepared.

* More precise inventory locating systems needed to be created.

* More care was needed in the reporting to the systems.

* Employees needed more job training.

* Housekeeping needed to take on the image of part of the job not something extra.

Company #1 was the leader in the use of cube all along, but they found they could compress their inventory even more by doubling pallet racks in the random accessed stockroom. This did require the purchase of an additional forklift truck with "reach" capability. The cost of this truck was offset by the fact that a new piece of equipment was required anyway to replace an existing truck which no longer functioned properly and that the space created by the new layout saved more in one year than the new equipment cost. It is surprising to note that even though the amount of inventory stored in the building has gone up by 30%, it still does not look chaotic. Space used efficiently coupled with good housekeeping is the key.

They have computerized many of their functions and soon will have their locator systems on the computer as well. Cycle counting is being groomed to replace the annual "wall to wall" physical inventory. Inventory accuracy is reported at 98%.

Safety classes are still conducted and each employee is responsible for the housekeeping in a specified area of the building.

Sales orders are still picked by hand, but by taking advantage of computer analysis of product sales activity, they will soon cut down on the amount of walking an order filler must do. As 10% of the instruments account for 75% of the business. The 10% will be moved to fixed locations at the beginning of the picking aisles. The business has grown but the staff size has remained constant. The operation has been streamlined and is more effective. Management here recognizes that space management cannot only reduce the cost expended for warehousing space, but that controlling inventories can be easier when you go up in your building and not out.

In Company #2 a more effective plant layout has put all materials within reach of one of the three bridge cranes. The main advantage of these cranes is that they can give complete overhead lift service to a large rectangular area. They make possible the moving of items over the top of work and storage areas without regard to aisles. They permit very high utilization of floor space because the aisles can be as narrow as two feet, and working areas do not have to include allowances for floor-based handling equipment such as forklift trucks. Another important advantage of the use of the cranes is that they can handle loads at higher elevations with greater safety and with more efficiency, this permits better utilization of vertical warehouse space. They are also the best equipment for the handling of the unwieldly loads which this company must move. Conveyors now move lengths of steel to and through automatic saws and welding and splicing machines. Needless to say, injuries have gone down.

Standard pallet racks did not suit this operation, but the acquisition of custom made cantilever and "A" frame racks did allow for the more effective use of the cube in the warehouse building. Both of these racks are well suited for storing long narrow shapes such as tubing, bar, and rod stock. The "A" frame is simpler in design, and can be easily constructed in the warehouse from some of their own steel stock if more are needed in the future.

All materials are now housed inside. The only company assets now found "out in the yard" are the company tractors and trailers. The old log book is gone and in its place is a perpetual inventory card file that doubles as the locator system. Material receipts are logged in daily by date and location while cutting lists and customer order quantities are deleted and removed from the locator as the requests move down to the floor. The new layout has helped increase inventory accuracy to 92% and the weekly inventory has been eliminated in favor of cycle counting. With the locator system now in effect, any employee can find and count the inventory and with the new racks in use stock can be rotated as desired. Computerization of the inventory is planned for 1985.

Inventory investment is down by 50% while customer service levels have risen by 85% and they still have plenty of room for growth within the space they now have.

Company #3 did need additional space. At first management proposed building a new warehouse. They recognized that it need only be of shelter-type construction. Plumbing and heating would not be required. However, a careful study of existing buildings showed an area of cellar space which if cleaned out, deepened and floored would solve the space problem quite nicely. A ramp could be constructed connecting production and machine shop areas with this warehouse so that existing material handling equipment could be used. The only additional costs involved would be for racks and shelving.

The most important functions this warehouse was to perform were the following:
* Provide for efficient handling and displaying of the tooling inventory stored there.
* Provide flexibility for needs brought on by additional growth.
* Provide the foundation for complete random accessed location of all tooling whether it be stored in the warehouse or on the production floor.

It took a full year to remodel the area and to move the tooling; cataloging was done as a routine part of the move. The trust in the system is now so high that the only tools that are in the production area are the ones which are necessary for the next 24 hours of operation.

Yes, men were needed to maintain the system, but management feels that, even with one part-time and two full-time employees handling the tooling area, they are still saving money.

Another interesting twist has been added, cycle counting. Yes, they cycle count their tools. Even the customer auditors have been impressed by the results.

Having all of the tools in one area available for study has also been useful to the manufacturing engineers. There have been times when a look at a tool provided an idea for a new set-up where merely seeing documentation did not.

This new warehouse has relieved all of the congestion and chaos and has encouraged good housekeeping and safety practices in the employees which could not have been hoped for in the past.

SUMMARY

Whenever the question of space arises it might be wise to see whether you are using all of your assets wisely.

There is certainly no single formula that will fit all warehousing operations. Each operation must be carefully designed to perform the services needed in the individual company. There are however some factors which should be considered no matter what the application may be. They are as follows:

* Know what you are storing.
* Understand what you have for storage space.
* Establish procedures and controls.
* Take an inventory of your material handling equipment.
* Take an inventory of available storage equipment.
* Review and revise your layout to fit your needs.

When you have completed all of the above, you may wish to consider your other assets. In my mind these are:

* Layout
* Procedures
* Equipment
* Methods of Storage
* People

Your layout needs to assure proper product flow, ease of handling, safety constraints and most important of all it must be three dimensional to ensure proper use of your available cube. Among the basic items to be considered in preparing the layout are:

* What types of items are to be stored, what is their volume, and how are they packaged?
* How they are handled, can they be stacked and how frequently they will need to be retrieved?
* What type of storage equipment is required and what type of locating and inventory control systems are needed?
* Are there any local, federal or industry codes which must be followed?
* Are there any special environmental issues to be resolved.

Another part of the layout process is the determining of the aisle patterns. It is common knowledge that aisles are not usable storage space. It is also true that too few aisles can landlock the inventory and make retrieval impossible. The aisles should be short and straight allowing for ease of use by both man and machine. If it is not possible to provide short aisles then it may be advisable to design in sufficient cross aisles to limit excess travel.

When you are figuring your total storage capacity, your warehouse height dimensions are just as important as your length and width. Furthermore, changing your height dimension has the least effect on building costs. Increased storage height can be one of the best and least expensive means of reducing the unit cost of storage. Until recently it was unusual to find inventory stacked higher than nine feet, keeping it within easy reach of the average man. Today, lift trucks that reach over twenty feet are standard with all manufacturers and are safe and reliable.

Let's compare two buildings.

The problem is to store 200,000 cubic feet of inventory allowing 35% of the total area for aisles. Which building would be most economical?

Building #1 has a usable height of 12 feet. If we allow the 35% for aisle space, we would need 25,641 square feet of space. If the cost is $9.00 per square foot, the cost of the warehouse space would be $230,769.

Building #2, on the other hand, has twice the usable height of 21 feet. Allowing the same 35% for aisle space we would only need 14,652 square feet of space. Resuming the cost remains at $9.00 per square foot, the cost of the warehouse would be only $131,868.

If you are able to store your product in pallet racks and take advantage of the cube, obviously Building #2 would be your choice.

Your procedures need to be well documented so that they are easy to follow. The simple block diagram has been effectively used by two of our three case companies. The aircraft house has decided to use more formal procedures in keeping with its military nature.

Though it is a fact that is not usually recognized, storage equipment is often as important to the total success of the warehouse operation as is the handling equipment. Companies will give more consideration to how the inventory will be moved about as to how it will be stored. They will spend all sorts of time with material handling experts before buying a forklift truck, but when questioned about racks or shelving will reply

"That can wait until we see what things look like". Both need careful advance consideration. In the selection of material handling equipment it may be that some activities will always be best carried out by hand. Equipment should only replace or assist manual work when it is the best alternative.

How should you decide which equipment to buy? Listed below are some guidelines which should be given consideration when you are selecting warehouse equipment.

* What is to be done?
* Will this equipment save money, lives, products?
* Is this the right equipment for the job, or is it a salesman's dream?
* Can operating costs be accurately estimated?

After you have obtained your equipment you need to decide what approach you will take in maintaining it. There are really two alternatives. The first is to make repairs as needed, and the second is to have a preventive maintenance program in operation. If you can afford to be without the equipment for an hour, a day, a few weeks, perhaps the repair-as-needed program will work for you. If on the other hand losing the piece of equipment will mean downtime in the operation, then perhaps you should take the time to set up a periodic maintenance program. This program is not difficult to set up once you know what all your equipment is and you have a file containing all of the documentation necessary for maintaining the equipment. There are many benefits to be reaped from a preventive maintenance program, but the most often discussed are listed below:

* Longer equipment operating life.
* More economical and reliable equipment performance.
* Safer operation.
* Better operator performance due to higher morale.

We defined our methods of storage at the start of this paper and it is important to review that the method to be used will vary with the type of warehouse you are operating. You have many choices, fixed location, random accessed, a combination of both, and yes chaos if you prefer it.

And people, the greatest asset or liability your company can have. The choice in this case is really up to you. A group of employees who are properly trained and motivated to work safely are worth their weight in whatever carries the highest value in today's market. The cost of properly motivating your employees is really quite small when it is compared to the savings and profits your employees can generate. Recognize your workers. Let them know you value them. Let them know you care about their well-being by enforcing safety rules. Take the time to manage by walking around. As was written in the book The One Minute Manager, "Help people reach their full potential, catch them doing something right". Let them know they are free to ask questions and make suggestions. It will pay off.

One final note, good housekeeping not only looks good, but it promotes safety and lifts morale.

ABOUT THE AUTHOR

Katherine A. LeBeau is currently Materials Manager for the Industrial Products Group at CTI-Cryogenics, A Division of Helix Technology Corporation. Kay has previously held the position of Manager of Training, Production and Inventory Control Supervisor, Senior Supervisor, Distribution Services, Production Planner, and buyer in several firms.

Kay holds a B.S. in Transportation and Traffic/Industrial Management from Bryant College and is presently a candidate for an M.B.A. degree.

Kay is active in APICS, currently serving as a Director on the Board of the New Bedford Chapter. She is a past president of the Boston Chapter and has served on the Region I Board as Secretary-Treasurer and Director of Education and Research. She is a member of the APICS Chapter Motivational Counseling Team and has been a seminar and training leader in both Distribution and Production and Inventory Control techniques at various APICS, college and business conferences.

A ROBOTICS PRIMER: FROM THEORY TO APPLICATION

Edward H. Szkudlapski
Scott Paper Company
Savas Ozatalay, Ph.D.
Widener University

INTRODUCTION

The purpose of this paper is to provide the potential robot user with a comprehensive yet simple presentation of the robotics field from theory to application. In the first part, a general overview of the evolving robotics industry, both in the United States and abroad, will be presented. This will be followed by the discussion of topics such as the history of robots, the current robot population, robot technology, and the socio-economic impact of robots. The second part will take a more detailed look at the opportunities and economic justification criteria for the applications of a particular member of the robot family - the industrial robot. Finally, opportunities for robot applications in a particular segment of the manufacturing sector, the sanitary paper industry, will be analyzed in micro terms. Using the "case study" approach, a particular robotics application will be identified and then scrutinized using common financial evaluation techniques.

The overall result of this three-step approach will be to raise the reader's understanding of a current and complex business issue: the selection, justification, and implementation of modern robot technology.

AUTOMATION: THE ROOTS OF ROBOTICS

The roots of today's industrial society go back to the early 1800's where the most important phase of the "industrial revolution" was taking shape. In that period factory automation was introduced. Today, nearly two hundred years later, everybody is engaged in the discussion of a yet new era in industrial structure: the robot. Some see the robot as a science fiction creature that will do anything that human beings do not want to do, others see it as a device of recreation, and still some see it as a threat to their future jobs. To a certain extent all these views may be right.

Robotics is probably best defined as a subdivision of the science of automation. Charles G. Andrew and Dr. William A. Kraus define automation in the following way: "Automation, or high technology,... has five distinguishing characteristics: (1) Automation is a process in and of itself, an integrated system, or more properly a subsystem, having inputs, processes, and outputs; (2) High technology assumes that there are discernible patterns and actions which are capable of routinization; (3) Automation has a feedback loop; (4) There is human control in the sense that a person instructs or programs the system, using judgement; and (5) Automation today has flexibility -- that is, it can do a variety of jobs or tasks and meet a variety of objectives." [1 ;p:44]

The following chart illustrates the proper place of robotics in comparison to automation [8 ;p:36]:

Figure 1: Automation and Robotics

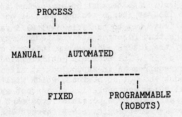

ROBOTICS: THE BEGINNING

The term "robot" was introduced into the English language in 1921 by Karel Capek, a Czechoslovakian playwright. In his play entitled "R.U.R." (Rossum's Universal Robots), Capek wrote of chemically-controlled machines that resembled humans, but worked much harder. He called them "robots", derived from the Czech word "robota", which means "forced labor". Although Capek's robots were externally identical to humans, their simplistic internal design enabled them to work much more efficiently than people, with many fewer distractions. This image of robots, similar to yet very much unlike humans, was accepted and perpetuated in books, plays, and movies for many years. Only since the advent of very unhuman-like industrial robots in the early 1960's has a new image of robots and their capabilities emerged.

In its simplest form, a robot is nothing more than a mechanical device programmed to perform some useful act requiring movement or manipulation. Since the first industrial robot was manufactured in the United States in 1961, robots have been designed to satisfy many diverse needs and as a result come in a wide variety of sizes and shapes.

In an effort to provide some direction to the emerging field of robotics, the Robot Institute of America (RIA), which was founded in Dearborn, Michigan in 1974, proposed the following definition: "A robot is a reprogrammable, multifunctional manipulator designed to move materials, parts, tools, or specialized devices through variable programmed motions for the performance of a variety of tasks". This definition has become widely accepted among both researchers and practitioners in the robotics field.

The RIA definition of a robot contains two key terms, reprogrammable and variety, which distinguish robots from other modern machines. While automated machines are designed to repeat a specialized operation, robots have the capacity to be reprogrammed to perform a number of different tasks. These tasks do not necessarily have to be similar to those for which the robot was initially intended, but can involve a variety of new and different operations.

Estimates of the world robot population as shown in Figure 2 indicate that there are over 27,000 robots (as defined by the RIA) in use in seven countries. Japan, which is regarded as the leader in robotics applications, has over 15,000 robots, followed by West Germany (6,000), and the United States (5,000) [6 ;p:48]. The, the robot population in the United States more than doubled between 1979 and 1981 and according to the estimates obtained by Bache Halsey Stuart Shields Inc. is expected reach to 8,100 by 1985 [11;p:8].

Figure 2: World Robot Population

Country	Human Population (Millions)	Robot Population
Japan	108.0	15,000
W. Germany	59.0	6,000
Sweeden	8.0	700
Norway	4.0	200
Finland	4.7	130
U.S.A.	210.0	5,000
England	56.0	200

Through 1981, nearly 90 % of all robot applications were in manufacturing, particularly in the automotive industry. Spot welding alone accounted for about 40 % of all robot applications. Other common uses of robots were for materials handling (including machine loading and unloading), paint spraying, arc welding, and assembly. More recently, however, robot technology has been extended to many non-manufacturing areas, most notably the scientific, military, and medical fields.

MODERN ROBOT TECHNOLOGY

Allen G. Dunn [4] classifies industrial robots into three categories.
(1) Fixed sequence (non-servo controlled)
(2) Variable sequence (servo-controlled)
(3) Multi-legged robot (functionoid)

The first category contains those robots which are not "servo" controlled. The movement of these robots is powered directly, without a feedback or the capability for self-correction. Such low-technology robots are limited to a relatively small number of program steps and thus provide the user with good repeatability.

The next level of sophistication contains robots of medium technological capability. Robots in this group contain microprocessors or minicomputers as the basic control element and are easily reprogrammed to perform new tasks. These robots utilize servo mechanisms for accurate position and velocity control. Many of the robots in use today fall into this category.

The third and final classification includes only the most sophisticated "high technology" robots. Robots in this category posses all the capabilities of medium-technology robots, but also contain one very important attribute, the external sensors. Sensors provide the robot with information about the external environment, similar to the human senses of sight, touch, hearing, etc.. Applications for multi-sensory robots may be in agriculture, sea, land and space exploration, security, surveillance, and defense.

Regardless of their level of technological sophistication, all robots must possess a common set of attributes in order to be of any practical use. These attributes, as described by Joseph F. Engelberger [5 ;p:5] are:

(1) a hand to grip a workpiece
(2) an arm to move the hand in three planes
(3) a wrist with two or three articulations
(4) sufficient power to move limb and workpiece around
(5) manual controls so that an operator can control limp motions
(6) a memory to store a sequence of instructions
(7) a means of executing a sequence of instructions stored in memory
(8) ability to function at speeds equal to or greater than a person
(9) reliability

The absence of any of these attributes makes a robot of little or no practical value to the user.

Despite all the advances made in robot technology in recent years, today's robots are still limited in their uses. Most are blind, deaf, mute, and clumsy, and have little or no sense of feel. Robots operate successfully when they are properly programmed to do so, but they have no ability to think or act on their own. The common computer notion of "garbage-in garbage-out" is equally applicable to robotics. Therefore, roboticists are concentrating their efforts on increasing the capability of robots to "learn" and "know".

Current research, however, is not limited to efforts to improve a robot's intelligence. Many areas of a robot's "anatomy" are being explored as well. Robots, for example, although much heavier than humans, have a much poorer strength-to-weight ratio, which causes them to be very energy inefficient and costly. Not only are robot arms inefficient, but they are also very rigid. Efforts are underway to design arms which are more compatible (lightweight and flexible) with modern sensing and control techniques.

The dexterity and mobility of robots are also being improved continually. Future robot arms will allow smoother motion by providing more degrees of freedom, and new end-effector design will replicate the flexibility of the human hand as roboticists try to develop a general, all-purpose robot hand.

Improved mobility is another specialized area of research. Many factors are interrelated in researching robot mobility -- intelligence, energy efficiency, memory capacity, and strength-to-weight ratios. Other developments in robot configuration are anticipated, such as providing the robot with two hands or two arms and making them smaller to take up less floor space.

Finally, efforts are underway to standardize robotic subsystems, improve robot-control languages, and distribute intelligence. Robot subsystems need to be standardized in order to integrate them successfully with other modern technologies such as computer-aided design (CAD), computer-aided manufacturing (CAM), and flexible manufacturing systems.

Although the commercial success of all the mentioned research and development efforts cannot be guaranteed, a great leap in coming years in the capability of robots is almost a certainty. Researchers and users alike hope that the technological gains resulting from ongoing research efforts will be a higher standard of living and an improved quality of work life.

SOCIO-ECONOMIC IMPACTS OF ROBOTS

Many reasons have been posed for the sluggish response of the United States to implementing robot technology despite a greatly heightened interest level. Among the most commonly cited causes [9 ;p.359-362] are: management resistance, plentiful supply of labor, lack of understanding and technical knowledge, and people's fears of being displaced.

The greatest impact of robotics in the United States so far has been in jobs that are undesirable to human workers because they are monotonous, repetitive, and/or in harsh environments. Most proponents of robotics are optimistic that the proliferation of robots will be beneficial for society. The majority believe that robots will actually create more jobs than they will eliminate. However, George Brosseau of the National Science Foundation is more cautious and questions "In the past whenever a new technology has been introduced, it has always generated more jobs than it displayed. But we don't know whether that is true of robot technology. There is no question but that new jobs will be created, but will there be enough to offset the loss?" [9 :p.361].

There has been little agreement as to the number of workers that will be replaced by robots. A comprehensive study undertaken at Carnegie Mellon University in 1981 estimated that servo-controlled robots could replace up to 3 million out of 8 million operative workers in manufacturing over the next twenty years. On the other hand, Peter Blake, in a study performed at the University of Michigan for the RIA, reported that by 1990 only 440,000 jobs currently held by human workers will be filled by industrial robots. Of those displaced, most will be retrained by their employers and only 22,000 may actually lose their jobs. [7 :p.5]

Robots will contribute to a safe workplace by taking over many dull and hazardous jobs, and may free workers for better jobs. New jobs and occupations will likely emerge as a result of introduction of robot technology.

One of the more controversial and emotional issues emerging from the expansion of robot technology is the retraining of displaced workers. The retraining problem is compounded by the fact that the first workers displaced by robots are generally the most unskilled and difficult to retrain.

Obviously, business and labor will have to work closely together to reduce the impact of introducing new technologies, or the inherent advantages of using robots may be wasted. Although the impact of robots on society cannot be predicted with certainty, there are certain economic factors at work which will be instrumental in forecasting future trends. These include the cost of robots, prevailing labor rates, pressures of foreign competition, and the ability to use robots effectively after purchase.

ECONOMIC JUSTIFICATION OF ROBOTS

As robots have become more capable and more widely available, increasing numbers of decision-makers have been forced to investigate for the first time the potential benefits resulting from a capital investment in robot technology. Robots are attractive is industrial uses for many of the same reasons as traditional fixed machines: dependability, repeatability, sturdiness, insensitivity to the elements, etc. Should then the cost justification process for an industrial robot pattern that for an investment in any other machine? According to most roboticists, the answer is no. To do so would be to overlook the additional capabilities brought by a robot to a given application. Robert L. McMahon, Jr. believes that robotics justification must be approached appropriately. "You must look at things besides just direct cost, which is the traditional way to justifiy capital investments. ... Many things that robotics and new technology and the factory of the future address are indirect cost areas"[10:p. 56]. The economic justification of a robot therefore requires an in-depth look at all of the factors, both obvious and not so obvious, which will be affected by the installation and operation of a robot system.

Any analysis of a possible investment in a "steel collar" worker must begin with a through evaluation of all the direct and indirect costs associated with its purchase and installation. The initial capital outlay varies with the size and complexity of the particular robot selected, ranging from $6,000 to $120,000 or more. Figure 3 provides a summary of recent robot prices [2 :p. 32]. Added to the purchase price must be the cost of engineering and installing the robot system, freight from the manufacturer's facility, and applicable taxes. Depending on the situation, spare parts may also be purchased "up front". Special tooling and interface equipment needed to operate the robot should also be included. Experience has shown that the cost of the robot alone accounts for only thirty to fifty percent of the actual cost of a robot system.

Figure 3: Approximate Prices of Robots

Degrees of Freedom	Mechanical (Limit Switches)	Programmable by Tracing Movements	Programmable With Separate Software
1 - 3	$ 6,000 - $13,000	--	--
4 - 5	$13,000 - $30,000	$17,000 - $25,000	$ 60,000 - $100,000
6 +	--	$25,000 - $90,000	$ 65,000 - $120,000

On the other hand, two factors should be considered which may actually reduce the cost of the initial outlay. The first is the salvage value, if any, of the equipment that the robot will replace. The other is the financial benefit resulting from existing investment tax credit regulations.

An analysis of post-installation operating costs is very important. These costs should be properly estimated and compared with the costs of the labor and/or equipment replaced. Operating costs may be segregated into four broad categories: energy, maintenance, depreciation, and other. While labor costs have risen sharply in recent years, robot operating costs have remained relatively stable. According to industry reports, the only component of a robot's operating costs that has risen significantly in the last ten years is energy [2 :p. 32].

In analyzing a robot installation, particular consideration must be given to maintenance costs. Automotive industry users report that annual maintenance costs often exceed ten percent of the total initial purchase price. These costs have also become a minor stumbling block in robot justification because they are highest for the first robot. Most maintenance cost components, such as the wages of service personnel, are reduced only as they are spread over additional units.

Once the major cost components have been described, the benefits side of the justification ledger is analyzed. Historically, the most frequently cited and significant economic benefit of a robot installation is the reduction in labor costs. This is not surprising, since the thrust behind the development of robot technology has been to design, develop, and make commercially available a mechanical alternative for human workers. However, to stop at labor savings would be a big mistake since many other economic benefits have been confirmed by experience. In fact, a recent survey of industrial robot users has revealed that the attention given to the flexibility of robot systems has not gone for naught. Results of the survey indicate that manufacturing flexibility is now the key benefit sought by industrial robot users, with the reduction in labor costs being second [12].

The further benefits of a robot can conveniently be segregated into two categories: those impacting on productivity and those affecting material cost. Simply defined, productivity is the ratio of output to input. It can be measured in countless ways, for example units per manhour, depending on the peculiar requirements of the manufacturing firm. In addition to the reduction in direct labor already mentioned, many factors related to productivity are favorably affected by robots. Robots can [6 :p.48-49]:
(1) reduce or eliminate the need for a backup work force to cover absenteeism, training, and turnover
(2) lower the costs of maintaining a personnel department (and other staff departments) due to fewer workers
(3) reduce the number of machines or work stations necessary to maintain a given level of production
(4) increase output without purchasing additional equipment or incurring overtime costs.
(5) lessen floor space requirements and extend the useful life of an existing facility

(6) reduce costs of complying with safety and environmental regulations
(7) decrease the number of worker's compensation claims
(8) simplify operations by completing work sequences that human workers would be unable to perform
(9) extend the useful life of tooling and related equipment or parts

In the area of material savings, robots can be equally beneficial. Robots reduce costs because they are able to:
(1) reduce the number of rejected parts and amount of wasted material
(2) minimize the need for reworking sub-standard parts
(3) simplify inspection and testing procedures
(4) reduce inventories of raw materials and work-in-process
(5) reduce overruns, reorders, or duplicate set-ups due to shortages
(6) minimize delays in shipments to customers and partial shipments
(7) improve product quality and eliminate variability

While the preceding lists are not comprehensive, they do represent a sampling of additional benefits (cost savings) that should be included in the economic justification for a robotics installation. There are other factors peculiar to a given application that can be identified and incorporated to provide a thorough cost/benefit analysis.

Although this analysis is simplistic, it is intended to reinforce an important guideline in robotics justification -- that direct labor savings are just "the tip of the iceberg". For example, Kelly suggests that [6 :p.48] "Perhaps the greatest contribution of robotics to date is that it has been a very effective catalyst and driving force for making engineers and managers rethink the ways that they have been doing things".

Once the costs and benefits have been thoroughly analyzed, the "attractiveness" of a robot project must somehow be determined relative to other uses for the same capital. Such an analysis usually involves one or more of the commonly-used financial evaluation techniques: payback period, net present value, or internal rate of return. The techniques used differ with the individual firm depending on managerial preference, regulations, etc.

CASE STUDY: SANITARY PAPER INDUSTRY

The sanitary paper industry encompasses many degrees of technological sophistication. It is an industry in which fifty-year-old paper machines run side-by-side with high-speed machines employing modern, state-of-the-art technologies. It is a capital intensive industry as well, which requires a heavy investment in paper machines, converting equipment, energy, and other facilities. The result is a potpourri of manual, semi-automatic, and automatic operations which must be integrated in a cost-effective manner.

Any industrial situation which possesses the following characteristics is a likely candidate for robotization:
    or uncomfortable working conditions; repetitive tasks; difficult handling; multi-shift operation. A number of situations that satisfy these conditions can be identified in the sanitary paper industry.

One potential robotic application is in the "transfer of product". When they are ready to be converted into a final product, napkins, for example, large rolls of papern stock are mounted into the unwind stands of a folding machine, or "folder". A common folder design involves three parent rolls in series, each the width of an unfolded napkin. The three sheets pass through the folder simultaneously, first over bars which orient the sheets properly, then down over pans which give them the correct fold. After the three-sheet-thick web is folded, it is slit into individual napkins which are discharged from the folder through three separate two-napkins-wide lanes. The napkins are then transferred to a wrapping machine that wraps and seals individual packs. The packs proceed to a unit which accumulates the appropriate number of packs, orients them properly, and loads them into a corrugated case. The case moves along a conveyor belt into a case sealer, which applies glue to the top and bottom flaps and seals them, and then to the warehouse for storage.

The operation just described can range from fully automated to labor intensive depending on the age and the sophistication of the mechanical equipment. The first phase in which folded napkins are produced as the large rolls are unwound and passed through the folder is an automatic process. The second phase, in which napkins are transferred

from the folder discharge lanes to the wrapper's infeed
conveyor belt, varies in degree of sophistication from
fully-automated mechanical transfer to a manual
operation. Similarly, the loading of packs from the
wrapper's discharge belt into cases, or third phase,
may be automatic or manual. The case glueing and sealing
step is typically automatic. The two transfer points
described (the second and third phases) are often manual
because of mechanical intricacies or marketing demand,
which may require that different brands be produced on the
same napkin line. However, advances in the capabilities of
industrial robots-- particularly in their flexibility and
programmability-- make such transfer operations good
candidates for automation using robot technology.

Typically one of the operators working on a line
producing napkins is responsible for manually transferring
napkins from the discharge lanes of the folder to the
conveyor leading to the packing unit. An opportunity exists
for automating this operation by using a robot. The
transfer operation simply involves grabbing a pre-counted
(by the folder) pack of napkins, lifting and turning it,
and placing the pack properly on an indexing belt conveyor
that leads to the pack-wrapping unit. This is a simple,
repetitive motion, which must be sustaines ad long as the
folder is running.

Given the range and frequency of motions required a
cylindirical-coordinate robot with six axes of motion is
recommended. A servo-controlled robot should be used to
preserve future operating flexibility. Based on current
prices and industry averages, costs of purchasing,
installing, and operating such a robot are summarized in
Figure 4.

Figure 4: Cost of Robotics Application for Product
        Transfer

Initial Cash Outlay
Purchasing price
    Robot (manipulator) $ 25,000
    Gripper   19,600
    Controls and software   40,000

                               $ 84,600

Engineering, Installation, Debugging $ 20,000
Special Tooling and Fixtures   15,000
Spare Parts   8,500
Training   5,000

                TOTAL $ 133,100

Annual Costs
Operating, Programming, Energy $ 48,000
Maintenance
    Scheduled $ 7,800
    Unscheduled   6,000

                                 $ 13,000

                TOTAL $ 61,800

The major benfits of such a replacement will be the
labor cost savings. Assuming that direct and indirect labor
cost savings are $ L per hour and that the department
operates three shifts per day, five days per week, than
total annual savings will be X= 6240xL.

Now that the benefits and costs of the application
have been identified, the "attractivenss" of the investment
relative to other potential uses for the same capital must
be determined. Two of the most commonly used finacial
evaluation techniques are payback period and the internal
rate of return. The payback period is the simpler of the
two methods and provides a quick measure of the amount of
time that will elapse before the resulting savings will
offset the required initial cost. This period is usually
expressed in years. Typically, a two or three year payback
period is considered to be acceptable.

Bublick provides a general formula for calculating the
payback period for a proposed robot installation [3 :p.6]:

$$Y = \frac{C}{WS +RS +AS +DE(R) -RM -RO}$$

Y = Payback period, years
C = Total first cost (robot, accessories,
     controls)
WS = Wages and benefits saved
RS = Annual robot savings (material, quality,
     energy, OSHA)
AS = Annual savings (operating and maintenance)
DE = Robot depreciation expense
R = Tax rate
RM = Annual robot maintenance costs
RO = Annual robot operating and programming costs

Using the data provided for this particular case and
assuming straight-line depreciation, a useful life of eight
years, and a tax rate of fifty percent, the payback period
at different labor cost savings per hour is shown in
Figure 5.

Figure 5: Payback Period and Internal Rate of Return

Hourly Labor Cost Savings	Payback Period	Internal Rate of Return
$ 15	2.716	17 %
16	2.409	24 %
17	2.165	36 %
18	1.965	44 %
19	1.800	
20	1.660	
25	1.195	
30	0.933	

As shown in Figure 5, for an hourly labor cost savings of $
18+ will result in a two year payback period. The second
common financial evaluation technique is to calculate the
internal rate of return (IRR) of a proposed investment. The
IRR is the discount rate that equates the present value of
future cash flows to the cost of investment. If the IRR
exceeds the firm's marginal cost of capital, which s
defined as the cost of borrowing its next dollar or
capital,then the project should be accepted. For the case
presented, the IRR is calculated for different levels of
hourly cost savings and the results are shown in Figure 5.
For hourly costs over $19 per hour, the IRR exceeds 50 %.
Assuming that the firm's marginal cost of capital is lower
than 17%, this project should be accepted if the hourly
labor costs savings are $ 15.

SUMMARY AND CONCLUSIONS

As defined at the outset, the intent of this paper was
to raise the reader's (and potential user's) understanding
of a current and complex business decision--the selection,
justification, and implementation of modern robot
technology. The level of presentation was directed to the
first-time user who is looking for a simple yet
comprhehensive discussion of the robotics field from theory
to application. Admittedly, no paper of this length could
exhaustively cover all of the topics addressed. However, a
number of important conclusions can and should be drawn
from the material presented:
  (1) robots will have a significant social and economic
      impact on our society
  (2) the number of robots in use will grow as the user's
      knowledge and understanding of robot technology
      improves
  (3) robots will become increasingly more visible in
      non-manufacturing applications
  (4) the next generation of robots will be significantly
      more capable and sophisticated than today's models
  (5) robots will never be able to replace humans
Obviously, no one can predict with certainty what the
impact of robots on our society will be. Leading studies
to-date have been inconsistent in forecasting the number of
jobs that will be affected by the anticipated robotics
boom. In fact, there is much speculation as to whether the
proliferation of robots will actually increase or decrease
the number of jobs available to the human labor force.

Proponents and opponents alike, however, expect the resulting socio-economic impact to be significant.

As potential users become better versed in the capabilities of modern robot technology, the number of robot installations should increase rapidly. In this regard, a parallel can be drawn between the computer and the robot. There was much fanfare when mainframe computers were introduced, but the actual benefits of this technological breakthrough were first limited primarily to those large organizations that had the resources available, both human and financial, to harness and apply the computer's tremendous capabilities. As research, development, marketing, and manufacture of computers continued, however, many more people were exposed to the benefits to be gained from the use of computers. Interest in computers has continued to grow and with the advent of the personal computer has reached an all-time high. Is it unrealistic then to imagine an era, in the not too distant future, marked by personal robots?

The greater the number of people that are exposed to robots, the more opportunity there is for their creative application. Researchers and practitioners alike are already extending the benefits of robots that had been previously limited to industrial users into a number of new areas. Space exploration, undersea mining, medical uses, and the military are just a few examples. The diversity of future applications might only be limited by the imagination and ingenuity of users themselves.

Vision, proximity and tactile sensing, hearing, and two-way communication are just some of the areas currently receiving considerable attention among researchers and academicians. While some of these new capabilities are still limited to laboratory experimentation and testing, others are becoming commercially available. These new robot senses will present potential users with an even greater array of new opportunities for application. Like other technological breakthroughs, such as airplanes and computers, continued research and development efforts will lead to increasingly more powerful and sophisticated generations of robots.

Despite all their newfound capabilities and uses, robots will never be able to completely replace the human worker. The human senses are so refined that they are not likely to be reproduced in the foreseeable future. Perhaps the biggest advantage of human workers is their ability to learn. Robots are still decades away from replacing the human capability to change or react to a dynamic environment.

These are just a few of the conclusions that may be drawn from the material researched and presented, although many other observations can be made about the emerging robotics industry. Despite all the speculation and uncertainty about robots and their future, one thing appears likely-- that we as a society will have to adapt to an increasing number of robots in our midst.

REFERENCES

[1] Charles G. Andrew and William A. Kraus, "The Human Face of Automation", P&IM Review and APICS News, July 1983, pp:44-46.

[2] Barry Bronstein et al, "Robotics: Its Technology, Applications, and Impacts", Battelle Technical Inputs to Planning/Report No. 27, March 1982

[3] Timothy Bublick, "The Justification of an Industrial Robot", AFP/SME Technical Paper, 1977

[4] Alan G. Dunn, "Industrial Robots: What are the True Costs?", APICS 1983 Conference Proceedings,pp:171-175

[5] Joseph F. Engelberger, Robotics in Practice, American Management Association, 1980

[6] Robert T. Kelly, "A Systems Approach to Staying Competitive", Assembly Engineering, May 1983, pp:46-54

[7] Gail M. Martin, "Industrial Robots Join the Workforce", Occupational Outlook Quarterly, Fall 1982, pp:2-11

[8] "Robotics... Start Simple", Mack Corporation, P&M Review and APICS News. June 1983. pp:36-38

[9] Jean Rosenblatt, "The Robot Revolution", Editorial Research Reports, Vol I, No. 18, May 14, 1882, pp:347-363

[10] Rita R. Schreiber, "Robotics Roundtable", Robotics Today, August 1983, pp:54-59

[11] The Robots are Coming and They are Bringing a New Industrial Revolution",Barrons, April 11, 1983, pp:8-9,37

[12] Willard Wilks, Technology Forecasts, Volume 15, No 9, September 1983, p:7

ABOUT AUTHORS

Ed Szkudlapski is currently Distribution Operations Manager at Scott Paper Company in Philadelphia. Ed joined Scott Paper in 1979 following his graduation from the Pennsylvania State University with a Bachelor of Science Degree in Industrial and Management Science Engineering. He has his MBA degree from Widener University. Ed is a member of the Institute of Industrial Engineers.

Savas Ozatalay is a Professor and the Head of the Department of Management at Widener University. Prior to joining Widener, he worked at University of Chicago, Middle East Technical University, and University of Illinois-Chicago Circle. He has a B.Sc. in economics and statistics from the Middle East Technical University, and M.A. and Ph.D. from Northwestern University. Dr. Ozatalay holds memberships in APICS (Southern Delaware Valley Chapter), ORSA, TIMS, American Economic Association, and the Project Management Institute. He has published in the production/operations management area.

THE ROLE OF P&IC IN ENGINEERING CHANGE MANAGEMENT

Andru M. Peters
Centigram Corp.

INTRODUCTION

The role of the Production and Inventory Control Practitioner in Engineering Change management is an important function. This role is a direct involvement in the analysis, agreement, and implementation of the engineering change into the manufacturing process. The P&IC Practitioner is the individual with TOTAL responsibility in making the approved engineering change a reality. The objective of this paper is to present to the reader, the author's experience in implementing the engineering change into the manufacturing process.

The topic areas to be addressed in this paper include: First, a review of the kinds of engineering documentation a P&IC Practitioner will encounter in their firm and their involvement with these various documents. Secondly, the activities and responsibilities of the practitioner in the analysis and implementation of the engineering change will be addressed. The third area addressed by this paper is the involvement and interface by the Practitioner with those functional areas who may have a direct/indirect interest in the engineering change being reviewed. Finally, the Fourth area to be developed is the study of the reasons for change and the role the Practitioner must play in analyzing these reasons in preparing the effectivity date of implementation, based on the manufacturing environment and personality trait displayed by their firm.

BACKGROUND

In reviewing, analyzing and implementing the engineering change, the Practitioner must understand the concepts and philosophies of engineering changes. One can define the definition of an engineering change as: "A revision to a standard, released document such as bill of materials, parts lists, or drawings generated and approved by the Engineering Department and identified by a document identification control number. Changes may be classified by:

* Safety changes,
* functional changes, or
* cost revision changes.

Other classifications of change may vary from company to company. Some firms list their changes as MAJOR, to indicate complex changes, or MINOR, to indicate an easy incorporation of a change. A large number of companies will use the guidelines established in DOD-STD-480A and expand for their use and identify the class of change by using the Roman numerals I, II and III. This identification is defined by:

* CLASS I Effects form, fit, or function and the rule of interchangeability is affected. This class may be further sub-divided into EMERGENCY or URGENT changes.

* CLASS II Incorporates change at the ease of manufacturing. This may be called a ROUTINE change.

* CLASS III A document change only, and no material is affected by this type of change.

The understanding of the definition of change and what the company's definition of the classifications for change, must be understood by the Practitioner in order to effectively review and analyze the engineering change as submitted for approval. This understanding will allow the Practitioner to develope the appropriate materials action in support of the class of change noted on the document. Refer to Figure 3 which illustrates typical kinds of action required for the various material locations.

In reviewing the various types of engineering change documents, the P&IC Practitioner must understand which part of the Documentation Release and Change Cycle the applicable document comes under. Documentation changes will fall into three categories:

* RELEASE Which is the initial release of the new part number and its' related documents which include: Drawings, specification sheets, Bill of Materials, Standard Operating Procedures, Production processes,etc.

* CHANGE Which is the major reason for engineering changes in which a problem has been identified and an agreeable solution is required to correct this problem and formally documented as an approved change.

* IMPLEMENTATION Which is the physical incorporation of the change into the manufacturing process.

Figure 1 illustrates the categories of change and types of documents which may be used in recording pertinent data in support of the reason for change.

With this understanding and background, the P&IC Practitioner can intelligently review the engineering change as written and provide the appropriate material actions, such as release, cancel, or reschedule orders, scrap or rework items, to effectively implement the change into the manufacturing process.

TYPES OF DOCUMENTS USED

There are many kinds of engineering change documents that may be utilized in recording data in support of the engineering change. The names and use of these documents varies from company to company. Figure 1 illustrates a sampling of engineering documents which may be used in documenting an engineering change within the change cycle to provide an overview in documenting a problem into an approved engineering change.

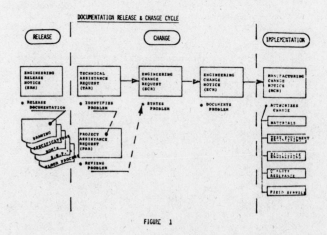

FIGURE 1

In reviewing the various documents used in documenting a change, the sequence illustrated in the documentation release and change cycle will be used.

American Production & Inventory Control Society

RELEASE

* Engineering Release Notice (ERN) This is
  the initial engineering document which is
  used to release a part number for the first
  time and is usually supported by drawings,
  specifications sheet, bills of material,etc.
  The Practitioner prior to sign-off of this
  engineering document, must create an item
  master record data sheet which includes the
  part number, description, unit of measure,
  lead times, standard cost data, and other
  data necessary to support a computerized
  data base.

CHANGE

* Technical Assistance Request (TAR) This document is used to identify and document a
  potential problem involving a released part
  number. Generally, this affects a process
  related problem and on few occassions, impacts materials.

* Project Assistance Request (PAR) This document is used when Design Engineering action
  and assistance is required and is usually
  prompted by an approved TAR. Engineering,
  upon their review of the perceived problem,
  will initiate an ECR if the problem has been
  determined valid.

* Engineering Change Request (ECR) This document is the most commonly used document to
  state the problem in presenting the change
  before the Engineering Change Review Board.
  The ECR can be generated by any individual,
  but must require engineering approval prior
  to submission to the Change Review Board.
  The Practitioner should be involved in the
  review of this engineering request, in that
  preliminary investigation and data gathering
  may be required to assist in the materials
  analysis and financial impact in determining
  if the change is economically desireable.
  This of course is tempered by the class of
  change desired, in which Class I change
  would make the action mandatory and required
  which would definitely have a financial impact to the manufacturing process. The
  Practitioner must bear in mind a Class I
  change is in most cases required as a result
  of a safety or major functional problem with
  the product and must be reacted upon accordingly. A Class II change would be reviewed
  with the incorporation of the change taking
  place with the next work order or the next
  purchase order.

* Engineering Change Notice (ECN) This document is the final approved engineering change
  and is signed off by the Change Review Borad.
  The document is used to notify Manufacturing
  of a change to the standard document and
  documents the problem as identified by the
  use of the aforementioned documents. Some
  companies use this document to incorporate
  the change into the manufacturing process
  and initiate the material changes required
  to support the ECN disposition. The Practitioner, upon signing off of this document,
  has made all of the material related activity
  analysis and upon final approval, initiates
  all of the appropriate activities to implement the change. There are industry applications in which there exists two data bases
  Engineering and Manufacturing in which when
  upon approval of the ECN document, is for-
  warded to Manufacturing Data Control who then
  initiates the MCN form.

IMPLEMENTATION

* Manufacturing Change Notice (MCN) This document when used in a seperate data base environment, upon receipt of the ECN, transfers
  data into manufacturing terms which also includes all of the detail instructions for

incorporating the change into the manufacturing process. The Practitioner plays an important part in affecting changes to work
orders, purchase orders, rework/scrap of
material per the instructions of the disposition, serial number effectivity and the
date for implementation.

* Engineering Change Order (ECO) This engineering change document is widely used by
  many companies and in this article presentation would encompass both the ECN and MCN
  documents as described in this article. In
  all three documents, ECN,MCN and ECO, the
  P&IC Practitioner has a large role in determ-
  ing the effectivity of implementation of the
  change into the Manufacturing process.

* Field Change Order (FCO) This document is
  used when product in the field must be
  upgraded per the instructions of the ECO.
  The FCO will contain abbreviated instructions
  on how to incorporate the change, a parts
  list of materials required to perform the
  change in the field and instructions on how
  to dispose the material removed as a result
  of the change.

OTHER

* Engineering Parts List This list is used in
  conjunction with the applicable drawing and
  the references within the drawing correspond
  to applicable items as listed in the parts
  list.

* Manufacturing Parts List This list is constructed as how the product is manufactured
  and is the basis for the generation of kit
  lists used for picking of manufacturing work
  orders.
       NOTE: It should be noted, that the
              Practitioner should insure that
              the engineering parts list is
              in concert with the associated
              drawing before it is converted
              into a manufacturing parts
              list.

* Materials Inventory Analysis Worksheet An
  inventory analysis worksheet should be utilized in reviewing and recording data in preparation of setting the effectivity date and
  determining the materials activities required
  and the cost of incorporating this change.
  This worksheet should become part of the
  final approved engineering change package
  when the document, ECN,MCN, or ECO, is released. The Practitioner will, upon release,
  place in effect all of the necessary activities to comply with the instructions and effectivity date as established.

     These are examples of kinds of engineering
change documentation that may be used in identifying, reviewing, stating and documenting the
problem. By understanding the use and purpose
of these documents, the Practitioner can effectively analyze the proposed change to determine
the effectivity date.

PRACTITIONERS' ACTIVITIES AND RESPONSIBILITIES

     With an understanding of the kinds of en-
gineering change documents used and the interpretation of the classes of change, the Practitioner can now analyze and determine the
material activities required to facilitate the
change as approved. One of the major responsibilities of the Practitioner, which many firms
call an Engineering Change Coordinator, is to
control the data and information as presented
and to insure the item master data base has been
updated in accordance with the language of the
engineering change. In addition, another major
responsibility of the Practitioner is to gather
and analyze inventory availability data for effective implementation of the approved change.

Typical activities performed by the Practitioner in analyzing the engineering change includes a review of material availability of gross inventory impact of:

* purchase orders,
* work orders,
* stock,
* material reject bond stock,
* finished goods, and
* field inventory.

Other analysis of data would include a re-review of lead times, standard cost data, as well as other pertinent data required to maintain an accurate item master data base.

Based on the class of change, the Practitioner with the inventory availability position data, refers to the Materials/Manufacturing Calendar, refer to Figure 2, determines the effectivity by week and serial number. This calendar should be prepared for one year, similar to the Master Schedule horizon, and prepared in concert with the Master Schedule.

This is another factor, many times overlooked, as a reason to minimize the number of changes to the Master Schedule. In addition to the most common known reason for schedule stability, minimize inventory replanning and rescheduling, the establishing of the calendar to establish future serial number effectivity and date implementation would stabilize configuration control guidelines or the data as pre-determined would be distorted and create numerous material related problems as a result of the many schedule changes. An example, using Figure 2, of effectivity problems would be reviewing a change package in Week 8436 and based on the class of change and inventory position, the effectivity was set for October, Week 8501, serial number 1259. The Master Schedule was changed in July by an increase of 100 units, thus causing the change to be implemented much sooner than the material plan was set for. The serial number of the unit and the corresponding effectivity week do not correspond and thus material availability problems would occur. Additional purchasing activities would have to be generated against the affected part number as called out in the engineering change.

Materials/Manufacturing Planning Calendar

MONTH	MANUFACT. WEEK	WEEK BEG.	SERIAL NUMBER	MONTH	MANUFACT. WEEK	WEEK BEG.	SERIAL NUMBER
JUN (37)	8436 8437 8438 8439	6/4 6/11 6/18 6/25	1084 1093 1102 1111	DEC (60)	8510 8511 8512 8513	12/3 12/10 12/17 12/24	1369 1384 1399 1414
JUL (48)	8440 8441 8442 8443 8444	7/2 7/9 7/16 7/23 7/30	1121 1130 1139 1148 1157	JAN (70)	8514 8515 8516 8517 8518	12/31 1/7 1/14 1/21 1/28	1426 1443 1457 1471 1485
AUG (50)	8445 8446 8447 8448	8/6 8/13 8/20 8/27	1169 1181 1194 1206	FEB (70)	8519 8520 8521 8522	2/4 2/11 2/18 2/25	1499 1516 1534 1551
SEP (40)	8449 8450 8451 8452	9/4 9/10 9/17 9/24	1219 1229 1239 1249	MAR (70)	8523 8524 8525 8526	3/4 3/11 3/18 3/25	1569 1586 1604 1621
OCT (50)	8501 8502 8503 8504 8505	10/1 10/8 10/15 10/22 10/29	1259 1269 1279 1289 1299	APR (80)	8527 8528 8529 8530 8531	4/1 4/8 4/15 4/22 4/29	1639 1655 1671 1677 1693
NOV (60)	8506 8507 8508 8509	11/5 11/12 11/19 11/26	1309 1324 1339 1354	MAY (90)	8532 8533 8534 8535	5/6 5/13 5/20 5/27	1719 1741 1764 1786

FIGURE 2

The other overlooked problem is that the configuration control guidelines would be in contradiction with the established effectivities

and the Engineering and Quality Assurance functions would have problems in interpreting the efficient and effective implementation of the change. This would also affect the field inventory if the change was a Class I change.

The last activity to be performed by the Practitioner are the desired actions required to implement the approved changes. Actions required by Class change are:

CLASS I	* close workorders,
	* cancel purchase orders,
	* change purchase orders,
	* open rework work orders,
	* scrap material,
	* RTV material,
	* open new work orders,
	* re-identify stock,
	* update computer database,
	* field retrofit required, and
	* expedite/de-expedite materials.
CLASS II	* change purchase orders,
	* cancel purchase orders,
	* open rework work orders,
	* scrap materials,
	* RTV material,
	* re-identify stock,
	* update computer database, and
	* expedite/de-expedite materials.
CLASS III	* update computer database.

A summary of activities required by change classification is illustrated in Figure 3.

ENGINEERING CHANGE IMPLEMENTATION MATRIX

CHANGE CLASSIFICATION	AREAS REQUIRING ACTION				
	ON ORDER	STOCK	WIP	F/G	FIELD
I	YES	YES	YES	YES	YES
II	YES	YES	NO	NO	NO
III	NO	NO	NO	NO	NO

FIGURE 3

INTERDEPARTMENT INTERFACES

The interface of the Practitioner with other functional departments include those functions represented on the Engineering Change Review Board. The involvement by the Practitioner with these functional areas varies with the Class of change of the approved engineering change document. These interdepartment interfaces include:

* Materials Department Material Control and Purchasing interface is essential because of effect to the material availability and disposition determined activities as cancel/reschedule/open purchase orders and interface with Production Control to cancel/reschedule/open production work orders and all of these functions in obtaining inventory status data to determine an appropriate effectivity date and corresponding unit serial number.

* Engineering- Design Review the change with the originator or with the engineer who authorized the change to be made, to insure that the Practitioner understands the language of the engineering change document as submitted.

* Engineering- Manufacturing Review the change with the Manufacture Engineer to verify the effect of the change in the manufacturing process and other in-process related problems which would provide

additional insight in analyzing the change.

* Engineering- Test Review with the test department the impact the change will have as to lead time, rework and additional or changed test equipment requirements.

* Quality Control/Assurance Review with the QA/QC function the ramifications of the change as to configuration control, and what documentation they require to insure the language of the engineering change has been implemented per the effectivity as established.

* Marketing/Customer Service Review with the service department as to the impact of the change to products currently in the field and determine what retrofit kits will be required to implement the change into the units all ready in the field.

* Traffic Review with the traffic department the different modes of transportation that can be utilized in expediting the receipt of materials into the factory and effective return of field product which may be required to be returned for repair per the instructions of the Class I change.

* Finance Review with finance as to the method/means of capturing appropriate inventory and labor costs in the implementation of the approved engineering change.

The majority of the functional areas the P&IC Practitioner interfaces with, are usually members of the Change Review Board. The Board should meet at least on a weekly interval with advanced copies of the proposed changes given to the Materials Department to prepare in advance of the meeting. This will allow the P&IC Practitioner gather data for all the Change Board attendees to review the inventory position and the material availability/cost impact to effectively implement the change per the language of the engineering change.

THE ROLE OF THE P&IC PRACTITIONER

The major role of the Practitioner is the management of the implementation of the engineering change into the manufacturing process. This role is one of leading, controlling, and directing the activities and course of action in the effective implementation of the change into the manufacturing process. A crucial matter in directing the activities as a result of the review and analysis of the engineering change is the determination of the effectivity date and the serial number of the final level system to begin the incorporation of the change.

The setting of the effectivity date provides the base point for all activities to be in place and the base point for configuration control of the product affected. Quality Assurance personnel will insure that the language of the engineering change has been implemented per the instructions of the approved change and the product meets the pre-established quality parameters prior to shipment of the product to the customer.

Another role the Practitioner has, is assisting in the material analysis to determine the material cost/benefit relationship the engineering change proposes. This includes such concerns as to the cost of rework of the affected material, scrap costs of the material, purchase order cancellation costs, increased or decreased unit cost of components which affect the standard cost of the product, and costs of purchasing material within standard lead times and premium costs associated with purchasing material within standard lead time parameters. In summary the role of the Practitioner is to define the material cost impact of implementing the proposed engineering change.

As a result of the financial impact the proposed change would create, primarily if the cost of the porposed change would be expensive, the effectivity and disposition of the material may be tempered as to minimize the cost of implementing the change. It should be noted, the Class of change would dictate as to whether a change should be affected by the material/labor cost implications as determined and identified. Obviously a Class II change would dictate a re-evaluation of the effectivity date if the proposed change would be costly to implement. The Class I change would have to be further analyzed as to whether the effectivity and material disposition should be modified in terms of the reason the change was proposed. The reasons for change would include:

* customer requested,
* field failures,
* WIP failures,
* Federal government requirements such as GMP/FDA, FCC, etc., or
* independent agencies requirements such as U.L., CSA, or state, city requirements.

Other considerations which may be required in the re-review of a change, with assistance from other functional departments, would include the perfromance of the product, the affect of the "form, fit or function" guidelines for change and the effect of product pricing as proposed by the change. The cost of implementing one engineering change into the product may have minimal financial impact, but the Practitioner should raise concerns when the proposed engineering change is, for example, the 10th major engineering change to be incorporated into a particular assembly within a 3-4 week period. This raised concern should be part of the engineering change package analysis in which the Practitioner may recommend a product hold for further re-evaluation of the design of the affected component.

SUMMARY

The role of P&IC in Engineering Change Management is, the Practitioner successfully managing the implementation of the approved engineering change into the manufacturing process. The Practitioner defines the course of activities to be performed and insures these activities have been initiated and implemented. To quote one of Murphy's Laws: "Anything you try to fix will take longer and cost more than you thought." would summarize the importance of the role of the Practitioner in the review, analysis of the engineering change to prevent Murphy's Law to prevail. With the understanding of the use of the many engineering change documents and forms available, the understanding of the reason for change, the understanding of classes of change, and the effect of the change to the manufacturing process and to the customer, the Practitioner can establish an effective material effectivity date and corresponding serial number for implementation of the approved change.

BIOGRAPHICAL SKETCH

Andru M. Peters is currently Materials Manager for Centigram Corp., and has 20 years of experience in Materials Management both as a consultant and a practitioner. He also teaches Traffic, Physical Distribution and Materials Management at DeAnza College.

Andy is Past President of the Silicon Valley Chapter of APICS and he is a frequent speaker at APICS International Conferences and local APICS Chapters. He has a B.A. Degree in Economics from Macalester College and is a candidate for a M.S. Degree at the University of Southern California.

SHOP PAPERWORK ARCHITECTURE—PREREQUISITE TO SUCCESSFUL MRP

Gene Thomas
Thomas-Laguban & Associates, Inc.

The author's 30 years of experience, associated with the implementation of mechanized MRP systems, long ago lead to recognition of the most critical element -- communication. This is finally expressed as shop paperwork. The process begins with Engineering Design, but ends only when shop workers and customers can build product or order repair parts. Until these chains-of-events are properly thought through, any company is risking a severe gap in their exposed "closed-loop" system.

The purpose of Engineering Records is to communicate beyond just other Engineers. The communication, to be effective, must go all the way downstream to ME's for manufacturing procedures, IE's for estimates or standards, Cost Accountants to establish and measure cost performance, shop personnel to identify and learn fabrication and assembly specifics, QC to to inspect for conformance, and finally to customers who may need repair parts. While in-office communications are important, the real test is at the shop floor level where a multitude of personnel are in constant need of retraining. The comprehension capabilities at this level often require an evolutionary rather than revolutionary approach.

Shop floor workers have memories like an elephant. Any screw-ups will be remembered at least for a generation. Your first implementation has to work. Second chances are rare!

In the "olden days" of punched cards, fabrication and assembly firms were generally successful with shop travelers for production quantities that could be quantified, tracked thru multiple operations and "completed". Process firms in those days didn't relate -- especially to batch control. Shop travelers, normally moving with the processing of the parts, often contained an extended Bill-Of-Material for a pick list, a routing sheet for operational instructions, and pre-punched "turn-around" labor tickets for reporting quantities produced or scrapped including actual labor or machine hours. I'm sure many production control people even remember the days of the Ditto Master prior to these punched card innovations.

Picking transactions, often utilizing issue card turn-arounds, were processed (maybe even daily) -- providing a stockroom inventory status. Cost accounting also used these transactions to move cost from Raw Material to Work-in-Process (WIP). The labor tickets were often filled out by shop workers or time-keepers and clocked in or out to verify actual hours worked and pieces produced. These were subsequently processed (more than likely daily) to balance portal attendance time to the labor hours distributed. Employee and departmental efficiency performance against I.E. standards was also reported.

A major problem often appeared in those days, however. It took too long to prepare the travelers. Therefore, the temptation was to make them up earlier. This made them vulnerable to last minute process changes and order quantity "replanning". As the reliability of this method of communication deteriorated, companies often became sloppy about expectations of accuracy representing configuration of the product and replanned (alternate) operation schedule dates. Computer programs were also generally not powerful or sophisticated enough to relate non-stocking or made-to-order levels to each other. This resulted in planning lead-time offsets too loosely and developing unrealistic due dates.

There was also the problem of just too much paper. Often in the attempt to produce a complete turn-around labor ticket down to the operation level of a traveler, multiple tickets per operation had to be anticipated and stuffed into the packet. Of course, this created a need for handwritten tickets if the operators ran out, or unneeded tickets littering the floor. Early solutions to this problem produced the "spread ticket" format where all the operations were abbreviated and printed on the turn-around tickets, requiring the worker to merely circle the appropriate operation. He would then apply his man number, quantity and on or off time -- just as with the operation level procedure. The tickets could also be used for moves or identification. Since the "spread tickets" applied to any operation on the traveler, the amount of extra or unused tickets was drastically reduced.

Another "solution" was to utilize Data Collection terminal stations whereby the employee provided the "key punching". By using a pre-coded badge card and a job card (back now to the operation level) he would enter his transaction along with quantity. Time stamping and daily collection was automatic. This "solution" however has generally caused anguish as well as false starts due to the tremendous "revolution" in training effort required. Often, due to slow processing cycles, the only people pleased with the information were the cost accountants. Production management lacked a profitable return on the investment of their thorough support.

In order to provide production's support for this effort, a dispatching function often was attempted. This involved selection and verification of job sequencing for each work center significantly raising the data processing support required. In the early 60's data collection terminals were combined with manually maintained centralized WIP card files. This effort fostered production's support because the transactions were posted immediately -- normally by their own personnel. Although this procedure was somewhat cumbersome by today's standards, the verification of "cherry picking" out of planned sequence could be successfully monitored. Computers (programmers included) were not reliable enough or up-time dependable to assist this "real-time" technique until the mid-70's. This experience did, however, provide an uncomplicated evolutionary exposure to shop floor "discipline" and the benefits of accuracy that set the stage for Computerized real-time support.

BREAK-THROUGH

An early break-through occurred at the Vollrath Company in Sheboygan, Wisconsin in the mid 70's. Vollrath had previously built computer reliability with dual CPU availability. They also had 10 years of prior centralized dispatching/data collection terminal experience. Job selection and operational instruction were married based upon recognition that blue prints (as opposed to expanded verbiage about each operation) were needed on only the beginning 20% of the operations. A real-time dispatch list for each workcenter was displayed on shop CRT's for the foreman to make job assignments. He entered the first and enough subsequent assignments for each worker directly to the operations displayed for a horizon unique to his department. Enough assignments could be made for each worker for the next half shift, full shift, next shift, or tomorrow (if the foreman plans to arrive late). When the worker arrived he merely entered his employee number and the

CRT returned the preselected operation with full verbiage concerning job instructions. After reading the instructions on the CRT he hit "enter" and was automatically clocked on. For 80% of the operations, where a blue print was not required, Vollrath had the "touted" paperless factory. Where blueprints were really required, such need would be called out in the instructions and prints would be issued with the tooling for the operation under appropriate engineering change revision control. Upon completion of the operation, or at the end of shift or partial completion, the worker returned to the CRT and again keyed in his employee number. Once more the instructions were returned for verification or Q.C. and he only needed to enter pieces completed plus any non-standard events such as scrap, day-work, down-time etc. As he "clocks off" on the CRT the next job assignment would appear and he would repeat the cycle. This system has been fully implemented for over 6 years!

NEW CAPABILITIES - MATERIAL TRACKING

With computer capabilities such as indicated above, many additional variations have been successfully implemented over the past several years.

1. Pick paper is being generated in the stock room utilizing on-line terminal printers, sorted by aisle-bin location.

2. Since pick paper is generated only at the last minute, hard allocation of on-hand stock room balances is reviewed just prior to printing. Any potential shortage can be evaluated for order cut-backs or partial picks and changes made immediately.

3. Because of this thorough short-term evaluation of component balances the likelihood of "complete order" picks is raised to almost 100%.

4. With "complete order" picks, "full screen" issues or transfers to WIP occur, and only one on-line entry is required to disburse all components. This reduces issue transactions to a bare minimum, thus significantly increasing accuracy.

5. Because hard allocations (printed pick paper) is reduced to only the lead time to physically pick parts, cycle count cut-off reconciliation is practically eliminated. This generally eliminates the biggest factor contributing to cycle count work load and provides time for more counts. Tooling allocations, picks and returns, are handled in the same fashion.

6. Bulk issues to floor stock or flow transfers at key check points and cell input/output operations can be effectively monitored on-line to prevent tracking inaccuracies such as negative or excessive balances.

7. By building non-stocking network levels in the WIP order data base, transfers without physical stocking moves can be made "assumptively". This means that subsequent transactions would force previous transactions assuming they have happened. A multi-level Order-in-Process ("OIP" string) can accept transactions at any part number change level or any operation within a part. This facilitates migration from job-lot control to parts selected for JIT flow-control tracking.

FUTURE SHOCK CAPABILITIES - LABOR AND COUNT TRACKING

Because transactions can be delayed somewhat, material tracking can generally be supported with imperfect CPU up-time. Labor

transactions, on the other hand, are usually time dependent. If you lose the clock on-off time, you've lost the transaction. Many schemes to distribute the WIP data base to smaller dedicated (usually redundant) CPU hardware merely complicates the interfacing of the integrated re-planning MRP system. A tightly coupled shop floor labor/count on-line, real-time terminal system significantly increases the risk factor due to its technical complexity. There are, however, several on-line "crawl before you leap" steps that have been implemented since the mid 70's that provide the solid base from which to jump ahead.

1. Shop travelers can be printed in a format to provide "spread" turn-around labor transactions using gummed labels, preprinting order numbers, abbreviated operations, and extended instruction verbiage. The labels can be pulled and stuck to daily attendance cards for collection at the end of the shift. This procedure is similar to piece work bundle systems in the soft goods industry.

2. Labels can be pulled and collected several times per shift for entry and verification before the worker leaves. This accomplishes the discipline, and subsequent accuracy, of cumulative attendance balancing and prior operation count editing. This technique requires that these transactions update the WIP data base as they are entered during the shift. Normally a time-keeper makes the rounds of the shop floor collecting the transactions and entering them during the shift. This provides an opportunity to correct any variances and "confront or counsel" any perpetrator of errors before the transaction is "history". Next day is hardly sufficient! Batch updates (normally at night) are not sufficient.

Real-time WIP operation update via CRT is a minimum requirement! Several such systems have been operating since 1975 where a time-keeper can enter between 1000 and 1500 labor transactions per shift. A transaction includes order number, operation, employee, on/off time and count. CPU down-time exposure problems are minimized because on/off time is time clocked or hand written and the time-keeper is the only shop floor person interfacing to the system. Worker training is minimized! High return on reasonable investment hand-in-hand with real-time CRT entry and edit!

3. Labor tickets or labels can be printed for wand-reading. This normally appears to be an advanced sophisticated capability, but can have a questionable return when you consider that the only pre-determined data can be the order number and/or operation sequence number. Think twice (or more!) before you invest in wanding or data collection terminals when direct time-keeper entry, with attendant worker - friendly editing, provides the same function! You probably will require a time-keeper type of function anyway to make adjustments and monitor accuracy!

4. The same technical capabilities supporting on-line material pick paper can be utilized to produce labor tickets and copied orders of subsequent operations for rework or splits. Nothing should move on the shop floor without attendant order paper work - now that the paper work can be streamlined, and is convenient to obtain.

THE FUTURE IS NOW!

When you reconsider the technical limitations that have restricted successful shop tracking systems, aside from all the management issues, CPU or program up-time reliability is probably the biggest problem to overcome. The advent of Personal Computer (PC) types of hardware capabilities, with their down loadable highly intelligent terminals, will change this drastically. Systems are now being implemented that utilize the best of all previous experience gained in the never-ending struggle to avoid down-time risk. Feature this scenario as pragmatic capability -- and implementable in 1985:

1. A mainframe CPU powerful enough to handle a multiplant, completely integrated, company data-base consisting of Sales Order-A/R, MPS integrated to unload ATP on-line and drive MRP, Purchasing-Receiving-A/P, SFC-Dispatching and MRP.

2. CAD systems from multiple vendors depending on unique applications -- but with a common interface to a mainframe data base providing on-line Bill-of-Material and note maintenance. Components of any part, whether assembled or fabricated from raw-material, do not appear on drawings. They are maintained in the mainframe and printed separately with the Bill-Of-Material when drawings are required.

3. PC type hardware (factory hardened) with line switching can retrieve CAD Graphics and/or Bill-Of-Material for downstream communication.

4. CAM systems from multiple vendors depending on application specialty -- but interfaced to an integrated mainframe data base. CAM graphics unloaded from CAD system's, same or interfaced hardware, to reduce redundant geometry. Manufacturing process drawings are more likely to increase and foster better communication now that the ME.'s have more capability and are not beholding to Design Engineering drafting resources. This may also reverse, however, as process drawings are not needed because of further machine tool and QC inspection automation.

Routings are developed and maintained utilizing mainframe power to select, from a classification system, similar features, standardized procedures and standards data. "Same-as-except" feature to copy routings, help set up new part routings and develop estimates or standards. The capability to programmatically generate complete routings is still too far off for serious consideration for most companies. All Routing text data will be maintained in a mainframe data base, copyable to other plants, but interfaced to CAM (similar to CAD) for PC viewing on the shop floor.

5. Complete integration of CAD thru CAM to factory machine tool control and scheduling will develop piecemeal as experience is gained and the capital expenditure is justified.

6. The P.C., or similar type hardware, can provide practically all formal shop floor communication. This hardware approach will not complicate the architecture of the integrated MRP data base. In this time frame we will still do everything we can to avoid "distributing" the main data base because of risk of questionable performance and response times. We will, instead, "extract" a very short-term picture of the dispatching data base, i.e. the planned queue for a work center, and bring it into the PC with a short range of preceding and succeeding operations. The next step is to reprioritize the limited horizon (several shifts) keeping the due dates as planned, but matching set-ups and worker availability. Then the job assignment sequence, by worker, can be entered for the shift horizon and procedures displayed as per the Vollrath experience.

The breakthrough opportunity that now offers itself, reducing the down-time vulnerability risk of the mainframe plus the peak loads generated at end-of-shift, is the capability to "asynchronously" maintain the

single integrated data base as the need occurs. "Asynchronously" means, in laymans language, accepting transactions at the rate of absorption, letting them stack up until they can be handled by the CPU. This is similar to the time-keeper's solution of going on a coffee break if the CPU bogs down. The PC can handle the time dependent transactions itself, such as time stamping on/off times, and can stack them in queue for transmission to the CPU (normally just a few seconds). At shift end a tremend us peak load occurs that may require several minutes to absorb. If the CPU goes down, the horizon originally brought down to the PC, should be sufficient to sustain job assignment and reporting until the CPU comes up again (generally less than a shift). If a PC, goes down the workers can perform their transactions temporarily in an adjacent department from a refreshed pull down of the original queue, or a physical floppy transfer from the backed-up P.C.

As the price of PC type devices comes down and functionality increases, every foreman's high school kid will be suggesting new scheduling techniques within due-date limitations -- probably much to the Old Man's chagrin. We will be entering this era in 1985. Exciting!

Gene Thomas is Founder and CEO of Thomas-Laguban & Associates, Inc. (TLA), a consulting and software firm of 120 professionals. Formerly with IBM for 15 years, he invented the IBM "Bill-of-Material Processor" (BOMP) Package and initiated the "PICS" packageable program development. While at the IBM Rochester plant, Gene developed the first Control- Center-Dispatching Data Collection Terminal System, and the "Dock-to-Stock" on-line receiving and stockroom system. He also directed the first installation of the "Kraus/CLASS/CAPOSS" series of Finite capacity scheduling systems in the U.S. Gene has often been a National APICS Conference speaker and is past president of the Baltimore APICS Chapter.

USING PLANNING BILLS OF MATERIAL TO SCHEDULE PRODUCT OPTIONS

Rick Morgan, CPIM
R. J. Morgan Company

INTRODUCTION:

Do you have 15,000 possible end items but only sell 100 a month? Do you try to schedule the "standard product" only to find out that the sales orders call for something different and you don't have the parts to ship the product when the customer wants it? Or, do you schedule all 15,000 end items and have high inventories on infrequently used parts?

These are not uncommon problems. This presentation will offer some practical solutions to these problems through the use of bill of material modularization and planning bills of material. A tie-in with master production scheduling is also discussed.

APPLICABILITY

The techniques presented here are applicable to a wide range of companies. It doesn't matter how you make a product, i.e. mix, blend, mill, drill, weld, solder, etc., or what the components are, e.g. liquids, steel plate, powder, leather, paper, etc. The point is, to make a finished product you use some sort of manufacturing sub-assembly. Your company may call it an intermediate, semi-finished, bulk, etc. But you take these sub-assemblies made from purchased and manufactured parts and combine them to make a finished product with a bill of material - and many times these products have different configurations. You should not think of your company as "unique". Look for the similarities between your product and the examples used - not the differences.

Here is an example of a product you wouldn't normally think of as having many options:

Athletic Jersey Options

- Short sleeves
- Long sleeves
- Material
- Trim color
- Neck style
- Color
- Team insignia
- Player number

THE PROBLEM

In any company there are sometimes conflicting objectives. Let's review some of the typical WANTS in a company.

MARKETING - They want everything! Sufficient inventory to cover all customer needs.

FINANCE - They want as little as possible or nothing! High inventories mean more taxes, carrying costs, etc.

MANUFACTURING - They want just enough! They want the right parts at the right time to build the product.

ENGINEERING - They want immediate action! Part obsolescence and scheduling problems are not their concern.

These conflicting objectives are highlighted even more when a product has many options from which the customer may choose. So then, here is the problem that is being faced.

"In a product with many options, how do we coordinate and plan the options so we can ship the final configuration on time to the customer?"

SOME SOLUTIONS

1. Have the customer wait the full lead time to purchase, fabricate, and assemble the product. This solution is fine if your customers are willing to wait that long - many are not.

2. Forecast all end items. This is practical if your company has 5,000 end items and sells 3,000 a week for example. There is a good history to fall back on.

But if 15,000 possible end items exist and sales are only 10 a month, you've got a real problem in forecasting.

3. Build a "standard product". Many times a company will try and outguess the customer by making and actually assembling what they call a "standard product". This is what the sales orders call for frequently. However, when a customer orders something with a different final configuration, more often than not the parts aren't available and the customer has to wait.

4. Forecast and master schedule the options using modularized bills of material and a planning bill of material. This is the desired solution and is the focus in the remainder of this presentation.

THE SOLUTION

A good way to handle the problem raised is to modularize the bills of material, create a planning bill of material, and use this in master scheduling to help schedule the options.

Modularizing Bills of Material

This is a way to structure bills of material that aids in better planning and scheduling of options and option sensitive parts using MRP.

It is the process of grouping parts in a product by the option they go with.

Steps

1. Identify the options.

2. Group the parts according to which option they go with.

3. Collect all the different parts for an option under a single part number (called a phantom).

4. Develop a planning bill of material.

COMPREHENSIVE EXAMPLE

This material uses an overhead projector as an example. The four steps in modularizing a bill of material are illustrated.

Step 1 - Identify the options. Figure 1 identifies the options in this example. The number is limited to keep the example clear and concise.

MODEL 500 PROJECTOR OPTIONS

- Single Bulb
- Dual Bulb
- Regular sensitive (normal lighted image)
- Hi-sensitive (brighter image)
- Flat black
- Flat brown

Figure 1

Step 2 - Group the parts by option. Figure 2 is a partial list of parts that is used. Figure 3 shows those parts listed under their option.

1050	single socket mount
1060	dual socket mount
1065	black leg covers
1066	black carrying case
1067	black cabinet
2010	hinges
2015	handle
3116	hi-lo sensitive switch
3128	lense
3150	dual bulb switch
3155	power/on-off switch
4000	brown leg covers
4010	brown carrying case
4015	brown cabinet
5111	single socket
5112	dual socket
5150	standard cooling fan-reg. sens. option
5155	large cooling fan-hi sens. option
6023	standard motor-reg. sens. option
6024	hi-power motor-hi sens. option
6029	regular bulb
6030	hi-intensity bulb

Figure 2

SINGLE BULB	DUAL BULB	HI-SENSITIVE	REG. SENSITIVE
1050	1060	3116	5150
5111	3150	5155	6023
	5112	6024	6029 (2)
		6030 (2)	

FLAT BLACK	FLAT BROWN	COMMON
1065 (4)	4000 (4)	2010 (2)
1066	4010	2015
1067	4015	3128
		3155

Figure 3

Step 3 - Collect all the parts for an option under a phantom part number.

PHANTOMS - A phantom is not a bill of material, it is an item! It is used to:

   a. identify a group of parts that cannot be assembled but must be forecasted and master scheduled as a group.

   b. identify a common parts group.

   c. identify transient sub-assemblies that could have residual inventory.

Items a. and b. are the situations we are dealing with in the projector. Figure 4 shows this in a bill of material format as a visual aid. All of the other parts are still "hooked up" to the phantom part number. They are not shown here for ease of illustration.

MODEL 500 PROJECTOR

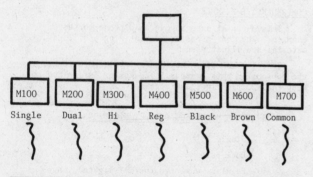

Figure 4

Step 4 - Create a planning bill of material. If you notice in the bill of material in Figure 4, there is something missing - a quantity per assembly. To create a planning bill, you need to determine an option's popularity expressed as a percentage, i.e. 50% of the time customers will order the single bulb option or 90% of the time they will order the flat black option. It is an option forecast. This percentage is then put in as the quantity per assembly of that option. Since common parts are used regardless of what options are chosen, their quantity per is 1. Figure 5 shows the completed planning bill of material.

MODEL 500 PROJECTOR

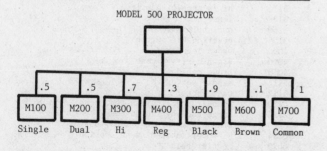

Figure 5

TWO LEVEL MASTER SCHEDULING

Now that the planning bill has been created, let's see how it's used in the master scheduling function. Figure 6 shows the master schedule for the Model 500 Projector. By knowing how many projectors are going to be made, the gross requirements for the options can be calculated by multiplying the option percentage times the MPS quantity for the projector. As illustrated in Figure 6, in week 1, if 100 projectors are going to be made, then 90 (100 X .9) sets of parts for the flat black option are needed that same week. Similarly with weeks 3, 5, and 7.

MODEL 500 PROJECTOR

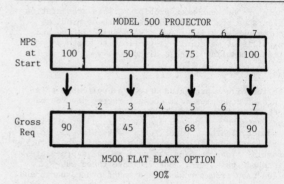

Figure 6

Carrying this concept down another level, Figure 7 shows how the gross requirements for the parts are determined. Once the requirements for the option are known, the master schedule can then be determined. These calculations to actually arrive at the MPS are not covered here to keep the example clear and concise. In Figure 7 the MPS is shown for the flat black option. Again using standard MRP logic, the parent planned orders (the MPS in this case) become the component gross requirements. We have now determined the requirements of the components needed to support the MPS.

M500 FLAT BLACK OPTION

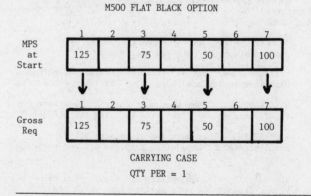

Figure 7

There are three main ways this technique has helped the master scheduling function:

1. Helps coordinate the options better.

2. Easier to do overplanning if needed.

3. Provides better visibility.

However, don't use this as a solution if your company doesn't have the problem! Some companies feel this is a prerequisite for doing MRP - it's not. Only use this technique if you have the problems mentioned earlier.

HOW MODULARIZING HELPS OTHER AREAS IN A COMPANY

<u>Master Scheduling</u> - This area probably has the most benefits as discussed previously.

<u>Sales</u> - Forecasting and order entry.

<u>Engineering</u> - Adding new options and easier bill of material maintenance.

<u>Stockroom</u> - Shortages are reduced and now a picking list can be generated.

<u>Finance</u> - Costing is simplified.

<u>Shop Floor</u> - Shortages are reduced eliminating the extra work of "parts chasing".

SUMMARY

Modularizing bills of material and creating planning bills to aid in master scheduling is a technique that can be used in a wide variety of products that have many options. To evaluate whether this is applicable in your environment, analyze the products and see if your company is having the difficulties mentioned at the beginning of this presentation. Get together a group of knowledgeable people - don't forget the Shop Floor, and actually go through and modularize a product line as a test pilot. This will show you the problem areas and the areas that need concentration. Gradually all product lines can then be cut over. But remember - don't use this as a solution if you don't have the problem!

ABOUT THE AUTHOR

Rick Morgan is President of R.J. Morgan Company. His company provides MRP consulting services to companies implementing MRP or companies wanting to upgrade to Class A.

In addition to his MRP consulting services, Rick has been an MRP Education Consultant for Oliver Wight Video Productions, Inc. In this capacity he provided educational assistance to companies on their in-house and outside MRP education programs.

At one company Rick was involved with the MRP implementation from its inception. Rick's positions were Manufacturing Systems Analyst, Production Planning Supervisor, and Manager of Manufacturing Systems. He co-chaired the MRP Project Team where he designed and implemented Inventory Control systems at all levels, a Master Scheduling system, Work In Process, and was also responsible for working with Manufacturing and Engineering on structuring the bills of material. This company became a Class A user. Rick was also heavily involved with the entire MRP education program. At another company he co-chaired the MRP Project Team in another MRP implementation and was the driving force in the project.

Rick has a B.S. degree in Mathematics from the University of New Mexico and is Certified by APICS. He is President of the Pikes Peak Chapter of APICS in Colorado Springs.

ENGINEERING CHANGE MANAGEMENT: A COMPLETE DEFINITION

Tom Bechtel
Northern Telecom Canada Limited

INTRODUCTION

This paper explores the nature and impact of product change in an industrial setting. An environment of change can be a violently shifting mix of excitement and frustration. The intent of this presentation is to share ideas that will enable us to minimize the agony and maximum the ecstacy. The pleasure inherent in effective management of change is that of seeing your company meet the challenge of remaining or becoming a winner. If change is not managed, a company can crumble. Change must and can be managed because change is here to stay. As defects are said to be viewed as treasures in the Japanese mind set, likewise should change be viewed as good unless shown otherwise.

The objective of this paper will be to describe what change is; the cause of change; the ensuing benefits or consequences and associated costs; methods, tools and techniques for review and control; implementation strategies and a macro look at what change means to the business.

An effective change management system is mandatory for successful business operations.

DEFINITION OF CHANGE

We are always considered to be a changing society - our morals, standards and work ethics are always shifting. Our manufacturing environments are in need of change to remain competitive in this world of high technology and automation. The factory of the future must be one that links all possible elements into a fully integrated local area network of information and control. The heart of such a factory of the future will not be the main frame colossus designed to hold and process all this good information but rather the embracing of the integration concept itself.

The true marriage of functional disciplines long since divorced will provide the power necessary to run the automated factory. Truly integrated management of both the product and the process are required to make the manufacturing business successful. Hi-tech has to be equated to not only the product but also to the manufacturing process. A synergistic approach by all functional parties is required to make our companies profitable today in light of the very serious competit on surrounding us.

A starting point might simply be acceptance of a change to how we talk about change to products. The most commonly used term is engineering change. This instantly puts the design engineering group in the spotlight as being the perpetrator of the crime.

CAUSES OF CHANGE

We are deeply immersed in the electronic revolution whether we like it or not. Some of us make products totally dependent on state of the art electronics, others may not ever have electronics as their products but instead will find them in the equipment on their factory floor, in the office or at a minimum, at the check out counter of their local supermarket. These knowledge intensive, electronic laden products have horribly short life cycles. One reason for change, therefore, is simply the absolute necessity to keep up with the lightning-like advances of the electronic age if we hope to remain competitive.

Studies over five years in a telecommunications company have shown that over 75% of product changes have been due to discontinued or unreliable components, design errors, requirements to meet product specification and requirements to meet increased market demand. These changes therefore satisfy engineering design, field service and marketing demand requirements. Reference Figure 1. To make products to the performance requirements of the market place as quickly as they are demanded places a tremendous burden on our businesses.

So, are product changes good or bad? It's not so much that they are bad but that it's unfortunate that they couldn't have been avoided or planned into the product design from the beginning. By default we have to declare that they are good because without them our products won't sell. We will continue under the premise that product changes will always result no matter how well we plan.

In fact, the best plan is probably one that allows for a certain level of product change activity.

How about the other 25% of product changes? What are their causes? This category is that of manufacturing requirements versus engineering design, field service and marketing needs. These changes are required to make products compatible with the manufacturing process. The incorporation of such changes will provide the opportunity for manufacturing to actually build the product as it was perhaps originally intended.

Manufacturing has to go through the painful process of requesting consideration of a change to the engineering created and released drawing package. Are these changes good or bad? They are changes that would have a direct impact on operations effectiveness. They are changes that should have and could have, in most cases, been designed into the product but weren't because the product design process is not an integrated one! Nonetheless, they are changes required to enable us to survive in a world of ever-increasing demand for cost competitive and flexible products and as such have to be considered necessary and thereby good.

Is the product design group responsible for all changes? They are simply the ones who have to field all the questions and requests relating to marketability, productability and serviceability and translate them into altered, varied, modified, transformed designs or as we bucket them - engineering changes. However, the changes are not necessarily because of technical design reasons and therefore should not be called engineering changes. They are product changes caused by the need to make the product in harmony with the requirements of all functional groups: Marketing, Service, and the Manufacturing world of Materials, Quality, Production and Manufacturing Engineering.

The engineering design group is responsible for translating change requests to enable incorporation into the product design. The company is responsible for it's own success and therefore should not rely on just one functional group to be responsible for so critical an issue as product change management. The concept of review and control boards and committees is covered later.

EXTERNAL REASONS FOR PRODUCT CHANGE

- improve reliability in the field
- maintain competitiveness in terms of customer options
- maintain certain image in market place
- meet regulatory requirements

Figure 1

The needs of manufacturing are unfortunately too often overlooked until the costs of operations finally erode all of the profit margins. Manufacturing is then singled out as being too inefficient and attempts are made to improve the elements of operations. Techniques of value analysis and productibility are too often employed only as a result of crisis management. They should be planned and integrated activities.

CONSEQUENCES OF CHANGE

We have now discussed the nature of change - what it is, why it happens and why it should be considered good until justified otherwise. What are the ill effects or consequences of product changes? Change would certainly be considered bad if customer options were deleted or reliability was diminished but these situations are the exception rather than the rule. Product changes consume engineering design capacity and that definitely becomes an issue. The primary, short term impact is on manufacturing - both inventory and labour. The major effects are noted in Figure 2.

IMPACT OF PRODUCT CHANGE ON MANUFACTURING

- shipment interruption
- additional one-time rework
- additional sustained direct labour time
- scrap/obsolete materials
- inactive materials
- excess materials
- increased documentation costs
- increased test equipment costs
- increased material cost   Figure 2

In a high-value, knowledge intensive product oriented company, inventory cost management is paramount. It is not

94

American Production & Inventory Control Society

uncommon for materials to be 80 to 90% of total cost of goods manufactured. The labour side of the equation doesn't look nearly as significant until all of the normally hidden costs of labour are uncovered - tools, space, training, benefits, etc. The point is, the cost impact of product change on manufacturing is enormous. Millions of dollars are lost with a single subsitution of one device for another if not properly planned. A choice of one component over another may double or triple the labour content in a certain phase of assembly. Why are these events possible? Because we are not managing product change.

MANAGEMENT OF CHANGE

To manage product change we should consider the steps outlined in Figure 3.

PRODUCT CHANGE MANAGEMENT
CRITICAL ELEMENTS

1. Clearly identify the desired/required change (inc. products affected).
2. State reasons why it is being considered or has to happen.
3. Justify why it should be approved.
4. Determine time fences as guidelines.
5. Document the above.
6. Determine how to incorporate change and document.
7. Determine exact timing.
8. Implement.

Figure 3

These major steps can't be done too quickly. We know it is best to make an informed decision and in the case of a normal product change, a fair bit of data and information is required. However, how often do we skip steps 2 through 7?

Why do we not properly cover these elements? Time, policy, discipline, understanding. These are the terms that come to mind.
Time is a big issue. Everyone says they are going to take a time management course or read a book on the subject or just go to an evening presentation to learn more about it, but how many follow up? We waste so much time that it should actually scare us. If you have a product change review committee you are probably scorned for tying up so much time discussing change.
This is where policy becomes an issue. If there is no upper management support or commitment to proper attention to change, the rank and file will never do justice to managing change no matter how well intended.
In the case of change management, the policy simply has to be a statement of direction and support of multi-functional group participation in planning and controlling product change. All parties have to be convinced that it deserves each of their attention and that as much as required will be supported. With a top level policy statement the next required ingredient is discipline.
The responsibilities of people involved in product change management include a dedicated diligence in their efforts and an optimum sense of urgency. We just can't waste time incorporating change. Some types of change can be done over a more relaxed time frame but others may need urgent attention. The change management responsibilities therefore have to lie with keen individuals or a select group of same. Disciplined professionals are needed.
All the time, policies and disciplines in the world won't matter if there is an air of confusion about why product change management is such a big deal.
The final ingredient then may be understanding.
Only 25% of product changes are triggered by manufacturing but about 90% of changes impact manufacturing. Some changes only affect archived bills of material or product in the field but the majority of product changes will have some impact on inventory, production or quality.
A product change from the design engineering point of view has an impact on one of three key parameters: part number, description and quantity per parent part number. Engineering drawings also must be updated. What has to be realized next is the potential impact on manufacturing. Unfortunately, manufacturing people often don't have a proper understanding of their own network. Materials people don't always appreciate the impact of their decisions on Production and Manufacturing Engineering, etc.

MANUFACTURING SYSTEM IMPACT

We know that bills of material are an integral part of any manufacturing system. We know that product change impacts these bills. To accent the need for understanding manufacturing we will look briefly at the nature of bills of material.
What we now commonly accept as a bill of material has a wealth of manufacturing data. Many think that bills of material are created by Design Engineering. If that were the case, what would they look like? What information is guaranteed to be on them? What you will find as a minimum are the items pointed out earlier as key concerns of Design, accented in Figure 4.

PRIMARY DESIGN INPUTS TO A BOM

- part number
- description
- quantity per
- parent part number

Figure 4

What else is on a bill of material? Consider Figure 5.

BILLS OF MATERIAL FILE STRUCTURE

FIELD NAME	ORGINATOR DEPARTMENT
PARENT PART NUMBER	DESIGN ENGINEERING
COMPONENT PART NUMBER	DESIGN ENGINEERING
DESCRIPTION	DESIGN ENGINEERING
REVISION	DESIGN ENGINEERING
QUANTITY PER	DESIGN ENGINEERING
EFFECTIVITY START DATE	MANUFACTURING
EFFECTIVITY CLOSE DATE	MANUFACTURING
ISSUING STORES	MATERIALS
ROUTING	INDUSTRIAL ENGINEERING
MANUFACTURE LEAD TIME	INDUSTRIAL ENGINEERING
PROCUREMENT LEAD TIME	PURCHASING
LEAD TIME OFFSET	INDUSTRIAL ENGINEERING
UNIT OF MEASURE	PURCHASING/MANUFACTURING
PRODUCT CODE	DESIGN ENGINEERING/MAKETING
COMMODITY CODE	PURCHASING
SOURCE CODE	MANUFACTURING
TYPE CODE	MATERIALS
ABC CODE	MATERIALS
PLANNING CODE	PRODUCTION PLANNING
LOT SIZE	MATERIALS
YIELD	QUALITY ASSURANCE
SHRINKAGE	MATERIALS
PRODUCTION CONTROL CODE	MATERIALS
MATERIAL CONTROL CODE	MATERIALS
BUYER CODE	PURCHASING
SHIP LEVEL CODE	MANUFACTURING
SPARES CODE	MATERIALS

Figure 5

About 15 of these factors would be considered critical to the effective running of an MRP system yet only 5 are designengineering oriented. Therefore, one might say that Design Engineering builds only the core or about 1/3 of the bill of material. What they are actually providing is an engineering parts list. With the addition of other key data and a bit of structuring, this list becomes a manufacturing structured bill of material.
It is this level of BOM that is useful for management of the business. The engineering parts list is certainly important and it could be used for gross requirements planning but it is hardly enough information to warrant being called a bill of material. The BOM as we need it in operations has to be developed and controlled in manufacturing. Design Engineering has to understand that there are at least 10 other important parameters from manufacturing in our bills.

PRODUCT CHANGE MANAGEMENT SYSTEMS

The design of a product change management system will depend on the size of the company. If a large company, you may be dealing with a design authority that supports 3 plant locations. If a small company, your engineering and manufacturing efforts may be in the same group. We will look at a possible set up for the larger company environment.

Even in larger companies, the product change management system is often only a sophisticated review board which has only as much effect on change control as it is allowed. The system that works best will be one that has the proper delineation of responsibilities and authority, sense of urgency, discipline and support.

It has to be built such that it allows for a balance of the three primary business objectives: stated in Figure 6.

PRIMARY BUSINESS OBJECTIVES

- maximum customer service
- minimum inventory investment
- maximum operating efficiency

Figure 6

The product change management system must include all functional groups within the company: Engineering, Manufacturing, Marketing, Field Service/Customer Engineering, Legal, Finance, Strategic Planning and Human Resources. But how can you possibly take the time necessary for all these groups to be involved? Review and critique is one of the most powerful techniques a businessman could employ. The review portion covers the critical need for awareness and communication. The critique portion creates the opportunity for input and contribution. Together, they offer the potential for balance, compromise and harmony in direction taking and decision making. The small company environment forces the issue whereas the large company atmosphere unintentionally discourages it. Therefore, the large company normally resort to the board or committee approach in an attempt to embrace the doctrine of review and critique. To involve all the functional groups mentioned, two tiers of review are often necessary.

The first tier of review and critique should be a feasibility filter. A proposed change has to be judged on its worth to the company and relative importance. This review or review board must consist of representatives from each of the 7 or 8 major functions in the company. The review is in essence setting the limits or levels of product change activity. In other words, the review board approach has the greatest effect if it not only acts as a screen but also as a forecasting and planning body. The output of the first review should be a macro plan of product change activity. The use of change classification, normally denoting maximum allowable implementation time, helps build this plan.

Those changes allowed to filter into the mainstream then have to be scheduled in more detail. No change approved via the initial screening should be rejected at the second level unless there was gross misrepresentation of projected achievability and costs. Change activity is scheduled within the boundaries of the product change activity plan.

The first review and critique has to put a price tag on each proposed change along with a dollarized perceived benefit. This sizing has to be done quickly and comprehensively. For larger changes, the 'business case' approach may be desired.

The cost of implementing should include an estimate of impact on manufacturing in terms of production efficiency and inventory investment. Other factors to consider would be design engineering, field service and manufacturing support group time required to set up and implement the change. The cost of not implementing would include an estimate of lost market share and sales. Impact due to fines and legal action need to be considered when change is a regulatory issue.

The sizing exercise answers our worth to the company question. Relative importance has to then be determined in order to label the change with a classification or a 'degree of urgency.' Factors to be considered include market share and sales impact, manufacturing efficiency and inventory investment impact, safety and health impact, regulatory requirements and reliability. Figure 7 lists typical change classifications.

PRODUCT CHANGE CLASSIFICATIONS

A - Immediate implementation due to hazardous or inoperative condition.
B - Mandatory implementation due to potential hazardous or inoperative conditions.
C - Unsatisfactory operation due to improved design or new features.
D - Cost reduction phase-in or new drawing releases

Figure 7

The most striking feature of these classification types is de-emphasis or lack of priority for manufacturing issues. The fact that inventory investment or labour efficiency problems can be far more costly to a company than perceived unsatisfactory product operation is essentially ignored. The first stage of review and critique has to have very sound manufacturing representation and the rest of the functional partners have to be willing to listen.

The second tier of product change review must also be multi-functional but from a manufacturing perspective. Included should be: Production, Manufacturing Engineering, Quality Assurance, Materials and Finance. Such a review, or better stated, a control board or committee, has objectives as shown in Figure 8.

MANUFACTURING PRODUCT CHANGE CONTROL BOARD OBJECTIVES

- Setting of effectivity dates
- Identification and summary of risks, constraints, opportunities
- Detailed assessment of cost impact
- Definition of an implementation plan

Figure 8

A traditional problem with the manufacturing review of proposed product changes is the narrowmindedness of the people involved; or the problem is simply that the right people are not involved.

Even in my declaration of who should be involved a fair bit of ambiguity exists. For example, we mentioned Manufacturing Engineering. The Materials representative may feel that the board should go to an ME rep only if required. Many review boards are Materials based. The irony of such an attitude is very visible in a high-tech environment where MANUFACTURING ENGINEERING usually consists of Product Support Engineering, Test Engineering and Industrial Engineering, each of whom may be represented on a review board. In fact, the most effective review boards are potentially those in which Materials/Purchasing people are in the minority. The best functional make-up of a manufacturing product change control board might be as displayed in Figure 9.

MANUFACTURING PRODUCT CHANGE CONTROL BOARD
REPRESENTATIVES

- Material Planning/Purchasing
- Production Control
- Manufacturing Systems Support
- Quality Engineering
- Industrial Engineering
- Test Engineering
- Product Support Engineering

Figure 9

Too often, decisions regarding scheduling, capacity, and product introduction are based primarily on material availability. If we can get the materials in we feel we can do anything. This is so wrong in today's factories. Capacity constraints, other than material availability, have emerged as a function of new manufacturing technology emergence. That is, the factory of today, and certainly the factory of the future, is and will be heavily dependent on special tools and robots and software. Test, QC and assembly equipment requires fixtures and programs that are not available overnight. The 'new' fixture may be the upgrade of the old therefore presenting a major scheduling challenge, e.g. how to get the old revision work order finished in time to allow the fixture to be pulled off-line to get it upgraded in time to accommodate the new revision work order.

The normal mode of managing product change in manufacturing can probably be safely summarized as shown in Figure 10.

NORMAL REQUIREMENTS OF CHANGE

- recognition of causes/benefits/consequences
- acceptance of its continuance
- review and control of its introduction
- implementation

Figure 10

We spend a great deal of time reviewing and controlling. Most of the tools and techniques designed are for this

96

portion of product change management - data collection forms, BOM change forms, implementation schedules, MRP effectivity dates, review boards, policies, procedures.

What do we need to consider in order to go from 'normal' to 'total' management of product change?

MARKETING IMPACT

The impact of change on the macro elements of the business has to be considered. We can start by looking at customer service. Product change may enable us to deliver exactly what the customer wants but perhaps not when. We may want to consider sacrificing features for on time delivery. Late delivery has extremely dire consequences as shown in Figure 11.

CONSEQUENCES OF LATE SHIPMENT

- late cash inflow
- lost sales
- loss of credibility
- loss of market share
- lawsuits

Figure 11

INVENTORY IMPACT

What does change do to inventory investment? Changes for cost reduction purposes should result in a net positive impact on inventory but only if properly analyzed and implemented. For example, a change might introduce a lower cost component. However, the stock on hand status, anticipated usage and timing of the change the change have to be such that we don't actually lose money by introducing the new part. Do we have parts in our stores account with more than 1 year usage? Improperly planned change may cause material shortages. This may help keep our raw material level down but what happens to work-in-process?

We know that product changes cause material shortages that cause work orders to crash on the shop floor. Work in process increases because we keep releasing work to the shop (push, push) and we probably release some jobs earlier to fill in the 'gaps' caused by stalled work orders. Is this how it works?

What other inventory accounts are effected? What happens when we choose a new component to get a better price but we don't get the proper quality or manufacturing suitability? That is, the part has a lower P.O. price but it never gets past QC incoming or it doesn't fit in the assembly fixture or it craps out in test. Where does this part end up - material review board stores account, scrap account, obsolete account. How much does it really end up costing us after we add in inventory carrying costs of making it past QC or work in our fixtures?

There is a need to recognize the true material cost of our components and assemblies. We have to look beyond standard costs. What is our purchase price variance? What causes it? Excess freight, set up or ordering charges due to urgent need or smaller than economical lots due to improper implementation of change. Inventory carrying costs may change from one part to the next because of different storage and handling requirements, rates of deterioration and obsolescence. Cost of repair or rework to make the part acceptable may be absorbed internally. Extraneous costs may be incurred such as need to modify equipment, fixtures and methods required to handle the new part. These costs would be considered as we look at the impact of change on our third major business objective, manufacturing efficiency.

MANUFACTURING IMPACT

Manufacturing efficiency is optimised if we work on the right parts at the right time at the right place. This means that we have parts that fit and work, are neither early nor late and are delivered to the right spot. Product change has been seen to effect 'right part', what impact does product change have on schedules? Schedules are based on material availability and capacity availability. Material availability we have seen is effected by proper setting of effectivity dates. Is there a capacity impact?

Capacity is determined by consideration of bottlenecks and productivity. Does product change help clear up bottlenecks or does it cause them? We know that the answer is both, the challenge is to have the mix in favor of the clearing up benefit. How does product change effect productivity? To be productive, we must work on good product at a good rate. We must minimize incorporation of change, repairing or retesting.

SUMMARY

So what's new? A lot of motherhood here. What do we do about it, we have control boards looking at all of these things. Maybe! The review committees and control boards can only do so much. Back to an earlier question, who is really responsible for product change management? The whole company of course because everyone is either on the cause or effect side of the equation. How can you possibly raise the issue to the proper height? We must show how product change fits in our hierarchy of business performance and then monitor and display our plans to improve.

The importance of product change management has to be proven and accepted. It has to be included in all of our business reports, be they engineering, marketing, finance or operations initiated. It has to be forecast just as we attempt to forecast product demand. It has to be treated as a change in how we utilize our resources including capital. It has to be recognized as a potential cash flow drain. It has to be accepted as a deterrent to achieving profitability. It must be factored in to how we manage our people, it's a drain on shop floor personnel, engineering and manufacturing support group productivity.

One of the realities of the manufacturing world is change. It must be understood and truly managed and not treated as a short term exception or secondary priority.

ABOUT THE AUTHOR

Tom Bechtel is Manager of Materials Planning for Northern Telecom Canada Limited. He is located at the Digital Switching Division in Bramalea, Ontario, Canada.

Previously employed at Mitel, Canadian General Electric and General Electric, Tom has gained experience in industrial engineering, new plant planning, new product introduction, human resources, and materials management.

Tom is a graduate of Penn State University in electrical engineering. He has also done graduate work at The University of Toronto.

Tom is a member of APICS, AIIE and SME and is a CPIM and an instructor of the 'Principles of Production and Inventory Management' course.

AUTOMATIC REAL TIME TRACKING AND CONTROL IN THE MANUFACTURING PLANT

Bert R. Willoughby
Accu-Sort Systems, Inc.

ABSTRACT

A case study that describes how a Fortune 50 company was able to achieve manufacturing excellence by:

- Insuring accurate inventory counts--finally they were able to reconcile work in process inventory totals with production counts. Daily physical inventories were no longer necessary.
- Eliminating critical final assembly part shortages--no more assembly line "shutdowns" or part substitutions.
- Increasing labor efficiency--real time automatic tracking of warehouse personnel transactions helps establish realistic labor standards and improve operator performance.
- Substituting day old detailed production reports with concise current "exception" reports--management was able to pinpoint potential production shortages and make scheduling changes to accommodate final assembly requirements.
- Knowing the exact location of on-hand inventory--random computer directed space assignment has optimized warehouse space and eliminated safety stock requirements due to anticipated shortages from misplaced product.

Traditional manual procedures using the familiar perforated work ticket, clipboards, expeditors, inventory clerks, and records keeping personnel are contrasted with an automated system that integrates the bar code, automatic laser scanning, sortation controllers, special horizontal transportation equipment, automated guided vehicles, real-time on-line man/machine communications, and nonstop computer processing.

PRE SYSTEM SURVEY

The case study presented in this paper takes place in a TV manufacturing plant. Over 13,000 TV sets "roll-off" assembly lines during two 8-hour shifts. There are many components that must be delivered "just-in-time" to meet production schedules. One of the most critical components is the TV cabinet. There are hundreds of different model numbers each requiring a specific cabinet. The following scenario describes the manual procedures observed during the on-site visit.

TV cabinets with the same model number were removed from plastic injection moulding machines and placed in large cardboard containers (57" x 37" x 42"). A three part ticket identifying a seven digit model number was attached to the container. Material tracking and data recording was performed by removing ticket stubs at critical transaction points. Warehouse personnel used the ticket stubs to record production counts by part number for each of the three--8-hour production shifts.

The containers were then transported by tow cart and conveyor to a staging area where warehouse personnel sorted the containers into pairs with the same part numbers. This procedure was followed to make efficient use of forklift trucks which are capable of transporting two containers. Warehouse recording operators assigned storage space by writing the section/hole location on the ticket stub. Warehouse personnel were responsible for taking a daily physical inventory to insure that adequate quantities of specific model numbers were on hand to meet final assembly requirements. Ticket stubs removed during picking for final assembly were used to decrement inventory counts. A warehouse clerical staff generated reports to track labor efficiency and on-hand inventory.

Analysis of the manual operating procedures point out that they were labor intensive and highly susceptible to error. Incorrect tallies by part number was a frequent occurrence which resulted in inaccurate production counts; transposition of digits by warehouse labor, sorting containers, resulted in containers being placed in the wrong location; ticket stubs were found lost in the aisles which rendered the task of reconciling production counts with on-hand inventory virtually impossible; and errors in manual calculations by the clerical staff often resulted in an insufficient quantity of cabinets being available for final assembly.

Objectives for the automated system were established. They included: (1) Elimination of labor required for performing: production counting, sortation, daily physical inventory, assigning/maintaining warehouse space and on-hand inventory by part number, and calculations and generating management reports. (2) Reduction in errors. (3) Minimize inventory. (4) Optimize warehouse space. (5) Elimination of the manual reporting procedures. (6) Maintain an audit trail of driver transactions.

Meeting these objectives requires the identification and tracking of containers from production to bulk storage and final assembly. Automatic identification, real-time data processing, man/machine communications, controls, and material handling technology are the tools available to the systems analyst. The following checklist serves as a guideline for addressing the key considerations within each of these technologies.

SYSTEM DESIGN CHECKLIST

Overall System Design

_____ Have you described in writing exactly what it is you hope to accomplish (objectives and scope). Don't forget Peter's Principle! If you don't know where you're going, you'll probably end up somewhere else.

_____ Have you put together a cost justification for the proposed system? "You can't talk productivity without talking profits."

_____ Have you written a functional specification that describes how the proposed system will operate? Remember a system must be a simulation of reality! It must be compatible with the operation of your existing facility.

_____ Have you discussed the transaction flow with the people who will be responsible for making the system "work"? WHO needs WHAT information WHEN?

AUTOMATIC IDENTIFICATION TECHNOLOGY

Which automatic identification technology should I use?
_____ voice
_____ magnetic
_____ radio frequency
_____ optical character recognition (OCR)
_____ vision
_____ surface acoustic wave (SAW)
_____ magnetic ink character recognition
_____ bar code

BAR CODE TECHNOLOGY

Selecting a Symbology

_____ How much information should I encode in the symbol? Number of characters.
_____ What is the data content? Alphanumeric/numeric
_____ How much space is available for the symbol?
_____ Which code format makes sense? Code 3 of 9, I 2 of 5, UPC, EAN, Codabar, Binary, Code 93, Code 128,...
_____ Do I need to use a check digit?
_____ What are the symbol dimensions?
_____ Is the code bi-directional?

Generating Bar Codes

_____ Off-Site Printing
Flexography, letter press, film masters, photo composition, ion deposition
_____ On-Site Printing
Impact, dot matrix, thermal, inkjet, electrostatic, laser, embossing, moulding, stamping
_____ Label exposed to weather, harsh environment
_____ 'X' dimension
minimum bar width
_____ Quantity of labels/day
_____ Label content
Lines of human readable, graphics,...
_____ Special Reader Requirements
Raster pattern_____, omnidirectional_____, shadowscan_____.
_____ Options
Memory_____, special program_____, relay output_____, code output (parallel/serial)_____, keypad_____

Applying Bar Codes

_____ Hand or machine applied
_____ Thruput speed for print and apply
_____ Direct application
_____ "Ladder" or "picket fence" orientation

Verifying Bar Code Readability

_____ Bar/space dimensions within tolerance

American Production & Inventory Control Society

_____ Print contrast ratio acceptable
_____ Clear areas on both sides of code adequate
_____ Specular reflection
_____ Label/printer/applicator cost

Reading Bar Codes

_____ Hand operated or automatic wand, gun, portable, fixed position.
_____ Visible or infra-red wand
_____ Fixed or moving beam scanner
_____ Automatic Scanning Performance Requirements
_____ Height-of-scan_____, Scan rate_____, optical throw_____, depth of field_____
_____ Symbol Presentation
_____ Tilt, Pitch, Skew
_____ Read reliability
_____ "Voting Logic"

COMPUTER/COMMUNICATIONS TECHNOLOGY

Functional Considerations

_____ Current data processing (DP) system architecture
_____ DP system interfaces
_____ Host CPU, local CPU, printer and other peripherals (name, model#)
_____ Nonstop processing
_____ Redundancy_____, "Hot" back-up_____
_____ Device concentrators
_____ # channels_____, data buffering_____, polling_____, read and transmit "immediate"_____
_____ Bi-directional communications
_____ Download, upload
_____ Transmission data integrity, word parity, LRC, CRC
_____ Electrical interface
_____ RS232, 20 mA C1, RS422
_____ Software protocol
_____ Asynch, Bisynch, SDLC, device emulation
_____ User Access Required
_____ Real time data base_____, Report generation_____

MATERIAL HANDLING/CONTROLS TECHNOLOGY

System Flow

_____ Blueprint layout available
_____ Deployment of readers and controls?
_____ Delivery system interfaces, conveyor, AS/RS, Monorail, AGVS, industrial trucks (manufacturer/type)

Tracking

_____ Sortation
_____ Field proven software?
_____ Vendor supplied
_____ Carton/object
_____ Spacing_____, speed_____, Leading vs. Trailing edge_____
_____ Photoeye "inputs"
_____ presence detection_____, update-location_____, lane full_____, divert confirmation_____, induct point_____
_____ No read handling
_____ Special lane_____, recirculation loops_____
_____ Jam detection and restart required
_____ Speed/distance calibration
_____ Shaft pulse encoder_____
_____ Lane assignment from Host?

Input/output interfaces

_____ Programmable controller
_____ Serial, parallel, BCD, ASCII
_____ Relay Outputs
_____ Diverters, alarms, motors

SYSTEM OPERATION

A robot removes TV cases from a plastic injection moulting machine, places them on a small conveyor which delivers the cabinet to an inspection station. An inspector examines the cabinet for defects and places acceptable parts in a cardboard container. When the container has been filled with the required quantity, the inspection operator attaches a bar code label to the container (Figure 1 Ladder orientation). The bar code replaces the three part ticket. An Interleaved 2 of 5 code format is used to encode a seven digit part number followed by a modulo 10 check character. A dot matrix printer is used to generate the label. The 'X' dimension

(dimension of the narrowest bar/space) is .030" with a wide bar to narrow bar ratio of 3:1.

Figure 1

Figure 2 is a graphic illustration of the system components and material flow. Containers travel by automated tow carts from the inspection station (Robot) to a 90 degree pop-up-chain transfer station where they are automatically transferred onto a power driven roller conveyor.

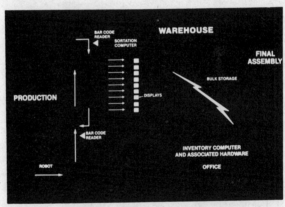

Figure 2

Moving Beam Bar Code Reader-Production Counting

Containers are conveyed (60 fpm) past the first moving beam laser scanner (Figure 3). The scanner is mounted so that the laser beam sweeps through a vertical axis (height-of-scan) 360 times per second. The scanner is configured for an optical throw of 20 inches; a depth of field of 10 inches; and a height-of-scan of 22 inches. Designing the system with a bar code ladder orientation and a 40 inch height-of-scan, permits a wide variation in symbol placement along the Y axis. This practice is frequently followed when bar code labels are "hand applied." Bar code label size, scan rate, and container speed are parameters that have been optimized to accommodate a tilt angle of ± 40 degrees (clockwise or counter-clockwise rotation of the symbol). Code reading accuracy and reliability have also been enhanced by programming the decoder to compare multiple scans (voting logic) before acknowledging a successful read.

The part number is next transmitted in real time via an RS232 output from the scanner to the warehouse computer (Figure 4) which updates a production count.

Material Handling - Sortation

Containers continue by conveyor and travel past a second bar code reader interfaced to a sortation controller (Figure 5). The sortation controller is installed in a NEMA 12 enclosure, and uses the second laser scanner, tracking software, photoeye inputs, and relay controls to divert containers into one of nine accumulation lanes. Photoeyes spaced along the conveyor and a conveyor drive shaft pulse encoder assists the tracking software in escorting containers to their final destination. Confirmation photoeyes signal the sortation controller when a container has been successfully diverted.

During the pre-system survey we observed that people were sorting containers into parts to expedite forklift truck put-away. The sortation controller has been programmed to permit a high volume of containers to circulate a pre-set number of times waiting for a match before diverting them into the same accumulation line.

Figure 3

Figure 4

Figure 5

Radio Frequency Communications

The sortation controller now signals the warehouse computer that a match has been found and a display at the accumulation lane is illuminated with the part number. Forklift truck drivers now proceed to lighted display lanes and using on board radio frequency terminals (Figure 6) receive instructions from the warehouse computer (Figure 4) through a base station link. The warehouse computer communicating through an rf terminal dispatches the drivers to either move the material to final assembly or assigns the warehouse section/hole in which the containers are to

Figure 6

be placed. Concurrently, pickers operating forklift trucks are instructed via the radio link the fetch locations for containers required by final assembly. Prompting messages and help routines assist the drivers through interactive responses. The rf terminal located on board the lift truck has a full alphanumeric keypad with a 40 digit LCD display. Transmission speed from the warehouse computer to the truck mounted unit is 300 bps.

Real Time Nonstop Data Processing

The warehouse computer system which is "driving" the warehouse operation is configured with a primary and secondary processing unit. Information in both units is current. In the event of a failure in the primary unit, the secondary system can take over with no degradation to warehouse operation. Both the primary and secondary units consist of Intel based microcomputers, an Electromagnetic Sciences, Inc. rf base station which transmits to the microcomputer at 2400 bps, and bulk storage units (primary--10MB CDC disc) (secondary--floppy disc). Other peripherals include a CRT and hard copy printer.

Reports
System Design--"Who needs What information When"?

Both on-demand and automatic reports are available at either the CRT or printer. Production counts by part number and shift are reported. Production schedulers input final assembly requirements by part number and an exception report is printed to point out insufficient quantities of on-hand inventory. Labor efficiency reports and forklift truck driver audit trails are also available from the system. File maintenance routines permit updates to the warehouse plan-o-gram and valid part number file.

Benefits/Savings

Have you put together a cost justification for the proposed system? You can't talk productivity without talking profits. Effective integration of field proven technology has provided this implementer with "tighter and better" operating controls. Tangible savings from the elimination of labor to:

    count product
    sort product
    assign and maintain warehouse space locations
    perform a daily physical inventory and
    maintain on-hand inventory

translates into a system payback period of less than a year. Furthermore, intangible savings are anticapted from

    enchanced accuracy of on-hand inventory and
    production counts and
    enhanced accuracy of real-time production scheduling.

Bar code reading machines, robots, automatic guided

vehicles, sortation, rf communication, and computers are the technological tools of today. Integrating these tools into a coordinated harmonious system can help you increase labor productivity, reduce inventory, optimize warehouse space, reduce scrap, and improve your company's profitability.

Biography
    Mr. Willoughby is Vice President of Marketing Accu-Sort Systems, Inc., Telford, Pa. Incorporated in 1971, today Accu-Sort is an established leading supplier of automatic identification equipment and systems for use in both manufacturing and distribution applications. Customers include many Fortune 500 companies.
    Recent articles that Mr. Willoughby has authored appeared in "Industrial Engineering" and "Plant & Inventory Management Review." Mr. Willoughby has served on the faculty of the Institute of Industrial Engineering Material Handling Management Course. He is also a frequent guest speaker at seminars and symposiums sponsored by SME, IEE, and AIM.
    A graduate of Fairleigh Dickinson University, he has held engineering and marketing positions with Bell Laboratories, Sperry Univac, and RCA where in 1973 he was a member of the team that installed the first supermarket scanning system.

BAR CODING—A DEEPER UNDERSTANDING
Jack Loeffler, CPIM
Ford Motor Company

Why is there so much interest in bar coding and the other automatic data capture techniques? Are they solutions looking for problems? I believe there are real problems that automatic data capture techniques can solve. Most businesses have become more productive and efficient by using computers. They rely heavily on information systems, but these systems are lacking in three general areas:

. There is much information and data about the business that management needs if they are to manage better. In the past, however, businesses could not afford or could not justify obtaining this information.

. When businesses can afford to capture data, too often managers don't get the data soon enough, when they really need it. There is an increasing need for real time systems.

. When businesses can afford to capture information and have it when needed, it is too often wrong. Inaccurate data result in expensive mistakes, expensive correction procedures, and a mistrust of information which results in very expensive "CYA" decisions.

Automatic data capture techniques, especially bar coding, help to solve these problems which are associated with computer systems. Additionally, they address a business' number one problem - productivity. Unmanned laser scanners collect data without labor. And hand held scanners increase worker productivity. Most likely these problems and productivity opportunities really exist but are not easily recognizable. For many, the first challenge is to highlight and bring about an awareness of them and the benefits for resolving them.

A common misunderstanding that warrants clarification is that there are no automatic data capture or bar code systems as such. As stated earlier, bar coding is a technique not a system. Most existing information systems today can be improved by using bar coding or other automatic data capture techniques. But don't be mislead. When implementing automatic data capture tecniques, one also must consider the impact on the rest of the system as well as the potential impact on other systems. And by other systems, I mean already existing systems as well as potential systems. To be more specific, here are some examples of situations you must be aware of:

. If you have a batch system today and want a real time system, the cost and effort related to bar code equipment and procedures may be minor compared to the cost and effort, i.e., the hardware and software, to make this information available after it's captured.

. Data communications and the associated protocol requirements may present special problems. After implementing a data collection program that provides accurate data in real time, it would be a crime to lose some of the data when communicating it to a host computer. Data communications are an important part of the total system and must be carefully planned.

. At times, it seems that there are more computer systems and programs than basic data. The same data often are needed in many different systems and programs that are used by different departments, divisions and companies. The same labels should feed the same data to all of these systems. Additionally, most automatic data capture applications, especially bar coding, capture data by reading some form of label. Generating readable labels is one of the most costly and difficult aspects of bar code applications. The overlapping uses of data among different systems and different activities, and the cost and work required to generate usable labels, make label development critical. Labels should be carefully planned, so that they can be used by and for different activities and different systems.

DECODING BAR CODES

The secret to bar code reading devices is based on optics. A reader or scanning device emits a beam of light at a bar code symbol. A sensing device within the reading device measures the amount of light that is reflected back from the bar code symbol. The reading device then develops an analog signal, which in a sense is a chart of reflected light. Two key measurements are charted. The first is the difference between the amount of light that is reflected when the beam is aimed at a space versus the amount of light that is reflected when it is aimed at a bar. When aimed at a space (generally white) there is high reflectence. When the beam is aimed at a bar (generally black) there is low reflectence. This means that the background label material or substrate must reflect light well, and the ink or material that forms the bars must absorb light and give low reflectence. This is how a reading device knows whether it is looking at bars or spaces. A second important measurement that is charted is the length of time that the reading device is aimed at a bar or space. This means that the light must be moved across the bar code symbol at a constant speed. In this way, the reading device determines whether it is aimed at wide or narrow elements (bars or spaces). This also suggests that all narrow elements should be identical in width. The widths of wide elements should not only be consistent, but signficantly larger than the narrow elements. It is generally recommended that the ratio of wide to narrow elements be three to one.

Once the reading device determines the pattern of bars and spaces, a decoding process can be accomplished. In decoding Code 3-of-9, most scanners use a binary numbering system process. This process assigns the number one to all wide elements and the number zero to all narrow elements. The pattern of wide and narrow (1's and 0's) for both bars and spaces are compared to a lookup table which associates that pattern with a specific alpha or numeric character.

Just as there are many different speaking languages, there also are many different bar code languages or symbologies. It has been estimated that there are over 50 different bar code symbologies.

SYMBOLOGY SELECTION

Because there are so many different bar codes symbologies, i.e., UPC, Codabar, Code 3-of-9, Code 128, Telepen, etc., and because each have different characteristics, symbology selection is a key issue. In evaluating different symbologies, the following issues should be carefully considered:

. Character Set - Will the encoded messages require numeric, alphanumeric, or all ASCII characters?

. Density - Bar code symbols take up a lot of real estate. Will the information you want to encode fit on the size label you need?

. Security/Reliability - How accurate must the data be that is captured?

. Acceptance/Experience - Is the symbology new or have several activities used it effectively?

. Equipment Availability - Will most printers and scanners handle the symbology?

. Industry Standards - Has your industry already established a symbology standard?

. Equipment Needs - What type of printing and scanning equipment do you expect to use?

These are the major issues to be addressed in choosing a symbology. There are other symbology characteristics such as continuous versus discrete, fixed versus variable length, etc., but most of these relate to the issues listed above. If it becomes difficult choosing a symbology, an evaluation technique to consider is to assign importance (on a scale of 1 to

10) to each of the symbology characteristics or issues. Then each different symbology can be rated (on a scale of 1 to 10) against each characteristic. The importance-ratings and evaluations can be multiplied out to obtain a weighted average evaluation.

SYMBOLOGY SPECIFICATIONS

One might consider the symbology as the "language" and symbology specifications as the "handwriting rules". Examples of subjects covered under the symbology specifications include code configuration, code density and dimensions, bar and space width tolerances, reflectivity and contrast, bar edge roughness, substrate materials, etc. Generally if you have problems with a bar code application, the problem is with the labels. Clearly defined symbology specifications tell users how to properly print bar code symbols. If bar code symbols meet these specifications, scanners should be able to read. If not, there is something wrong with the scanners.

The American National Standards Institute (ANSI) has established a set of standards for some bar code symbologies. Every company that uses bar codes needs to follow a set of specifications. They should adopt ANSI's specifications, their industry's specifications if available, or develop their own.

Two of the most important specifications for bar code symbols are the print contrast requirements (see Figure 1) and the bar and space width tolerances (see Figure 2).

PRINT CONTRAST SIGNAL

$$\text{PCS} \atop (75\%) = \frac{\text{SPACE REFLECTANCE} - \text{BAR REFLECTANCE}}{\text{SPACE REFLECTANCE}}$$

FIGURE 1

The formula in Figure 1 calculates the percentage difference of light that is reflected from bars versus spaces. The print contrast signal is generally specified at 75%.

Recalling how a bar code scanner works, the light from the scanner must be reflected back from spaces and absorbed by the bars. Two of several important variables in this process are the light source and the bar material (ink). Until recently, scanners emitted a helium-neon, visible red beam (electromagnetic wave length of 633 nanometers), or a gallium arsenide, infrared beam (electromagnetic wave length of 900 nanometers). Now, other types of light sources (most notably solid state lasers) are emitting electromagnetic wave lengths around 800 nanometers. The important issue here is that light is absorbed by carbon inks but infrared and similar wave length lights are not absorbed by most dye inks. Visible red light is absorbed by most inks, including most dye inks and especially black inks. As a result, the type of scanner used must be coordinated with the ink and label materials used.

Bar and space width tolerances are a function of the average width of narrow elements and the ratio of narrow to wide bars. Of course knowing the proper specifications and making sure all labels meet these specifications are two different issues. Once symbology specifications are established, there are checking devices on the market that can be programmed with your specifications. Bar code symbols can be scanned with a checking device and, if not within specifications, the device can identify exactly what requirement is not met. Using these devices to spot check labels at the printing source, out-of-spec labels can be avoided. Using statistical process control techniques, adjustments to the printer and ribbon changes can be made at the proper times.

BAR AND SPACE WIDTH TOLERANCES

TOLERANCE = ± 4/27 X (RATIO - 2/3) X NOMINAL WIDTH

GIVEN: .020 INCH NARROW ELEMENTS
3 TO 1 RATIO

TOLERANCE = ± 4/27 (3 - 2/3) .020 INCHES
= ± .0069

FIGURE 2

LABEL LAYOUT

After the rules for properly printing bar code symbols are established, a label layout can be designed. A crucial issue is: What information should be contained contained on the label? Only essential data should be on any label. Labeds generally carry both bar coded data and human readable data. You should bar code the least amount of data possible. This often sounds like a simple task, but often ends up to be one of the most difficult steps in a bar code application. Bar code symbols take up a lot of real estate. To demonstrate, see Figure 3.

CHARACTER LENGTH

PARAMETERS

SYMBOLOGY	:	CODE 3-OF-9
RATIO	:	3 TO 1
NOMINAL ELEMENT WIDTH	:	.020 INCHES
INTERCHARACTER GAP	:	.020 INCHES

CALCULATIONS

NARROW ELEMENTS	:	1 X 6 X .020" = .120"
WIDE ELEMENTS	:	3 X 3 X .020" = .180"
INTERCHARACTER GAP	:	1 X .020" = .020"
TOTAL CHARACTER LENGTH	:	.320"

FIGURE 3

In the example of Figure 3, the symbology is Code 3-of-9 and the ratio of wide to narrow bars is 3 to 1. Using a smaller ratio will take less real estate, but will reduce both readability and the allowable tolerances. The nominal or average width of the narrow elements is .020 inches. This dimension is a function of the printing device and the type of scanning. If laser scanning is desired, a wider narrow element will increase the depth of field. Wider narrow elements also increase allowable printing tolerances. Because Code 3-of-9 is a discrete code, there is an intercharacter gap generally specified as the width of a narrow element. Based on these parameters, the character length is .320 inches.

If every character is .320 inches when printed in bar code form, the total field size for any bar code symbol can be calculated as shown in Figure 4.

BAR CODE FIELD SIZE

PARAMETERS

SYMBOLOGY	: CODE 3-OF-9
CHARACTER LENGTH	: .320 INCHES
CHARACTERS	: DATA, START/STOP, IDENTIFIER
QUIET ZONES	: (2) X .250 INCHES

CALCULATIONS FOR 12 DIGIT PART NUMBERS

$$\left(\frac{S/S}{(2} + \frac{I/D}{1} + \frac{DATA}{12)} \right) X \frac{C/L}{.320"} = \frac{B/C\ LENGTH}{4.8"}$$

$$\frac{B/C}{4.8} + \frac{Q/Z}{.5} = \frac{TOTAL\ FIELD\ SIZE}{5.3"}$$

FIGURE 4

In this example, the characters that are included in bar code form represent the basic data (i.e., a part number), the start and stop characters, and a field identifier. The field identifier in this example is a single character which tells the system what type of information is included in the bar code symbol. These are only necessary when more than one type of information is being fed into a system. In environments where there are many bar coded labels in the area, field identifiers may prevent operators from reading the wrong labels. In the example, 14 characters result in a bar code symbol that is 4.8 inches long. Because quiet zones, typically specified as .25 inches on either side, are needed to read a bar code, the total field size required is 5.3 inches for a 12 digit part number.

The above example should highlight why the information that is bar coded should be kept to a minimum. To accomplish this, a serialization technique is often used. In this technique, a unique serial number is used as a key or "license plate" for various types of information that are printed on the label (in human readable form) and stored in a computer system at the time the label is generated. This serial number can also be a key to additional information that is added to the system. For example, a container of parts may have a label that has part number, quantity, manufacturing location and tag number in human readable form. The tag number (may also be considered a serial number) is the only information that needs to be bar coded. At the time the label is printed, all information can be stored in the system database. At the time the container of parts is manufactured, an operator can add to the database such information as date manufactured, tooling used, equipment used, shift number, operator number, inspector number, lot number, etc.

These have just been examples of some of the issues that must be addressed when designing a bar coded label. Label location, substrates, adhesives, and protection requirements used are among the many other issues that must be considered. With that many issues to consider, there are many alternative solutions. The better you understand the technology, the better you can design labels that will support an effective bar code application that will support an effective total system.

BAR CODING—THE CATALYST: THE OPPORTUNITY FOR OBTAINING MAXIMUM PRODUCTION BENEFITS

Eugene F. Baker, CMC
E. F. Baker & Associates, Inc.

A large segment of the world's industry is rushing to implement Bar Coding because of customers' requirements to deliver products with Bar Code labels attached. However, only a small percentage of these companies are anywhere near approaching the maximum potential benefits which Bar Coding offers for their internal production, distribution and other related operations management. In this discussion the approach for using the Bar Coding techniques as a catalyst for improving productivity, production control, and manufacturing activity scheduling and control is explored. The new methods, changes in management disciplines and the requisite systems to support the decision making process, which have resulted from Bar Coding and the small computers, is reviewed. The importance of Bar Coding in the "Just In Time" procedure and the "Zero Inventory" philosophy is shown.

The Motivation

The recent recession highlighted several weaknesses in our manufacturing activities and indicated that if changes were not made, many companies and industries would not survive. As the result, a considerable number of American companies are looking for a "quick-fix" to their problems. They have rushed headlong into Bar Coding without investigating their respective fundamental problems and the opportunities afforded by these new techniques. In addition, the advent of the micro-computers, which frequently were indiscriminately purchased, has materially changed management practices and also has had a major effect on the use of Bar Code.

Our country's industry has the highest hourly wage rate in the world and thus places us at a disadvantage with imported products. However, the imported items have additional transportation costs, fees and duties which raises the effective labor rate and thus the labor dollar content in the products. An analysis of several imports has shown that the largest differential is not necessarily in the wage rate but rather in the labor hour content in the imported item. In effect, the productivity of the producing company has a greater effect on the product cost than the basic labor rate in many products.

This condition can be seen in Exhibit 1 where there is a comparison of the U.S. versus the Japanese hours, space and work-in-process for the production of a compact car.

It is well known that during the last five years we have had very small productivity growth, in fact negative growth in some years, while the overseas operations have had major improvements in productivity. Some studies have shown that we are obtaining as little as five and a half to six hours of effective work from an employee in an eight hour shift. Recently it has been said that the United States needs an 8-1/2% productivity improvement to catch up with the other world leaders and greater than that to go ahead.

There is little we can do about the basic wage rate. Therefore, we must meet this competitive cost difference through other methods; namely, that of improved productivity and increased use of inventory.

An area where we need to make major improvements is in the use and reduction of work-in-process inventory. We hold or have in effect four to five times the inventory of our major foreign competitors. The emphasis which has been placed on the "Just In Time" system and the philosophy of "Zero Inventory" has in effect said that inventory is no longer an asset, but rather is a liability. Mr. Robert D. Stone, Vice President of Materials for General Motors, says that "Inventory Is Evil." Studies of the work in-process inventory show that in the average manufacturing environment over 85% of the time the materials are standing in queue or some other area and are not being handled in any manner whatsoever. If we are going to reduce both work in-process and finished goods inventory, and receive our purchased materials and parts just in time, we must sub-

EXHIBIT 1

Comparison
U.S. Versus Japanese Production Time and Space Requirements

	JAPANESE WORKER HOURS	U.S. WORKER HOURS
ASSEMBLY	14.0	33.0
ENGINE MACHINING & ASSEMBLY	2.8	6.8
STAMPING OF BODY PARTS	2.9	9.5
INVENTORY CARRIED PER CAR PRODUCED	$150	$775
APPROXIMATE PLANT SIZE	1.5 MILLION SQ. FT.	2.0 MILLION SQ. FT.

SOURCE: *FORTUNE*, February 8, 1982

SET-UPS	FREQUENTLY MINUTES 10% to 25% of U.S.	USUALLY DAYS or HRS. 400% to 1000% of Japanese

©Copyright 1984
E. F. BAKER
All Rights Reserved

stitute something in their place. In lieu of the inventory which has served as a cushion, up-to-date and reliable information is required. Then we can carefully manage the entire closely integrated thru-put process and have instantaneous signals the moment that potential problems are occurring. To accomplish this end it is necessary to have a real time environment with fast and accurate up-to-the-minute input. Bar Coding allows this condition to be met.

Bar Coding and the micro-computer is forcing, in some cases unknowingly, a change in management style, method and discipline. These changes include organizations wherein there is a greater decentralization of the decision making process and delegation of authority, the true advent of distributive processing, production activity management and not just control, real-time flow reporting in place of batch processing, and of flexible production mangement in lieu of just "milestone" schedules, monitoring, dispatching and expediting. An American Industrial Renaissance is here.

The major role that Bar Coding plays as the catalyst and technique used for productivity increases and management improvement is the main theme of our discussion.

Bar Code Methodology and Uses

Prior to our discussion of the various ways in which Bar Coding can be used in numerous applications to obtain maximum benefits, let us take a look at certain key factors in Bar Coding. Bar Codes in themselves are nothing more than Identifers. If either a numeric or alpha oralphanumeric code can be assigned to any article, decision, account, process, document, or any event, response, or any other item regardless of nature, it can be Bar Coded. However, since Bar Codes only identify, they do nothing unto themselves and are dependent upon a system to utilize their input. Bar Codes are used primarily as an input or an output and their generation is usually initiated by a computer output or instruction. The basic flow in the use of Bar Codes is shown in Exhibit 2.

In the use of Bar Code you have at least two numbers. The first is the base number, which is the item to which something is performed or reported upon. The second is the action number, which describes what has been performed upon the base number or to report location, accounts, or other activities relating to the base number. There can be no more than one action number reported simultaneously concerning the base number. An example would be the reporting of the completion of an operation on a part and the location of the part in the same series of Bar Code entries into the computer system.

EXHIBIT 2
Basic Use of Bar Codes

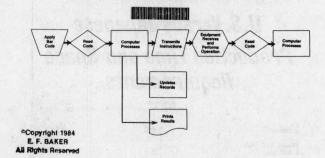

©Copyright 1984
E. F. BAKER
All Rights Reserved

Anything that we handle or have in manufacturing can be Bar Coded. Bills of material, routings, tools, dies and fixtures, reject and rework, locations, employee numbers, accounts, prints and change notices, storage locations, and many other aspects of the manufacturing and inventory procedures can be Bar Coded. The emphasis is where it can be effectively and profitably utilized and not if it is possible.

Our most urgent need in order to meet foreign and domestic competition, and to improve our productivity, is that of fast and accurate data retrieval for immediate and profitable decision making processes. While there are many options available to us, Bar Coding appears to be the one that most nearly meets all of the requirements for the manufacturing environment. Some of the reasons for the selection of Bar Coding are as follows:

. Proven highest level of reliability

. Can be used in almost an environment - not affected by magnetic or electrical fields

. High tolerance to oil, grease, moisture, direct and foreign materials

. Does not have to make physical contact

. Can be read up to five feet distance with laser reader

As shown in Exhibit 3, many types of defects can occur in a Bar Code and it is still readable.

EXHIBIT 3
LOCALIZED DEFECTS

i.e.   Spots and Voids in the Printed Code.

Major advantage of Bar Code is that a scan or rescan can avoid a problem area.

Typical Bar Code Symbol

Possible trace of a scanning beam through the symbol.

* A B C *

However: Magnitude and Frequency of Defects Affects:

1.   First Read Rate

2.   Substitution Error Probability

The fundamental applications of Bar Coding which later can be put into various functional systems are as follows:

. Accounting
. Data collection
. Information call-up
. Signaling to conveyor or other mechanical systems
. Send ahead orders and instructions
. Update of records and accounts
. Machine instruction selection and control
. Production line
. Robot instructions and control

Bar Codes are being applied by some of following ways:

. Printed adhesive label
. Matrix printed instruction and Bar Code
. Hand set stamping device
. Laser etching
. Time clock
. Preprinted code on package or carton
. Commercially printed codes, usually with other identifiable information.

Some of the places where Bar Code is currently being applied are as follows:

. Package
. Part or finished product
. Tray or bin
. Tag traveler, labor ticket
. Job card
. Receiver
. Bin identification
. Time card
. Employee badge
. Tools, dies and fixtures
. Bill of materials
. Routings
. Prints
. Picking ticket or lists
. Inspection reports
. Payroll checks
. Accounts payable checks
. Invoices
. Shippers
. Purchase orders
. Raw materials
. Supplies
. Decisions
. Accounts

EXHIBIT 4
INTERLEAVED 2 of 5

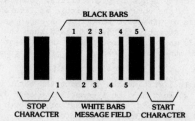

BLACK BARS

STOP CHARACTER | WHITE BARS MESSAGE FIELD | START CHARACTER

DIGITS per INCH	NARROW BARS	WIDE BARS
10.1	.010	.030
4.3	.021	.063
2.7	.030	.090

The decision as to what code should be used has become quite simple since two codes have been accepted as an American standard and also by the automobile industry. They are, namely, Interleave 2 of 5 which is shown in Exhibit 4 with some of its specifications. If you desire numeric only coding, or for alpha numeric, Code 3 of 9 or 39 as it is frequently called. Its example and specification are shown in Exhibit 5. Much of the equipment that is on the marketplace reads either of the codes automatically without any setting on the part of the operator, and therefore causes little problem in the area of code selection.

Approaches and Decisions

The biggest problem that any company now faces is to what extent they are going to use Bar Code. A "band-aid" approach can be taken which is that of merely changing the input/output procedures and leaving all other of existing management and functional programs in place. However, this does not maximize the potential use for management. Also, in conjunction with a mini-computer, it does not build a new flexibility system which allows for flexible management in order to meet the present and future challenges of domestic and foreign competition. Corporate managements are now at the crossroads to being very viable and competitive organizations or fastly becoming mature and sunset companies.

EXHIBIT 5

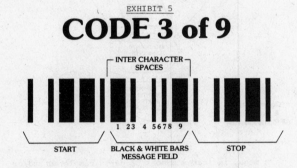

CODE 3 of 9

DIGITS per INCH	NARROW BARS (inches)	WIDE BARS (inches)
9.4	.0075	.0168
5.4	.0115	.0345
3.0	.021	.063

If the only reason for considering Bar Code is because of customer labeling requirements, such as that of the Department of Defense in accordance with its Military Standard 1189, then the only action required is to obtain a label printer, print labels for identification in the prescribed Bar Code format, and place on the outgoing packages or parts. A printer can be purchased and the vendor can hook up a tube or supply a printer with a built-in keyboard for production of the labels. If this approach is followed, nothing is gained for internal operations from the introduction of the Bar Code procedure.

A second approach, which is considered only an input/output substitute, is that of putting Bar Code on as many as possible of the documents from which you are collecting data, and using this as an entry method into the existing basic system and the accompanying computer program. In such a program you have advanced from strictly meeting customer demands to making some in-house use of the Bar Code through its reading capabilities, but the greatest potential for its use still has not been initiated. If this procedure is followed you will not materially improve your operations since in effect you are using the same basic programs and Bar Coding is only changing your input and output procedures. While your input will be read faster and its accuracy will be greater, nothing will improve in the basic results except in the areas of speed and accuracy. If your present system is generating a lot of "GIGO" the introduction of Bar Code will not change it to "FRUIT SALAD."

To accomplish the maximum with Bar Coding, major changes in the functional systems and their integration is necessary. These changes are necessary prior to the application of any software revisions or replacement. Regardless of what the final management decisions may be as to

methods of management and administration, it must be realized that with the introduction of Bar Coding in an on-line real-time environment, more information will be processed than in former systems. Also a large amount of localized simulation can be performed as a regular on-going procedure. Because of this increased amount of data and its evaluation into various formats for higher echeleons of management, many changes in management style will occur. A major change in management style and method will occur in executive and supervisory discipline and approach to the operation of a corporation. Management decisions will be made on the up-to-the-minute information which has been evaluated from a larger base of input and frequent simulations resulting from a more flexible base of operations. The concepts which are generally found in most present systems were developed based on what was affordable and timely using the techniques available in the mid-70's. At that time volume data retrievable on a real-time basis was not either possible or affordable. In that period, during the time span required to collect, process and implement the results, its usefulness lost significance. Therefore, it was not incorporated into the systems and management decisions were made on less information and evaluated alternatives than are available today. Bar Coding has caused a revolution in this area, and with the micro-computer has changed the decision process.

Integrated Systems Operations

One of the most important things to be considered in the new systems utilizing Bar Code is the integration of the various functions and their related programs in order that a single entry can update the maximum number of records and cause succeeding events to be started. By doing this we are maximizing the use of the computer memory and speed, and minimizing input and output which it is well known are the computers poorest operations. In order to have a successful operation, however, it is necessary that all output from the computer on which people must have an index number which is tied to the stored structure as to how the output was developed. This output number applies whether it be only on the CRT or on a printed form.

The most important tool needed in the manufacturing environment today is the completely integrated picture in order that moment-to-moment planning can be accomplished and proper work releases generated. To accomplish this all of the systems that have been mentioned, plus the status of rejects, rework, receipts, etc., must constantly be available to the individual responsible for the activity. In Exhibit 6 the previously mentioned indexed summaries, output numbers and a sample integrated information flow for manufacturing is illustrated.

EXHIBIT 6

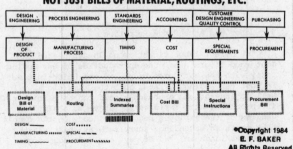

All these records need to be accurate and current at every moment in order that such decisions can be made based on the latest status, or up-to-the-moment simulation of the effect of tentative decisions can be run immediately. Bar Coding provides this input with the timing required if the necessary basics and management philosophy are in place with the accompanying software programs.

The introduction of the "Just In Time" system by major manufacturers such as General Motors, General Electric and similar companies is creating the necessity for greater flexibility and quick action in the production environment. As an illustration, General Motors will now change order content and delivery schedules on two or four hour notice. They will not allow the build-up of inventory in trailers or in any other forms in their yards, nor pay for any storage.

Therefore, in order to have the information to make rapid changes and schedules, most data must be in the electronic form with rapid up-to-the-minute input. This is provided by Bar Coding methods in which immediate entries can be made by any employee who has had about five minutes of training.

Functional Applications

1. Inventory and Stockrooms

Initially the greatest use of Bar Code was in the inventory area. This occurred primarily because of the UPC code used in supermarkets for their pricing and stock replenishment programs. While industry has started to use Bar Codes in materials and parts storage areas, the greatest emphasis to date has been primarily on the finished goods and the related shipping functions. It has not been expanded extensively into all the ramifications in the raw material and parts stockroom. In the stockrooms where it has been installed, Bar Coding has generally been handled by a modification of an old method such as pick sheets with Bar Codes on them. Other functions have not been built into the new system. One of the biggest changes which Bar Code has provided is to pull stock without the use of a pick list in the most orderly fashion and in the least possible time. In addition, multiple picking of orders at the same time or area picking is very feasible. This procedure can be accomplished by having the industrial engineering group determine the best sequence for picking orders on an engineered basis and to install these rules into the computer memory. Next, instead of producing pick lists, the computer can download the requisitioned items into a portable Bar Code scanner in the sequence in which they should be picked with their identified locations. The portable scanner, which is programmed, can lead the stock clerk to each location in the best sequence, inform him of the item to be taken from the shelves, verify such picking, and lead the individual to each successive item to be obtained. Upon return to the staging or shipping area, the items picked will be loaded back into the computer system. It will then place, in list forms on the screen, what items go to which staging location. At this time a listing can be made as desired. The same fundamental procedure can be used in any stockroom situation whether it be maintenance, manufacturing supplies or any other stockroom or issuing function.

In Exhibit 7 there is shown some of the procedures and systems followed in a maintenance stores stockroom, but it can be used in any storage area.

2. Labor and Attendance Reporting

The direct labor ticket is no longer needed on most shop floors since the introduction of Bar Coding. Today with the Bar Coded badge and the built-in timer in most Bar Coding systems, both the time clock as well as the job and attendance card can be eliminated. The procedure that replaces the above is a simple wanding of the employee badge and a code on the menu that it is an attendance entry such as shift start, lunch out/lunch in, end of day, etc. In addition, changes in normal assignments, such as direct labor to indirect, or department changes, can be handled by wanding the employee badge and the transfer of labor class and department on a menu that would carry this data. For job control, incentive pay, labor utilization and machine utilization, the employee is issued a job operation identification card, as shown in Exhibit 8, which has a unique number in Bar Code. The employee wands his badge and the card number when he starts the operation. Upon its completion, he again wands badge number and completion code and from

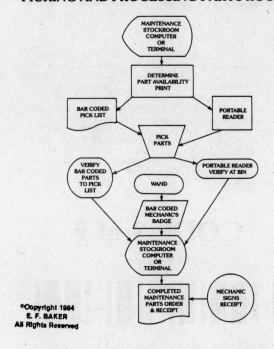

EXHIBIT 7

MAINTENANCE STOCKROOM BAR CODE PICKING AND PROCESSING PARTS ROUTINE

a menu, indicates number of parts completed and/or rejected, or any other information. Many people can work from the same card if the operation being performed is identical on the same order number. With this system all of the labor card handling is practically eliminated. In addition, as jobs are completed, the shop load is relieved, the order status is immediately know, parts locations are designated, and the value of the work added is included in the work-in-process value in the computer. Another advantage to this approach is that at any time an order may be split and its status known without additional paperwork since the "send ahead" items would be wanded in and out on every respective operation and no extra paperwork would be required. This same approach is used for simultaneous operations wherein a batch is not completed prior to starting on a second operation.

EXHIBIT 8

DIRECT LABOR TICKET ..... #3603			
SO #	**START**	**FINISH**	**QTY.**
7781	8/05	8/06	40
S/A OR P/P	**DESCRIPTION**		
01-13675-8	HEADER BAR		
DEPT.	**W/C**	**OPERATION**	
16	183-1	GRIND 3/8 x 1-1/2 x 5-3/16	
OPER #	**SEQ #**	**STD. RATE**	**SETUP RATE**
1670	115	.470	.200

Again, control is accomplished through the wanding of the quantity of items "off" an operation and the quantity "on" to each succeeding operation. Exhibit 9 shows this method of operation. An additional feature which has been added into many systems is that of the material handler indicating, through wanding, that he has a certain lot of material removing it from one department or work center and that he has dropped it in another. This is a very inexpensive procedure since cheap satellite wands are used for this purpose.

EXHIBIT 9
OVERLAPPING SCHEDULING

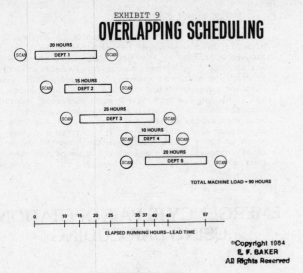

ELAPSED RUNNING HOURS—LEAD TIME

TOTAL MACHINE LOAD = 90 HOURS

3. Tool, Die and Fixture

One large problem we are finding in manufacturing is that of the scheduling and control of tools, dies and fixtures. Frequently these items are not available when a job is ready to go. Starts are made and then stopped because tools are not available to work on the assignment. The introduction of Bar Coding into tool rooms has saved money in the control and issuance of the items. Also, the integration of the tool room information into the total manufacturing system allows the flow manager/production scheduler to determine if the necessary tooling is available prior to the issuance of the instructions to commence operations. Also by having this information, production planning as well as the Flow Managers can place reservations on the needed tools, dies and fixtures in the same manner that they would schedule a piece of machinery. The introduction of this type of system in many companies has produced many million dollars of savings in loss labor time, machine utilization, as well as tool procurement, sharpening and repair.

4. Bills of Material

The coding of documents issued to the shop floor will vary by the type and size and procedures the company will follow. In small job shops the leveled bill of material will generally be Bar Coded and issued for direct read of the code through a matrix printer or a good copying device. In larger organizations with higher volumes, the previously reported procedure for use of the portable scanner would more generally be used for stock pulling purposes.

5. Routings

The routings will also vary by size of the company. In the case of a large organization, the above described method of issuing an operation identification card will be more generally found. In the smaller organizations, the routings themselves will be Bar Coded (see Exhibit 10) in a manner similar to the bill of material and will be issued in the typical job packet to accompany the job through the shop.

6. Prints

One of the biggest problems on the shop floor has always been that of producing to the latest print revision or engineering change order. By placing a Bar Code on these documents, they can be scanned on the shop floor and the computer can check if they are the latest revisions prior to their issuance to an employee for work.

7. Purchasing and Receiving

The question is frequently raised as to where to start from scratch on the installation of a Bar Coding system. The answer to this, of course, is where

---

EXHIBIT 10
ROUTING

DEPT. 10		PART NO. 01-2346-3 MATERIAL NO. 00-0926-4		PART DESCRIPTION—SHROUD STEEL, GALVANIZE—20 GA. SHEET		
SEQUENCE NO.	OPERATION NO.	MACHINE NO.	OPERATION, DESCRIPTION & SPECIFICATION	STD. HRS. S/U	RUN	TOOL NO. DIE NO. FIXTURE NO.
10	1000	001-0	SHEAR-936	.1	1.2	T101
20	1102	100-2	DRAW-109	.25	5.0	D296 F062
30	2390	200-1	FORM-296	.6	10.5	—
40	3333	240-0	PUNCH-500	1.1	6.8	F286

everything begins, namely, the receiving areas where the material and parts first enter the factory and are processed. To accomplish this effectively the Purchasing Department must perform certain operations in order that the incoming material is identified. At the present time most companies cannot and will not put part numbers or Bar Coded labels on their shipments. Therefore it becomes incumbent on the buyer to furnish any such identifying material to the supplier. Only the giants of industry and the government can force their suppliers to follow their requests. One very effective method which is being followed is to include in the purchase order set sent to the vendor one or more Bar Coded order identification slip. In Exhibit 11 the flow chart for such a system is shown.

EXHIBIT 11

Bar Code Requirements
planning and purchasing.....

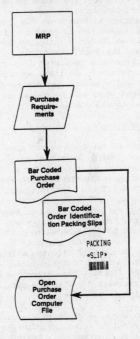

These Bar Coded identification slips contain instructions to include them with the packing slip papers accompanying the shipment. Of course this same purchase order should be entered into the computer with the appropriate number. Upon receipt of the order, the identification slips' Bar Code is wanded on the receiving docks and the items which are ordered are shown on a screen. After one of several methods of inventorying the items is completed, they are entered into the computer system on the shipping docks. A schematic diagram for this procedure is shown in Exhibit 12.

EXHIBIT 12

Bar Coded Receiving System with portable readers

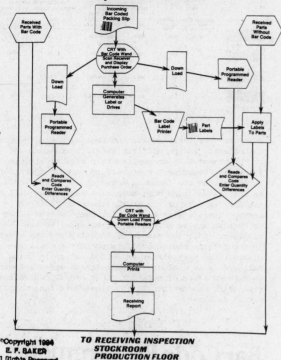

**TO RECEIVING INSPECTION
STOCKROOM
PRODUCTION FLOOR**

These entries immediately update the stock status records, open purchase order files and determine if there are still any items to be received. Upon review of the screen an entry can then be made as to the number of labels of each item desired. A label printer attached to the tube will print the necessary labels which can be attached to all items prior to leaving the dock. From this point on the items can be tracked and receiving inspection can use the Bar Code systems to indicate acceptance or rejection of items and also its recommended disposition. Then the received items can be placed in the stockroom and recorded in the computer by thier respective location.

8. Maintenance

One of the more recent areas to introduce the use of Bar Coding is that of maintenance planning. The maintenance departments are placing Bar Codes on all of the equipment lists in the manner as on a bill of material. These lists are used both in the regular maintenance planning and the emergency maintenance procedures. In the case of regular maintenance procedures, the plan and dates are established the same as would be for scheduling production, and the items which are regularly replaced during a maintenance procedure are wanded from the maintenance equipment list and transmitted to the maintenance stockroom with the desired dates. These items are then made available and are ready for when the particular maintenance function is to occur.

In the case of emergency maintenance or problems discovered in a regular maintenance check, the procedure is diagrammed in Exhibit 13.

Upon opening up of a particular piece of equipment and defective parts are found, the equipment list is scanned for the Bar Codes for the items needed and then transmitted to the maintenance stockroom for immediate pickup or delivery. The experience of companies using such a procedure has been that of considerable improvement in the length of waiting time at the maintenance stockroom for the obtaining of the necessary parts and improvement in the stocking level which is necessary to be carried in order to properly support the maintenance requirement of the fully operating installation.

9. Conveying and Stacking

Heavy users of conveyor systems which contain gates or other methods of changing direction of the flow of a package or item are starting to heavily utilize Bar Code equipment. In fact, one manufacturer of conveyor equipment recently purchased a Bar Code scanning company. Under these systems the computer has established a routing for each number in order to take the item to its ultimate destination, whether it be a work center or the stockroom. Laser scanners are placed along the line which reads the Bar Code which in turn is transmitted to the computer which sends instruction to the next point where the direction of the package will be changed. This is accomp-

EXHIBIT 13

EMERGENCY REPAIR OPERATION USING BAR CODING

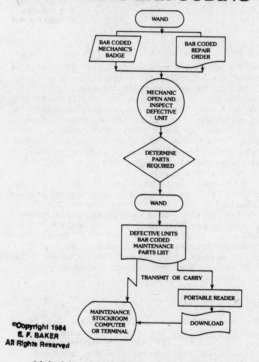

lished by the throwing of gates or the activation of a pusher to shove the item off the conveyor system at a particular point. A schematic of this procedure is shown in Exhibit 14. In the case of stockrooms, several systems are now in existence which read the Bar Code and the automatic stacking system takes the particular carton and places it in the exact bin or shelf which has been assigned to it by the computer system. Automated retrieval of the stock is also being handled, and verifying of the pick through the use of Bar Code. With the greater use of the "Just In Time" system, companies are going to have greater activity on their receiving dock since there will be more frequent deliveries of smaller quantities. This means there will be an increase of material handling activity on the shop floor which may in many instances be too great a load for the existing aisles and other facilities.

Therefore, it can be expected that in many plans overhead conveyor systems will probably be installed to directly carry the material to the work center and its point of use. In order to effectively utilize such a system some method of identification, such as Bar Code described above, will be necessary to accomplish the desired end.

10. NC, CNC, Equipment and Robots

The new numerical controlled machines are either controlled by a computer or stored programs within the machine. The machines may have as many as thirty programs or more stored in them, which are then

EXHIBIT 14

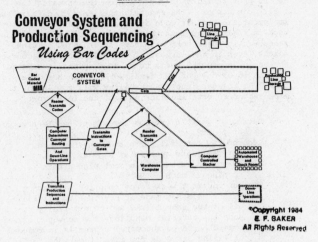

Conveyor System and Production Sequencing *Using Bar Codes*

selected for the appropriate operations. As was mentioned earlier, one of the uses of Bar Coding is to select particular functions to be performed. In order to accomplish the desired functions on the numerical controlled machines, the identification of the part number through the reading of Bar Code can select the appropriate NC program from its stored memory, or in the computer.

In a manner similar to that of numerical controlled machinery, we now have the instruction of the multi-purpose robot. In Exhibit 15 both the procedure for NC and Robot instructions in conjunction with a conveyor system is shown. According to a recent report, about 40% of the robots produced today require specific instructions as to what they are to do and are not just controlled by a certain sensing, weight, light interruption, or similar single or limited purpose devices. The multi-purpose robot must be instructed as to what to do. Its instructions are stored in the computer or the unit as to certain procedures which it must follow in order to accomplish its desired purpose. Again, like in the numerical controlled machinery, this identification and pulling out of the proper set of instructions can and is being accomplished in many cases by Bar Code.

EXHIBIT 15

ROBOT AND CNC OR NC MACHINE CONTROL USING BAR CODES

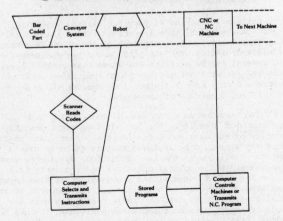

11. Paperless Factory

The paperless shop floor control system, as shown in Exhibit 16, has come into being through the use

of Bar Code and other computer and data collecting systems. The conditions have been limited to the cases where certain instructions and prints are still necessary to be in the departments in order to accomplish the various operations or assemblies. However, the introduction of Bar Code has given a new dimension to shop activities whereby even the prints and instructions no longer need to be issued on paper. Instead they can be generated and displayed on a tube in front of the operator. To accomplish this result and to obtain the maximum flexibility, it again is necessary for identification to be made as to the item which is to be fabricated or assembled in order that the computer can select the appropriate routing instructions and, if necessary, parts list. Therefore Bar Code, because of its great capability of identification, comes very much into play. Under this system the Bar Code is wanded on each part as it comes into a worker position. This scan causes the computer to generate the instructions on the screen in front of the operator. Therefore a complete interchange and mix of what's going down the assembly or other type of production line, or at a fabrication type machine, can occur and does not require everything to be produced in lots. Under this procedure, because of the mix, the operators do not have to pull out instructions and prints each time a different part comes into the position. The information requirements are all portrayed on the screen in front of them. In large assembly type operations, particularly in electronics, a considerable amount of preparation and setup time is avoided through the introduction of this procedure.

EXHIBIT 16

PAPERLESS Shop Floor Control System

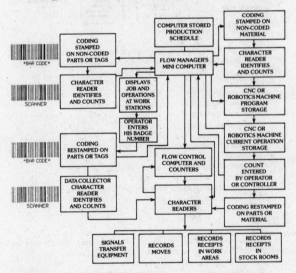

A total network for a Flow Manager in which he directs all activities in an assigned area and controls the entire machine network in this area is shown in Exhibit 17.

Space allowance does not provide for further detailed description of applications and case studies which will be presented in the live session. Diagrams, flow charts and operating Bar Code equipment will be used to illustrate many of the points.

Functions, Procedures and Processes for Bar Coding

A few of the areas where Bar Code should be considered are as follows:

Accounting - cost, payables, receivables
Production control
Inventory control
Flow Management - Shop Floor Control

Production processing
Materials handling
Purchasing - Receiving
MRP
Capacity planning
Quality control
Production planning and scheduling
Shipping
Labor planning and control
Sales
Engineering design
Industrial and process engineering
Stockrooms and warehouses
Rework - scrap
Tool - die - fixture planning and control
And many others

EXHIBIT 17

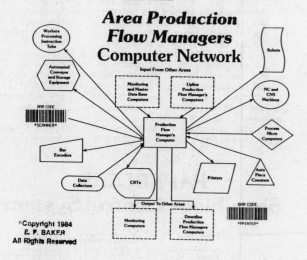

Area Production Flow Managers Computer Network

©Copyright 1984
E. F. BAKER
All Rights Reserved

Some of the ways within a process in which the particular procedures and processes may be applied are as follows:

Data collection
Document coding
Time recording
Counting
Identification
Verification
Indexing
Equipment and robot instruction
Conveyor control
Automated stocking and selection instruction
And others

Summary

The overall productivity improvements which are being experienced in many companies are as follows:

Decreased worker time for clerical functions
Less waiting time for jobs
Improved material, machine, tool, labor coordination
Faster total through-put, less queue
Current, rapid and information for management decision

Summing up opportunities which are available through the use of Bar Coding are:

Reduced lead time
Improved tracking
Smaller EO
Elimination of batch processing
Reduced material handling
Employement of the Just In Time" system
Utilization of multi-purpose robots
Enhanced Flow Management
Higher inventory accuracy
Higher capacity utilization
Higher manufacturing flexibility
Complete functional integrated systems
Responsive customer service
Less repetitive clerical functions
Improved total accuracy

The biggest question always asked is what is going to be the profitability or payback from the installation of a Bar Code system. The general experience to date in the implementation of Bar Code systems has been that the payback is realized in less than one year. In fact, in many cases, it is quite common to have it in eight or nine months, even in the largest of installations. Of course, the basic "homework" needs to be done on the fundamental systems in advance of the final work on the Bar Code systems. As to where the profitability will come from, the more recent reports indicate some of the following:

. Decreased work in process investment has been reported up to 65%.
. Reduced raw material parts and finished goods inventory are running as high as 50%.
. Less paper processing. In some plants this is running as much as 90%.
. Smaller indirect work force required. In some plants this has made it possible to eliminate all of the shop clerks and to materially reduce the material handling if a conveyor or some other type automated system is introduced utilizing Bar Code for identification.
. Increased output from existing capacity is running as much as 35%.

All indications are that similar results will be obtained in many additional places. However, the amount depends on the existing conditions of each and every facility. You must be selective as to where you will install the system and management must be in agreement with the new approach to management and control of the production facility.

I recently returned from New Zealand, Australia, Southeast Asia and Taiwan and found that while they are considerably behind us in the use of Bar Code, it is beginning to be introduced at the present time. They are utilizing the same codes that we are and are labeling the products which are being shipped to this country as many of their customers have a Bar Coding requirement. Many of the companies are branches of U.S. organizations and are being required to introduce Bar Code into their manufacturing area in order to have a unified manufacturing control between the overseas and domestic operations. There is also a desire for greater flexibility in their operations. Therefore, several companies are in the process of developing and installing the Flexible Production Management system utilizing Bar Code.

Our government is using Bar Coding in many of its various departments and bureaus at the present time. Investigations have been under way concerning the use of the code in the Customs operation. This is another reason for the overseas companies becoming extremely interested in learning and adaptation and use of Bar Code. They believe it will enhance their position from an import point of view and the clearing of Customs. We can expect that the Pacific countries will be utilizing as much Bar Code as we are within a very few years.

European countries already are extensively using Bar Code. In some areas they are considerably ahead of us. Many transportation organizations already have Bar Code on bills of lading, freight bills and other documents, and several of the airlines even have them on the passenger tickets. We will not get any break from being ahead of Europe and only have a minimum lead against the other industralized countries of the world.

The question is often asked, where is Bar Code going now and what else is on the horizon that might possibly compete or supplant Bar Code. At the present time there does not appear to be anything that is going to make a serious challenge to the use of Bar Code within the next ten years. While optical character reading is in existence for certain specialized pruposes, it is also being replaced by Bar Code in other areas. The magnetic stripe will continue to be used on credit cards, although Bar Code is expected to be added as an additional feature for compatibility within certain business systems. However, in the production area, the magnetic stripe card is fast disappearing in lieu of Bar Coding.

A voice system would be an ideal situation, but after many years of work, it has just reached a point to a very limited usable vocabulary from a single person and does not have great universal usage. Some day voice may be the method we use, but it is not foreseen within the next ten years. There does not appear to be any other system "in the wings" at the present time.

Bar Coding has finally established an American standard for symbology, which is expected to be shortly accepted in European operations. Therefore, most of the rest of the world will no doubt utilize these symbologies or ones that are compatible. The symbology and methodology appears to be pretty well established for some period of time. There no doubt will be major improvements in equipment that will do an improved job of printing, increase its speed, allow for greater density in printing,

scanning and become integral parts of other pieces of machinery, such as sorting equipment, specific types of material handling, communications, and other electronic and mechanical equipment. However, there is nothing to indicate that the present equipment will become outmoded and non-compatible with any of the new operations since the sumbology has been standardized. The limitations would primarily be those of density in the label of newer printing compared to existing equipment. But this is a matter of choice as to label densities and the requirements for extremely high density printing. There is not any fear in proceeding today into Bar Coding with an idea of obsolescence or gain by waiting. Time lost and delay today is money lost and increased profitability and efficiency in most operations.

BIOGRAPHY OF EUGENE F. BAKER, CMC

Eugene F. Baker is a certified management consultant and President of E.F. Baker & Associates, Inc., Northbrook, Illinois, an international counseling and training firm. His consulting experience includes all phases of production and inventory control, shop floor control, systems, cost, Bar Coding and data processing. He has been a production supervisor, production and inventory control manager and corporate director of Management Information Systems. An active member of APICS, Mr. Baker received the F. Norman Stewart Communication Award, primarily for his work in developing and communicating a major addition to the body of knowledge in shop floor control. In 1969 he developed and presented the first known program on Shop Floor Control, which he has continually updated and taught to date. In 1978 the concept of "Flow Management" was developed, which enhances shop floor control to meet "Just In Time" needs. This has further been enhanced to "Flexible Manufacuturing Management." Mr. Baker has kept pace with the application of minicomputers and Bar Coding to the manufacturing environment and has worked with various companies, societies, and universities around the world discussing their role. He is a member of the Production and Material Control Advisory Committee for the Department of Business and Management, University of Wisconsin-Extension, and an approved arbitrator of the American Arbitration Association's Commercial Panel. Approximately seventy-five days each year Gene conducts seminars in Bar Coding, Flow Management, Flexible Manufacturing Management, MRP, Computer in Manufacturing, and related Materials Management subjects. In 1982 he conducted Production Manufacturing Management seminars in various countries in Southeast Asia and in 1983 and 1984 seminars in Bar Coding and Flexible Manufacturing Management were conducted in the U.S., New Zealand, Australia, Southeast Asia, Hong Kong and Taiwan. He has written many articles on P & IC subjects, some of which are "The Changing Scene on the Production Floor" and "Management Giving Production Planning Bigger Role in Shop Floor Operations." At the present time he is preparing the Bar Code chapter for the soon to be published APICS Production and Inventory Control Handbook, and a Bar Coding application booklet for the AMACOM Publishing Division of the American Management Association.

BAR CODING SAVES THE D.O.D. HUNDREDS OF MILLIONS

Charles A. Horne
Randall K. Love, CPIM
Arthur Andersen & Co.

Barcode applications have saved the Department of Defense (D.O.D.) hundreds of millions of dollars primarily through improved productivity, timelines and data accuracy associated with material ordering, processing and control. The techniques used to implement these various barcode applications at D.O.D. installations are proven technologies capable of increasing productivity in virtually all Production and Inventory Control systems. Barcoding is easy to understand and implement with many obvious benefits.

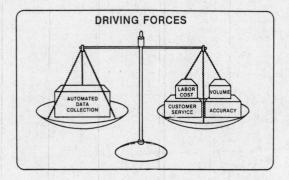

DRIVING FORCES

The requirements for accurate and timely data collection are essential for successful manufacturing system operation and overall management control. Automating this data capture process through the integration of barcoding has an immediate bottom line effect. Substantial benefits in the reduction of labor costs increased production volume and operations throughput, results in lower manufacturing costs, reduced lead times, and improved customer service.

The retail industry has lead the way in the past in the automated data capture processing and "worked out the bugs". Several data collection alternatives were implemented and are all proven technologies available for current use. These alternatives range from keystroke data entry to punched cards, mark sense cards, magnetic stripe cards/tape, optical character recognition (OCR) and barcoding. Each of these alternatives have positive and negative characteristics related to costs of implementation, flexibility, error-rates, speed, applicability to need, etc.

The advantages of barcoding in relation to the other alternatives are primarily the data entry speed and productivity, high accuracy rate (minimum of one error in three million reads), relatively inexpensive equipment/media, and is a widely accepted standard throughout the manufacturing industry. Several advantages include the inability of humans to read the data without decoding, special printers and/or software and the positioning of the barcode for accurate and timely reading.

The D.O.D. has been the driver in the evaluation of automated data collection techniques and standardization of symbologies and procedures as they relate to the manufacturing industries. The study results of the Joint Steering Group for Logistics Application of Automated Marking and Reading Symbols (LOGMARS) were presented in 1981. Two key instructions were established within the Government to standardize the specification of the barcode itself (MIL-STD-1189) and barcode label contents and placement on government material (MIL-STD-129H). Total implementation of barcoding as defined

by the Joint Steering Group was projected for 1985, although the schedule is behind at this point.

LOGMARS PILOT FINDINGS

10 PILOT PROJECTS

* 100%-400% PRODUCTIVITY INCREASE
* 99%-100% ERROR REDUCTION
* 90% REDUCTION IN DATA ENTRY TIME

INTANGIBLE BENEFITS

- DATA ACCURACY
- INCREASED ASSET VISIBILITY
- REDUCTION IN DOCUMENTATION REQUIREMENTS
- FEWER TRAINING REQUIREMENTS
- CONTROL AND ACCOUNTABILITY
- REDUCED LEAD TIME
- PAPER REDUCTION
- OPPORTUNITY TO PROVIDE DETAIL TRACKING

LOGMARS COST/BENEFIT STUDY

FUNCTION	TOTAL ESTIMATED DOD SAVINGS
DEPOT LEVEL MAINTENANCE	$ 59,273,000
AMMUNITION INVENTORY	29,663,000
SERVICE STORE INVENTORY/ISSUE	13,847,000
WHOLESALE RECEIVING	4,672,000
WHOLESALE SHIPPING	2,755,000
AIR TRANSPORTATION	1,229,000
RETAIL RECEIVING	1,159,000
DISTRIBUTION SORTATION	675,000
WHOLESALE INVENTORY/LOCATION AUDIT	212,000
WHOLESALE DISPOSAL	183,000
TOTAL YEARLY SAVINGS FOR 10 FUNCTIONS (D.O.D. WIDE)	113,868,00

Barcoding technology and standardization has matured to the point of being a natural data collection means for many aspects of the factory of the future. Data capture for systems such as CAD-CAM, JIT, Group Technology Automated Material Handling, MRP and Robotics have been integrated with barcoding around the world. The technologies behind these systems compliment each other and are moving closer to standard interfaces which will ease integration.

The most popular barcode symbology used today within the manufacturing industry is "3 of 9". This symbology has been adopted by the D.O.D. and the automotive industries primarily for its flexibility, alphanumeric capabilities, and ease of understanding and use. Other less popular symbologies within the manufacturing industry are "9 to 3" (interleaved, alphanumeric, relatively new); "2 of 5" (simpliest, numeric only); and interleaved "2 of 5" (higher density).

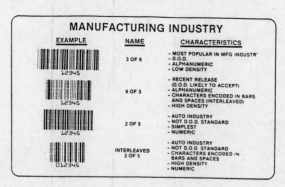

MANUFACTURING INDUSTRY

EXAMPLE	NAME	CHARACTERISTICS
12345	3 OF 9	- MOST POPULAR IN MFG INDUSTR' - D.O.D. - ALPHANUMERIC - LOW DENSITY
12345	9 OF 3	- RECENT RELEASE (D.O.D. LIKELY TO ACCEPT) - ALPHANUMERIC - CHARACTERS ENCODED IN BARS AND SPACES (INTERLEAVED) - HIGH DENSITY
12345	2 OF 5	- AUTO INDUSTRY - NOT D.O.D. STANDARD - SIMPLEST - NUMERIC
012345	INTERLEAVED 2 OF 5	- AUTO INDUSTRY - NOT D.O.D. STANDARD - CHARACTERS ENCODED IN BARS AND SPACES - HIGH DENSITY - NUMERIC

Barcode symbologies used substantially in other industries include the Universal Product Code (UPC) in the retail industry and CODABAR used by the Library of Congress and the Medical industry.

OTHER INDUSTRIES

EXAMPLE	NAME	CHARACTERISTICS
‖‖‖‖‖ 12345	CODABAR	- MEDICAL INDUSTRY - NUMERIC
0 ‖‖‖‖‖ 12345 67890	UPC	- RETAIL INDUSTRY - NUMERIC - TYPE VARIES BY PRODUCT - FIXED LENGTH

The technical aspects of printing the barcode, reading it and interfacing the data with the related applications are integral parts of the P. and IC system design and implementation. The selection of the barcode-related equipment must address key design issues including barcode density, reflective capability of the media (paper, metal, plastic, etc.) volume of labels required, number of reads required per label, and the working environment. The technology of the barcode equipment to properly address these design issues is steadily improving and changing.

The barcode terminal/reader has a wide and varied spectrum of capabilities to best meet the functional and technical design requirements of the system. Key functions to be considered are whether physical contact of the wand is required, fixed versus movable equipment and material, density of the barcode, operator prompts for data entry and data storage and transmittal. As you can see, a thorough analysis of requirements and design of the system applications are required for proper selection and implementation of barcode equipment.

The costs involved in the design and implementation of barcoding with P and IC systems vary with the level of integration and overall functions performed. For data entry, normal MRP-type screen changes are not required with adjustments necessary only to procedures and documents for barcode placement and usage. If barcodes are used beyond simple data entry to represent groups of data and direct system processing, redesign is normally required to screens, data basis and overall system architecture.

Similar to the results of the LOGMARS study the applications of barcodes within P and IC are unlimited. Material, labor and operations data capture are primary candidates for barcoding. Material receipt, issue, inspection, storage, counting, moves, and quality control require timely and accurate control. Personnel related elements such as labor cost, time and attendance and security are areas where barcoding can be employed. Order entry, status, material routing, processing instructions and machine/tool usage all have substantial opportunity for productivity improvements.

COMMON ELEMENTS BAR CODES REPRESENT

MANUFACTURING FUNCTIONAL AREA	PART	LOCATION DESIGNATION	OPERATION	PERSON	JOB . . .
INVENTORY CONTROL	√	√		√	√
SHOP FLOOR	√		√	√	√
MATERIAL HANDLING	√	√			
SECURITY				√	
TIME AND ATTENDANCE			√	√	√

Barcode applications in these areas have tremendous benefits, if properly implemented. Barcoding must become a "natural" part of the daily routine, not a "spur". The characteristics of barcoding alone allow for success -- reduction of manual efforts through automated data collection. Within the D.O.D., these reductions amount to hundreds of millions of dollars.

SUMMARY

The estimated savings from implementing barcoding techniques are real and obtainable not only throughout the D.O.D., but the manufacturing industry as well. The impact on the productivity of people, processing of paperwork and the speed and accuracy of communication is substantial.

BIBLIOGRAPHY

Charles A. Horne, CPIM and Randall K. Love, CPIM are members of Arthur Andersen & Co.'s Management Information Consulting Division. Mr. Horne is a partner in the Dallas office with 16 years of consulting experience in the manufacturing industry and is a frequent APICS speaker on the local and national level. His primary focus is on the design and installation of computer based manufacturing planning and control systems and executive education.

Mr. Love is a senior manager consultant in the Los Angeles office and is the current Chairman of the Board of the Los Angeles chapter. His consulting experience of nine years has been primarily with large manufacturing corporations with major concentration on the Department of Defense engagements for the Navy to improve production and efficiency.

CRITICAL FACTORS ASSOCIATED WITH THE SUCCESSFUL IMPLEMENTATION OF A BAR CODE DATA COLLECTION SYSTEM

J. H. Leckenby
General Dynamics Corporation

OVERVIEW

Four years of experience designing, implementing and operating manufacturing control systems using bar code data collection has shown that the success of the program is, in large part due to the efficient interlock of the supporting activities of the system with the inherent advantages of bar code data collection. This paper identifies and discusses in detail the critical elements which have contributed to the success of these bar code data collection systems.

As the result of an innovative Plant Manager's decision, bar code data collection was designed into an upgrade of a manufacturing shop control system in 1978. At that time there was no precedents on which to base the methods to be used in applying bar code to data collection in a manufacturing control system. Even portable readers which, at that time, were thought to be an essential part of the system had not been exposed to a heavy industry manufacturing environment.

In spite of the lack of experience the first system was designed, installed and implemented using Bar Code 39 format with a degree of success which confounded the most pessimistic critics.

A second bar code data collection system using job tickets was installed early in 1983. The installation followed the same guidelines of the first system and the results in throughput, data accuracy and user acceptance have again been extremely favorable. As was found in the first system there were paybacks which had not been anticipated when the systems were designed.

System number three using laser printed pick lists will be installed in July 1984.

Systems four, five and six will be installed in late 1984 and early 1985 and there is no reason to doubt that they will be successful even though they will use new techniques, new equipment and will service areas with different requirements from the existing systems.

Why were the first two systems successful and why is there so much confidence that the follow-on-systems will also be successful?

An in depth analysis of the installed systems showed that there was no one reason for the success. Instead, it was a combination of interlocking disciplines - a team effort - of hardware, software, and peopleware which contributed to the success of the system. The basics used in the first two systems are being followed in the new systems and barring unforeseen circumstances these systems will also be installed without major problems.

It is appreciated that all the elements which contributed to the success of the systems to be described may not apply to other manufacturing control systems. However, it is hoped that this paper will lead designers and implementation personnel to look more closely at the total system to determine if an upgrading of peripherals can enhance the inherent benefits available from bar code data collection.

CRITICAL ELEMENTS OF BAR CODE SYSTEM

The critical elements of the systems have been broken down as follows:

- Bar Code Labels
- Bar Code Forms
- Data Input
- Location Patterns
- System Flexibility
- Data Integrity

BAR CODE LABELS

The first use of bar code was in a hostile environment where the identification media was subject to immersion in a caustic solution for up to one hour at a temperature of 180°F. Up to the introduction of bar code labels the only label to meet the hostile environment was an embossed stainless steel plate which was produced manually at a rate of about twenty per hour. Bad numbers were frequent and caused serious problems on the production floor. The sharp edges of the label caused many accidents and the workers hated to handle slippery material with these labels attached.

In 1979 a high density impact printer was the only equipment available that could efficiently produce alpha numeric bar code labels to meet our requirements. After a lengthy test period in which the adhesive, paper and film manufactures co-operated a satisfactory label was produced which has given excellent results and exceeded all our expectations.

The label carries the computer line identity in the bar code and the plan and part number in the line above the bar code. The label is capable of being read visually in dim light and is purposely uncluttered. A very desirable attribute of the strip printer is that there is no relationship between the top line and the bar code.

The one mil mylar film protecting the print is "fisheye free" to ensure no distortion in scanning the code bars. In certain cases it is not practical to stick the label directly on to the material for several reasons:

1. Not all the material has a smooth flat surface.
2. On large assemblies it would be difficult to find the label, let alone scan it.
3. In rework heat could destroy the label.

To overcome these problems the label is stuck on to a plastic plate which is in turn attached to the assembly by nylon ties. The plate can be turned for better scanability. (Figure 1)

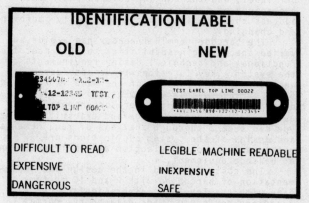

Fig. 1 Comparison Between Old & New Labels

There have been no reported accidents attributable to the use of the tag and, in the infrequent event of the tag being attached to an incorrect assembly, the system is so designed that the problem can be corrected within minutes of the mistake being found.

PAINTING OVER BAR CODE LABELS

Some of the assemblies have to be painted. Prior to painting, a 1" low tack translucent colored tape is stuck across the bar code label. After painting, the tape is removed with no damage to the bar code label underneath.

BAR CODE JOB TICKET

The introduction of a tab card printer with sixty four characters of bar code and ten lines of print opened the way for a second generation system of shop floor control using bar code data collection.

Fig. 2 Job Ticket

The original method of control was a five part computer printed form. The new form is a single white card (See Figure 2). A rough draft of the form was printed and shown to all personnel who would be working with it. After 20 changes the form was finalized and not one adverse comment has been received on text or layout. In all cases where the employee suggestion could not be used, a reason was given for the non-acceptance.

Bar code data collection using this form has raised both data credibility and material traceability from 80% to better than 99.5%.

BAR CODE PICK LIST

The advent of the medium cost laser printer allowed phase three of the bar code data collection system to be designed for service in July 1984.

The existing pick list was computer generated and was strictly an information document. Before any attempt to design a new document was made, material picking personnel were questioned on the type of document and layout which would be best applicable to their job. Six experienced material controllers were asked how they thought through the material collection process - location, part number, type of material, quantity, etc.

Their input was incorporated into a computer designed form. The basic form went through thirty-four changes before it was accepted by all the people who would use it in their day to day operations (See Figure 3).

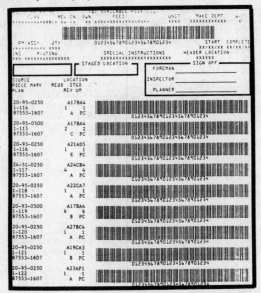

Fig. 3 Part of a Laser Printed Pick List

The form is designed to track six sequential operations all bar coded. Space is available for signatures and final storage location.

The interest generated in the development of the form together with an analysis of the problems associated with collecting and recording job progress was such, that when a form is required for a different type of material collection, the same formula will be followed and the form will be custom made to that operation.

DATA INPUT

Single Entry

The changeover from keypunch to real time bar code data entry resulted in a dramatic upgrade in data integrity. The old method of data input used a source document which had to be sent to a centralized data input to be processed. Problems with data integrity were common due to keypunch errors, legibility of handwritten location, identity and human error. Inevitable delays and excessive expediting was also experienced because of document loss and a normal turnaround of up to three days.

The new system allows the person handling the material to wand the transaction into the system with three strokes as shown in Figure 4.

The "MOVE" and "TO SUBSTORES" bar code labels are mounted on a board adjacent to the bar code terminal. The

terminal is designed to beep 3 times for an accepted read and six times for a bad read. There are no prompts in the terminal equipment.

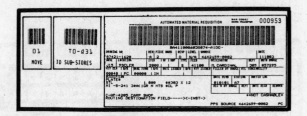

Fig. 4 Wanding Material to Sub-Stores

Batch Wanding

Batch wanding i.e. moving many pieces to the same location, is available at all work stations. The operator wands the control (MOVE) and location (TO-Q31) once, then all requisitions for that location. The average speed of batch wanding is 20-30 transactions per minute but can go as high as 60-80 when the operators hold a friendly competition to see who will buy the coffee.

Multiple Entry

When a control area has to ship or control material to a number of stations the multiple entry bar board is used (Figure 5). The labels are large and placed in their own individual rectangle. Boards with as many as thirty bar codes are in use. Wherever possible descriptive information is printed beneath the bar code.

Fig. 5 Multiple Entry Bar Board

There have been no known cases of wrong codes being wanded in over three years of operation. Watching the operation from a distance has revealed that if the worker is not satisfied with what he or she had wanded they will return to the terminal and rewand the transaction. The program is designed to accept without question the second transaction and overlay the previous transaction without any kickouts.

One of the benefits of this system is the standardized input. Illicit transactions made by keypunch will often not match the bar code input and can be readily identified.

The most durable bar board consists of a sheet of aluminum to which is attached, with double sided sheeting a transparancy printed with the blocks only. The bar code labels are stuck on the blocks from which they can be cleanly removed for replacement. The cushioning effect of the double sided adhesive and transparancy provides a smooth surface without the wear problems found when the label is attached directly to a firm base. Replacement labels are never stuck over used or torn labels. The surface of the labels would be uneven causing less than excellent ready and as the label stock is translucent the covered label could affect the read rate.

Labels attached directly to metal boards tend to leave their adhesive on the board when removed and the replacement label will not be smooth due to the adhesive beneath causing an uneven surface and excessive wear.

Bar Code and Manual Wanding Assist

When it is not practical to wand the location bar code

at the point of origin the job ticket carrying the bar code I.D. of the item being stored is marked with the location. The ticket is taken back to the bar code wanding terminal where it is entered into the computer system as follows (See Figure 6).

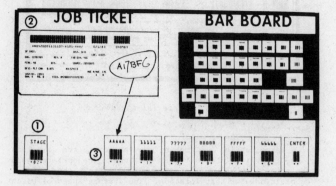

Fig. 6 Bar Code and "Manual" Wanding

The operator wands 1 "STAGE", 2 the I.D. on the workpaper and 3 the location characters from bar code labels on a special bar board. The system is designed for a six character location field and the individual characters are preceeded by a space which tells the system there is more to come until an "ENTER" character is received.

The system is in use where a 99.5% material location credibility is being maintained. There has been very few discrepancies between the paper and the bar code entries.

Training on this system is minimal. As the persons wanding also pick material, they know that incorrect entries may cause them future frustration so they are careful to wand accurately.

Bar Code Update On A Terminal CRT

Bar code update on a terminal CRT was not thought to have a major role in the systems design. This is no longer true.

The bar code data collection systems in operation control and track many thousands of individual jobs a week going through the shops.

Because of the overload of the transactor accepting the wanding information, it was decided to equip one CRT terminal with the requisite equipment to accept wanded information. The transactions would be slower than direct input (10 seconds against 1-2 seconds) but the accuracy and real time input were of overriding importance.

The paperwork for jobs going to the shop floor is routed to a CRT terminal equipped with a bar code wand.

Bar code labels on the display terminal plus the I.D. of the job read through the transparant envelope provide the information to the computer to activate the system.

The wanding of bar code labels brings up the line item on the CRT. The status of the item is checked and if OK the next set of bar code labels change the status to "ISSUED" which means that the job has been issued to the shop floor. The job packages are wanded in batches of one hundred and then sent to the shop floor input control.

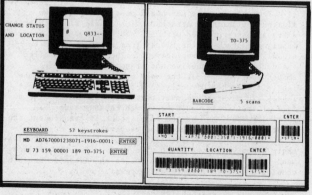

Fig. 7 Comparison Between Manual Keypunch Data Entry & Bar Code Input to Computer Terminal

The first days operations showed ten duplicates being issued for work already in process or already made.

Investigation showed a fault in the system which until that time had never been realized.

Now at key points CRT wanding will be used to check system integrity. Some terminals have a switch to allow both high speed direct to transactor wanding and CRT display wanding. Figure 7 shows the comparison between manual and bar code entry into a CRT terminal.

LOCATION PATTERNS

Location identification patterns are one of the most critical and least looked at areas of a storage system. The placing of bar code labels in any storage area is a time consuming and tedious job. Should a location identification pattern not be easily expandable the location idents tend to be "hangons" or "X, Y, Z" additions.

Before any bar code systems are introduced the area should be relabelled and an inventory taken. BAR CODE SYSTEMS DO NOT UPGRADE EXISTING POOR INVENTORY SYSTEMS.

The system to be described has been in place for four years and is running at better than 99.5% credibility with very large inventories.

Standard Location Pattern

The standard pattern used in the following examples is six characters alpha and numeric. The following alphas are not used in the system: I O U The alphas Q and V are only used in the first position of the pattern.

The first character is always an alpha and it identifies the department controlling the stored material. The identification patterns within the remaining five blocks are as follows:

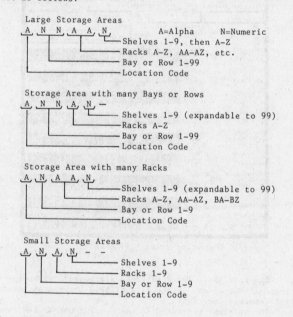

Location Identification Codes

Before allocating location identification codes to work with the bar code system the total system must be examined in detail and the following questions answered.

Are there existing identification patterns which can be retained?

Does the computer system contain alphas which can be used as location, shop or even work center locators?

Is there confliction with location codes at other sites?

Can the system be structured to cover expansion or rearrangement?

Can the location be linked with the shop code?

Can the first character of the building name be used as a designator?

Figure 8 shows an example of an area with signficant identification codes for locations and work centers.

Work Center Identification Codes

Work center identification codes should be standardized before systems are installed. A combination of locat-

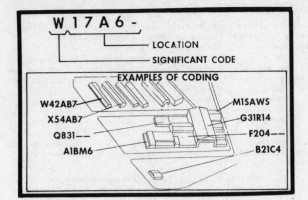

Fig. 8 Significant Identification Codes

or and work center codes is an advantage. The length of the code should be kept as short as practical, any spaces being filled in with "-".

Examples for a six-character field: Q831-- M42--
The availability of "-'s" in the code can be put to use as will be shown in the paragraph "System Flexibility" which follows.

An area of identification which is often overlooked is the possible conflict between similar areas. As an example Shop A has an input buffer area designated A1xxx-through A10xxx.Shop A send its output to a holding area.

The bays in the holding area should be designated x30xxx - x40xxx This will eliminate all chances of confliction between the two areas, and still allow each area to expand by 300%.

Layout of Material Storage Areas

Material storage areas must be laid out in a modular pattern. Figure 9 illustrates a simple case where expansion or change can take place without massive relabelling. Racks can be placed against the walls-in bay 28 they can be labelled E through G without disturbing existing rack codes. Similarly additional racks can be placed in the lower row of Bay 27 without changing existing rack codes.

Bar Code Label Displays Material Storage Areas

The layout of material storage areas (see previous paragraph) together with the design of location bar code label boards plays a significant part in maintaining accuracy of material location being fed to the computer.

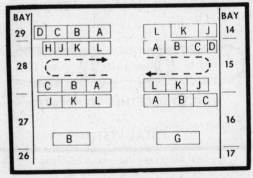

Fig. 9 Storage Area Identification Layout

There is no standard way of attaching the bar code label to the rack. The type of rack, the kind and size of material being stored, the lighting, access and other factors can affect the way the bar code label is installed.

The following example shows one method of placing bar code labels on a pallet rack. Safety rules preclude placing individual labels on each shelf above 6' high.

The racks in Fig. 10 are 12' high and the bar boards are located on metal backboards attached to the rack uprights by countersunk bolts. The rack and shelf designators are printed on a waterproof plastic paper on a drafting machine. In one area the bar boards were installed ahead of the system and location credibility improved. The material controllers when questioned judged that this improvement was in part due to the bar label board giving them Bay, Rack and Shelf I.D.'s on each rack.

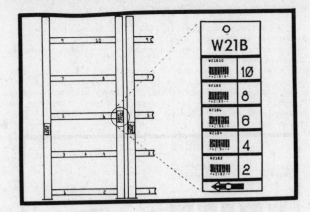

Fig. 10 Bar Code Boards On A Pallet Rack

SYSTEM FLEXIBILITY

Changes in the information being fed to the computer can be introduced in the time it takes to print a label and add it to a bar board.

The following are two of the many innovations which have been introduced into working systems.

Material Control

The foreman had decided in the original system design that there was no need to individually control work going to each of his saws. After the bar code manufacturing control data collection system was introduced he realized the simplicity of the system and requested bar code labels for each machine. Within 30 minutes the labels were available and jobs already in the queue were bar coded to their individual machine by means of a portable scanner. Computer runs which used the machine code as a sort now break the jobs into SAW1, SAW2 and SAW3 (Figure 11).

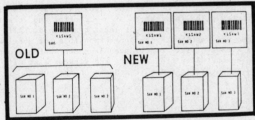

Fig. 11 Changing the Reporting Status
From A Group of Machines to an Individual Machine

Work Center Control

Jobs are normally wanded into a work center by a material controller. A request was received to wand the job to the mechanic in a work center. A set of labels bearing the work center code Q833 followed by the mechanics' codes (P1 through P8) was placed on a bar board in the work center. By means of a portable scanner jobs coming into the work center are scanned to the mechanic and later fed into the computer.

Figure 12 shows the two wandings, the first by Material Control who moves the job to the work center and the lower scan by the work center control who allocates the job to the mechanic.

Fig. 12 Job Wanded To Mechanic

Downloading to a Micro Computer

In a system designed in 1982 for a production shop provision was made for downloading information from the main computer into a shop floor control system by means of bar code information.

Fig. 13 shows the job ticket with the I.D., start date and routing bar coded. This information is fed to the microcomputer shop floor control system by bar code wanding. The main system records entry onto the floor. When the job is completed it is wanded out of the floor system back into the main system.

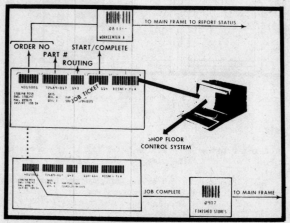

Fig. 13 Schematic Showing Bar Code Input
To A Micro Shop Floor Control System

DATA INTEGRITY

Bar Code Printers

The total bar code system is driven by the bar code labels produced by an inhouse printer connected to the manufacturing system computer.

Access to this printer for manually created labels is restricted. The information of new control and location labels are co-ordinated by at least two people. All changes are sent to the person responsible for purging the daily kickout list. Experience has shown that the person scanning the daily transactions and kickout list will spot a new code the first day it appears on the run.

Kickouts

The daily kickout report is a major control point in the system. Depending on the program installed the list will show all the deviations from normal practices. These can include:

- Incorrect wanding sequence
- Wanding from wrong terminal
- Incorrect number of characters received
- Bad reads (normally caused by line problems)
- Item not found in main file
- File shows item wanded is already complete (duplicate)
- Incorrect quantity

The corrections have a high priority for attention preferably same day action and each area has a designated person to resolve any problems and correct misoperation.

Terminal Hierarchy

Terminals must be given unique identification codes in order to control levels of input. This is especially important when using portable scanners.

If only one of the transactions sent to the computer by the portable has been already wanded into the system at the next level of operation, that portable transaction must be blocked and fed to the kickout list.

The levels of heirarchy can be as follows:

Production Planning	1x	Transfers	4x
Production Control	2x	Assembly	5x
Work Centers	3x	Test	6x

A feature which can be readily controlled is the legitimate return of a job to a lower level. This is performed by means of an "OVERIDE" control.

The "OVERIDE" wanding is normally performed by a supervisor. The computer is updated with the new location but a kickout warns the data entry control to check all the parameters of the transaction and make changes where necessary.

CONCLUSION

This paper has described some of the high points - the critical items which have played a significant part in the successful implementation of bar code data collection in manufacturing control.

Each of the items described have worked because people made them work. From the very first concept for installing a bar code data collection system the interaction with the people inputing and supporting the system has been paramount.

It has not been easy. The many changes to the forms (Figs. 2 and 3) caused much comment. The location identification pattern (Fig. 9) was extremely difficult both to sell and install. In discussing bar code with shop floor personnel they were reluctant to break the job reporting into smaller parts (Fig. 11).

There was no problem encountered with hourly personnel. They were encouraged to use the suggestion award system to upgrade the bar code system in their area. One suggestor received a monentary award for a very simple idea which was put into use within an hour of the bar code data collection being implemented.

It is PEOPLE who have made the systems described in this paper work with so much success. As Figure 14 depicts it is "PEOPLEWARE" linked to HARDWARE and SOFTWARE which has contributed to an outstanding level of credibility in both data and material location integrity.

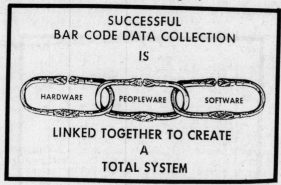

Fig. 14 The Links That Make Bar Code
Data Collection Successful

CREDITS

I wish to express my sincere thanks to Gerald Faella CPIM for his valuable suggestions in the planning of this paper and for his conscientious review and positive comments in proofreading the documentation and illustrations.

IMPROVING PRODUCTIVITY IN DISTRIBUTION

Charles A. Snyder
Auburn University
James F. Cox, CPIM*
University of Georgia

INTRODUCTION

Distribution entails many diverse activities in most manufacturing and service firms and these activities are typically not thought of as a unit, but studied as separate functions. This piecemeal approach results in a suboptimal solution to the overall system problems. Additionally, several specialized skills are required to sufficiently integrate these varied activities into an efficient operating system. Logistic networks, information systems for order entry, processing, shipment and record retention, inventory systems, packaging, and scheduling for workers and product delivery are critical areas that must be analyzed. These activities must be examined with respect to each other and the overall efficiency of the system in order to insure success of the organization.

This paper presents the results of designing, implementing, and operating a direct delivery system for small electronic equipment. The purpose of the paper is to provide an approach for analyzing a distribution system to identify deficiencies. An application of the methodology is provided.

In the case organization, an order processing center was established in a centralized facility to receive customer orders from a five state region via computer printers. The processing center ordered the required equipment, packaged and shipped the equipment and tracked the return of any defective equipment.

METHODOLOGY

The proposed approach to analyzing and improving a distribution system is provided in Table 1.

FORECAST OF DEMAND

First, a long range forecast of the demand for the product or service should be constructed. This forecast should provide the basis for analyzing physical changes in the information system and production system. Additionally, in analyzing any distribution system two flows should be examined in detail--the information flow and the product flow. Improvement and standardization of these flows are essential to increasing productivity. Process flow charts should be constructed to identify the present and proposed methods of producing the service or product and the present and proposed methods of handling the needed information.

The forecast should be far enough into the future to provide an indication of the size of the distribution facility and information system required. Time-phasing of changes in demand is essential to planning expansions of and changes to the distribution system. Additionally, changes in product demand influence information requirement substantially.

Table 1

Systematic Procedure for Improving Distribution System

1. Forecast demand for product(s) over estimated life of system.
2. Study logical foundation of system in terms of the objectives of the organization.
3. Examine present information system and identify deficiencies.
4. Examine present physical system and identify deficiencies.
5. Design new system with standardized forms, flows, methods, procedures, etc. in both information and product systems.
6. Identify objective productivity and quality performance measures for both the distribution and information systems as they interface and collect measures to establish benchmarks.
7. Feasibility/cost-effectiveness evaluation.
8. Implement new distribution system.
9. Measure performance.
10. Audit information and product flow systems.

LOGICAL FOUNDATION OF SYSTEM

In examining the distribution system, one must build an understanding of the system in terms of the organization's objectives. This understanding should encompass the goals, objectives, and functions of the total distribution system. In addition, the specific contributions of the system to the attainment of overall organizational objectives need to be determined. This determination means that the analyst must have a clear understanding of both the organizational goals and the distribution system goals. Frequently the analyst finds that the organization may have poor or nonexistent documentation in these areas. However, the statement of goals and objectives is needed for building the logical model that will serve as the foundation for the design of a new system. Unless there is a clear understanding of the logical basis for the distribution system, it is difficult or impossible to design an adequate system. In addition, shortchanging the study of the logical system can easily lead to "solving" the wrong problem.

EXAMINE PRESENT INFORMATION SYSTEM

The information flow should be analyzed with respect to the business objectives, needs, accuracy and timeliness. Non-essential data should be identified and eliminated from forms, reports, and files. Redundant data and files should be identified and summarized in a list of system deficiencies (documentation of the existing system). Outputs of the information should be reviewed in detail with the users to ascertain format, content, and usefulness. The timeliness and periodicity of inputting data and outputting detailed and summary reports should be analyzed. Additionally the level of detail or aggregation of data is important and should be examined with respect to the needs of the various levels of management in the organization. If several different forms are used to collect data on similar activities or functions, an examination of these activities should be conducted to ascertain the likelihood of standardizing and consolidating activities.

The description of the existing information system should contain sufficient detail to support conducting a cost-benefit analysis and provide a clear understanding of those procedures that should be retained in the revised system. In addition to the description of the existing physical system, a logical model, stressing the system objectives and functions and the manager's decision support requirements, should be constructed.

It is useful to employ a checklist in conducting the analysis of the existing system. Such checklists are readily available in systems analysis and design texts. Typical categories to be investigated are:
   a. Existing Policies and Procedures
   b. Present System Outputs
   c. Present System Inputs
   d. Examination of Data Stores (Files)
   e. Description of Peripheral Systems That Must Interface

At the end of the examination of the present information system, there should be a fairly comprehensive documentation file. This documentation should provide the basis for new system requirements and new system design activity.

EXAMINE PRESENT PHYSICAL SYSTEM

The product flow should be examined in great detail. A layout of the present facilities should be constructed. Process flow charts of the activities related to providing each good or service should also be constructed. Flow diagrams of each type of order processing should be drawn. A flow diagram illustrating the movement of orders and goods through the facility should help to identify existing and potential bottlenecks, inefficient material flows as well as space and capacity problems. Capacity available and required for the present physical system and the capacity required for the proposed physical system should be ascertained. Lead times for order processing should be identified and analyzed with respect to the timing and relationship of its components (queue, set up, processing, etc.). Streamlining and standardizing procedures reduce both lead time and in-process inventory levels. An analysis of the need for supplies, raw material, in-process and finished goods inventory should be conducted. Both the inclusion of and elimination of these stages in the distribution system should be studied. The tradeoffs between inventory, lead time and customer service should be examined.

Manpower requirements should be determined in addition to the timing of any additions or deletions to the work force. The decision of using overtime versus hiring additional workers should be evaluated. Daily demand patterns should be studied to determine the scheduling of pickups and deliveries and the scheduling of workers. Man/machine boundaries and interfaces should be identified. In addition, control points and control mechanisms throughout the process should be identified and analyzed. In particular, the efficacy of these controls must be evaluated and any deficiencies identified.

IDENTIFY OBJECTIVE PRODUCTIVITY AND QUALITY PERFORMANCE MEASURES

Productivity and quality performance measures should be identified and measured to provide a benchmark to compare present and proposed operations over time. Lead times, customer service levels, inventory turns, and labor cost per unit are a few of the more common performance measures. It should be noted that typically the use of only one measure can distort overall system performance. For example, customer service levels can be extremely high if inventory levels are high or expediting is prevalent. A set of productivity and quality criteria should be established and measured simultaneously to prevent an unrealistic picture of system performance.

Examine the process flow charts for both the information flow and product flow in an effort to streamline and standardize methods and procedures. Forms should be combined and standardized to eliminate the need for separate types of paperwork for each product/service. In some cases forms and procedures might be eliminated entirely through proper design of the data base, information flow and production process.

FEASIBILITY/COST-EFFECTIVENESS EVALUATION

Usually project feasibility is evaluated along four dimensions. The technical feasibility dimension is determining if the project can be done. For instance, the project must be amenable to the proposed solution and tested technology must be available for the application. Operational feasibility is assessed by ascertaining if a technically feasible system can be operated with existing or prospective system resources. Schedule or time feasibility addresses whether the proposed system can be installed and implemented within the time constraints of the project. A fourth feasibility dimension is cost or economic feasibility. Can the proposed system be afforded? Even if a sufficient budget exists, it is necessary to evaluate the expected benefits. Both tangible and intangible benefits should be assessed to determine the expected return to the firm.

DESIGN NEW SYSTEM

The physical flow of each product should be analyzed. Can activities be eliminated or combined? Which operation is the bottleneck? Does the capacity available match the capacity required? Can workers or equipment be used more effectively? Is inventory used effectively? What are individual item lead times? What customer service level is expected, required and cost-effective?

IMPLEMENT NEW DISTRIBUTION SYSTEM

An implementation plan should be constructed which defines the timing of and manpower required for the activities associated with implementing both the distribution system and information system. Conversion to the new system should be in accordance with a careful plan. While some systems require a pilot, others may be directly cut over (usually a dangerous strategy). Still others may be best converted by a phased or modular changeover or must be cut over in a parallel manner when backup is absolutely essential. Well planned implementation strategy is critical to the overall success of the new system. The implementation plan should be monitored to ensure timely project completion.

MEASURE PERFORMANCE

Once the distribution and information system is operational, a monitoring system to measure the performance of each should be set up. What is the product lead-time both in-house and in-transit? Customer service level? Inventory investment? Inventory turn-over rate? Cost/unit in labor and in shipping? What is the system bottleneck? Does capacity available match capacity required? These are a few of the questions that should be answered about the distribution system's functioning.

Performance measures for the MIS should be monitored. Is the information timely? Accurate? Useful? Is more or less information needed? Continuous evaluation of both systems for productivity and quality performance is essential to ensure overall distribution system effectiveness. Standards of performance help to insure that the total system operates in accordance with plans.

AUDIT INFORMATION AND PRODUCT FLOW SYSTEMS

The flow of information, its accuracy, use and timeliness should be checked periodically to ensure proper use of the system. Employee turnover and changes in demand, product mix, etc. cause personnel to short-circuit the information and product flow systems and disrupt the distribution system. A periodic audit using the process flow charts and performance measures should be conducted. In addition, the audit provides a vehicle for re-evaluation of the performance standards for appropriateness.

AN APPLICATION

The approach described in the previous section was applied to an existing distribution system. The system had lead-times of up to five days in getting the part or equipment to the customer after the order was received. From a centralized location, a direct delivery center processed small electronic equipment ordering, replacement, and return orders for a five state area via UPS and USPS. The processing was manual order entry, inventory packaging, follow-up and returns systems. Current demand levels were over 1,100 items per day. A forecast of immediate and medium range demand levels is provided in Table 2. Based upon these demand levels and product mix, the present distribution system, both product flow and information flow, were analyzed.

Table 2

Summary of Short-Range Daily Demand on DDC

| | New | | Replacement | |
	Standard	Custom	Parts	Order/Day
September	100	10-20	750 4-500	1260-1370
October	200	90-100	800 4-500	1490-1600
November	300	150-200	800 4-500	1650-1800
December	600	150-200	800 4-500	1950-2100
Jan-Dec 1983	3000	90-100	2000 6-700	5690-5800

In Figure 1, the five different equipment/parts flows are diagrammed. Trouble reports were received from customers who were having problems with their existing equipment. These orders could require either the replacement of the entire unit or the replacement of an expendable part. If a swap was necessary, the order was processed and entered on a returns log to ensure the equipment was returned. Replacement sets were shipped by United Parcel Service (UPS) and replacement parts were shipped by mail (USPS) and no return was required. These flows are depicted graphically in Figures 1a and 1b.

The second type of order was the service order and was used for customers to order new equipment, replace existing equipment and return old equipment. A returns log was maintained for replacement orders and returns orders. The equipment flow networks for these transactions are provided in Figure 1c through 1e.

No inventory was maintained; however, because of proximity of the major supplier's warehouse, most equipment could be ordered one day and received the next day. The lead time associated with processing an order was three days in the order processing center and one to two days in transit to the customer. Few standard procedures existed or were followed if they existed and excessive overtime was required to process orders.

122

Figure 1   Equipment Flow Diagrams

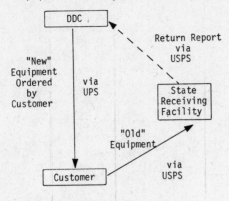

a. Defective Equipment Replacement Orders

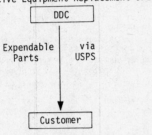

b. Parts Only Orders

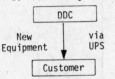

C. New Equipment Orders

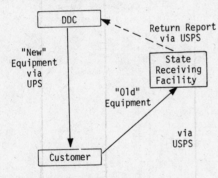

d. Change Equipment Orders

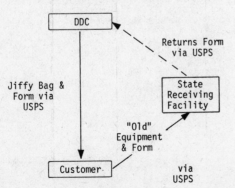

e. Return Equipment Orders

Process flow charts of the existing order processing system for each type of order and of the processing and packaging of the various types of products were constructed. A layout of the order processing area and packaging area was constructed in addition to a flow diagram and equipment list. The bottlenecks were identified. Present capacity was ascertained for both systems and compared to projected capacity.

The addition of an inventory system was studied. Table 3 and Figure 2 summarize the results of the inventory analysis. The addition of an inventory system and other changes decreased lead time by 1.5 days and the inventory turnover rate increased to over 125 turns per year.

Table 3

Summary of DDC Inventory Analysis[1]

Service Level	Safety Stock		Average Inventory		Maximum Inventory	
%	n	$	n	$	n	$
50	0	0	376	8,590	765	17,180
70	439	10,627	815	19,217	1,204	27,807
80	551	13,323	927	21,913	1,316	30,503
85	682	16,496	1,058	25,086	1,447	33,676
90	839	20,302	1,215	28,892	1,604	37,482
95	1,081	26,171	1,458	34,761	1,846	43,351
97	1,232	29,819	1,608	38,409	1,997	46,999
99	1,527	36,957	1,903	45,547	2,292	54,137

[1]Analysis is based on August 1982 daily demand.

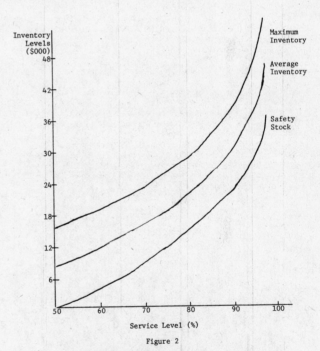

Figure 2

Dollar Investment in Safety Stock, Average Inventory and Maximum Inventory for Various Levels of Service

Information requirements were identified and the information flow was analyzed and activities combined, eliminated, simplified and standardized across the various types of orders. Rescheduling of order processing and shipping pickups, in addition to improvements in order processing and packaging, substantially improved performance measures. As demand increased, overtime decreased to an average of three hours per week. A 98% customer service level was established: orders received by three o'clock one day were delivered the next day. Labor cost per unit decreased significantly as returns from shipping incorrect material decreased also. Performance measures of investment in inventory, inventory turns, customer service level, labor cost/unit, and lead time were collected.

These measures were monitored over the implementation of the improvements in the layout, order processing, information flow, inventory system, etc. Periodic audits of the distribution system and MIS were conducted to ensure proper operation and maintenance of the systems.

CONCLUSIONS

A systematic approach to improving distribution systems helps to assure increased productivity. Such an approach was outlined and the results of employing the procedure were reported. The case organization's centralized direct delivery system was redesigned using the systematic methodology to result in a cost-effective configuration with improved inventory turnover, management control, product processing, information flow, and high service levels. The systematic procedure was thus shown to be effective in a dynamic, real-world environment.

IN SEARCH OF MRP II

Stephen A. Melnyk, Ph.D., CPIM
Richard F. Gonzalez, Ph.D., CPIM
Michigan State University

One year ago a team from Michigan State University completed a study (sponsored by APICS) of six firms regarded to be Class-A MRP II firms. [4] The Production-Inventory Manager in each firm was a critical agent in the implementation of MRP II. We propose to share their experiences with you. Specifically we'll be telling you:

- That tough as competition is today, it's going to be a lot tougher tomorrow.
- The key to survival is technology.
- The management technology called MRP II is uniquely suited to the manufacturing environment of the future.
- What you always wanted to know about MRP II, but were too embarrassed to ask.

THE MANUFACTURING ENVIRONMENT--TODAY AND TOMORROW

In a 1983 study, "The Changing U.S. Automotive Industry," Arthur Andersen & Co. concluded that Japanese auto manufacturers enjoy a 1500 to 2000 dollar cost advantage per vehicle in competition with U.S. manufacturers. [1] Understandably concerned, U.S. managers have trekked to Japan in large numbers to witness the marvels of Japanese manufacturing methods. Upon their return, many rushed to emulate the layout, material planning systems, quality circle, or whatever aspect of Japanese technology and organization they deemed to be transportable. All the while the arguments continue about the factor(s) that explains the Japanese success--people, culture, exchange rate, infrastructure, and so on.

If Reich [2] is correct the Japanese can not afford to rest on their oars. Their mastery of the repetitive manufacturing environment is being challenged not only in the U.S. and Western Europe, but by a number of manufacturers in the so-called less developed countries. Already the latter are making their presence felt in markets for raw materials, most significantly raw steel. Not long ago Japanese steel manufacturers asked for relief from South Korean competition. The Japanese complained that Korea enjoys lower labor and energy costs which should somehow be offset to the benefit of Japanese producers. The Japanese also sought its government's ok to delay installation of a turn-key mill for finished steel products--a mill which they contracted to sell to Korea.

Japanese steel makers will conclude, as have U.S. steel men, that they cannot compete against raw steel producers in Korea, Brazil, Mexico, and other developing countries. Rather, they will import raw steel to make high-margin finished and specialty steel products.

Our manufacturing environment is changing in fundamental ways. What we observe in worldwide markets for raw and finished steel will be replicated in other markets, particularly those in which the developed nations now enjoy success--automobiles and other standard consumer durables. In other words, the technology of repetitive manufacturing is easily transported to those countries now classified as less developed.

The relevant product classification in manufacturing today is:

- Raw Materials
- Standard Products
- Special Products

The progression from raw materials to standard products to special products is marked by increasing need for technology. It is the developed nations which can afford the investment necessary to discover and apply the technology to support the production of special products, i.e., products made to customer order, usually in small quantities. Reich describes the opportunities for the U.S. in the following way: [2,p.13]

> The industries in which the United States can retain a competitive edge will be based not on huge volumes and standardization, but on producing smaller batches of more specialized, higher value products--goods that are precision-engineered, that are custom tailored to serve individual markets or that embody rapidly evolving technologies.

Such products will be found in high value segments of traditional industries (specialty steel and chemicals, computer-controlled machine tools, advanced automotive components) as well as in new high-technology industries...

The manufacturing environments described above are the make, assemble, and engineer-to-order environments in which process flexibility and responsiveness to the marketplace are the keys to survival. The manufacturing system will have to simultaneously achieve or provide:

- Low Production Costs
- Flexible Production Processes
- High Product Quality
- Good Customer Service
- Employee Satisfaction

Just a few years ago it was generally conceded that trade-offs were unavoidable. High quality meant high production cost. The same was true for flexibility and responsiveness. If a customer wanted a special item on short notice, the price was high because processing and distribution costs were high. The only way to justify design and set-up costs was to produce standard items in large batches. In today's markets, trade-offs are not permitted. Management must devise systems for quickly producing high-quality, low-cost products to customers specifications.

TECHNOLOGY

How to achieve production systems of the kind described above is the challenge we face. And survival is the issue. Recently, F. James McDonald and Roger B. Smith, president and chairman respectively of General Motors Corporation put it this way:

> All business today competes in a worldwide technological race. It's a race that affects not only the products we make and how we make them, but also how we run our businesses and even our personal lives. This worldwide technology race is a race for survival--a race some companies won't be around to finish...the winners will be the companies who bring advanced technology to market in an affordable word-class quality package--one that gives true value to the customer. [3,p.2-3]

Note that McDonald and Smith use the word, technology, when referring to:

- Products -- What We Make
- Processes -- How We Make Them
- Management -- How We Run Our Firms

We are familiar with "high tech" products and processes. Too often we misplace our faith in product or process technology. To survive, management must exploit product, process and management technologies. The personal computer industry is strewn with the bones of firms whose products were technologically superior, but which reached the market late, were incorrectly priced, or were targeted at the wrong market. Similarly, we can think of firms with state-of-the-art process technology which can't meet product specifications on two successive units of output.

Management technology is the sum of the processes routinely used to plan and carry our organizational activities. MRP II is such a technology. It's well defined, standardized and easily understood. MRP II is not well defined. No two MRP II systems appear to be the same. Most of all, this technology is to many people difficult to comprehend.

WHAT YOU ALWAYS WANTED TO KNOW ABOUT MRP II

- MRP II, don't you mean Manufacturing Resource Planning?
- Isn't MRP II something the consultants cooked up to keep clients on the string?
- MRP II is pretty fuzzy, isn't it?
- What do I get from MRP II that I can't get from MRP?
- What about JIT, FMS, OPT, CAM, Q-Control, "Factory of the Future?"
- Will I have to scrap my present system and start all over?
- What are the costs?
- How am I (a PIM) affected?

The foregoing are typical of the questions voiced when MRP II is brought up. Developments in manufacturing management are revolutionizing the field. Acronyms are bandied about in a way that guarantees confusion. For the production-inventory manager who has come to terms with MRP, CRP, RRP,

MPS, and so on, the invitation to consider MRP II is unsettling. More distrubing to PIMs is the suggestion that they become part of an information-decision system which takes them outside the familiar confines of the production-inventory control department. Our purpose in this paper is to answer the questions raised by the PIM.

WHAT'S IN A NAME?

Unfortunately the labels "material requirements planning" and "manufacturing resources planning" contribute to the confusion about the two techniques and their relationship. APICS would have us avoid the use of the acronym MRP II which apparently is identified with The Oliver Wight Companies. "MRP II" is proprietary in the minds of some, yet it's convenient and its use is widespread. One of several alternatives is the label, "Business Resources Planning." Offhand we can't think of a better label for the technique than "manufacturing resources planning." We would not discourage the use of the acronym "MRP II." The lesson for the future is to avoid acronyms in which roman numerals are required.

A CONSULTANT'S FABRICATION?

Our research [4] indicates that a number of companies, each in its own way, developed MRP II in response to particular needs. These firms had called on consultants to help implement components (especially MRP) of a system which later became an MRP II system. Just as MRP was created in the 1960's by PIM's, then later standardized and marketed by the consulting fraternity, so MRP II had its origins in the work of a few thoughtful practitioners. In our judgment they took the lead in building systems while consultants provided the theory. The job of popularizing, standardizing and helping the large majority of companies acquire MRP II competence will again fall to consultants and professional associations like APICS.

A FUZZY CONCEPT?

The concept of MRP II is clear. It's the implementation which produces the impression of fuzziness. Users agree rather well about the kind of system they want.

> MRP II is a formal information-decision system which integrates strategic and operational planning. Realistic, detailed, time-phased resource requirements are planned in support of the business (strategic) plan of the manufacturing firm.

Each company is a unique mix of history, customs, personnel, environment and MRP II architect. MRP II firms did not all begin the MRP II journey from the same point. Their experiences along the way were different. Their rates of progress and the time spent on the journey were different.

One shouldn't expect to find uniformity of experiences as in the cases of MRP users. As management technologies go, MRP is a relatively small and special purpose example. Its use is pretty well restricted to the manufacturing organization. Those who work with MRP speak a common language—the language of manufacturing. They share a common vocabulary. The process by which MRP generates planned orders or exception messages is well understood—the process or system is said to be transparent. There is confidence in MRP.

MRP II embraces the entire firm. All functions interact. All support the firm's game plan—the business plan. Functional groups have deep suspicions about each other's processess. Manufacturing questions marketing's forecasts. Sales questions PIM's master schedule. Engineering's ECO process is a mystery to everyone. Cost accounting is uncomfortable with PIM's on-hand inventory numbers. Suspicions abound because functional groups do not understand the processes (technologies) used by others. What's more, the plans of the several groups traditionally are expressed in different units. In sales it's dollars. In manufacturing it's units. In PIM it's a synthetic unit (in one firm) called "model unit count."

To create an MRP II system, this tower of Babel must be torn down. A common vocabulary is needed. Data formats useful to everyone must be designed. Data, formerly the sole property of one group, must be made available to all. The system must provide for easy conversion from the unit of measure of one group to that of another.

It's the experiences of MRP II firms when resolving the many difficulties that gives MRP II the look of fuzziness and non-uniformity. The implementation of MRP II is unique to each firm. Each makes whatever changes are necessary to achieve the desired system. Rarely will two firms have the same experiences.

UNIQUE BENEFITS OF MRP II?

The confusion about the benefits of MRP II, vis-a-vis MRP results from confusion about the nature of MRP II. The confusion is found even in firms identified by knowledgeable observers as Class-A MRP II firms. When asked to describe their MRP II systems the first response was, "We don't have an MRP II system." They responded to our question only after we defined what we meant by MRP II.

The APICS Dictionary defines Manufacturing Resources Planning as follows.

> A method for the effective planning of all resources of a manufacturing company. Ideally, it addresses operational planning in units, financial planning in dollars, and has a simulation capability to answer "what if" questions. It is made up a variety of functions, each linked together: Business Planning, Production Planning, Master Production Scheduling, Material Requirements Planning, Capacity Requirements Planning and the execution support systems for capacity and material. Output from these systems would be integrated with financial reports such as the business plan, purchase commitment report, shipping budget, inventory projections in dollars, etc. Manufacturing Resource Planning is a direct outgrowth and extension of closed-loop MRP. [5, p. 18]

We would like to simplify this definition of MRP II by saying that it is the closed-loop MRP system, with which you are familiar, plus the strategic planning system.

MRP is one part of MRP II. MRP was conceived as a material-priority planning system at the operational level. Given a production plan and master production schedule, MRP planned acquisition or production of material. Where the MPS is realistic, the benefits are impressive and have been well documented. Typically, substantial reductions of inventory and stockouts result as well as improved customer service. Note that inventory, shortages, and delivery performance are operational measures. They measure how well the operating system (purchasing, manufacturing) is executing the material plan (MPS, MRP). In contrast, MRP II requires us to focus not only on operations, but also on strategy.

By strategy we mean the statement of who we are (organizationally) and where we are going (objectives). The statement of strategy is formulated by the CEO, usually with considerable help from chief functional officers. The objectives may be stated generally, even abstractly. For example, the latest strategic declaration from General Motors is the following:

> "...our goal is to be the world's leader in all technologies appropriate to us."
> [3, p. 5]

More often the strategy of a firm is stated in terms of products and markets. Objectives might well be expressed in marketing and financial terms, i.e., market share, sales growth, return on investment, and so on.

Strategic plans provide identity and direction. They may provide measurable objectives so that future performance can be evaluated. But strategic plans have little meaning to operating managers and hourly paid workers. How do we achieve a sales volume of 500 million dollars, market share of 30 percent, leadership in product innovation or quality, return on investment of 10 percent? Strategic plans must be restated in operational terms. Whatever the corporate objectives, the first pass at rendering strategic plans operational results in a sales plan. The sales organization plans the sale of product lines in sufficient volume to achieve the strategic objectives, i.e., sales volume, market share, etc.

Next, the sales plan is translated into a production plan. This is the first of a series of material requirements plans. The production plan is evaluated in terms of the resources necessary to execute it. In addition to materials, labor, capital equipment and working capital are calculated. Long term capacity problems are resolved at this time.

American Production & Inventory Control Society

Depending on the manufacturing environment (MTO or MTS), the difference between the sales and production plans is an inventory or backlog plan. As a matter of strategy, inventory or the backlog is managed to achieve the desired level of customer service.

When the production plan has been developed so that it is both feasible and strategically satisfactory it is disaggregated into the master production schedule. Requirements stated by product lines in monthly time buckets are restated as end items in weekly buckets. From this point the now familiar detailed material and capacity plans are generated.

MRP II is the capability of transforming the strategic plan into specific, detailed material requirements that operating people can execute. More importantly MRP II can answer the CEO's "what if" questions.

- What if we change the production mix?
- What if we delay (or expedite) the introduction of a new product?
- What if we adopt a new pricing policy?
- How can we service customers in the event of a strike by our workers?
- What's the effect of price increases announced by our suppliers?

These and other questions can be answered by MRP II by modeling the proposed change as sales, production and inventory or backlog plans. MRP II computes resources requirements and stimulates the results of the execution of the proposed plans. Those results are expressed in pro forma accounting statements and schedules. The CEO can then decide whether a proposed strategy is acceptable.

MRP II makes use of accounting information. In fact some practitioners describe MRP II as the marriage of the manufacturing and financial information systems. Both share common files. Eventually, in MRP II firms, accounting concedes that manufacturing's numbers are better for projecting revenues, inventory valuation, purchasing commitments, and so on. On the other hand, manufacturing relies on the data maintained by cost accounting. The hallmark of the MRP II system is the corporate data base.

The question asked earlier was about the benefits of MRP II apart from those claimed for MRP. The operational benefits from MRP are limited and dependent on the quality of the production plan and the master schedule. The benefits of MRP II have to do with achieving the strategic objectives. Because the objectives may be broadly stated it's not possible to say that a firm can precisely attribute profit, market share, or return on investment to its MRP II system. Survival, growth, leadership, competitiveness, and responsiveness are the variables used when planning strategically. These variables are not easily scaled. We must rely on managers in MRP II firms to assess the system's value. Without exception, in the firms we surveyed, the system was seen as a technology for managing the whole company, for creating game plans in which all participated during formulation, and to which all could enthusiastically subscribe. The benefits are tangible although difficult to quantify. Specific benefits cited by MRP II users include:

1. RATIONALIZATION OF PRODUCTION In one firm management recently reassigned certain product lines among its various production facilities. The need to reassign was flagged by financial reports produced by the MRP II system which indicated to management a deteriorating profitability of these lines. The product lines affected consisted of high volume, low unit profit standard items. These lines required unskilled labor. Before reassignment, these lines were produced at the firm's main plant with a skilled unionized labor force. Management realized that labor costs at this plant were eroding profits.

Having reassigned the standard product lines to lower cost facilities, management next considered the question of which product lines to reassign to utilize capacity at the main plant. It was decided that low-volume orders requiring design modifications or special processing would be build there. As a result production was rationalized. MRP II not only alerted management to the need to re-examine the existing assignment of product lines, but it was also used to decide better product line assignments.

2. LEVELING EMPLOYMENT In several of the firms, management's policy was to provide level employment for its work force. In these firms, management attributed its success in maintaining level employment to MRP II. They believed that the system gave them a better handle on the business. For example, manufacturing managers were able to show departments such as marketing the need to level their

weekly demands against manufacturing. With MRP II the effects of different Master Production Schedules could be demonstrated in terms of sales and manufacturing capacity. In one case, marketing actively participated in smoothing the MPS by negotiating order backlog with its customers. During the recent recession marketing moved orders in to assure manufacturing of level demand. Marketing assumed responsibility for providing manufacturing with at least 40 hours of work per week.

3. MANAGING LABOR DISPUTES MRP II enhanced management's ability to reduce disruptions created by labor problems. One company's main facility was organized by a large international union. Historically, the company was struck every time the contract was renegotiated. Except for the last strike, previous strikes were short-lived, lasting about three weeks. Management would not tolerate a long strike because the company's market position could be severely damaged. A year before the last strike management examined the problem of meeting deliveries to customers should a strike occur. MRP II was used to identify strike-induced capacity shortages and to schedule vendors to make up the capacity shortfalls. Management created a strike contingency plan. When the strike was called the company was able to meet its production commitments. During the thirteen week strike, not one delivery was late.

4. MANAGING PRODUCT DEVELOPMENT AND INTRODUCTION MRP II enabled firms to compress the lead time to introduce new products. This was evident in two firms. In one, a new product incorporating a process computer was developed. The product gave the firm a four-year head start over its competitors. Management explained that it was able to introduce this new product early because MRP II linked material planning and product engineering. Development through prototype and pre-production stages was tracked (by special codes) by the material planning system. Material and operating personnel were formally joined in the development committee. Materials for development and pre-production requirements were planned by the system. Once the product design was approved it was brought on-stream very quickly. Marketing was informed of the product's development and availability.

5. MANAGING THE FIRM DURING A RECESSION Several managers observed that the power of MRP II was most evident during a prolonged recession. Several of the firms experienced significant declines of sales. In contrast to many of their competitors these firms were better able to control costs and minimize losses. The reason given by these managers was that they had the tools in the form of MRP II with which to manage the firm. They no longer had to rely on fire fighting.

In one firm, the finance department informed manufacturing what current inventory investment would put the firm in the best tax position at year's end. By means of full simulation and conversion capabilities of the system (i.e., translating operating numbers into financial terms), manufacturing determined how best to plan its inventory finance's goal.

6. MANUFACTURING AN ASSET NOT A MILLSTONE Managers of the marketing departments of two firms stated that MRP II significantly improved the performance of manufacturing. In both of the markets served by these firms it was essential that promised due dates be met. Manufacturing's ability to deliver on time provided marketing a competitive edge. They could offer what their competitors could not -- reliable manufacturing performance. As one marketing executive put it, "We sell our customers the known credibility of our manufacturing department."

Another advantage cited by marketing managers was the close tie between marketing and manufacturing. Manufacturing really understood marketing's needs and constraints (and vice versa). Marketing consulted manufacturing when accepting new orders. For example, the sales manager of one firm had an opportunity to obtain a large contract. Before accepting it, however, he contacted manufacturing. Manufacturing evaluated the order in terms of planned capacity and existing load. It was determined that the order could not be accepted given current conditions. Sales and manufacturing managers examined the existing load and by rescheduling orders were able to accept the proposed order. Generally, there was sufficient evidence that marketing managers were beginning to understand how manufacturing gave them a competitive selling point.

7. IMPROVEMENTS IN THE MANAGEMENT ENVIRONMENT Finally we noted that MRP II served to reduce stress within the firm. The integration of major functions and the exchange of information worked to remove many of the frustrations previously experienced. One major frustration was the feeling that no one understood manufacturing. Several production managers noted that corporate objectives via MRP II are now stated in terms meaningful to manufacturing. The resource plans also made manufacturing's role and contribution apparent to those outside manufacturing.

It may be simplistic to suggest that only MRP II is a comprehensive management system and all other techniques address specific operational problems. We can't perceive a forced choice, lets say, between MRP II and JIT. Even defining it broadly, JIT and MRP II serve different manufacturing environments. Yet, it's conceivable that if JIT is regarded to be a material planning system, it could be incorporated into MRP II. The latter requires a formal material-capacity planning module. We have not seen an MRP II system without MRP, but conceptually it's possible. Techniques such as FMS, GT, OPT and so on can be reconciled with the use of MRP II. None impinges at the strategic planning level which gives MRP II its unique charter.

WHAT'S THE COST OF MRP II

We must answer this question in the same way we responded to the benefits question. MRP II is not like MRP. It is not a package that one purchases and for which a price can be determined. [6] The cost depends on the system you have in place. The firms in our study had smoothly running closed-loop MRP systems to which they added the link to strategic planning and established a corporate data base. One could argue that they had already made a substantial investment. Most, although not all, had upgraded hardware and software during the 10 years or so in which the system was developed.

When the question of cost is raised, the answer sometimes heard is, "Can you afford to be without it [MRP II]?" That's flip, but realistic. Which of you would go back to the material planning systems you used 20 years ago? You can only afford less than the best if your competitors are also using 1950's state of the art systems.

The question of cost is tough to answer except on a case by case basis. But there are costs which are not apparent. These may well be greater than the costs of education, software and system maintenance. We have in mind the organizational costs of MRP II.

1. OVERCOMING RESISTANCE. A new system requires new relationships which some people will not acknowledge. In such cases the viability of the system depends on a "champion" who has the clout to bypass or remove obstacles in the way of implementation. We have observed various tactics to isolate or render impotent those managers who refuse to buy into MRP II.

2. FORMING NEW LINKS. MRP II is a company-wide system, not simply a manufacturing system. At the strategic planning level manufacturing must work closely with sales, engineering, purchasing and so on. Interaction must be regular and formal. Achieving this requires that new positions or committees be created. Our study revealed various instances of new organizational units particularly to do forecasting and master production scheduling.

3. A CORPORATE DATA BASE. The costs here are both tangible and intangible. How does one effect the transfer of files from functional units to a central department managed by a newly created "Director of Corporate Data and Information Systems?" Discipline is necessary to maintain good quality data and prevent users from maintaining islands of information scattered around the firm.

4. TOP MANAGEMENT. Despite the imperative that top management be strongly committed to MRP, top management could avoid becoming involved. With MRP II we take the essence of the CEO's job and embed it in the information-decision system of the firm. The CEO can't help but become regularly involved. Perhaps this is the largest hidden cost--the time and attention of the CEO and the principal functional officers.

IS EXPERIENCE WITH MRP GOOD PREPARATION FOR UNDERSTANDING THE OPERATION OF MRP II?

Let us begin by stating that MRP is not a necessary condition for the development of MRP II. As we observed in our study, MRP II requires an effective material planning formal material planning system. MRP is one of the best known examples of such a system. Those managers who are familiar with MRP should find that many of their experiences are transferable to MRP II. There are strong parallels present. The following are some of the most significant parallels.

DRIVING THE FORMAL PLANNING SYSTEMS

For an MRP system to function effectively, it needs a Master Production Schedule. In MRP II, the parallel to the MPS is the Business Plan. Without a Business Plan, there can be no formal planning of corporate resources.

THE PLANNING SYSTEM AS A SIMULATOR

One of the major advantages of MRP is its ability to simulate and represent, in a time-phased fashion, the effects of a given plan (MPS or Production Plan) on manufacturing resources (materials, capacity and tooling if we are referring to the Closed Loop MRP sytem). Similarly, MRP II offers the user the ability to simulate and represent, in a time-phased fashion, the effects of a specific Business Plan on all of the corporate resources (materials, capacity and capital). This capability gives top management the same power to evaluate the Corporate Plans in advance of implementing them that PIM's have previously enjoyed with MRP.

DEVELOPING A FEASIBLE PLAN

A major concern of the MRP system is that the shop floor works with a "doable" MPS. The Closed Loop MRP system evaluates the doability of a given MPS by testing it against a set of checks reflecting material, tooling and capacity constraints. Any problems with the MPS are resolved before the plan is released to the shop floor. This concern with doability is also present in MRP II.

In converting the Business Plan into progressively more detailed operational plans, MRP II uses its checks and balances to ensure (1) that the operational plans are accurate representations of the Business Plan; and, (2) that the Business Plan is consistent with current and future levels of corporate resources (i.e., capacity, material, tooling and capital). Planning problems identified at higher levels are resolved before the resulting plans are passed on to the lower levels.

FORMALIZING THE PLANNING PROCESS

MRP has helped to formalize the manufacturing planning process. That is, MRP has provided the manufacturing planning process with an effective planning structure previously lacking. In this structure, the formulation and review of the MPS is linked formally and on a regular basis to the material and capacity planning systems and ultimately to purchasing and the shop floor. Similarly, MRP II formalizes the corporate planning process. It links on a regular basis operations planning and strategic planning. Furthermore, it forces top management to view the process of formulating and reviewing corporate strategy and the Business Plan as a formal activity which must be carried on a regular basis. In some instances, the Business Plan was reviewed once a month.

There are other parallels that can be drawn between the operation of MRP and MRP II. The presence of these parallels should not be interpreted to mean that MRP II is nothing more than a "grown-up" MRP system. This is not the case. Instead, the point to be made here is that the lessons learned by Production Inventory Managers in manufacturing planning are also applicable to the task of corporate plan. MRP II provides one means of applying these lessons.

REFERENCES

1. Arthur Anderson & Co., "The Changing U.S. Automotive Industry," Chicago, 1983.

2. Reich, Robert B., The Next American Frontier, Times Books, New York, 1983.

3. "GM Corporate Report for First Quarter," General Motors Corporation, Detroit, 1984.

4. Melnyk, Stephen A. and Gonzalez, Richard F., "Manufacturing Resource Planning: Insights into a New Corporate Way of Life," APICS, 1984.

5. Wallace, Thomas F., Editor, "Dictionary Fifth Edition," APICS Inc., Falls Church, Virginia, 1984.

6. Anderson, J.C., Schroeder, R., Tupy, S. E., and White, E. M., Material Requirements Planning A Study of Implementation and Practice, Washington, D. C.: American Production and Inventory Control Society, 1981.

ABOUT THE AUTHORS

Richard F. Gonzalez is professor of materials and logistics management. He is the coauthor of 5 books in operations management and systems analysis.

Steven A. Melnyk is assistant professor of materials and logistics management at Michigan State University. He has also authored articles appearing in The International Journal of Operations and Production Management, International Journal of Production Research and Production and Inventory Management. Currently, he is a coauthor for the chapter on Production Activity Control to be published as part of APICS' revised Production and Inventory Management Handbook.

RESULTS FROM IMPLEMENTING MANUFACTURING RESOURCE PLANNING

Arno A. Th. de Schepper
Coopers & Lybrand Associates

OBJECTIVE

From 1979 until 1983 a project was undertaken with Philips' Telecommunication Industry (P.T.I.) in the Netherlands, to improve the planning and control of the goods flow along the entire product line incorporating marketing, development and production activities. The project was called POLIS (P.T.I. Overall Logistics Information System). A closed loop MRP system was implemented in P.T.I.'s five Product Groups.
A detailed estimation of costs and benefits was made at the start of this project. Also included were targets for the reduction of throughput times and for the improvements in delivery reliability. The paper describes how these estimates were made and the targets formulated. In addition, results calculations are presented, as there has been:
- a reduction in leadtimes from 9 to 4 months;
- an improvement in delivery performance by 50%;
- a reduction in stock level of $ 25 million;
- a reduction in obsolescence of $ 1 million per year.
It is demonstrated that quantification of results is essential for getting top management's commitment for an MRP project.
Finally the favourable impact of high level computer languages on system development cost is described.

PHILIPS' TELECOMMUNICATION INDUSTRY

Philips is a diversified multi-national, European, electronics enterprise. The Concern has 12 Product Divisions, responsible for the creation of profit potential, and National Organisations in 60 countries, responsible for making the most of that potential.
The Board of Management resides in the Netherlands in Eindhoven. In 1981, 56% of the $ 14 billion turnover was realized in Europe. Of the total number of employees worldwide (367,700), 68% worked in Europe.
The Telecommunication Systems Division, called Philips' Telecommunication Industry (P.T.I.), had its headquarters and factories in five different cities in the Netherlands. Turnover in 1981 exceeded $ 350 million (of which 50% in Europe). The number of employees in the Netherlands was 6,400.

P.T.I. was organized into five different Product Groups. In 1982 the Product Groups were:
- Public Telephony (exchanges for national networks);
- Private Telephony (exchanges of smaller size);
- Transmission (telephony transmission equipment);
- Data Telecommunications (e.g. telex networks);
- Traffic Systems (traffic control systems).

Product Group management reports directly to top management. Within each Product Group there is a Development Department and a Commercial Department (Sales and Technical Sales Support). The departments Pre-Development and Order Installation & Service are designed to provide a service for all Product Groups. Within the departments Product & Factory Engineering and Production, a subdivision is made per Product Group.

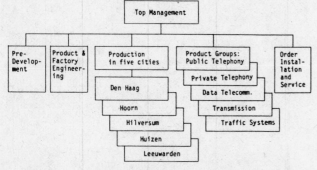

Figure 1   Organization structure of P.T.I. in 1982.

CHARACTERISTICS OF THE GOODS FLOW CONTROL

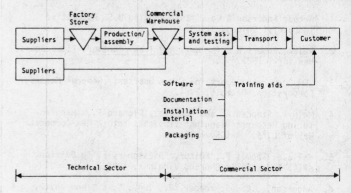

Figure 2   Survey of P.T.I.'s goods flow.

P.T.I.'s goods flow control is complicated. Some 1980 data:
- 9,500 production end-products (type-numbers in Commercial Warehouse), 1,750 were actually on order;
- 350 stores receipts and 3,500 material issues per day;
- 120,000 items to be controlled: 55,000 assemblies; 25,000 purchased components and 40,000 local building blocks;
- 900,000 bill of material lines, of which annually 45,000 are changed.   The average number of levels in the production bill of material is 3, the maximum is 9.

There exists a basic difference in character between production/assembly and system assembly. Production is characterized by batch production, while system assembly is via unit production, mostly to customer order, which is controlled by project control techniques.

Two important characteristics are long customer delivery times and high stocks. The delivery times, from receipt of a customer order until delivery, differ for the various systems. At the beginning of the POLIS project, in 1979, they varied from 6 to 20 months. Stock level is indicated in Table 1.

Table 1   Total stocks of P.T.I. at the end of the relevant year, as a percentage of turnover.

Year	1975	1976	1977	1978	1979
Stock percentage	63.0	61.7	62.1	51.6	53.0

In the same period, stocks in the Technical Sector were 40% of total stocks (20% in factory stores and 20% work-in-process stocks). Stocks in the Commercial Sector, where risks of obsolescence are high, were therefore 60% of total stocks. This resulted in high obsolescence.

Table 2   Written-off obsolescence per year, as a percentage of stocks at the end of that year.

Year	1975	1976	1977	1978	1979
Obsolescence percentage	3.3	1.7	2.7	5.3	3.9

BUSINESS REQUIREMENTS FOR POLIS

A number of different external and internal factors forced P.T.I. to give more attention to goods flow control.

- Increasing competition.
  High costs for product development and the saturation of home markets resulted in more intensive international competition. This competition necessitated reliable and short delivery times and cost control, i.e. logistics savings.

- Higher degree of complexity of the goods flow control.
  The complexity of telecommunication systems increased over the years. Another complicating factor is the fast progress of technology. The life-cycles of the systems decreased, while considerable periods of subsequent after-sales obligations still existed. This led to an increase in the number of product changes and, consequently, in the number of items to be controlled.

- Changed organizational set-up in the Technical Sector.
  In 1974, top management issued the directive that the

American Production & Inventory Control Society

goods flow control activities, which were up to that moment centralized at its headquartes, should be handled decentrally in the factories. Up to 1974 the factories were only responsible for detailed production planning and for handling materials supplied by headquarters. The new organizational set-up made changes to the existing logistics information systems necessary.

- Functional and technical deficiencies in the automated information systems.
  . The frequency of automated information processing was too low.
    Examples were monthly requirements calculation, monthly issuing of material and bi-weekly update of stocks and bills of material
  . The information systems had no replanning facilities.
  . Sufficient simulation features were not available. For example, it was not possible, prior to shop order release, to check the availability of materials.
    The process of making a Master Production Schedule was very labour intensive and had a long throughput time.
  . There were no facilities for the detailed calculation of required capacities in the factories and for work-in-process registration per capacity group.
  . Only a few performance indicators were available.
  . The information systems were batch systems based on a sequential file organization.
  . Old programs made quick and efficient adaptions almost impossible, resulting in high maintenance costs and a low degree of user acceptance.

OBJECTIVES OF THE POLIS PROJECT

From the foregoing, the conclusion could be drawn that the information systems, especially in the Technical Sector, required upgrading. The most important logistics problems were considered to be the excessive throughput times and the long delivery times. As well as unreliable delivery times, these factors caused high, unbalanced and obsolete stocks. We would like to stress, with the help of Figure 3, the prime importance of decreasing throughput times.

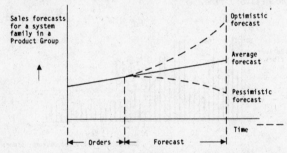

Figure 3   Sales forecast reliability in relation to time.

Plossl (1) drew attention to the relation between forecast reliability and forecast horizon at the APICS Conference in 1972. From the trumpet curve of Figure 3, the negative effect of long throughput times becomes clear. The longer the throughput times the less reliable the sales forecasts on which operational logistics activities, like releasing shop orders or buying materials from vendors, are based.
Figure 3 also shows the necessity for P.T.I. to plan flexibility in order to arrive at a realistic plan. However the shorter the throughput times, the less need there is for flexibility because uncertainty, with respect to specific customer demand, decreases in the shorter term. Also the absolute delivery reliability decreases with shorter throughput times. It has been experienced that fluctuations in deliveries increase as throughput times increase.

Further, the stated problem of unbalanced and obsolete stocks, is also reduced by shorter throughput times. This occurs in different ways. A shorter throughput time makes it easier to define decoupling points in the goods flow control chain. The need for buffer stocks (to overcome market demand fluctuations) will decrease and therefore also the risk of unbalanced and obsolete stocks. In some cases, it is also possible to have stocks at a lower bill of material level when throughput times are short. These stocks are less specific and can therefore be tuned more easily to market demand. Finally, it is envisaged that

shorter throughput times result directly in lower inventory levels.

In an early stage of the POLIS project the major objective was framed as follows:

Improvement in planning and control of goods flow per Product Group within P.T.I. in order to obtain a production process better tuned to market demands, sufficiently flexible to respond to customer orders with acceptable delivery times, and at acceptable costs.

The derived objectives were:

- improved delivery reliability of P.T.I. towards its customers, and of its production centres;
- reduction of throughput times;
- better balanced stocks along the entire route.

The main objective indicates that control must take place primarily per Product Group. For the greater part, however, goods flow control was centralized for P.T.I. For these reasons a re-organization was unavoidable. The MRP philosophy also had a considerable influence on the elucidation of the main objectives. The market constituted the driving force. The market dictated the required degree of flexibility and acceptable delivery times (i.e. as derived from competitors' delivery times).

QUANTIFICATION OF EXPECTED RESULTS

The quantification of expected results is one of the following nine key factors playing a role in the effective improvement of a logistics system.
- Management Support.
- Project Management.
- Organization Structure with respect to effective control.
- Logistics Methods and Procedures.
- Adequate Information Systems.
- Education and Training.
- Accurate Data.
- Management Information.
- Quantification of Expected Results.

The contracted external consultant Hal Mather, was the first to emphasize the usefulness of giving time and attention to the quantification of the targeted results. It is necessary to quantify the results for at least four reasons:
- to obtain support for the project, which means employing the best people and preventing their redeployment elsewhere during the project;
- to provide the possibility of measuring the project results during the project, thereby allowing for re-adjustments to be made;
- to stimulate management support for a short project throughput time;
- to be able to determine succes or failure of the project.
In the POLIS project quantifications have been made for throughput times, delivery reliability, stock savings, obsolesence, additional costs, and automation costs.

REDUCTION OF THROUGHPUT TIMES

During the discussions about the objectives of the POLIS project, it has already been indicated that the reduction of throughput times was very important. In Table 3 the throughput times expressed in months for information flow (left) and goods flow (right) are indicated.
The POLIS target was a throughput time reduction of 5 months (from 9 to 4 months in total).

Table 3   Throughput time for information and goods flow, existing situation (first line) and the POLIS targets (second line).

INFORMATION FLOW			S U P P L I E R S	GOODS FLOW				
Comm.& Fact. Plan.	Mat. Req. Calc.	Mat. Con-trol	Pro-cure-ment	Goods in-ward	Sta-ging	Expe-di-ting	Dis-patch stock	As-sem-bly
2.5	1			0.5	1	1	1	2
0.5		0.25		0.25	0.5	0.25	0.25	2

The average throughput times for information and goods flow have been analyzed in various operational situations and, from the results, targets have been defined for the average throughput times in the final POLIS situation. Table 4 gives detailed objectives for the various Product Groups.

Table 4   Throughput times, existing and POLIS targets, per Product Group expressed in months.

Product Group	Data Tele-comm. OLD/NEW		Public Tele-phony OLD/NEW		Private Tele-phony OLD/NEW		Traffic Systems OLD/NEW		Trans-mission OLD/NEW	
Total through-put time	9.7	4.2	9	4	7.5	4.5	11	5	9	5
Through-put time reduction	5.5		5		3		6		4	

The monthly physical staging of materials from the factory store in order to indicate material shortages and to chase suppliers accordingly, has been replaced in POLIS by a material availability simulation preceding the weekly release of shop orders. The result was a considerable reduction of the throughput time in this route. The reduction in the route Material Requirements Calculation, Material Control and Material Procurement, was obtained by:
- switching over from monthly calculation of the material requisitions to a (in the end) weekly material requirements calculation;
- faster processing of the data by the various Materials Management departments, especially the Material Control and the Material Procurement department.

As can be concluded from Table 4, there were considerable differences in the targets for the throughput time reduction in the logistics routes concerned. This was the result of the differences existing in the situations preceding the POLIS project.

PLANNING AND EXECUTION OF THE THROUGHPUT TIME REDUCTION

The reduction of the throughput times is to be done step-by-step. The planning of this throughput time reduction was set up accordingly. As an example, Table 5 shows the planning in the Main Factory of the Product Group Data Telecommunications. From Table 5 it becomes clear that the reduction of the throughput time of the information flow could be achieved soon after the implementation of POLIS. The realization of the throughput time reduction of the goods flow takes considerably longer. Reduction of the throughput time in this factory has in general been realized according to this plan.

Table 5   Throughput times expressed in months in the existing situation (first line) and in the planned situations (following lines).

plan date	INFORMATION FLOW				S U P P L I E R S	GOODS FLOW			
	Comm.& Fact. Plan.	Mat. Req. Calc.	Mat. Con-trol	Pro-cure-ment		Sta-ging	Expe-di-ting	Dis-patch stock	As-sem-bly
exist.	1.5	1	1	0.25		1	1	1	3
mar 81	0.75	-	0.5	0.25		1.5	1		3
dec 81	0.5	-	0.5	0.25		1.5	-		2.5
jun 82	0.5	-	0.5	0.25		1	-		2.5
dec 82	0.5	-	0.5	0.25		0.5	-		2.5

INCREASING THE DELIVERY RELIABILITY

The measurements of delivery reliability are to be categorised as follows:
- delivery reliability of the type-numbers from the assembly factories to the commercial warehouse with respect to the Master Production Schedule;
- delivery reliability of customer orders, which means the throughput time from receipt of the customer order until the moment of delivering the system to the customer.

Two examples (Figures 4 and 5) from the Product Group Data Telecommunications are used to explain the method of reporting the delivery reliability.

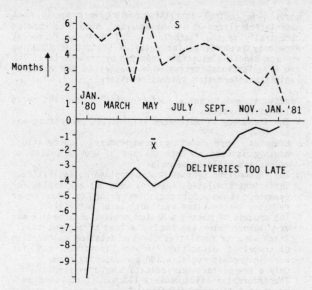

Figure 4   Backorder position with respect to the MPS and dispersion in delivery times of the factory.

For the type-numbers delivered to the Commercial Warehouse, the actual delivery dates have been compared with the delivery dates according to the Master Production Schedule.

In the delivery sequence of customer orders the time period between receipt of the order and the delivery of the systems concerned has been traced for each order. In Figure 5 the average delivery time as well as the dispersion around this average have been indicated. For this system family three months was agreed as a norm for the delivery time.

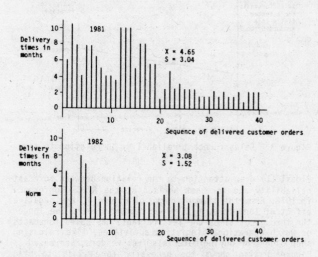

Figure 5   Actual delivery times of customer orders for a system family in 1981 and 1982.

In order to enable the measurement of the impact of an MRP project on the delivery reliability it is recommended that data concerning the actual delivery reliability is collected immediately at the start of the project.

METHOD FOR CALCULATING SAVINGS ON STOCKS

In the Public Telephony, Traffic Systems and Transmission Product Groups an analytical method has been used to determine stock savings. The agreed targets concerning the reduction of throughput times (see Table 4) formed the basis for these savings calculations. The method used is explained with the throughput time reduction in the Transmission Product Group but with simulated figures for material turnover, work-in-process stock, and the obsolete inventory in the commercial warehouse. Calculations were based on the influence of the POLIS implementation on the stocks in the factory store, on the work-in-process stocks as well as on Commercial Warehouse stocks.

THE INFLUENCE OF POLIS ON THE STOCKS IN THE FACTORY STORE

The throughput time reduction from staging until delivery at the commercial warehouse resulted in a reduction of the flexibility stocks available in the factory store. The planned throughput time reduction was 3.5 months (from 8 to 4.5 months).
The Transmission Product Group was already operating with a flexibility stock, of 15% of the annual material turnover. To determine the flexibility stock actually available it is assumed that half of this stock is in the factory stores and the other half on order. So the material flexibility stock present in the old situation could be estimated as: Material turnover x 15% x 0.5 (factory store) = $ 400,000.

Figure 6 shows the situations before and after the POLIS implementation, indicating a 15 % flexibility stock for covering 9 months uncertainty. After POLIS implementation the uncertainty to be covered is 3.5 months less. Therefore the required flexibility stock becomes: (5.5/9) x 15% = 9%, and the resulting flexibility stock saving will be: (3.5/9) x $ 400,000 = $ 156,000.
Due to of the relatively small size of the resulting cost saving, this has not been used further in the cost/benefit analysis for the various Product Groups.

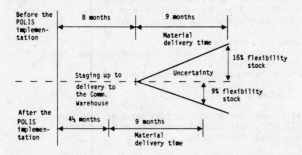

Figure 6   Reduction of the required flexibility stock as a result of reducing the throughput time from staging until commercial warehouse delivery.

THE INFLUENCE OF POLIS ON THE WORK-IN-PROCESS STOCK

The factory throughput time in the Transmission Product Group had to be reduced from 6 to 3.5 months. The decrease of the work-in-process caused by this reduction is explained from Figure 7.

Starting with $ 3.6 Million as work-in-process, the work-in-process decrease is:
(6-3.5)/6 x $ 3.6 Million = $ 1.5 Million.

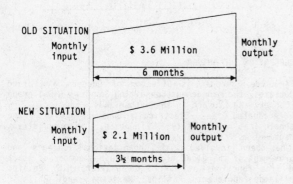

Figure 7   Decrease of the work-in-process stock resulting from the factory throughput time reduction.

THE INFLUENCE OF POLIS ON THE COMMERCIAL WAREHOUSE STOCK

The Commercial Warehouse stock includes the following

components: obsolete stock, slow-moving stock and miscellaneous stock. For the determination of the decrease of the obsolete stocks in the Commercial Warehouse we considered that no obsolete stocks could be generated if the throughput time in the factory was zero months, because then production would be to customer order. Moreover, the obsolescence risk was considered as a linear function of this throughput time. The value of obsolete stocks destroyed each year amounted to $ 640,000 in the example (8 months throughput time). When this throughput time is reduced from 8 to 4.5 months, obsolete stock would decrease with (8-4.5)/8 x $ 640,000 = $ 280,000.

For the reduction of the slow-moving stocks (stock exceeding two years consumption) a similar approach to that above was applied.

Miscellaneous Commercial Warehouse stocks were divided into: lot sizing stocks, work-in-process stocks in the Testing Department, in packing and in forwarding, half a month of stock for balancing the Testing Department, and safety stocks. Only for the safety stocks was a decrease in the Commercial Warehouse inventory, resulting from the throughput time reduction, given consideration. The result of this reduction has also been included in the benefit calculations.

ADDITIONAL COSTS AND BENEFITS IN THE PRODUCT GROUPS

At the start of the POLIS activities in the various Product Groups a rough estimate of costs and benefits was presented. These estimates included:
- coverage of POLIS budget (with depreciation over 5 years);
- change in annual costs for:
  . information systems and personnel;
  . logistics and material management personnel;
  . interest on stocks in the Technical Sector;
  . interest on stocks in the Commercial Sector;
  . obsolete technical stock;
  . obsolete commercial stock.

During the POLIS project each Product Group gave detailed estimates of the costs and benefits of implementing POLIS. For the savings on stocks the method discussed in the previous paragraph was used in the Public Telephony, Traffic Systems and Transmission Product Groups. The results of the detailed estimates of the savings were set as targets for the POLIS project. In Table 6 the agreed targets for the total benefits per Product Group are compared with the rough estimates.

Table 6   Agreed targets for total benefits of POLIS as percentage of rough estimates per Product Group.

Product Group	Public Teleph.	Private Teleph.	Traffic Systems	Trans-mission
Total benefits	310%	76%	421%	107%

From Table 6 we conclude that, before starting an MRP project the intended results must be estimated in detail. A rough approach to these results is just not sufficient. To defend this policy statement further, a comparison is made between the estimates and the targets agreed, concerning the influence of POLIS on the stocks for the various Product Groups.

Table 7   Comparison of estimates and targets of stock and obsolescence reductions resulting from POLIS.

Reduction of	Estimate when starting the POLIS project	Targets agreed by the Product Groups
Technical stocks	$ 5 Million	$ 9.5 Million
Commercial stocks	$ 10 Million	$ 15.9 Million
Obsolesence		
- in Technical stocks	$ 0.23 Million	$ 0.03 Million
- in Commerical stocks	$ 0.5 Million	$ 0.8 Million

Again we see the considerable differences between the original estimates and the agreed targets. Furthermore, clear and detailed insight is necessary in order to be able to achieve these results.

ESTIMATES AND REALITIES OF AUTOMATION COSTS

During the preparatory phase of the POLIS project (in 1980) the management of the DP department made a rough estimate of the exploitation costs in the final situation. It appeared that a cost increase of 50 to 100% had to be expected. As the main reasons for this cost increase, the higher run frequencies and the cost of the on-line real-time facilities in the future situation were mentioned.

Table 8 gives the latest estimates of the automation costs. The total of the first column of this table has been set at 100%, other data being related to that.
In the first column of this table the exploitation costs of the old systems which were replaced by the POLIS sub-systems have been given. It can be concluded that the original estimate of a 50 to 100% higher cost level was rather high.

Table 8   Comparison of the operational automation costs
            in percentages, based upon the 1983 price level.

Elements	Costs former situation	Sept.'82 estimate of POLIS costs in final situation
Mainframe	34%	37%
Network, VDU's, printers	19%	35%
Maintenance	47%	35%
Total	100%	107%

Table 8 also shows that terminal equipment is responsible for the increase in automation costs. Table 9 gives a survey of the successive estimates of numbers of VDU's and printers.

Table 9   The final number of screens and printers as
            estimated in 1980, 1981 and 1982.

Elements	Sept.'80	Sept.'81	Sept.'82
VDU's	115	112	178
Printers	9	11	10

Table 9 shows the difficulty of estimating the numbers of VDU's. It can be seen from Tables 8 and 9 that it is important to review the estimates in detail, with respect to the related costs. When the information systems are actually in use in the organization, the demand for terminals will increase.
From Table 8 it can also be seen that the maintenance costs (being costs of DP personnel and costs of computer resources for program development) have decreased. The cost reduction could be achieved mainly because of the application of the MIMS software package.

IMPACT OF HIGH LEVEL COMPUTER LANGUAGES ON SYSTEM DEVELOPMENT COSTS

POLIS was developed using the MIMS (Mitrol Industrial Management System) software package; now provided by Geisco. During the POLIS project MIMS proved to be capable of fulfilling a threefold role:
- a ready-made program for calculating capacity and materials requirements. In applying this program, time horizon, time buckets etc., are determined with the aid of parameters, while there is freedom to specify a company-oriented data base structure;
- a DBMS with CODASYL and relational properties;
- a very-high-level language. Compared to COBOL, about eight times fewer program lines are needed.

MIMS was chosen in order to develop a complex MRP II system quickly.... and it worked. During a careful test at the beginning of 1979, an MRP I system was realized using the MIMS Starter System.
Based on the results obtained, MIMS was accepted, together with its limitations. In deciding to make use of MIMS, the close collaboration between the users' management and DP management was of great importance. Where the advantages of a software package lie with the user, while the risks of technical failure are borne by DP, such decisions are not easily arrived at.
Following the choice of MIMS, the POLIS project could really start. The experiences gained were used to realize a broader-based system, as was required for MRP II in the multiplant-control situation at P.T.I.
The Starter System available in 1979 could be used for test purposes and practice.

According to some people, MIMS can be thought of as belonging to the fourth generation of data base management systems and programming languages. Application of MIMS meant, among other things, that the data-processing department did not form a bottle-neck during radical organizational and procedural change in a company.
Merely applying the MIMS DBMS and language (i.e. without the ready-to-use program products for calculating capacity and material requirements) already meant something like a three to tenfold improvement in productivity, system development time and costs, as compared with the classic COBOL approach. MIMS is of course not unique. There are other software tools on the market which produce comparable results.

The high productivity obtained through the use of MIMS had of course its impact on initial system development costs. By mid-1983 P.T.I.'s DP department had spent 46 manyears on the POLIS project, spread over 45 months at a (charged) cost of $ 3.1 Million, including costs of computer usage for on-line programming and testing. This corresponds to a staff of 12.3 persons over that period.

The old system had been in use for more than 10 years, but the average maintenance effort over the last 10 years (1970-1980) in manpower terms had been a staff of 14.2 persons. If the old system had been continued, and adapted to organizational changes (not included MRP II), then much higher maintenance would have been required. At the start of the POLIS project, the maintenance of the old system could be eliminated, because the users were concentrating on the new system that promised results for the first Product Group within a year.

Comparing continued use of the old system and its maintenance with designing the new systems, mainly with MIMS, it is safe to say that the initial costs of the new systems have proved to be less than zero.

LITERATURE

(1) Plossl, George W., Getting the most from Forecasts, 1972 APICS Conference, Production and Inventory Management, March 1973.

(2) Tromp, Ing.Jan G., P.T.I.'s POLIS; technical implications, Philips VISA (Views & news on information systems & automation), May 1983.

(3) Schepper, Dr.Ir.Arno A.Th.de, Gewenning aan logistieke planning, Samsom, Alphen a/d Rijn, 1983
(to be published in english as "Implementing logistics planning").

BIOGRAPHY OF THE AUTHOR

Dr.Arno de Schepper is Director of Coopers & Lybrand Associates, the Management Consulting Services (MCS) group of Coopers and Lybrand in the Netherlands.
He graduated in Electrical Engineering at the Technological University, Eindhoven, with Business Management as a subsidiary subject.
He has been involved with organizational changes and improvement of the goods flow control in a number of staff and line functions at N.V. P.de Gruyter, N.V. Philips Gloeilampenfabrieken, Philips Mexicana and Philips' Telecommunication Industry B.V.
He is a member of the Education Committee of the Dutch Society for Logistics Management, the NEVEM, and lectures on organization and information systems and Manufacturing Resource Planning (MRP II). He is also editor of the Samsom's "Guide Book on Goods Flow Control".
From 1979 until 1983, he managed the POLIS project.